MULTINATIONAL HUMAN RESOURCE MANAGEMENT AND THE LAW

MULTINATIONAL HUMAN RESOURCE MANAGEMENT AND THE LAW

COMMON WORKPLACE PROBLEMS IN DIFFERENT LEGAL ENVIRONMENTS

MATTHEW W. FINKIN
JOEL CUTCHER-GERSHENFELD
University of Illinois, USA

With

TAKASHI ARAKI
PHILIPP FISCHINGER
ROBERTO FRAGALE FILHO
ANDREW STEWART
BERND WAAS

Edward Elgar
Cheltenham, UK • Northampton, MA, USA

Published by
Edward Elgar Publishing Limited
The Lypiatts
15 Lansdown Road
Cheltenham
Glos GL50 2JA
UK

Edward Elgar Publishing, Inc.
William Pratt House
9 Dewey Court
Northampton
Massachusetts 01060
USA

A catalogue record for this book
is available from the British Library

Library of Congress Control Number: 2013936176

This book is available electronically in the ElgarOnline.com Law Subject Collection,
E-ISBN 978 1 78100 412 8

MIX
Paper from responsible sources
FSC
www.fsc.org
FSC® C013056

ISBN 978 1 78100 411 1 (cased)

Typeset by Columns Design XML Ltd, Reading
Printed and bound in Great Britain by T.J. International Ltd, Padstow

CONTENTS

PREFACE AND ACKNOWLEDGEMENTS

This book began as an experiment – could a graduate seminar be structured around common legal problems placed in different country settings? It was first offered in 2009 to Master's degree students and law students in the School of Labor and Employment Relations and the College of Law at the University of Illinois. Then, in 2010, it was offered to mid-career professionals engaged in a special program at the School of Labor and Employment Relations (LER). Aspects of the course have been offered in other settings as well. Based on the high levels of engagement generated, we were convinced that a book manuscript was appropriate.

We sought to identify easily recognizable, potentially common problems that we anticipated would reveal the variation in legal contexts and underlying values and assumptions. The problems were vetted by our participating human resource (HR) professionals. Some early problems were omitted as unreflective of real world issues and others put in place more representative of what multinational managers and their lawyers actually confront. In addition, the problems had to be manageable, "teachable" within the space and time available – which meant that some pressing and fascinating issues simply could not be taken on. The distinction between an "employee" and an "independent contractor," for example, vexes virtually every legal system. But because it *is* so vexing, because the law is so highly nuanced and the literature so extensive, we concluded, with real regret, that it simply could not be taken on. Nevertheless, we believe the problems we set out, real in every sense as the appended comments of our participating managers evidence, have the necessary sweep and depth.

Five nations were selected, based on both the diversity of legal contexts and there being sufficient maturity in the systems to allow for answers across the many different topical areas. These are Australia, Brazil, Germany, Japan, and the United States. In each case, the countries are relevant both as important settings for investment by multinational corporations *and* as representative of a larger set of nations. Thus, the Australian legal system has close correlates in New Zealand and analogues to various degrees across the former British Commonwealth. The Brazilian system is, in part, reflective of legal challenges across South America and other rapidly developing nations, though there are also echoes of Portugal in this system. Germany is a lead case, of course, for most of Northern Europe and, to various degrees, for other parts of the European Union. Japan was first among Asian nations to be fully industrialized and the underlying Confucian values and assumptions can be found in China, Korea, and many parts of South-East Asia. The United States has a close correlate with Canada and features a language and culture that has come to play a dominant role in the global economy. The legal responses from these five countries will not precisely apply in other countries, but can be taken as illustrative of general tendencies in other related nations.

Two major economies – China and India – would be worthy of inclusion in this volume based on their size, but the maturity of their legal systems and the degree to which these systems do not fully operate under the rule of law would make it difficult to generate precise answers to many of the problems posed. Still, in these two cases, and in the case of other nations not included in the volume, we invite the generation of answers in additional contexts. *Indeed, instructors using the book in other countries are encouraged to generate answers to the questions in* their *legal system, which will add yet an additional opportunity to compare and contrast with the five countries selected here.*

The answers provided in this volume were generated by individuals who are each premier labor and employment law scholars in their respective nations. Not only did they provide precise and nuanced answers, but in many cases they provided the text of original primary sources (including excerpts from the law) and additional relevant references. We have kept the spelling of key words in the form used in each country – thus some entries will consider "labor" and others "labour" – and we have left the references in the formats used in each country. This means that even as the style of internal reference is not consistent across the book, the cultural integrity of each country entry is maintained. In this regard, we are bowing to the individual nature of each culture, rather than imposing a single consistent standard that would not honor local culture – a choice not unlike that faced by multinational corporations. However, references to supplemental references and readings are in uniform U.S. legal style for ease of access and consistency.

We are deeply appreciative of the engagement of the country experts – the task of responding to the many problems was a large one. The scope and depth of their work make an invaluable contribution without which this book simply would not exist. We are grateful for the assistance of the reference staff of the College of Law's library and LER librarian Yoo-Seong Song. Students in the various classes at the University of Illinois and the Interdisciplinary Center at Herzliya, Israel, where earlier drafts were taught, also advanced our thinking. We would particularly like to highlight the contributions of HR professionals participating in a special online offering of the course, many of whose comments can be found highlighted at different points in the text. These add the depth of practical experience to the rather more dry legal analyses. In that regard, we also want to acknowledge the assistance and input of Andrew Bartlow, Shari Calhoon Bennett, Pat Canavan, David Halleck, Gary Newman, Howard Salazar, and Marc Thompson.

Administrative assistance with the manuscript was provided in succession by Stacey Ballmes, Julie Knapp, and Kelly Downs, all of whom had to struggle with Finkin's scrawl as he refuses to enter the computer age. And, Tara Gorvine at Edward Elgar has been all that an editor should be – a helpful sounding board and appropriately aggressive in ensuring the manuscript is completed and advanced into production and use. A final word of appreciation to Eleanor and Susan who, as good moms, observed this book from conception through adolescence to adulthood.

ABOUT THE AUTHORS

Matthew W. Finkin holds a chair at the University of Illinois College of Law and an appointment at the University's Center for Advanced Study. He is the author of numerous books and articles and directs the College of Law's Program on Comparative Labor and Employment Law and Policy. Since 1997, he has co-edited the *Comparative Labor Law and Policy Journal* with Professor Sanford Jacoby of the Anderson Graduate School of Management at UCLA. Professor Finkin is a member of editorial boards of scholarly journals in the United States, Canada, Belgium, and Germany. He is a recipient of the Alexander von Humboldt Foundation's Research Prize and is a holder of honorary doctorates from the University of Trier (Germany) and the University of Athens (Greece).

Joel Cutcher-Gershenfeld is a professor and former Dean in the School of Labor and Employment Relations at the University of Illinois, United States. He is an award-winning author who has co-authored or co-edited eight books and over eighty-five articles on high performance work systems, transformation in labor-management relations, negotiations and conflict resolution, economic development, and engineering systems. Joel is the former president of the Labor and Employment Relations Association (LERA). His current research centers on stakeholder alignment in complex systems – the foundation for 21st century institutions. Joel holds a Ph.D. in Industrial Relations from MIT and a B.S. in Industrial and Labor Relations from Cornell University. Joel is also affiliated with the National Center for Super Computing Applications (NCSA) and the University of Sydney, Australia.

Takashi Araki is Professor of Law at University of Tokyo and former Dean of its Law School. He is an award-winning author of two comparative books on German, U.S. and Japanese labor and employment law. In Japan, he is currently a member of the subcommittee, Labor Policy Council in the Ministry of Health, Labor and Welfare, and former chairperson of the Labor Relations Commission in the Tokyo Metropolitan government. Internationally, he is the former vice-president of the International Society for Labor and Social Security Law and actively involved in comparative studies in labor law and industrial relations. He has been a visiting scholar and professor at several institutions worldwide, including Harvard Law School, the Catholic University of Leuven, Cambridge University and the University of Illinois College of Law.

Philipp Fischinger is Akademischer Rat auf Zeit at the University of Regensburg, Germany and is currently writing his "habilitation" (postdoctoral lecture qualification) in order to become a professor of civil, employment and labor as well as social security law in Germany. He has published three books and numerous articles, on issues including civil liability, strike law, bankruptcy law and family law. He holds a doctoral degree from the University of Regensburg and an LL.M. degree from the Harvard Law School. He was a visiting professor at the University of Illinois College of Law in 2012.

Roberto Fragale Filho holds a doctorate in political science from the University of Montpellier I (1997) and teaches sociology of law at the Universidade Federal Fluminense (UFF). He has been visiting professor at the University of Illinois College of Law (2006) and the University Paul Valéry–Montpellier III (2009 and 2010). Since 2004, he has been the Labor Judge of the First Labor Section of the city of São João de Meriti (RJ), and has been the educational coordinator of the School of Magistrates of Rio de Janeiro Labor Court since 2009. During 2010, he was also Chairman of the National Council of Labor Schools of Magistrates (CONEMATRA). He is a member of the *Comparative Labor Law and Policy Journal* Editorial Advisory Board and has authored four books and over fifty articles in labor relations, judicial training, researching and teaching of law. His current research centers on judicial training and the impact of technology on the judicial profession.

Andrew Stewart is the John Bray Professor of Law at the University of Adelaide, Australia, and President of the Australian Labour Law Association. The author of many books and articles on Australian labour law, his current research projects include examining the regulation of unpaid work experience, analyzing the extent to which the protective strength of labour laws varies across countries with different legal systems, and preparing a comparative study of the regulation of job loss. Besides his academic work, he helps advise employers and business groups through his position as a consultant to law firm Piper Alderman.

Bernd Waas is Professor of Law at Goethe University of Frankfurt, Germany. He is the author or co-author of several books on individual as well as collective labor law and has written more than 100 articles on German, European and comparative labor and civil law. Bernd is coordinator of the European Labor Law Network which comprises labor law experts from 31 jurisdictions in Europe (ranging from Portugal to Russia).

PART I

INTRODUCTION

The way work is structured and administered directly affects the economic performance of the firm, the quality of working life of the employees, and the very fortunes of a nation. With the globalization of markets and enterprises, multinational corporations face unique challenges in setting the terms and conditions of employment. No one consistent set of policies can span multiple national jurisdictions, yet employees often have assignments that involve rotation among various locations and working together in teams with people each operating in different countries. The result is a wide array of dilemmas and tensions that are brought into sharp relief by this coursebook.

The assumption of this volume is that a significant cohort of human resource managers are active in companies that function multinationally and that more are likely to be engaged in such enterprises. Consequently, lawyers are and will increasingly be called upon to advise managers about employment policies and practices in that environment. Even as corporations seek, if not complete uniformity, at least to harmonize their human resource (HR) policies, employment law and employment relations remain deeply rooted in the nation state. Thus HR policies within a single enterprise may differ because of the legislation, administrative policies, and court decisions these legal systems produce – especially as limits on what management would like to do: the very structure and assumptions on which these legal systems operate, the role of the rule of law in human resource management, can have centrifugal effects.

We have chosen five countries for comparative purposes. The United States has been chosen not because we view its law as in any sense a model – though, as will be seen, it does represent something of an economic neo-liberal outlier compared to the others – but because U.S.-based companies represent the most significant group in the multinational corporate universe. We selected four others, that number being manageable without overwhelming the student, for two reasons. First, for their educational value because their labor laws are quite distinct from one another. Indeed, the countries span different legal traditions (common law and civil law; English, French, and German legal roots). Second, the countries represent a range of economic and cultural contexts (liberal versus coordinated markets; developing versus developed economies; and Eastern versus Western cultural traditions). Third, these countries all host large numbers of outside multinationals. Just consider the data on U.S. and U.S.-affiliated multinationals hosted by these four countries.[1] The figures for the last year for which data are available are set out in Table I.1.

Table I.1 U.S. multinationals in comparison countries

	Number of U.S. affiliates	Number employed by them
Australia	828	312,200
Brazil	588	452,200
Germany	1,586	649,000
Japan	896	590,000

Source: U.S. Dept. of Commerce, Bureau of Economic Analysis, *International Economic Accounts* (Nov. 17, 2008).

These materials proceed on a problem-focused basis. We believe that in lieu of purely descriptive accounts, discussion of the law is enlivened by confronting it in application. It is often the case that different legal systems yield equivalent results, albeit by very different doctrinal means. The problem method draws out practical equivalence, doctrinal analogies, as well as differences in analyses and outcome. For a notable example in employment law *see* WORKPLACE JUSTICE: EMPLOYMENT OBLIGATIONS IN INTERNATIONAL PERSPECTIVE (Hoyt Wheeler & Jacques Rojot eds., 1992).[2] We have accordingly devised a set of problems that we thought would represent the kinds of real world issues HR managers and their lawyers confront. We have vetted them with a sample of mid-career and senior HR managers as well as lawyers in the U.S. and abroad in advance of submitting them to our panel of legal experts.[3] These responses are accompanied by additional references and suggested readings which, in turn, should stimulate further in-depth consideration of how, and why, these systems function as they do. But a caveat is worth mentioning here even if it will emerge

1 We considered China and India but chose not to include them. They are economically significant globally and will become even more so. Nevertheless, in both countries the content of the law, the ease of access to the law, and the effectiveness of enforcement are works-in-progress. We concluded, that, for the time being, the coverage we chose is adequate for systemic variety, and that Brazil stood in good stead as an important, rapidly developing country: hourly compensation costs in manufacturing increased in 2010 over 2009 in Brazil by about 24 percent in U.S. dollars while in the U.S. they increased by about 2 percent (Daily Labor Report, 245 DLR D-1 Dec. 21, 2011).

2 Other leading works featuring this methodology but only touching on issues in employment are GOOD FAITH IN EUROPEAN CONTRACT LAW (Reinhard Zimmermann & Simon Whittaker eds., 2000) and PERSONALITY RIGHTS IN EUROPEAN TORT LAW (Gert Bruggemeier, Aurelia Ciacchi & Patrick O'Callahan eds., 2010).

3 Because German law is so highly textured the assistance of two experts in German labor law was needed. Professor Waas attended to Problems 1, 2, 3, 4, 8, 10, 11, 12, 13, 16, 17, 18, 19, 20, and 21. Dr Fischinger attended to Problems 5, 6, 7, 9, 14, and 15 and also supplied a translation of the German "Social Plan" set out in connection with Problem 10.

with clarity as the problems are worked through: the bare fact that a practice or policy might be lawful speaks not at all to whether it is desirable – or tell us how employers, unions, and employees actually behave. *Can* does not imply *ought*. Put differently, the question might be posed in each case regarding how the law facilitates or hinders the implementation of best practices.

With the assistance of the consulting HR managers we identified six areas where the kinds of problems they confront are most common and where the differences – and similarities – are most salient:

- *Employee voice*. Does the law allow or require that employees be heard in company decisions? If so, on what subjects, by what means, and with what legal consequences?
- *Discrimination*. Most countries forbid discrimination by employers on some invidious, usually class-based grounds. How do these play out in commonly encountered scenarios? Do these vary from country to country? If so, why?
- *Privacy*. Over the past several decades demands for the protection of personal data have accelerated in tandem with the proliferation of technologies that make more and more data available and render employees more and more transparent. Does the law limit the deployment or utilization of these technologies? Does it protect employees against intrusion in the workplace or in private life?
- *Wrongful dismissal*. Does the law constrain the employer's ability to discharge an employee? On what grounds? Subject to what procedure? With what consequences?
- *Compensation and benefits administration*. Can a corporation have consistent compensation and benefit policies that span nations? How can pay and benefits be fair given different legal constraints across countries?
- *Global supply chain and labor standards*. Does the law – "hard law" – impose any obligations on companies vis-à-vis the labor standards of their foreign affiliates, contractors and suppliers? If not, does "soft law" – international norms or efforts by non-governmental organizations – affect what companies do in that regard? If so, how and with what consequences?

This is a time of fundamental change in the human resource function. Key elements, such as benefits, compensation, training, and HR analytics are increasingly being outsourced to external providers. At the same time, in a global knowledge economy, talent management and change management are more central than ever to the economic fortunes of a multinational corporation. Equally, virtually every nation sees human capital as the foundation for its future success in the global economy. The six problem areas selected for this volume are emblematic of a fundamental reality, which is that employers and employees have both common and competing interests. The law is the foundation on which these mixed motive relationships are navigated and mediates the degree to which the potential of human resource management is or is not realized. The primary purpose of this coursebook is to educate future professionals on this emerging and important domain at the intersection of national labor and employment laws, on the one hand, and multinational employment practices, on the other. A secondary, but perhaps further reaching purpose is to motivate broader debate and dialogue on these issues. The full array of cases and examples presented here point to limits in the institutional arrangements and alternative approaches, conceptually and in outcome. Additional notes, comments, and questions are appended to stimulate research, discussion, and thought. In larger perspective, this book as a whole can be understood as a problem statement for which we do not yet have the answers.

> The HR practitioner should help hone the founding concepts of the organization and ... ask tough questions ... holding companies true to these tenets. They have to make the C-suite aware of the impact of their decisions on consumers and employees in diverse environments. It is an awareness of social and cultural assumptions that could be very supportive or damaging to their ultimate goals ... it is HR's job to create insight and appreciation ... so that the mission, vision and values of the organization can best be realized.
>
> Vice President, Employee Relations, Health Care

A. SKETCHES OF THE LABOR AND EMPLOYMENT LAW SYSTEMS

The texture of a nation's labor and employment law is invariably complex and highly nuanced. It is hard enough to master one system let alone five. What follows are brief sketches to outline the structure of these countries' systems to put the reader on a map, so to speak. At the close of these sketches a brief statistical display of the demographics of the jurisdictions is set out. The content-specific aspects of the law will be dealt with in the course of analyzing the problems for discussion.

EMPLOYMENT LAW IN AUSTRALIA: A GENERAL INTRODUCTION

Political structure, governance and legal system

Australia is a federation, comprising the Commonwealth of Australia, six States (New South Wales, Victoria, Queensland, South Australia, Western Australia and Tasmania) and a number of Territories, of which the two largest are the Northern Territory and the Australian Capital Territory.

Australia has a written Constitution, which establishes a system of federal courts and confers power on a bicameral parliament to legislate on certain specified matters. Each of the States has its own Constitution, parliament and court system. State parliaments have a "plenary" or residual power to legislate on any matter, though if any of their statutes are inconsistent with a valid federal law, the federal law will prevail. The Territories have been afforded a measure of self-government, and also have their own legislatures and court systems. But their laws can be overridden by the Australian Parliament, which can legislate on any matter arising in a Territory. By contrast, the Australian Constitution protects the States in certain ways from the exercise of federal powers.

Although the Australian Constitution is loosely modelled on the US Constitution, the Commonwealth, States and Territories each operate a "Westminster" system of government, in which the executive government is formed by the party (or coalition) with a majority in the lower house of parliament. Hence there is no clear separation between the legislature and the executive.

Like the US and other former British colonies, Australia's legal system still accords an important role to the "common law" – judge-made law developed by reference to established principles and precedents. The common law can be – and often is – excluded or overridden by legislation. But important aspects of the law of contract and the law of tort (civil wrongs) are still governed by common law principles.

Responsibility for employment regulation

Australia's employment laws are amongst the most complex in the world. The reasons for this are many and varied. They include the absence of any clear demarcation in the Constitution between federal and State authority over employment matters, as well as a historical attachment to the use of compulsory arbitration by public tribunals to resolve labour disputes and regulate minimum wages, working hours and other employment conditions.

Importantly, however, the picture has begun to simplify in recent years, thanks to a series of major reforms that have culminated in the federal Fair Work Act 2009. With the cooperation of the States, and with effect from 1 January 2010, this statute now operates to regulate employment conditions and labour relations for *all* private sector (i.e. non-governmental) employers. The only exception is Western Australia, although here too all companies are covered by the federal statute.

For the most part, the Fair Work Act operates to the exclusion of any State or Territory labour laws. However, there are important exceptions. The regulation of occupational health and safety (OHS), workers' compensation, training and child labour, for instance, are all matters that are primarily left to the States and Territories. Hence a company that operates throughout Australia has traditionally had to comply with eight different OHS statutes, although a recent attempt has been made to harmonise those laws. Most States and Territories have now enacted a model Work Health and Safety Act to replace their former legislation. Discrimination or equal opportunity is another matter where federal, State and Territory laws may co-exist.

Minimum employment conditions

Under the Fair Work Act, all employees (including managers) are entitled to the benefit of the National Employment Standards (NES). These create minimum entitlements in relation to various forms of leave, as well as matters such as notice of termination and redundancy (severance) pay. They also cap working hours at 38 per week, plus reasonable additional hours.

In addition, most non-managerial employees are covered by a further and more detailed set of minimum entitlements, enshrined in an instrument known as an award. Traditionally, awards were made by industrial tribunals in settlement of labour disputes, and there were thousands of such instruments. However the award system has just been reviewed and radically simplified. Most employees are now covered (if they are covered at all) by one of the 122 "modern awards" that took effect on 1 January 2010 – although until 2014 it will still be necessary to refer to old awards for transitional purposes.

Each modern award is framed to cover specified types of work within a particular industry, sector or occupation. If a job comes within one of the "classifications" in an award, the employer must pay the minimum wage rate set for that classification. There are usually a number of different rates for each classification, based on the worker's levels of experience or training. Awards usually also have detailed provisions as to the range of hours employees can be expected to work, and typically impose loadings or penalty rates for overtime, shiftwork, evening or weekend work, or work on public holidays. "Casual" (temporary) employees are also usually entitled to a premium of 25 percent on their wages, in lieu of any entitlement to annual leave, personal leave or severance pay.

For employees who are award-free, including most managers, there is a statutory minimum wage. But for the great majority of lower-paid employees, it is an award that will set their minimum wage. And that minimum wage can and does vary according to the type of job, how much experience they have, and what sort of hours they work.

In addition to the requirements of the Fair Work Act, employers may have to comply with other labour statutes. For example, federal law generally requires employers to contribute a portion of each worker's ordinary pay into a superannuation (pension) fund on their behalf. The required percentage is currently 9 percent, but will rise to 12 percent by 2019. State and Territory laws also oblige many employers to provide "long service leave" to employees who have been continuously employed for (generally) 10 years.

Collective bargaining

Australia has a strong tradition of trade unionism and collective bargaining. Although union density has fallen to 13 percent in the private sector, it is still common for larger employers to negotiate collective agreements that set wages and other employment conditions. Since the early 1990s, it has become standard practice for these agreements to be registered under labour statutes. A registered agreement displaces the operation of any award(s) that would otherwise apply, and is enforceable under the statute in the same way as an award. It applies to union members and non-members alike.

There have been many changes to the rules relating to registered agreements over the past few years. But under the system created by the Fair Work Act, enterprise agreements (as they are now known) may be made for all or part of a single enterprise, or for a group of enterprises. They can have a nominal duration of up to four years. After agreements reach their expiry date, they continue in operation, but can be more easily replaced or terminated.

Enterprise agreements can be negotiated with one or more unions, or directly with a group of employees. Either way, the final text must generally be approved by a majority of employees in some sort of vote, before being submitted to Fair Work Australia (see below) for approval. An agreement will only be approved if it leaves each affected employee "better off overall" than they would be under an otherwise applicable award.

An employer cannot be forced to bargain, unless a majority of employees request an agreement. Once bargaining is initiated, however, all concerned must negotiate in good faith, though there is no obligation to bargain to conclusion. Employees may take "protected" (i.e. lawful) industrial action in support of a new single-enterprise agreement, though only after the expiry date of any existing agreement. Employers can only initiate a lockout in response to protected action by employees. Any other form of industrial action is unlawful.

Unfair employment practices

The Fair Work Act allows a dismissed employee who has served a minimum qualifying period to challenge the fairness of their dismissal. A successful claim may result in reinstatement (plus back pay), or compensation of up to six months' remuneration. Higher-paid non-award employees, including many managers, are excluded from making such a claim.

The Act also contains various "general protections" against discriminatory or otherwise wrongful treatment at work. For example, it prohibits an employer from taking adverse action against an employee or job applicant on the ground that they are a union member or non-member, or that they have or are proposing to exercise some sort of "workplace right." There are also a range of other federal, State or Territory laws that deal with discrimination on the grounds of race, gender, age, disability, and so on.

The employment contract

Each employee is considered to have entered into a contract of employment, whether this is formally documented or not. To the extent that the parties have not expressly reached agreement on matters such as the duration of the hiring, or the employee's obligation to comply with instructions, the common law will imply appropriate terms on these matters. In practice, detailed employment contracts tend to be written only for managerial or professional employees.

It should also be emphasised that relatively few employees in Australia are engaged on an "at will" basis. Assuming the hiring is not for a fixed term, an employer must generally give notice before dismissing an employee, other than in the case of serious misconduct. The one major exception may be casual employees. It is often assumed that a casual can simply be refused any further work, without any need for notice, although the issue has not been fully tested. In any event, there have been many examples of long-term casuals successfully bringing claims for unfair dismissal.

An employment contract can lawfully offer wages or benefits that are more favourable to an employee than the minimum entitlements set by the NES, an applicable modern award, or any other labour statute. But a promise to accept less than any of those entitlements is not enforceable.

Regulatory agencies

There are two main regulatory agencies under the Fair Work Act. Fair Work Australia (FWA, renamed the Fair Work Commission on January 1, 2013) operates for certain purposes as a tribunal, but in other ways through administrative decisions. Its responsibilities include:

- adjusting minimum wage rates;
- reviewing and updating awards;
- policing industrial action and other tactics used in negotiating enterprise agreements;
- helping to resolve bargaining disputes, including (though only in limited instances) through compulsory arbitration;
- scrutinising and approving enterprise agreements;
- resolving disputes arising under awards, enterprise agreements or the NES, where the parties have agreed it should have that role; and
- determining unfair dismissal claims.

The Fair Work Ombudsman promotes compliance with awards, enterprise agreements and other statutory obligations. Its inspectors have the power to enter workplaces, investigate breaches and launch prosecutions. It is also responsible for providing education and advice on workplace laws to employers and employees.

References

For a general overview of Australian employment law, including the Fair Work Act, see ANDREW STEWART, STEWART'S GUIDE TO EMPLOYMENT LAW (4th ed. 2013). An online supplement was accessed at www.federationpress.com.au/supplements/.

More detailed accounts can be found in BREEN CREIGHTON & ANDREW STEWART, LABOUR LAW (5th ed. 2010) and ROSEMARY OWENS, JOELLEN RILEY & JILL MURRAY, THE LAW OF WORK (2d ed. 2011).

Because of the massive scope of the recent changes to Australia's laws, not all accounts of Australian labour or employment law are up to date. *Care should therefore be taken when reading any material written prior to 2009.*

EMPLOYMENT LAW IN BRAZIL: A GENERAL INTRODUCTION

Political structure, governance and legal system

Brazil is a federation, comprising 26 States, its Municipalities and the Federal District (Brasília). It is a complex political structure, which concentrates power on the federal level. Its political structure may be attributed to historical reasons as the country was originally organized as a centralized empire after independence in 1822. Federal importance as a trend has thus survived the proclamation of the Republic in 1889 and the seven Constitutions the country has known since independence.

Brazil promulgated in 1988 its seventh written Constitution. This established a system of federal courts, with four different branches: federal (which examines cases that have a State agency as one of the litigants), electoral, labor and military (which examine, respectively, electoral, labor and military matters). The National Congress is a bicameral parliament entitled to a wide array of exclusive legislative competence, which may be delegated to the States through the approval of a specific statute by a higher quorum. The Union, the States and Federal District also have a concurrent legislative competence, though if any of their statutes are inconsistent with a valid federal law, the federal law will prevail. Accordingly, the States and Federal District may legislate on any matter which is not an exclusive prerogative of the Union or the Municipalities as the latter also have exclusive legislative competences. Each State has its own Constitution, parliament and court system.

The Brazilian system of government is presidential and elections are held every four years. The President is directly elected by the people and the electoral body is actually composed of 140,646,446 voters. As for the National Congress, the electoral system is purely proportional for a scenario of 30 political parties, the latest created in June, 2012. No party has been able to obtain a Congressional majority which has to be negotiated at the beginning of every legislature term. Hence there is a clear separation between the legislature and the executive.

Brazil's legal system is clearly civil based although a complex system of judicial precedents has been developed by the Higher Courts over the years.

Responsibility for employment regulation

The Constitution establishes that Brazil's employment laws can only be issued by federal authority and some labor rights have constitutional status. Although the Labor Code was issued in 1943, it is still valid in every aspect which is not contrary to the constitutional regulation. Discussions over the Labor Code reform have been on the public agenda for many years although no conclusion has been reached so far. Employment regulation is thus homogeneous for the whole country.

Brazil's Labor Ministry also has legal competence to regulate occupational health and safety (OHS) conditions. Over the years, it has produced a series of 35 OHS statutes that regulate most of the working conditions on the matter, the latest issued in March, 2012. Employers are compelled to enforce such administrative statutes which are verified by Labor Inspectors.

Public employees are not regulated by the Labor Code and have a specific regulation which replicates most of the labor standards. Federal public employees are thus regulated by the Federal Statute 8,112 (1990). States and Municipalities have their own Public Service Statutes. Nonetheless, all of them have to comply with constitutional labor rights.

Minimum employment conditions

Brazilian labor regulation does not have a specific statute that sets a minimum for employment conditions. Actually, all employers are bound by the Constitutional labor rights and the dispositions of the Labor Code. Among other rights, the Constitution entitles every employee to a minimum wage (which was last fixed in January 2012 at the equivalent amount of US$ 306.00 per month), 30 days of vacation with an additional payment of one third of the employee's salary, a 13th salary at the end of a year, a 30 day delay at least for dismissal, payment for overtime hours of at least 50 percent more than for normal working hours. It also caps working hours at 8 per day and 44 per week.

Every employee is entitled to an individual Time Service Guarantee Fund (FGTS) account to which the employer is required to contribute with a monthly deposit equivalent to 8 percent of the employee salary. Once the employee is dismissed the employer is required to make an additional deposit equivalent to 40 percent of all deposits previously made and the employee is allowed to withdraw all the savings in his FGTS account. The employee is also entitled to unemployment insurance which may last from three to six months according to the duration of his last labor contract. However, if termination is due to "just cause" (an employee's serious misconduct), none of these three benefits – additional employers' deposit, FGTS account withdraw, or unemployment insurance – is available.

A temporary job guarantee is an entitlement for union leaders from the time they present their candidacy until one year after their term if they are elected, for pregnant women from the time of conception until five months after the birth, and for victims of work accidents from the accident until their full recovery as attested by the Social Security services. A lifetime job guarantee is only available for public employees after they completed three years' experience.

Collective bargaining

Brazil has a unique situation as regards trade unionism and collective bargaining. Employers' and employees' unions are respectively established on an economic or professional basis. Thus, for example, collective bargaining in the civil construction area is done between the Civil Construction Industry Union and the Workers in the Civil Construction Union. Formerly, unions were required to have State approval before coming into existence. After the 1988 Constitution, State approval is no longer required. Still the Constitution has maintained the "unicity" principle which allows the sole existence of one single union for each economic or professional category in a given territorial basis which cannot be inferior to a Municipality. Unions are allowed to regroup themselves and create a confederation. As regards the requirements for the establishment of a confederation, they must: (a) reunite at least 100 unions from the five different Brazilian regions with a minimum of 20 unions in three different Brazilian regions, (b) cover five different economic sectors, and (c) represent at least 7 percent of all unionized workers in the country. Nowadays, there are six union confederations in the country which play an important role in Brazilian politics; but only five are officially recognized currently as the sixth no longer represents more than 7 percent of unionized workers. Union density is around 18 percent and regardless of being unionized every employee is required to pay an annual union tax equivalent to one day's pay. This peculiar scenario allows unions to exist regardless of their legitimacy and creates extremely difficult requirements for the making of a confederation.

Employers cannot be forced to bargain. Still, since collective bargaining may happen between unions that represent economic and professional categories entirely, a collective agreement reached in this manner will be enforceable in all labor contracts in their respective economic and professional category, regardless of the employers' and the employees' desires. Unions may also negotiate and establish collective agreements with single companies and in such cases their dispositions apply to all the labor contracts of the particular company. Collective agreements are valid for a maximum period of two years when they have to be renegotiated. In any situation, once bargaining is initiated, all concerned must negotiate in good faith, though there is no obligation to bargain to conclusion. Briefly, labor conditions are primarily defined by statute and collective bargaining is mostly used to enhance employees' rights. Therefore collective bargaining cannot result in a reduction in labor rights nor go against statute dispositions.

Unfair employment practices

Any employee is entitled to challenge the employer's practices as unfair or wrongful at any time. Labor Code dispositions forbid employers to discriminate on the grounds of race, gender, age, disability, and so on. Still a successful claim can only result in reinstatement (plus back pay) when the employee is in a job guarantee situation. Most claims end in compensation, which has no economic limit. This has led to a litigation explosion which is nowadays enhanced by the possibility of obtaining punitive damages for unfair or wrongful employment practices.

The employment contract

Employment contracts are supposed to be formally registered in the Employment Record Book. Yet the absence of such formality does not invalidate the existence of a contract. Employment contracts are usually signed for an indeterminate duration, although an experience period of 90 days is possible. If they are for a determinate length of time they may not exceed two years. Every modification in the employment contract is supposed to be written in the Employment Record Book.

Thirty days notice is required for dismissal during the first year of the employment contract if it does not have a fixed term or specify the end of the experience period. For every completed year of work, three more days have to be added to the notice period. However notice is not required in the case of serious misconduct, which is exhaustively defined by the Labor Code.

Labor justice

There are no regulatory agencies in Brazilian employment law. Employment litigation is settled in a federal specialized judicial branch which is structured in three levels: Labor Judges, Labor Courts and the Superior Labor Court. Labor Judges are attached to one of the 24 Labor Courts and have jurisdiction over one or more Municipalities. Labor Courts examine the appeals against Labor Judges' decisions. They also work as a first-level jurisdiction for litigation arising from collective bargaining. Labor Court decisions may be appealed to the Superior Labor Court, which decides every case in last resort. An extraordinary appeal may be made from a Superior Labor Court decision to the Brazilian Supreme Court if the case deals with constitutional matters.

Since 1941, the Labor justice system has examined over 70,000,000 cases. Still, more than half of these were filed over the last 14 years (1998–2011). Between 1994 and 2010, annual cases averaged 2,463,984.5, with no single year having less than 2,000,000 cases. Finally, by 2011, the cap of 3,000,000 cases was overcome as 3,061,172 cases were received. As "only" 3,016,049 cases were decided, by the end of the year the number of unsettled cases still stood at 1,450,197. The numbers are impressive and show not only that litigation is on the rise but also that almost every Brazilian employee has at least once in his lifetime had his day in a Labor Court.

References

For a general overview of the Brazilian legal system, see LIBRARY OF CONGRESS, THE LEGAL SYSTEM OF BRAZIL, accessed at http://www.loc.gov/law/help/brazil-legal.php.

EMPLOYMENT LAW IN GERMANY: A GENERAL INTRODUCTION

Political structure, governance and legal system

Germany is a federal state, comprising 16 partially self-governing States (*Länder*) ranging from so-called "city-states" (Berlin, Hamburg, Bremen) to "territorial states" like North Rhine-Westphalia, Baden-Württemberg and Bavaria.

Germany has a written Constitution, the so-called Basic Law (*Grundgesetz*) which was promulgated on 23 May 1949, as the fundamental law of those states of West Germany that were initially included within the Federal Republic. When the Communist regime in East Germany toppled in 1990 and the German Democratic Republic peacefully joined the Federal Republic of Germany, the Basic Law became the Constitution of the reunited Germany. The main body of the legislative branch is the *Bundestag*, which enacts federal legislation, including the budget. The *Bundesrat* represents the States and participates in federal legislation. The Basic Law fixes a number of matters such as foreign affairs and defense within the exclusive legislative power of the Federation. On matters within the concurrent legislative power, the States have power to legislate so long as and to the extent that the Federation has not exercised its legislative power by enacting a law. The Basic Law enshrines a number of basic (fundamental) rights which may be restricted only if certain requirements are met. In no case may the essence of such a right be affected. Basic rights are of major importance in the area of labor law for they bind the legislature, the executive, and the judiciary as directly applicable law. In particular, in those areas, like strike and lockout, where no statutory law exists, the respective lacunas are filled by judge-made law which is essentially derived from basic rights as well as fundamental constitutional principles such as the so-called "social state" principle.

Labor courts

There is an extensive system of labor courts with jurisdiction for both individual labor law – mostly concerning contracts but also including wrongful dismissal claims – and collective labor law, including the rights of both unions and works councils. These exist at three levels. The courts of first instance and the intermediate courts of appeals are state courts, called respectively labor courts – *Arbeitsgerichte* (cited as ArbG) – and Regional (or State) Labor Courts, *Landesarbeitsgerichte* (cited as LAG). At the apex is the Federal Labor Court (*Bundesarbeitsgericht*, or BAG), which hears appeals only on questions of law. All three courts are tripartite: ArbG and LAG cases are heard by a panel presided over by a professional judge and two lay judges, one selected through nomination by employers and the other by unions. The lay judges have the same authority as the professional judge. Appeals from the ArbG to the LAG essentially involve a *de novo* presentation of the case, but lawyers need not necessarily be involved. The BAG is also tripartite, functioning in panels, known as Senates, geared to particular sets of legal questions and the tripartite membership is enlarged. It is possible for the BAG to sit in a Grand Senate for especially important cases.

Responsibility for employment regulation

Labor law (including the organization of enterprises, occupational health and safety, and employment agencies, as well as social security, including unemployment insurance) is among the matters within the concurrent legislative power of the Federation and the States. Since the Federation has made ample use of its power to legislate, state laws barely play a role in this field, however. As opposed to many other countries, there is no uniform Labor Code in Germany. Statutory labor law is widely spread over various Acts. For instance, there are specific Acts on temporary agency work, fixed-term employment contracts and part time work. Dismissal protection is dealt with in the Dismissal Protection Act (*Kündigungsschutzgesetz*). The Works Councils Act (*Betriebsverfassungsgesetz*) establishes the so-called works constitution. Collective bargaining is the subject of specific legislation, too (*Tarifvertragsgesetz*).

Though various Acts exist in the field of labor law, some areas have not been addressed by legislation. This is why judge-made law plays an important role in Germany, with the rules primarily derived from basic rights and principles of the Constitution. Constitutional provisions are not directly applicable between employer and employee. They are, however, indirectly applicable because, according to the courts, they form the criteria for interpreting the so-called general norms of civil law like *bonos mores* and good faith.

Over the last few decades there has been an increased Europeanization of German labor law. A case in point is the General Act on Equal Treatment (*Allgemeines Gleichbehandlungsgesetz*) which came into force in 2006. The Act explicitly prevents employers from discriminating against job applicants or employees on the basis of gender, race or ethnic origin; religion or belief; age; disability; or sexual orientation. By passing this Act, Germany implemented four EU directives regarding anti-discrimination. Before that time, anti-discrimination rules in Germany were essentially based on human rights and the case law of the courts.

The employment contract

Between the employer and the employee a contract of employment exists. A person is in principle regarded as an "employee" if he or she is in a position of subordination. However, the courts take a "holistic view" which means that even subordination does not represent an indispensable requirement. Instead, various criteria are used as indicative of the existence of an employment relationship. Next to "employees" the law recognizes so-called "quasi employees" (*Arbeitnehmerähnliche*). Persons who belong to this category are economically dependent on another person and enjoy some labor rights. Contracts of employment are not required to be in writing. However, the employer is obliged to provide the employee with a written statement of all terms and conditions of employment.

As far as the employment relationship is concerned, freedom of contract is considered to exist only with some limitations. The Federal Constitutional Court once expressly stated that power was unevenly divided between the employer and the employee. Hence, freedom of contract could not guarantee a proper balance of interests. According to the court, the legislature has to step in to make up for a lack of protection.

The employment contract has many distinctive features. For instance, pay may be due even without work being performed by the employee. Such is true, for instance, in the case of sickness. According to German labor law there is a continuation of full salary payments for a period of six weeks if an employee is sick. Such is also true under the so-called doctrine of "works risks" which was developed by the courts. Under this doctrine an employee retains his/her entitlement to remuneration if, for example, lack of energy or raw materials makes it impossible to work. As regards holidays, a statutory claim exists for 20 working days' vacation per calendar year for employees who work a normal five-day week (i.e. four weeks' vacation). However, it is more typical for an employee to receive between 25 and 30 vacation days per calendar year, on the basis of collective agreements.

Under a five-day week, the average working time is between 35 and 40 hours. Daily working time generally may not exceed eight hours. Female employees are entitled to full paid maternity leave, starting no later than six weeks before the expected due date. All employees, both male and female, are entitled to a maximum of three years' parental leave per child.

Employees who perform work under a fixed-term contract must not be discriminated against either. The term of a contract may in principle be fixed only if there is a valid reason to do so (temporary business needs, substitution of another employee, etc.). Temporary agency workers in principle enjoy the same basic working and employment conditions for the duration of their assignment at a user undertaking that would apply if they had been recruited directly by that undertaking to occupy the same job.

In contrast to many other countries, there is no general statutory minimum pay in Germany. However, collective agreements constitute minimum terms and conditions of employment. In some areas collective agreements have been declared universally applicable by the state.

Dismissal protection

General legal protection against dismissals is based on the Dismissal Protection Act (*Kündigungsschutzgesetz*). The Act applies to employees with continuous service of at least six months as long as they work in an establishment comprising more than 10 employees on a regular basis. Under the Dismissal Protection Act a dismissal is null and void if it is not "socially justified". The substance of the law will be taken up in discussion of the problems under that head.

In addition to the Dismissal Protection Act which enshrines "general" dismissal protection, various other statutes exist that aim to fix specific dismissal protection for particular employees. Specific provisions exist *inter alia* for disabled persons, pregnant women and women on maternity leave, persons on family leave and persons on caring leave. What is more, there is specific legislation with regard to persons holding an office within the framework of workers' co-determination, in particular representatives of employees on company boards and members of works councils.

Finally, protective rules exist that are based essentially on judge-made law. These rules were established due to the limited area of applicability of the Dismissal Protection Act. According to the courts, every employee must be granted a certain minimum protection against dismissal under the fundamental right of profession as guaranteed by the Constitution. Accordingly, even if the Dismissal Protection Act does not apply, a dismissal may be found illegal by the courts for contravening the principle of good faith or being in breach of *bonos mores*.

Co-determination

The essential feature of the German employee representation system is the dualism of the representation of workers' interests by trade unions, on the one hand, and of works councils, on the other hand. Under German law works councils are independent legal bodies with the specific task of representing workers in the respective unit (the establishment in the case of a works council). Trade unions, on the other hand, have a more comprehensive task, namely to represent workers' interests at the bargaining table. Works councils form autonomous legal bodies which represent workers' interests independently. Workers' representatives at plant level are not necessarily members of a trade union, nor are they simply nominated by a trade union. Instead, they are essentially elected by all employees who work in a given establishment, irrespective of whether they are union members or not. The role of works councils will be discussed in several of the problems.

In addition to employee representation at plant level, there is a system of employee representation on corporate boards. While co-determination by works councils takes place at the level of the individual plant or establishment, the level of "entrepreneurial co-determination," as it is known in Germany, is the enterprise level, if not the level of a group of companies. Works councils' entitlements seek to restrict the powers of the employer in relation to (organizing and running) the establishment. In contrast, "entrepreneurial co-determination" aims at allowing employees (or their representatives) to participate in decisions that are taken in corporate boards. The extent of co-determination at board level depends on the size of the company concerned and its legal form. If, for instance, a stock corporation (*Aktiengesellschaft*) or limited liability company (*Gesellschaft mit beschränkter Haftung*) employs more than 2,000 persons on a regular basis, one half of the seats on the supervisory board of such company are reserved for workers' representatives. Since the chairman enjoys a double vote in case of a tie (and shareholders are in a position to ensure that one of their own is elected as chairman of the board), a slight (if determinative) predominance of capital owners is ensured.

Collective bargaining

Trade unionism and collective bargaining play an important role in Germany. Though union density has fallen to considerably less than 20 percent, around 60 percent of employees in the West and 50 percent of employees in the East of Germany are in one way or another bound to collective agreements. Only in relatively rare cases are collective agreements concluded by a trade union and an individual employer. The predominant level of collective bargaining is the individual branch or sector of industry, with collective agreements being concluded between employers' associations and trade unions. Collective agreements take normative effect. They are directly binding on employers and employees if both are members of the associations that have concluded the collective agreement. The employer must belong to the relevant employers' association and the worker must belong to the relevant trade union. Because only a minority of workers belongs to a union, collective agreements mostly become (indirectly) effective by being referred to in individual contracts of employment. Most employers are prepared to offer such reference in order to limit the willingness of their workforce to join a trade union.

Workers have the right to strike because bargaining without the right to strike would be no more than "collective begging," in the words of the Federal Labor Court. That the right to strike is based on the right to bargain collectively has an important consequence, namely, that the right to strike is guaranteed only insofar as the strike is related to that very purpose. A strike is lawful in Germany if and only if its underlying objective is to reach a collective agreement. As a result, "wild-cat strikes" are prohibited in Germany. When determining the lawfulness of a strike, extensive use is made of the principle of proportionality or *ultima ratio*. According to the courts, a strike is illegal if it is evidently neither necessary nor appropriate when taking the aim of industrial action into account. By assessing the lawfulness of a strike according to these standards, the courts are prepared to grant trade unions wide discretionary power and to exercise a considerable measure of self-restraint.

References

M. WEISS & M. SCHMIDT, LABOUR LAW AND INDUSTRIAL RELATIONS IN GERMANY (4th ed. 2008, Wolters Kluwer).

S. LINGEMANN, R. VON STEINAU-STEINRÜCK & A. MENGEL, EMPLOYMENT & LABOR LAW IN GERMANY (3d ed. 2012, C.H. Beck).

EMPLOYMENT LAW IN JAPAN: A GENERAL INTRODUCTION

Overview of the Japanese labor law system

The Japanese labor law is understood to comprise three major branches: individual labor relations law, collective labor relations law, and labor market law.[4] These three branches have their legislative basis in the Constitution promulgated in 1946.

The Constitution

The Japanese Constitution guarantees fundamental social rights in Articles 25 to 28. Article 25, commonly called the "right to live" provision, proclaims the principle of the welfare state.[5] Article 26 establishes people's right to, and obligation regarding, education.[6] Articles 27 and 28 deal directly with labor and employment relations as seen below.

These provisions on the fundamental social rights were influenced significantly by the Weimar Constitution in Germany. These social rights provisions in the Constitution provided an important political and legislative basis for developing social policy in Japan.

Individual labor relations law

Article 27 paragraph 2 of the Constitution ("Standards for wages, hours, rest and other working conditions shall be fixed by law.") requires the state to enact laws to regulate terms and conditions of employment. This article provides the legislative ground for individual labor relations law.[7]

---

4 Kazuo Sugeno (Leo Kanowitz trans.), JAPANESE LABOR AND EMPLOYMENT LAW (University of Tokyo Press, 2002); Takashi Araki, LABOR AND EMPLOYMENT LAW IN JAPAN 7 (Japan Institute of Labor, 2002).

5 Article 25: "All people shall have the right to maintain the minimum standards of wholesome and cultured living. In all spheres of life, the State shall use its endeavors for promotion and extension of social welfare and security, and of public health."

6 Article 26: "All people shall have the right to receive an equal education correspondent to their ability, as provided by law. All people shall be obliged to have all boys and girls under their protection receive ordinary education as provided for by law. Such compulsory education shall be free."

7 Art. 27 para. 3 of the Constitution, concerning prohibition of child labor ("Children shall not be exploited."), is incorporated into the child labor protective provisions of the LSA of 1947.

After World War II, the government established the Ministry of Labor in 1946 and enacted a series of worker protective laws. In 1947, the Labor Standards Act, the Workers' Accident Compensation Insurance Act, the Employment Security Act and the Unemployment Insurance Act were enacted. Among these, the Labor Standards Act (LSA) is the most important and comprehensive piece of protective labor legislation, establishing minimum standards of working conditions.

Subsequently, two chapters contained in the LSA were separated and became independent statutes: the Minimum Wages Act of 1959 and the Industrial Safety and Health Act of 1972. Other labor protective legislation followed, including the Security of Wage Payment Act of 1976, the Equal Employment Opportunity Act of 1985, the Child Care Leave Act of 1991 and so forth. The LSA underwent large-scale amendments in 1987, 1998, 2003 and 2008 to modernize its regulations.

Apart from labor protective norms sanctioned by the criminal penalties and administrative supervision, important rules governing individual labor relations have been established by the courts through the accumulation of judgments. To borrow a German expression, they are not *Arbeitsschutzrecht* (labor protective law) but *Arbeitsvertragsrecht* (labor contract law). In 2007, the Labor Contract Act (LCA) was enacted and some of the important case law rules were incorporated into the Act.[8]

Collective labor relations law

Collective labor relations are mainly regulated by Japan's Constitution, the Labor Union Act (LUA) of 1949 and the Labor Relations Adjustment Act of 1946.

The Constitution of Japan guarantees workers' fundamental rights. Article 28 of the Constitution reads, "the right of workers to organize and to bargain and act collectively is guaranteed." Any legislative or administrative act that infringes upon these rights without reasonable justification is therefore unconstitutional and void. Workers are immune from any criminal or civil liability for their engagement in proper union activities. Article 28 is understood to stem from the provision in the Weimar Constitution of 1919, which guaranteed freedom of association and created the "third-party effect" (*Drittwirkung*),

8 For the enactment and contents of the LCA, see Ryuichi Yamakawa, "The Enactment of the Labor Contract Act: Its Significance and Future Issues," 6(2) *Japan Labor Review* 4 (2009); Takashi Araki, "Enactment of the Labor Contract Act and its Significance for Japanese Labor Law," 32(12) *Journal of Labour Law* (Korean Society of Labor Law) 97–123 (2009).

regulating relations between private citizens. Thus, in the opinion of most, Article 28 is construed as regulating not only relations between the state and private citizens, but also relations between employers and workers. Consequently, workers have a cause of action against an employer who infringes upon their union rights. For instance, a dismissal of a worker by reason of his/her legal union activities is deemed as null and void because it amounts to a violation of the constitutional norm.

Article 28 is further interpreted as entrusting the Diet with the power to enact statutes to effectuate basic union rights. Accordingly, the LUA sets requirements for "qualified" unions, establishes the unfair labor practice system prohibiting employers' anti-union actions, gives collective bargaining agreements normative effect, and establishes the Central and Local Labor Relations Commissions. The Labor Relations Adjustment Act was also enacted in 1946 to facilitate the resolution of collective labor disputes. Under this Act, the Labor Relations Commissions are entrusted with the conciliation, mediation and arbitration of labor disputes.

From a comparative perspective, it is noteworthy that Japanese law not only gives civil and criminal immunity to proper acts of trade unions, but also encourages collective bargaining by imposing a duty to bargain on employers and by sanctioning it through the unfair labor practice system.

Labor market law

Article 27 paragraph 1 of the Constitution ("All people shall have the right and the obligation to work.") has been interpreted as requiring two political obligations on the part of the state.[9] First, the state shall intervene in the labor market so as to enable workers to obtain suitable job opportunities. Second, the state bears a political obligation to guarantee the livelihood of those workers who cannot obtain such opportunities.[10] This article forms the basis of "labor market law."

Corresponding to the first legislative mandate, various statues were enacted. The Employment Security Act of 1947 regulates employment placement services, recruitment and labor supply businesses. The Employment Measures Act of 1966 proclaims the general principles of labor market policies. Other

9 Sugeno, supra note 4, 15.

10 Art. 27 para. 1 also mentions the obligation to work. The literal meaning of the phrase implies industrial conscription. However, since that interpretation is not appropriate, "obligation to work" is interpreted to mean the state has no obligation towards those who do not have an intention to work. Thus, the availability of unemployment benefits is confined to those who intend to work.

examples include: the Act Promoting the Development of Occupational Ability of 1969, the Disabled Employment Promotion Act of 1960, and the Older Persons' Employment Stabilization Act of 1971. Corresponding to the second mandate, the Unemployment Insurance Act of 1947 and its successor, the Employment Insurance Act of 1974, were enacted.

Major laws regulating labor and employment relations in Japan

Constitution

Article 27: right to work, mandate to establish minimum standards of working conditions by statutes

Article 28: right of workers to organize and to bargain and act collectively

Individual labor relations laws

Labor protective laws

Labor Standards Act

Minimum Wages Act

Security of Wage Payment Act

Industrial Safety and Health Act

Workers' Accident Compensation Insurance Act

Equal Employment Opportunity Act

Part-time Work Act

Child Care and Family Care Leave Act

Labor contract laws

Civil Code Article 623–631 (Employment Contract)

Labor Contract Act

Labor Contract Succession Act

Collective labor relations laws

Labor Union Act

Labor Relations Adjustment Act

Labor market laws

Employment Measures Act

Employment Security Act

Worker Dispatching Act

Employment Insurance Act

Older Persons' Employment Stabilization Act

Disabled Persons' Employment Promotion Act

Regional Employment Development Promotion Act

Human Resources Development Promotion Act

Minimum standards of working conditions fixed by mandatory statutes

Worker protective laws

The individual employment relationship between an employer and a worker is regulated by labor protective laws such as the Labor Standards Act, the Minimum Wages Act, the Security of Wage Payment Act, the Industrial Safety and Health Act, the Workers' Accident Compensation Insurance Act, the Equal Employment Opportunity Act, and the Worker Dispatching Act.

As mentioned already, the most fundamental and important of these is the Labor Standards Act which establishes minimum working standards, such as employers' duty of full payment of wages (Art. 24), maximum working hours (8 hours a day, 40 hours a week, Art. 32), paid leave (10 to 20 days a year, Art. 39), special protection of young workers (Arts. 56–64) and pregnant women (Arts. 64–2 to 68), workers' compensation for work-related accidents (Arts. 75–88), rules of employment (Arts. 89–93) and supervision (Arts. 97–105) and penalties (Arts. 117–21).

LSA applies to all establishments which engage in the employment of workers irrespective of the number of workers. The exceptions are family businesses which employ family members only (Art. 116 para. 2), domestic workers (Art. 116 para. 2) and other employment relations for which special regulations apply, namely seamen (Art. 116 para. 1) and some civil servants. From a comparative perspective, the Labor Standards Act is very broad in its coverage.

Working conditions set forth by employment contracts, work rules and collective agreements that are inferior to the standards set by the Labor Standards Act are void and replaced by the Act's mandatory legal norms (LSA Art. 13[11]). Minimum standards prescribed in worker protective laws are enforced by the Labor Standards Inspection Offices, in addition to the sanction of criminal penalties.

To provide flexibility, the LSA allows deviation or derogation from the mandatory norms based upon a "labor-management agreement (majority representative agreement)." The majority representative agreement is different from a collective bargaining agreement concluded between employers and labor unions. The majority representative agreement is concluded between an employer and a "representative of the majority of workers at an establishment," namely a union organizing a majority of the workers in the establishment or a person representing a majority of the workers in the absence of a majority union. Deviation from the mandatory minimum standards is allowed when the Act explicitly prescribes such derogation. For instance, the LSA requires a majority representative agreement for deduction of wages, hours-averaging schemes or overtime work.

Labor contracts (individual employment contracts)

The LSA requires the employer to clarify the working conditions to the worker when concluding a labor contract (LSA Art.15). Article 5 of the Ordinance for Enforcement of the LSA (OELSA) enumerates matters which shall be clarified. In particular, clarification pertaining to the place of work, content of work, work hours, payment of wages, and retirement must be made in writing (OELSA Art. 5 para. 2).

It is, however, rather rare for an employer and a worker to make a written contract and prescribe concrete working conditions in detail. Workers merely agree orally that they will work for the company. To satisfy the requirement to clarify working conditions, the employer usually presents the worker with the work rules, which cover most items to be clarified. As long as the worker raises no objection to the content of the work rules, he is regarded as having agreed to the conditions. Thus, the conditions stipulated in the work rules become the substantive content of employment contracts.

---

11 Art. 13 of the Labor Standards Act stipulates that "A labor contract which provides for working conditions which do not meet the standards of this Act shall be invalid with respect to such portions. In such a case the portions which have become invalid shall be governed by the standards set forth in this Act."

Work rules

Work rules are the most important legal tools regulating terms and conditions of employment in Japan.

Duty to draw up work rules

Work rules are a set of regulations set forth by an employer for the purpose of establishing uniform rules and conditions of employment at the workplace. Article 89 of the LSA prescribes that an employer who continuously employs ten or more workers[12] must draw up work rules on the following matters: (1) the time at which work begins and ends, rest periods, rest days, leave, and matters pertaining to shifts, (2) the method of decision, computation and payment of wages, date of payment of wages and matters pertaining to wage increases, (3) retirement including dismissals, (3–2) retirement allowances, (4) extraordinary wages and minimum wages, (5) cost of food or supplies for work, (6) safety and health, (7) vocational training, (8) accident compensation, (9) commendations and sanctions, and (10) other items applicable to all workers at the workplace. Items 1 to 3 are absolutely mandatory matters which must be included in the work rules. Items 3–2 to 10 are conditionally mandatory matters which must be included in the work rules when the employer wants to introduce regulations concerning these matters.

When the employer institutes the work rules for the first time or when the work rules are altered, the employer must submit those new rules to the competent Labor Standards Inspection Office. The rules must also be made known to the workers by conspicuous posting, distribution of printed documents or setting up accessible computer terminals (LSA Art. 106, OELSA Art. 52–2). The duties for drawing up, submitting and displaying work rules are sanctioned by criminal provisions (LSA Art. 120).

In drawing up or modifying work rules, the employer is required to ask the opinion of a labor union organized by a majority of the workers at the workplace or, where no such union exists, the opinion of a person representing a majority of the workers. However, a *consensus* is not required. Even when the majority representative opposes the content of the work rules, the employer may submit them to the Labor Standards Inspection Office with such an opposing opinion and the submission will be accepted. In this sense, the employer can unilaterally establish and modify work rules.

12 Though it is not clear from the provision, it is generally interpreted that "ten or more workers" should be calculated not in the enterprise but in the establishment, on the rationale that work rules apply in each establishment and procedures for drawing up work rules presuppose each establishment as a unit (LSL Art. 90).

The legal effect of work rules and their unfavorable modification

The work rules apply to all workers in a workplace or establishment. Work rules cannot violate enacted laws or collective agreements applicable to the establishment (LSA Art. 92 para. 1). The LSA gives work rules an imperative and direct effect on individual labor contracts. Namely, the Act states that employment contracts that stipulate working conditions inferior to those provided in the work rules shall be invalid and that such conditions are to be replaced by the standards in the work rules (LCA Art. 12).

The LCA incorporates the established case law on reasonable modification of work rules. As a principle, the modification of work rules without a worker's consent is not binding but if the modification is reasonable, such modified work rules have a binding effect on all workers, including those who were opposed to the modification itself (LCA Arts. 9, 10). Underlying this ruling is a consideration for employment security and the necessity for adjusting working conditions. Traditional contract theory dictates that a worker who opposes the modifications of working conditions be discharged. However, according to the established Japanese case law, such a dismissal may well be regarded as an abuse of the right to dismiss. On the other hand, because the employment relationship is a continuous contractual relationship, modification and adjustment of working conditions are inevitable. In light of these circumstances, Japanese courts have given unilaterally modified work rules a binding effect on condition that the modification is reasonable. These unique rules can be called the Japanese version of "flexicurity," reconciling flexible regulation of working conditions with employment security.[13]

Collective agreements

The fourth vehicle for regulating the content of individual labor contracts is a collective bargaining agreement between the employer and the union.

Normative effect

According to Article 16 of the LUA, any portion of an individual labor contract is void if it contravenes the standards concerning conditions of work and other matters relating to the treatment of workers that are provided for in a collective agreement. In such a case, the invalidated parts of the individual contract are governed by the standards set forth in the collective agreement. Similarly, if there are matters that the individual employment contract does not cover, the same rule applies.

---

13 Araki, *supra* note 8.

Therefore, the "normative effect" actually consists of two legal effects: an imperative effect that nullifies the portion of an individual contract that contravenes the standards contained in the collective agreement, and a direct regulating effect that alters provisions of the individual contract.

Collective agreements not only supersede individual contracts but also invalidate work rules that contravene the collective agreement (LSA Art. 92).

Enterprise-level bargaining and legal effect of collective agreements

Almost all collective agreements in Japan are concluded at the enterprise level because unions are normally organized on an individual company basis. Consequently, in contrast to the practices in Western Europe, collective agreements can regulate not minimum, but actual working conditions. Therefore, according to the accepted interpretation,[14] the normative effect of collective agreements invalidates not only disadvantageous individual contracts but also advantageous contracts unless the collective bargaining agreement itself allows such contracts. In other words, *Günstigkeitsprinzip*, or the principle which permits more favorable individual agreements, is not generally accepted. Decentralized collective bargaining enables the parties concerned to adjust and determine working conditions in a particular company swiftly and appropriately.

Employer's duty to bargain collectively

In most industrialized countries, because employers have no duty to bargain, labor unions must put economic pressure on employers to make them come to the bargaining table. In contrast, the Labor Union Act imposes upon an employer a duty to bargain with a union in good faith, and a refusal to bargain is prohibited as an unfair labor practice (LUA Art. 7 no. 2).

The duty to bargain in good faith is not synonymous with the duty of co-determination. The employer must bargain in good faith, but he is not forced to make concessions or to reach an agreement.

As to the introduction of the unfair labor practice system, the Labor Union Act of Japan is modeled on the Wagner Act in the United States. However, the LUA does not adopt an exclusive representation system. Each union that meets statutory requirements enjoys full-fledged rights to bargain collectively and go on strike. Therefore, in Japan, there are neither elections to choose an exclusive representative of workers nor the notion of a bargaining unit. A union that organizes a few workers in a single company has equal bargaining rights with a

14 Sugeno, *supra* note 4, 589; Araki, *supra* note 8, 175.

union that organizes the majority of workers in the company (plural representation system).

A second difference is that, unlike the Taft-Hartley Act in the United States, the LUA does not impose a duty to bargain on labor unions.

Enforcement mechanism of labor law

Court system

Japan has no courts specially designated for labor litigation. All labor and employment related lawsuits must be filed in ordinary courts. The judges are professional jurists.

Japan has a three-tiered court system: district courts (including Labor Tribunals), high courts and the Supreme Court. The district court in each prefecture is usually the court of first instance.[15] A party may appeal from a judgment of the district court to the competent high court. It is possible for a party who is not satisfied with the judgment to make a further appeal to the Supreme Court. However, the grounds for appeal to the Supreme Court are limited to errors of interpretation of the Constitution or other violations of the Constitution in the original judgment (Code of Civil Procedure, Art. 312 para. 1). The Supreme Court also has discretion to accept appeals where the original judgment contradicts the precedents of the Supreme Court or involves other significant matters concerning the interpretation of law (Code of Civil Procedure, Art. 318 para. 1).[16]

Until 2006, Japan did not have a labor court system with lay judges like *Arbeitsgerichte* in Germany, Employment Tribunals in the UK, and *conseil des prud'hommes* in France. Faced with the rapid increase in individual labor litigation, however, Japan introduced a new labor dispute resolution system called the Labor Tribunal System (*Roudou Shinpan*) in 2006.

The Labor Tribunal System established in each district court in Japan is a procedure consisting of one professional judge and two lay judges recommended by labor and the management side respectively. In a sense, therefore, the Labor Tribunal System is a Japanese version of a tripartite labor court, although it is not a separate court but a forum established in an ordinary court.

15 Cases wher the amount at issue does not exceed 900,000 yen must be filed in a summary court. The cases filed in the summary court can be appealed to a district court and to an appellate court, but not to the Supreme Court.
16 Oda, *Japanese Law*, 64ff (2nd. ed. 1999).

Because the new tribunal is in principle aimed at overcoming delays in labor litigation, the Labor Tribunal must decide the case within three sessions. This means that a filed complaint will be disposed of within three or four months. Its hearings are informal and not open to the public. If either party rejects the Tribunal's decision, it has no effect, but the case is automatically transferred to the regular civil section of the same district court.

Since its coming into operation in 2006, the Labor Tribunal System has enjoyed a strong reputation for its expedited procedures and high performance with a high rate of settlement (80 percent).

Administrative agencies of the national government

The Ministry of Labor was responsible for the administration of labor law and labor policy until the end of 2000. However, as a part of the reform of Japan's central bureaucracy, the Ministry of Labor and the Ministry of Health and Welfare were merged and the Ministry of Health, Welfare and Labor (MHWL) was established in January 2001. Within the MHWL, several bureaus are in charge of the administration and implementation of labor laws. The MHWL maintains Prefectural Labor Bureaus in each of the 47 prefectures to implement the laws at local level.

The Labor Standards Bureau within the MHWL administers labor standards established by the Labor Standards Act, the Minimum Wages Act, the Industrial Safety and Health Act. The Labor Standards Bureau also administers the Workers' Accident Compensation Act. Actual implementation of this labor protective legislation occurs through the Labor Standards Inspection Offices in each prefecture. Approximately 3,500 Labor Standards Inspectors work at 343 Labor Standards Inspection Offices throughout Japan. The Labor Standards Inspectors are authorized to inspect workplaces, to demand the production of books and records, and to question employers and workers (LSA Art. 101). Furthermore, with respect to a violation of the LSA, Labor Standard Inspectors shall exercise the duties of judicial police officers under the Criminal Procedure Act (LSA Art. 102).

A worker may report violation of labor protective laws to the Labor Standards Inspection Office. Dismissal and other disadvantageous treatment by reason of such a worker having made a report is prohibited by criminal sanctions (LSA Arts. 104, 119 no.1).

The Equal Employment Opportunity Act is administered by the Equal Employment, Children and Family Bureau within the MHWL. Under its Prefectural Labor Bureaus, the Equal Employment Offices (*Koyo Kinto-shitsu*) are responsible for the daily enforcement of the laws related to employment equality and harmonization of work and family life.

The Employment Measures Act, the Employment Security Act, the Worker Dispatching Act and other labor market policy and regulations are administered by the Employment Security Bureau within the MHWL. The Public Employment Security Offices are responsible for public placement services, vocational guidance, and the employment insurance system, including distribution of benefits and grants to workers, as well as firms.

Labor Relations Commission (*Rodo Iinkai*)

The Central Labor Relations Commission at the national level and the Local Labor Relations Commissions in each prefecture deal with collective labor disputes. This commission is an independent administrative committee comprised of an equal number of commissioners representing employers, workers and the public interest.

The Labor Relations Commission has two main functions. First, it engages with collective labor disputes through conciliation, mediation and voluntary arbitration. Second, it adjudicates unfair labor practice cases and issues remedial orders when it finds that an unfair labor practice was committed by an employer.

References

For a general overview of Japanese labor and employment law, see KAZUO SUGENO (Leo Kanowitz trans.), JAPANESE LABOR AND EMPLOYMENT LAW (University of Tokyo Press, 2002); TAKASHI ARAKI, LABOR AND EMPLOYMENT LAW IN JAPAN (Japan Institute of Labor, 2002); TADASHI HANAMI & FUMITO KOMIYA, LABOUR LAW IN JAPAN (Kluwer International, 2011).

An English translation of Japanese laws is accessed at: http://www.japaneselawtranslation.go.jp/?re=02;

http://www.jil.go.jp/english/laborinfo/library/Laws.htm.

Useful English articles on Japanese labor and employment law and industrial relations are accessed at http://www.jil.go.jp/english/index.html.

EMPLOYMENT LAW IN THE UNITED STATES: A GENERAL INTRODUCTION

The United States is a federal structure composed of a national government and 50 states in addition to the District of Columbia and other possessions. The federal government is composed of an executive branch – including autonomous administrative agencies – a bicameral legislature and a three-tiered system of federal courts: district courts, circuit courts of appeals, and the Supreme Court. Actions of the federal government within its constitutional sphere are binding upon the states. Thus, federal legislation may preempt state action, that is, reserve a field of regulation to it exclusively, or allow the states to act so long as they do not contravene the federal scheme.

Each of the 50 states has its own three-branched governmental form: its own constitution, which may be more capacious in recognition of individual rights than is the federal constitution; its own executive, legislative, and judicial branches.

Unlike some countries where the constitution sets out labor rights or whose bill of rights is taken to be part of the order of legal values that infuse private employment relations – Germany is an example of this – with one exception, the abolition of slavery, the federal constitution controls public, not private centers of power. For example, an employee cannot invoke a constitutional right of free speech against an action of a private employer. In some states, however, the state constitution may act on the private sphere as, most notably, do some provisions in California.

Responsibility for employment regulation

Until the constitutional revolution of the New Deal in the 1930s, the power of Congress to legislate regarding the terms and conditions of employment, even of employees who worked for employers engaged in interstate commerce, was extremely limited: only if the employee actually crossed a state line in the performance of his or her work did Congress have any power. Thus, the basic regulation of employment fell to the states either by common law – contract or tort – or by legislation. In a scenario that is echoed in the global economy today, competition between the states could be conducive toward a "race to the bottom," for business to locate – or relocate – to states that allowed lower pay or poorer working conditions. That fact served as a barrier to such state reforms as the elimination of child labor or improving occupational health and safety. Interstate competition in labor protection generally, and especially hostility to unionization via so-called "right to work" laws, persists today.

Minimum employment conditions

Collective bargaining law

The law of collective bargaining is federal – in the Railway Labor Act (which, oddly, includes airline employees) and the National Labor Relations Act (NLRA), which includes many but by no means all private sector employees. It excludes, for example, independent contractors, domestic workers, and supervisors. The NLRA allows employees to engage in collective bargaining by a system of exclusive representation by majority rule – a model little followed elsewhere in the world. It prohibits conduct by employers and unions that interfere in the right to form a union (or to refrain from doing so) and regulates good faith in collective bargaining. The Act is administered by an administrative agency, the National Labor Relations Board (NLRB), which has regional offices throughout the United States. Critically, under the Supremacy Clause of the Constitution, the fact that the power to regulate employee representation is given to a federal agency has been held to preempt the states from taking any action, by legislation or by common law, that does or might upset or interfere in the federal system.

Union density in the private sector has been in steady decline since the mid-1970s. Today, unions represent about 6.6 percent of the civilian non-agricultural labor market; but, given the exclusions from coverage, union density with respect to those capable of exercising the right to engage in collective bargaining is actually a bit higher.

Other preemptive federal employment law

There are a variety of other federal laws that preclude state action but, with one exception, these tend to address narrowly defined and closely regulated subjects. The major exception is the Employee Retirement Income Security Act (ERISA) which broadly regulates pension and welfare benefits. It sets out a preemption clause that sweeps away all state law insofar as it "relates to" that which ERISA regulates, subject to exceptions.

Non-preemptive federal law

For the most part, federal employment law sets floors of rights. The states are accordingly free to echo that which Congress has established or go beyond it; and they do. Some of these federal laws are:

- The Fair Labor Standards Act (FLSA) which regulates child labor, sets out a federal minimum wage, and requires the payment of time and a half for work in excess of a 40-hour week, subject, however, to extensive and elaborate exemptions.
- The Occupational Safety and Health Act (OSHA), which establishes a command and control structure and a system of standards and sanctions.
- The Worker Adjustment and Retraining Notification Act (WARN), which provides for 60 days' notice of plant closing or mass layoff.
- The Family and Medical Leave Act (FMLA), which requires eligible employees to be given up to 12 weeks' *unpaid* leave for family and medical emergencies.
- Anti-discrimination in employment laws, starting with the Equal Pay Act in 1963, requiring equal pay for equal work for men and women (*not* comparable pay for comparable work, as in some countries), and expanding thereafter to prohibit employment discrimination on grounds of: race, sex, religion, national origin (all under the Civil Rights Act of 1964), citizenship (under immigration law), age (under the Age Discrimination in Employment Act), and disability (under the Americans With Disabilities Act). Again, unlike many countries no law requires employers to provide paid vacations or paid leave – for illness, childbirth or child care.

Employment law: state law and the "at-will" rule

The law governing the formation and existence of an employment relationship as well as the terms and conditions of it is largely state law. Who an "employee" is for federal statutory purposes is a federal question to be decided under each such statute. For the most part, U.S. law applies a more rigid employee/independent contract or distinction at both the federal and state levels.

Employees also confront the legacy of the late nineteenth century's embrace of *laissez-faire*. In that period the states adopted the rule that absent agreement on employment for a fixed term – or strong evidence implying such a term – the employment was indefinite and so terminable by the employer or employee without notice. To this the courts added the notion that the power to terminate was unfettered by law; it was irrelevant that the employer acted mistakenly, arbitrarily, or even maliciously. The "at-will" rule is much criticized today and has become riddled with exceptions, legislated and judge-made; but it persists, which, because of the many exceptions that can vary significantly from state to state, makes the U.S. law of employment almost bewilderingly complicated. Unlike Germany, Japan, Australia, Brazil, and a great many other countries, there is no general right not to be dismissed wrongly – aside from statutes in Montana and Puerto Rico.

State protective legislation

Many states do echo or go beyond non-preemptive federal law: they provide a higher minimum wage or add protected categories not included under federal antidiscrimination law, for example, marital status, sexual orientation, gender identification, obesity (Michigan), or "appearance" (District of Columbia). As a result, there may be a multiplicity of fora, administrative and judicial, federal and state, to which an aggrieved employee may have resort.

State laws deal also with such matters as: occupational safety and health, including mandatory rest periods; workers' compensation; unemployment compensation insurance (under a federal system but subject to state participation with considerable areas of state discretion); drug and alcohol testing; whistleblowing and other conscientious objection; plant closing; job references; wage payment; covenants not to compete; trade secrets; employee privacy; and a good deal more.

The common law

There is no federal common law of contract or tort. Federal courts may have jurisdiction to hear cases presenting such issues where the parties are from different states – for example, a Delaware incorporated corporation being sued by an Illinois employee – under so-called "diversity of citizenship" jurisdiction where the dollar amount is above a certain threshold, but the common law to be applied in such cases is that of the relevant state under the forum state's "choice of law" rules. Thus such matters as defamation, deceit, invasion of privacy, infliction of emotional distress, interference in prospective economic advantage, breach of loyalty or fiduciary duty are matters of state law. In some areas, the states generally take a uniform approach – indeed, there may be a "uniform state law" – but in others they differ, sometimes sharply.

Vindicating legal rights: courts, administrative agencies, and arbitrators

In some cases the aggrieved employee has available – or must resort to – an administrative agency. For example, claims that an employer has interfered in or coerced employees in their right to unionize or engage in other acts of statutory mutual aid or protection under the Labor Act must be made to the General Counsel's office of the NLRB which may – or may not – issue a complaint and pursue legal process. There is no private right of action under that law. Claims of unlawful employment discrimination under the Civil Rights Act must first be presented to the federal and any cognate state administrative agency; and if they decline to sue, which is most often the case, the individual has to secure counsel and bring a lawsuit on her own. The United States has no labor court, unlike, for example, Germany or Brazil. Consequently, resort must be had to state or federal court which, as a practical matter, means that the aggrieved individual must secure legal counsel.

A number of American companies have adapted policies that require non-unionized employees to forego access to the courts and submit all their legal claims to arbitration systems of the company's devising. The United States Supreme Court has upheld the enforceability of these plans under a 1925 federal law so long as due process is afforded. The states are not free to adopt policies disallowing employers that power.

References

There is no single comprehensive treatise on all of U.S. labor and employment law. Rather, there are comprehensive volumes treating the law of collective bargaining, employment discrimination, occupational health and safety, wrongful dismissal, covenants not to compete, and so on. The relevant references on U.S. law will be adverted to in the discussion of the problems that ensue.

B. SOME DEMOGRAPHIC CONTEXT

> [F]rom an HR practitioner ... perspective [it is important to understand] the demography of the labor markets that you choose to compete in. Whether they be existing markets and mapping trends, or analyzing information and trends as you aspire to new markets. These demographic realities shape the competitive and structural forces [to which] we will need to respond. Having a clear understanding of these trends can help identify ... potential shifts in protections or priorities for enforcement. Additionally, for a values-driven organization (as opposed to a purely bottom-line driven organization) understanding and being comfortable with these structural profiles can help drive policies relevant to your market space. Crafting these policies to reflect the demographic realities that you face can provide a significant opportunity to gain an advantage in attracting and retaining talent.
>
> Director, HR, Industrial Manufacturing Sector

More comparative data will be set out in connection with the discussion of specific problems. What follows will give a broad overview of the five countries presented for comparative study.

Table I.2 Workforce size, education expenditure, and UN education index by country (2007, estimated)

	Workforce size (m)	Education expenditure (as a percent of GDP)	UN education index
Australia	10.9	5.4	0.993
Brazil	99.47	5.0	0.891
Germany	43.63	4.5	0.954
Japan	66.07	3.5	0.958
United States	153.1	5.5	0.978

Sources: https://www.cia.gov/library/publications/the-world-factbook/geos/as.html. The UN education index is measured by the adult literacy rate (with two-thirds weighting) and the combined primary, secondary, and tertiary gross enrollment ratio (with one-third weighting). The adult literacy rate gives an indication of the ability to read and write, while the GER gives an indication of the level of education from nursery (UK & others)/kindergarten (USA & others) to postgraduate education.

Table I.3 Labor force participation, 2009

	Australia	Brazil	Germany	Japan	United States
Employment-population ratio – Total (Percent of civilian working-age population)	62.9	64.9	54.0	56.4	59.3
Labor force participation rate – Total (Percent of civilian working-age population)	66.7	70.7	58.5	59.3	65.4
Labor force participation rate – Men (Percent of civilian working-age population)	73.3	81.9	65.3	71.2	72.0
Labor force participation rate – Women (Percent of civilian working-age population)	60.1	60.1	52.1	48.2	59.2
Women's share of the labor force (Percent of civilian labor force)	45.5	43.7	45.9	42.1	46.7

Notes: The first row, employment-population ratio represents the total percentage of working-age civilians who were employed in 2009 (the balance were unemployed or not looking for work). The second row includes all participants in the labor force, employed and unemployed. The next two rows represent the same percentages, broken down for men and women. Finally, the women's share of the labor force represents the percentage of the civilian labor force (the middle three rows) who are female.

Source: U.S. Department of Labor, U.S. Bureau of Labor Statistics, Division of International Labor Comparisons.

Table I.4 Labor participation rate by gender (% female and % male, population aged 15+)

		2007	2008	2009	2010
Australia	Female	58	59	59	59
	Male	73	73	72	73
Brazil	Female	58	59	59	59
	Male	81	81	81	81
Germany	Female	52	52	53	53
	Male	67	67	67	67
Japan	Female	49	49	49	50
	Male	73	73	72	72
United States	Female	58	58	58	58
	Male	72	72	71	70

Source: The World Bank, World Development Indicators, http://data.worldbank.org/indicator/SL.TLF.CACT.FE.ZS.

Table I.5 Unemployment rate by gender (% female labor force and % male labor force)

		2007	2008	2009	2010
Australia	Female	4.8	4.6	5.4	5.4
	Male	4.0	4.0	5.7	5.1
Brazil	Female	10.8	9.6	11.0	–
	Male	6.0	5.2	6.1	–
Germany	Female	8.8	7.7	7.3	6.6
	Male	8.5	7.4	8.1	7.5
Japan	Female	3.7	3.8	4.7	4.5
	Male	4.0	4.1	5.3	5.4
United States	Female	4.5	5.4	8.1	8.6
	Male	4.7	6.1	10.3	10.5

Source: The World Bank, World Development Indicators, http://data.worldbank.org/topic/labor-and-social-protection.

Table I.6 Population age distribution by country (2008, estimated)

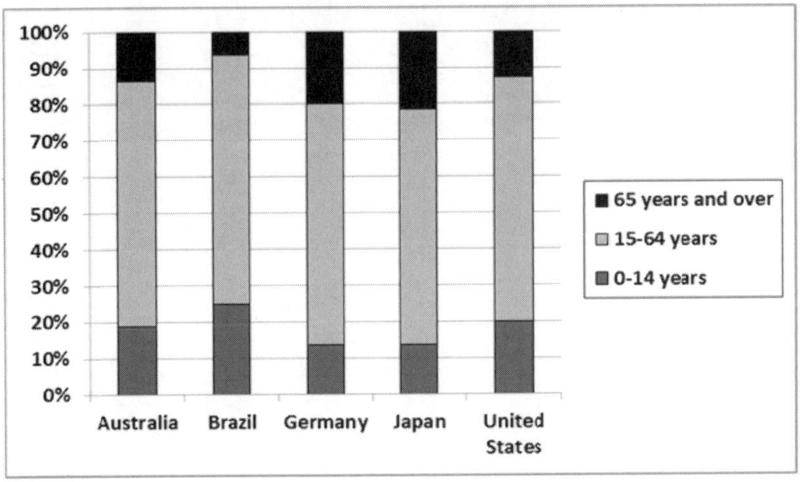

Source: Adapted from https://www.cia.gov/library/publications/the-world-factbook/geos/as.html.

PART II

EMPLOYEE VOICE: COLLECTIVE BARGAINING, CO-DETERMINATION, INFORMATION SHARING AND CONSULTATION

INTRODUCTION

The history of collective workplace protest – the demand to be heard on wages or working conditions – transcends history and culture. There is evidence of strikes in Roman Egypt and even of collective agreements in the ancient world. *See* W.H. Buckler, *Labor Disputes in the Province of Asia*, in ANATOLIAN STUDIES PRESENTED TO SIR WILLIAM MITCHELL RAMSAY Ch. III (W.H. Buckler & W.M. Calder eds. 1923). Labor protests were a feature of textile manufacture in the Middle Ages, but not in textiles alone. *See* Samuel Cohn, Jr., LUST FOR LIBERTY: THE POLITICS OF SOCIAL REVOLT IN MEDIEVAL EUROPE, 1200–1425 (2006). In eighteenth century Japan, peasant social protest, including refusal to work, reflected economic as well as social tensions. *E.g.* Anne Walthall, SOCIAL PROTEST AND POPULAR CULTURE IN EIGHTEENTH-CENTURY JAPAN (1986). One is tempted to consider the desire for voice an aspect of the human condition. In modern times, the International Labor Organization's conventions and numerous international declarations regard "freedom of association" as a human right.

With the rise of wage labor as the predominant form in which work would be done in eighteenth century Europe and North America, the law moved through three phases to deal with workers' demands for collective voice: repression, tolerance, and support. Today, the legal forms in which voice can be exercised vary: from forms of corporate governance, notably, employee representation on corporate boards; to collective bargaining; to co-determination by representative employee bodies "on the shop floor" or higher up in the enterprise's structure; to forms of "information sharing and consultation". These may be supplemented by less formal means little treated by law if at all, such as "affinity groups" and even less structured networks connected by social media. Many of these exist side by side.

The most common form in which legal support has been expressed has been in the provision for collective bargaining. But, there is enormous variation in how the right to bargain collectively is realized, in the manner and degree to which the representative is required to manifest its representative nature, in the architecture of a bargaining structure, in the extent to which the employee representative is or can be actively involved in the fashioning of employment or other corporate policy, and in the role of the state itself. *See generally*, Folke Schmidt & Alan Neal, *Collective Agreements and Collective Bargaining*, preprint from XV INT'L ENCYCLOPEDIA OF COMPARATIVE LAW (1984) (on the historical variety). In some systems, Germany and Brazil, for example, collective representation may or must transcend the individual firm. In others, Japan, for example, it is predominantly restricted to the individual firm. In the United States, bargaining structure is largely up to the parties to work out.

Tables II.1 and II.2 give a rough indication of union density in each of these countries and over time. We say "rough" because the data conflates public and the private sectors. In the United States, for example, private sector density is below 7 percent. As the note to Table II.1 explains, contract coverage can exceed the union's membership, sometimes rather significantly as in Germany. Nevertheless, despite these reservations the tables are instructive.

Table II.1 Union membership (combined public and private sector) as a percentage of the labor force

	1970	1980	1990	2000	2010
Australia	50.2	49.5	40.5	24.7	18.0
Brazil	19.6*	34.8*	38.1*	24.8*	–
Germany	32.0	34.9	31.2	25.0	18.5
Japan	35.1	31.1	25.4	21.5	18.4
United States	23.5	19.5	15.5	12.8	11.4

Note: Union membership (sometimes termed "union density") represents the proportion of union members relative to the labor force. Note that these figures have been adjusted by the source for the proportion of union members who are retired in each country. The proportion of the workforce covered by union-negotiated agreements – union coverage – will be larger in each case.

* Data for Brazil for time periods: 1976–80; 1981–85; 1986–90; 1991–95 from E.A. Lora and C. Pagés-Serra, *Labor Market Regulations and Institutions*, in ECONOMIC AND SOCIAL PROGRESS IN LATIN AMERICA – 2004 REPORT, October 2003, Inter-American Development Bank.

Sources: David G. Blanchflower, A Cross-Country Study of Union Membership, IZA DP No. 2016, March 2006, adapted from J. Visser, *Union Membership Statistics in 24 Countries*, MONTHLY LABOR REVIEW, January 2006, pp. 38–49; and, for 2010 data, OECD StatExtracts at: http://stats.oecd.org/Index.aspx?DatasetCode=UN_DEN.

Table II.2 Private sector union membership as a percentage of the labor force

Australia (2009)	13.2
Brazil (2009/10)	18
Germany (2003)	19.7
Japan (2009)	16.9
United States (2012)	6.6

Sources: Australian Bureau of Statistics, EMPLOYEE EARNINGS, BENEFITS, AND TRADE UNION MEMBERSHIP, AUSTRALIA (August 2011, released 27 April 2012); Roberto Fragale, "Employment Law in Brazil: A General Introduction," supra; Wolfgang Streeck, REFORMING CAPITALISM (2009), Figure 3.2, p. 97; Japanese Working Life Profile, 2000/2001 – Labor Statistics. U.S. Bureau of Labor Statistics, www.bls,gov/news.release/union2.ar0.htm

Provision has also been made for a variety of other forms of representation within the firm. These vary from systems of co-determination, as in Germany (and Austria), to systems of information sharing and consultation, as in the *comité d'enterprise* in France. *See generally*, Roger Blanpain, *Representation of Employees at Plant and Enterprise Level*, preprint from XV INT'L ENCYCLOPEDIA OF COMPARATIVE LAW (1994) (on the historical background). The latter has been pressed upon the Member States of the European Union by a Directive requiring them to make provision for such bodies where domestic law does not already so provide. (The Directive is appended at the close of this introduction.) Obviously, German law's more exacting system of co-determination via elected works councils goes well beyond the Directive's minima; but in other countries, where such provision was lacking, the United Kingdom, for example, the Directive has required legal change. *See* Simon Deakin & Gillian Morris, LABOUR LAW 913–69 (6th ed. 2012). Set out below is a snapshot of what corporate CEOs think of the nature of management-employee relations in the sample of countries taken up here.

Table II.3 Cooperation in labor-employer relations

Australia	4.3
Brazil	4.3
Germany	5.2
Japan	5.6
United States	4.7

Note: CEOs were asked "How would you characterize labor-employer relations in your country?" (1 = generally confrontational; 7 = generally cooperative). A weighted average for 2011–12 is shown (mean for 144 nations is 4.3).

Source: World Economic Forum, Executive Opinion Survey, Global Competitiveness Report 2012–2013.

The variety of approaches to collective representation is best introduced by a seemingly simple question, put by Problem 1. Some of the follow-on complexities of these approaches will be developed in the ensuing problems. For preparation the European Union's Directive on employee information sharing and consultation is set out below.

DIRECTIVE 2002/14 EC

Whereas:

(9) Timely information and consultation is a prerequisite for the success of the restructuring and adaptation of under-takings to the new conditions created by globalisation of the economy, particularly through the development of new forms of organisation of work.

(13) The existing legal frameworks for employee information and consultation at Community and national level tend to adopt an excessively a posteriori approach to the process of change, neglect the economic aspects of decisions taken and do not contribute either to genuine anticipation of employment developments within the undertaking or to risk prevention.

(27) Information and consultation imply both rights and obligations for management and labour at undertaking or establishment level.

Article 1

Object and principles

1. The purpose of this Directive is to establish a general framework setting out minimum requirements for the right to information and consultation of employees in undertakings or establishments within the Community
2. The practical arrangements for information and consultation shall be defined and implemented in accordance with national law and industrial relations practices in individual Member States in such a way as to ensure their effectiveness
3. When defining or implementing practical arrangements for information and consultation, the employer and the employees representatives shall work in a spirit of cooperation and with due regard for their reciprocal rights and obligations, taking into account the interests both of the undertaking or establishment and of the employees.

Article 2

Definitions

For the purposes of this Directive:

(a) 'undertaking' means a public or private undertaking carrying out an economic activity, whether or not operating for gain, which is located within the territory of the Member States;
(b) 'establishment' means a unit of business defined in accordance with national law and practice, and located within the territory of a Member State, where an economic activity is carried out on an ongoing basis with human and material resources;
(c) 'employer' means the natural or legal person party to employment contracts or employment relationships with employees, in accordance with national law and practice;
(d) 'employee' means any person who, in the Member State concerned, is protected as an employee under national employment law and in accordance with national practice;
(e) 'employees' representatives' means the employees' representatives provided for by national laws and/or practices;
(f) 'information' means transmission by the employer to the employees' representatives of data in order to enable them to acquaint themselves with the subject matter and to examine it;
(g) 'consultation' means the exchange of views and establishment of dialogue between the employees' representatives and the employer.

Article 4

Practical arrangements for information and consultation

1. In accordance with the principles set out in Article 1 and without prejudice to any provisions and/or practices in force more favourable to employees, the Member States shall determine the practical arrangements for exercising the right to information and consultation at the appropriate level in accordance with this Article.
2. Information and consultation shall cover:
   (a) information on the recent and probable development of the undertaking's or the establishment's activities and economic situation;
   (b) information and consultation on the situation, structure and probable development of employment within the undertaking or establishment and on any anticipatory measures envisaged, in particular where there is a threat to employment;
   (c) information and consultation on decisions likely to lead to substantial changes in work organisation or in contractual relations …
3. Information shall be given at such time, in such fashion and with such content as are appropriate to enable, in particular, employees' representatives to conduct an adequate study and, where necessary, prepare for consultation.
4. Consultation shall take place:
   (a) while ensuring that the timing, method and content thereof are appropriate;
   (b) at the relevant level of management and representation, depending on the subject under discussion;

(c) on the basis of information supplied by the employer in accordance with Article 2(f) and of the opinion which the employees' representatives are entitled to formulate;
(d) in such a way as to enable employees' representatives to meet the employer and obtain a response, and the reasons for that response, to any opinion they might formulate;
(e) with a view to reaching an agreement on decisions within the scope of the employer's powers referred to in paragraph 2(c).

Article 5

Information and consultation deriving from an agreement

Member States may entrust management and labour at the appropriate level, including at undertaking or establishment level, with defining freely and at any time through negotiated agreement the practical arrangements for informing and consulting employees .... .

Article 6

Confidential Information

[Provision is made for the respect of confidential business information.]

Article 7

Protection of employees' representatives

Member States shall ensure that employees' representatives, when carrying out their functions, enjoy adequate protection and guarantees to enable them to perform properly the duties which have been assigned to them.

Article 8

Protection of rights

(13) The existing legal frameworks for employee information and consultation at Community and national level tend to adopt an excessively a posteriori approach to the process of change, neglect the economic aspects of decisions taken and do not contribute either to genuine anticipation of employment developments within the undertaking or to risk prevention.

1. Member states shall provide for appropriate measures in the event of non-compliance with this Directive by the employer or the employees' representatives. In particular, they shall ensure that adequate administrative or judicial procedures are available to enable the obligations deriving from this Directive to be enforced.
2. Member States shall provide for adequate sanctions to be applicable in the event of infringement of this Directive by the employer or the employees' representatives. These sanctions must be effective, proportionate and dissuasive.

* * *

On February 19, 2009, the European Parliament called for a better implementation of this Directive. Among its criticisms were the failure of some Member States "to take account of certain young workers, women working part-time or workers employed for short periods on fixed term contracts" in their provisions for information sharing and consultation as well as better definition of the information to be shared, for requiring the provision of information "in good time," and in involvement of unions.

PROBLEM 1: COLLECTIVE BARGAINING AND A NEW "GREENFIELD" FACILITY

Your company has opened a new (or "greenfield") facility in each of these countries. The local managers have hired from 8 to 12 clerical and administrative employees and from 40 to 60 production workers, mostly skilled workers. A union has approached each of the local managements and demanded either to bargain or to insist that a collective agreement already in existence be applied. Must your managers bargain or abide by the collective agreement? Does it make a difference if the employees – a majority or a minority – are union members?

Problem 1 discussion – Australia

Collective agreements in Australia are generally now made, registered and given legal effect as "enterprise agreements" under Part 2–4 of the Fair Work Act 2009. (There are transitional arrangements for agreements made before the current Act took effect on 1 July 2009, but these do not affect the analysis that follows.) If the company had an existing business in Australia, and had already negotiated an enterprise agreement for that business, it is possible that that agreement could cover the new facility. This would depend on the "scope" or "coverage" clause in the existing agreement. For instance, if the agreement were defined to cover all of the company's operations, without reference to any specified locations, the new facility (and all its employees) might well fall within it. Similarly, if another corporation had been operating the facility and then sold it to the company, any enterprise agreement previously negotiated for the facility would becoming legally binding on the company, under the "transfer of business" provisions in Parts 2–8 of the Fair Work Act.

However, if the facility is a completely new one, and the company has not previously operated in Australia, there is no possibility of the company being obliged to comply with any existing agreement. Australian law does not provide for industry, regional or national agreements. Although a "multi-enterprise agreement" can be made under s 172(3), these can only apply to an employer that was involved in making the agreement, and whose employees vote to approve it (see ss 182(2), 184).

A company that intends to establish a new enterprise can make a "greenfields agreement" under s 172(2)(b). This is a special form of agreement that is subject to a separate set of approval requirements. But a greenfields agreement cannot be made if the company has already hired employees who will covered by the agreement. Furthermore, a greenfields agreement can only be made with one or more "relevant employee organisations" – that is, trade unions that are registered under the Fair Work (Registered Organisations) Act 2009, and whose rules allow them to represent employees doing the types of work to be covered by the agreement.

Since on the facts given the company has already hired a number of employees, it is too late to make a greenfields agreement. If any agreement is now to be made, it will be an ordinary (non-greenfields) agreement, most likely under s 172(2)(a) of the Fair Work Act.

If the company refuses to bargain, there are two options open to any union that is seeking an agreement – provided that the union's rules make it eligible to represent at least some of the workers to be covered by the agreement.

The first and more peaceful option is for the union to apply to Fair Work Australia (FWA) under s 236 of the Fair Work Act for a majority support determination. Section 237 requires FWA to issue such a determination if it is satisfied that a majority of workers in the relevant group want to make an enterprise agreement. The "group" in question might be all the non-managerial employees, or just the clerical workers, or just the production workers. (It is possible for an agreement to cover only part of an enterprise, provided the group in question is "fairly chosen": see s 186(3)–(3A). In practice it is not unusual for companies to have more than one enterprise agreement, defined by reference to locality and/or types of work. Any dispute about the coverage of a proposed agreement can be resolved by FWA making a scope order under s 238: see e.g. *United Firefighters' Union of Australia v Metropolitan Fire & Emergency Services Board* [2010] FWAFB 3009.)

Where a determination is sought, it is for FWA to decide what evidence of "majority support" it will require. In some cases, signed petitions may be sufficient. But if the issue is contested, it is common for a ballot to be required: see e.g. *Automotive, Food, Metals, Engineering, Printing and Kindred Industries Union v Cochlear Ltd* [2009] FWA 125. Note that a union can seek and obtain a majority support determination even if it does not have a majority of *members* within the group – it need in fact only have one member to make the application.

The effect of a majority support determination being issued is that it activates the good faith bargaining requirements specified in s 228 (see Problem 3). Where these requirements are not being met, a bargaining representative (see below) can apply to FWA under s 229 for a bargaining order that remedies the breach. Under s 230(2), such an order can generally only be issued if the employer in question has *agreed* to bargain, or been *compelled* to bargain by the making of a majority support determination or scope order.

Section 176 indicates that for any proposed agreement, the following are to be regarded as bargaining representatives:

- the employer (even if it has appointed someone else to represent it);
- a registered union that has at least one member who will be covered by the agreement, unless every such member opts not to be represented by the union; and
- anyone else appointed in writing by the employer or a relevant employee to be their representative.

Importantly, there is no concept under Australian law of a union being an *exclusive* bargaining agent for any group of employees. If, for example, an individual employee is appointed as a bargaining representative, whether by herself or by a group of her co-workers, the employer must recognise and bargain with that employee, alongside any union that is acting for its members. That does not change even if the union has a majority of members in the relevant group – although in practice a union with majority coverage is likely to be the dominant force at the bargaining table.

Where bargaining has commenced, s 228(1) requires the employer to meet with each bargaining representative and give proper consideration to their proposals. The employer must also be prepared to outline its own preferred agreement – in other words, it cannot just engage in "surface bargaining": see e.g. *Endeavour Coal Pty Ltd v Association of Professional Engineers, Scientists and Managers, Australia* [2012] FCA 764. But as s 228(2) makes clear, there is no requirement for the employer to make any particular concessions, or indeed to reach agreement at all. An employer is perfectly at liberty to engage in "hard bargaining", so long as it does not ignore employee representatives, act capriciously or seek to undermine the notion of collective bargaining.

It is also worth emphasizing that while bargaining is under way, an employer may still communicate directly with its workforce, rather than dealing only with the official bargaining representatives, so long as it does not seek to mislead or coerce its employees. Furthermore, even if consensus is not reached with those representatives, an employer may choose to put its own preferred agreement to a vote of the affected employees, so long as the bargaining process has been given a fair chance: see *Construction, Forestry, Mining and Energy Union v Tahmoor Coal Pty Ltd* [2010] FWAFB 3510. If a majority of employees in the relevant group approve the agreement, it does not matter that a union involved (or indeed any other employee representative) may not have given their consent: see e.g. *Broken Hill Employees Union v Barrier Social Democratic Club* [2012] FWA 1096.

The second option for the union is to organise "protected" industrial action, either to compel the employer to bargain, or to further its claims after bargaining has commenced. The taking or organisation of industrial action is generally unlawful in Australia. But under Division 2 of Part 3–3 of the Fair Work Act, protected (i.e. lawful) action may be taken in support of a new enterprise agreement, provided various requirements are satisfied. One of the key requirements for anyone taking protected action is that they (and/or their representatives) have been genuinely trying to reach agreement. This would usually require a bargaining process. However, in *JJ Richards & Sons Pty Ltd v Transport Workers' Union of Australia* [2012] FCAFC 53 it was held that where an employer has refused to bargain at all, a union that has made reasonable efforts to outline its claims may legitimately organise protected action – even if the union has not made an application for a majority support determination.

PRIMARY SOURCE

Fair Work Act 2009

172 Making an enterprise agreement

Single-enterprise agreements

(2) An employer, or 2 or more employers that are single interest employers, may make an enterprise agreement (a *single-enterprise agreement*):
  (a) with the employees who are employed at the time the agreement is made and who will be covered by the agreement; or
  (b) with one or more relevant employee organisations if:
    (i) the agreement relates to a genuine new enterprise that the employer or employers are establishing or propose to establish; and
    (ii) the employer or employers have not employed any of the persons who will be necessary for the normal conduct of that enterprise and will be covered by the agreement.

Note: The expression genuine new enterprise includes a genuine new business, activity, project or undertaking (see the definition of *enterprise* in section 12).

Multi-enterprise agreements

(3) Two or more employers that are not all single interest employers may make an enterprise agreement (a *multi-enterprise agreement*):
   (a) with the employees who are employed at the time the agreement is made and who will be covered by the agreement; or
   (b) with one or more relevant employee organisations if:
      (i) the agreement relates to a genuine new enterprise that the employers are establishing or propose to establish; and
      (ii) the employers have not employed any of the persons who will be necessary for the normal conduct of that enterprise and will be covered by the agreement.

Note: The expression genuine new enterprise includes a genuine new business, activity, project or undertaking (see the definition of *enterprise* in section 12).

Greenfields agreements

(4) A single-enterprise agreement made as referred to in paragraph (2)(b), or a multi-enterprise agreement made as referred to in paragraph (3)(b), is a *greenfields agreement*.

Single interest employers

(5) Two or more employers are *single interest employers* if:
   (a) the employers are engaged in a joint venture or common enterprise; or
   (b) the employers are related bodies corporate; or
   (c) the employers are specified in a single interest employer authorisation that is in operation in relation to the proposed enterprise agreement concerned.

176 Bargaining representatives for proposed enterprise agreements that are not greenfields agreements

Bargaining representatives

(1) The following paragraphs set out the persons who are *bargaining representatives* for a proposed enterprise agreement that is not a greenfields agreement:
   (a) an employer that will be covered by the agreement is a bargaining representative for the agreement;
   (b) an employee organisation is a bargaining representative of an employee who will be covered by the agreement if:
      (i) the employee is a member of the organisation; and
      (ii) in the case where the agreement is a multi-enterprise agreement in relation to which a low-paid authorisation is in operation – the organisation applied for the authorisation;

unless the employee has appointed another person under paragraph (c) as his or her bargaining representative for the agreement, or has revoked the status of the organisation as his or her bargaining representative for the agreement under subsection 178A(2); or

   (c) a person is a bargaining representative of an employee who will be covered by the agreement if the employee appoints, in writing, the person as his or her bargaining representative for the agreement;

(d) a person is a bargaining representative of an employer that will be covered by the agreement if the employer appoints, in writing, the person as his or her bargaining representative for the agreement.

Bargaining representatives for a proposed multi-enterprise agreement if a low-paid authorisation is in operation

(2) If:

(a) the proposed enterprise agreement is a multi-enterprise agreement in relation to which a low-paid authorisation is in operation; and
(b) an employee organisation applied for the authorisation; and
(c) but for this subsection, the organisation would not be a bargaining representative of an employee who will be covered by the agreement;

the organisation is taken to be a *bargaining representative* of such an employee unless:

(d) the employee is a member of another employee organisation that also applied for the authorisation; or
(e) the employee has appointed another person under paragraph (1)(c) as his or her bargaining representative for the agreement; or
(f) the employee has revoked the status of the organisation as his or her bargaining representative for the agreement under subsection 178A(2).

Requirement relating to employee organisations

(3) Despite subsections (1) and (2), an employee organisation cannot be a bargaining representative of an employee unless the organisation is entitled to represent the industrial interests of the employee in relation to work that will be performed under the agreement.

Employee may appoint himself or herself

(4) To avoid doubt, an employee who will be covered by the agreement may appoint, under paragraph (1)(c), himself or herself as his or her bargaining representative for the agreement.

Note: Section 228 sets out the good faith bargaining requirements. Applications may be made for bargaining orders that require bargaining representatives to meet the good faith bargaining requirements (see section 229).

182 When an enterprise agreement is made

Single-enterprise agreement that is not a greenfields agreement

(1) If the employees of the employer, or each employer, that will be covered by a proposed single-enterprise agreement that is not a greenfields agreement have been asked to approve the agreement under subsection 181(1), the agreement is *made* when a majority of those employees who cast a valid vote approve the agreement.

Multi-enterprise agreement that is not a greenfields agreement

(2) If:
  (a) a proposed enterprise agreement is a multi-enterprise agreement; and
  (b) the employees of each of the employers that will be covered by the agreement have been asked to approve the agreement under subsection 181(1); and
  (c) those employees have voted on whether or not to approve the agreement; and
  (d) a majority of the employees of at least one of those employers who cast a valid vote have approved the agreement;

the agreement is ***made*** immediately after the end of the voting process referred to in subsection 181(1).

Greenfields agreement

(3) A greenfields agreement is *made* when it has been signed by each employer and each relevant employee organisation that the agreement is expressed to cover (which need not be all of the relevant employee organisations for the agreement).

230 When FWA may make a bargaining order

Bargaining orders

(1) FWA may make a bargaining order under this section in relation to a proposed enterprise agreement if:
  (a) an application for the order has been made; and
  (b) the requirements of this section are met in relation to the agreement; and
  (c) FWA is satisfied that it is reasonable in all the circumstances to make the order.

Agreement to bargain or certain instruments in operation

(2) FWA must be satisfied in all cases that one of the following applies:
  (a) the employer or employers have agreed to bargain, or have initiated bargaining, for the agreement;
  (b) a majority support determination in relation to the agreement is in operation;
  (c) a scope order in relation to the agreement is in operation;
  (d) all of the employers are specified in a low-paid authorisation that is in operation in relation to the agreement.

Good faith bargaining requirements not met

(3) FWA must in all cases be satisfied:
  (a) that:
    (i) one or more of the relevant bargaining representatives for the agreement have not met, or are not meeting, the good faith bargaining requirements; or
    (ii) the bargaining process is not proceeding efficiently or fairly because there are multiple bargaining representatives for the agreement; and
  (b) that the applicant has complied with the requirements of subsection 229(4) (which deals with notifying relevant bargaining representatives of concerns),

unless subsection 229(5) permitted the applicant to make the application without complying with those requirements.

Bargaining order must be in accordance with section 231

(4) The bargaining order must be in accordance with section 231 (which deals with what a bargaining order must specify).

236 Majority support determinations

(1) A bargaining representative of an employee who will be covered by a proposed single-enterprise agreement may apply to FWA for a determination (a *majority support determination*) that a majority of the employees who will be covered by the agreement want to bargain with the employer, or employers, that will be covered by the agreement.

(2) The application must specify:
  (a) the employer, or employers, that will be covered by the agreement; and
  (b) the employees who will be covered by the agreement.

237 When FWA must make a majority support determination

Majority support determination

(1) FWA must make a majority support determination in relation to a proposed single-enterprise agreement if:
  (a) an application for the determination has been made; and
  (b) FWA is satisfied of the matters set out in subsection (2) in relation to the agreement.

Matters of which FWA must be satisfied before making a majority support determination

(2) FWA must be satisfied that:
  (a) a majority of the employees:
    (i) who are employed by the employer or employers at a time determined by FWA; and
    (ii) who will be covered by the agreement;
  want to bargain; and
  (b) the employer, or employers, that will be covered by the agreement have not yet agreed to bargain, or initiated bargaining, for the agreement; and
  (c) that the group of employees who will be covered by the agreement was fairly chosen; and
  (d) it is reasonable in all the circumstances to make the determination.

(3) For the purposes of paragraph (2)(a), FWA may work out whether a majority of employees want to bargain using any method FWA considers appropriate.

(3A) If the agreement will not cover all of the employees of the employer or employers covered by the agreement, FWA must, in deciding for the purposes of paragraph (2)(c) whether the group of employees who will be covered was fairly chosen, take into account whether the group is geographically, operationally or organisationally distinct.

Operation of determination

(4) The determination comes into operation on the day on which it is made.

408 Protected industrial action

Industrial action is ***protected industrial action*** for a proposed enterprise agreement if it is one of the following:

(a) employee claim action for the agreement (see section 409);

(b) employee response action for the agreement (see section 410);

(c) employer response action for the agreement (see section 411).

409 Employee claim action

Employee claim action

(1) *Employee claim action* for a proposed enterprise agreement is industrial action that:
  (a) is organised or engaged in for the purpose of supporting or advancing claims in relation to the agreement that are only about, or are reasonably believed to only be about, permitted matters; and
  (b) is organised or engaged in, against an employer that will be covered by the agreement, by:
    (i) a bargaining representative of an employee who will be covered by the agreement; or
    (ii) an employee who is included in a group or groups of employees specified in a protected action ballot order for the industrial action; and
  (c) meets the common requirements set out in Subdivision B; and
  (d) meets the additional requirements set out in this section.

Protected action ballot is necessary

(2) The industrial action must be authorised by a protected action ballot (see Division 8 of this Part).

413 Common requirements that apply for industrial action to be protected industrial action

Common requirements

(1) This section sets out the *common requirements* for industrial action to be protected industrial action for a proposed enterprise agreement.

Type of proposed enterprise agreement

(2) The industrial action must not relate to a proposed enterprise agreement that is a greenfields agreement or multi-enterprise agreement.

Genuinely trying to reach an agreement

(3) The following persons must be genuinely trying to reach an agreement:
  (a) if the person organising or engaging in the industrial action is a bargaining representative for the agreement – the bargaining representative;

(b) if the person organising or engaging in the industrial action is an employee who will be covered by the agreement – the bargaining representative of the employee.

Notice requirements

(4) The notice requirements set out in section 414 must have been met in relation to the industrial action.

Compliance with orders

(5) The following persons must not have contravened any orders that apply to them and that relate to, or relate to industrial action relating to, the agreement or a matter that arose during bargaining for the agreement:
   (a) if the person organising or engaging in the industrial action is a bargaining representative for the agreement – the bargaining representative;
   (b) if the person organising or engaging in the industrial action is an employee who will be covered by the agreement – the employee and the bargaining representative of the employee.

No industrial action before an enterprise agreement etc. passes its nominal expiry date

(6) The person organising or engaging in the industrial action must not contravene section 417 (which deals with industrial action before the nominal expiry date of an enterprise agreement etc.) by organising or engaging in the industrial action.

No suspension or termination order is in operation etc.

(7) None of the following must be in operation:
   (a) an order under Division 6 of this Part suspending or terminating industrial action in relation to the agreement;
   (b) a Ministerial declaration under subsection 431(1) terminating industrial action in relation to the agreement;
   (c) a serious breach declaration in relation to the agreement.

415 Immunity provision

(1) No action lies under any law (whether written or unwritten) in force in a State or Territory in relation to any industrial action that is protected industrial action unless the industrial action has involved or is likely to involve:
   (a) personal injury; or
   (b) wilful or reckless destruction of, or damage to, property; or
   (c) the unlawful taking, keeping or use of property.

(2) However, subsection (1) does not prevent an action for defamation being brought in relation to anything that occurred in the course of industrial action.

References and suggested readings

Fair Work Act 2009 (Cth) §§ 172(2)–(5); 176; 182; 230; 236–237; 408; 409(1)–(2); 413; 415 (Austl) (supra).

Andrew Stewart, STEWART'S GUIDE TO EMPLOYMENT LAW §§ 8.1; 8.3–8.26 (3d ed. 2011).

Anthony Forsyth, *The Impact of "Good Faith" Obligations on Collective Bargaining Practices and Outcomes in Australia, Canada and the United States*, 16 CAN. LAB. & EMP. L.J. 1 (2011).

Rae Cooper & Bradon Ellem, *Getting to the Table? Fair Work, Unions and Collective Bargaining*, in REDISCOVERING COLLECTIVE BARGAINING: AUSTRALIA'S FAIR WORK ACT IN INTERNATIONAL PERSPECTIVE Ch. 7 (B. Creighton & A. Forsyth eds. 2012).

Problem 1 discussion – Brazil

As was mentioned in Part I, Brazil's situation regarding trade unionism and collective bargaining is unique. Unions do not depend on workers' active engagement to exist or to bargain and have a guaranteed income out of union tax (a single work day per year) which every employee is supposed to pay regardless of membership. Of course, if a union has a high membership, its bargaining strength increases. But in this problem it does not make any difference whether a majority or a minority of the employees are union members. Actually, it would not make a difference if none of the employees were members or union supporters.

Employer and employee unions (in Brazilian usage) are respectively established based on an economic or professional basis; the outcome of the negotiation applies to all labor contracts in the economic category in the territorial base. In Problem 1, therefore, although company managers are not under any obligation to bargain, the first thing that they are supposed to verify is the existence of an employees' union in their economic category in the territorial basis of the new facility. If this is the case, there might be a collective agreement signed with the employers' union that will affect all labor contracts in the new facility. Its existence may be verified at the Labor Ministry which is supposed to register all collective agreements to ensure validity. Once the existence of such a collective agreement is confirmed, all of its provisions will apply to all applicable labor contracts of the new facility, unless the company engages in individual bargaining with the respective employees' union. In such a case, different dispositions may be negotiated, limited, nevertheless, by statutory provisions governing the issue. On the other hand, the idea of a union approaching the local management and demanding to bargain would only be reasonable as an attempt to improve either an existing "general" collective agreement or from some statutory floor.

As collective agreements are negotiated on a territorial basis, the existence of a collective agreement for another facility set in a different part of the country may be the trigger for a union to demand to bargain. In such a case, its demand might be for the extension of such provisions to the new facility. Still, in this case, local management would be under no obligation to bargain and the existing collective agreement would obtain only for the territorial basis in which it was originally made. However, if the parties do engage in a bargaining process, they are required to act in good faith even though they are under no obligation to reach a final result.

Suggested reading

Estêvâo Mallet, *Labour Law in* INTRODUCTION TO BRAZILIAN LAW Ch. 10 (Fabiano Deffenti & Welber Barral eds. 2011), provides a brief overview; Ana Virginia Gomes & Mariana Mota Prado, *Flawed Freedom Association in Brazil: How Unions Can Become an Obstacle to Meaningful Reforms in the Labor Law Systems*, 32 COMP. LAB. L. & POL'Y J. 843 (2011), provides a good, if critical, description of the "unicity system."

Problem 1 discussion – Germany

The essential feature of the German employee representation system is the dualism of the representation of workers' interests by trade unions, on the one hand, and of works councils, on the other. Under German law works councils are independent legal bodies with the specific task of representing workers in the establishment on statutorily enumerated subjects. Trade unions, on the other hand, represent workers' interests at the bargaining table, mostly regarding wages and hours.

Works councils form autonomous legal bodies which represent workers' interests independently. Works council members are not necessarily members of a trade union, though in practice a clear majority of works council members may belong to one or other trade union and may be nominated by a trade union. Works council members are elected by all employees who work in a given establishment, independent of whether they are members of a trade union or not. The electorate would include clerical as well as production workers and supervisors, but not higher executives. Under the Works Councils Act, works councils enjoy far-reaching co-determination rights and are empowered to enter into a specific kind of collective agreement (called a works agreement) with the employer. This will be explored according to its relevance to the text of the law in some of the problems to follow.

Trade unions, on the other hand, represent general workers' interests at the bargaining table. According to section 2 para. 1 of the Act on Collective Agreements (*Tarifvertragsgesetz*), collective agreements can be concluded by trade unions on the part of workers and employers' associations as well as by individual employers on the part of employers. However, a so-called "company collective agreement" (*Firmentarifvertrag*) that is concluded between a union and an individual employer, practically speaking, rather forms an exception. Most collective bargaining in Germany is still done by employers' associations, whose agreements an employer must obey if it is a full member of the relevant organization (see section 3 para. 1 of the Act on Collective Agreements). An employer who is bound by a collective agreement must apply its provisions. This is also acknowledged by the Works Councils Act. Section 2 para. 1 of the Act expressly states that "the employer and the works council shall work together in a spirit of mutual trust having regard to the applicable collective agreements and in co-operation with the trade unions and employers' associations represented in the establishment for the good of the employees and of the establishment."[1]

What means can be employed by a trade union to bring the employer (or the relevant employers' association) to the bargaining table? In contrast with many

1 Because both works councils and trade unions can conclude collective agreements, the question arises which collective agreements should take precedence in case of a (possible) conflict. This question is essentially addressed by section 77 para. 3 sentence 1 of the Works Councils Act. It states that "works agreements shall not deal with remuneration and other conditions of employment that have been fixed or are usually fixed by collective agreement". This means that if a works agreement is more beneficial for an employer than an applicable collective agreement, the latter agreement prevents the works agreement from becoming effective. Section 77 para. 3 of the Works Councils Act makes it clear that there should be no rivalry between works councils and trade unions with reference to collective bargaining. In particular, the legislator sought to ensure that works councils do not become "substitutes" for trade unions. In practice, however, recent years have witnessed considerable tension between the union and the works council as employers have sought to secure agreement on terms more beneficial to them for the sake of remaining competitive and works councils have acceded to that interest.

other countries there is no government agency in Germany which certifies the representativeness of a trade union or orders bargaining. As a consequence union recognition rests solely on the power of a union to compel the employer (or employers' association) to bargain. In order to achieve this goal the union is free to call a strike (or to threaten its counterpart with a strike). The right to strike is regarded as guaranteed for the very reason that it may be key to making collective bargaining actually happen. On the other hand, strikes are admissible only insofar as they aim to bring about a collective agreement. As a result, only trade unions which have the so-called capacity to bargain collectively (*Tariffähigkeit*), that is the ability to bring about viable collective agreements, enjoy the right to strike. As the capacity to bargain collectively requires a trade union to be sufficiently assertive (in terms of membership, for instance), a union which lacks that power is not allowed to call a strike. A trade union's capacity to bargain collectively is determined by the labor courts on the request of either another union, or an employers' association (or an individual employer) or the state. In determining whether a capacity to bargain collectively exists the courts are prepared to consider the past "bargaining record" of a union. If the *Tariffähigkeit* of a new union is at stake, the number of members forms a decisive criterion (Federal Labor Court 5.010.2010 – 1 ABR 88/09).

In recent years some employers have negotiated with unions they have sponsored or are otherwise rather close to – so-called "yellow unions" – usually resulting in terms very favorable to the employer, what in American parlance would be called a "sweetheart contract." These can be and have been successfully challenged by mainstream unions in the labor court on the ground that the union lacked the capacity to contract (*Tariffähigkeit*) for lack of membership, financial support, independence, and assertiveness.

Logically, a union represents only its members. As a collective agreement is binding only on the signatories, it does not apply to non-members of the union. For obvious reasons, employers apply the terms to all employees whether they are union members or not.

References and suggested readings

There is a rich literature in German on *Tariffähigkeit* – in legal commentaries on labor law in general and on the *Tarifvertragsgesetz* in particular. *E.g.* STEFAN GRENIER, *Der GKH-Beschluss – Evolution oder (erneute) Revolution der Rechtsprechung zur Teriffähigkeit?*, NEUE ZEITSCHRIFT FUR ARBEITSRECHT (NZA) 825 (2011); 825; MANFRED LÖWISCH & VOLKER RIEBLE, TARIFVERTRAGSGESETZ (3d ed. 2012). See also Bernd Waas, *Who is Allowed to Represent the Employees? The Capacity of Trade Unions to Bargain Collectively in Germany*, *in* LABOR MARKET OF 21ST CENTURY: LOOKING FOR FLEXIBILITY AND

SECURITY 164 (Tomas Davulis & Daiva Petrylaite eds. 2011). For a useful example of a union, "Medsonet," a denominated "Christian union" of health care workers, held to be lacking the capacity to make a collective agreement, *see* the decision of the Landesarbeitsgericht Hamburg of 21 March 2012, 3 TaBV 2011. The labor court's decision to the same effect was discussed by DANIEL ULBER, *Medsonet nicht tariffähig*, ARBEIT UND RECHT (AuR) 430 (2011).

Problem 1 discussion – Japan

In Japan, more than 90 percent of labor unions are organized at the enterprise level. Such enterprise unionism is not required by law, but is just a practice. Under such practices, it is very rare for a labor union from outside the company to approach and demand to bargain or insist on the application of a collective agreement already in existence. However, although their number is small, there are some local unions that organize workers across companies. Therefore, the situation in Problem 1 can happen sometimes.

If no worker in a company joins the union, the company is under no obligation to bargain with the union. Under the Labor Union Act, an employer owes a duty to bargain "with the representatives of the workers employed by the employer." The company is also under no obligation to apply the collective agreement to its workers because the collective bargaining agreement shall in principle apply only to union members.

However, if even one worker out of ten workers in the company joins the union, the company owes a duty to bargain with the union if the union demands collective bargaining. If the company refuses to bargain with the union without justifiable reasons, that constitutes one form of unfair labor practice. The administrative agency known as the Labor Relations Commission will issue a remedial order to bargain with the union in good faith.

In Japan, establishing a labor union is very easy. In order to be a qualified labor union under the Labor Union Act (LUA), majority support by the workers is not required. Thus, there is no definition of a bargaining unit nor are there any procedures, such as voting and card-check, to confirm the workers' majority support. A substantial number of members is not required. Just two workers can establish a legitimate labor union in Japan. Neither registration with nor permission from the government is required.

The LUA prescribes five requirements for a labor organization to be a qualified union enjoying statutory rights and remedies (LUA Arts. 2 and 5): (1) the organization must be primarily formed by workers; (2) the organization must be independent of the employer; (3) the main purpose of the organization must be to maintain and improve the working conditions and to raise the economic status of workers; (4) the entity must be an organization or a federation thereof, and to be deemed an organization, there must be more than two members; and (5) the organization must establish a union constitution which includes the items enumerated in Article 5 paragraph 2 of the LUA, which mainly relate to the democratic administration of the internal affairs of the union.

So long as an organization comprises more than two workers, is independent of the employer, and has a union constitution, it can qualify as a labor union under the LUA irrespective of the small size of the membership. Such a union can enjoy a full-fledged right to bargain collectively and go on strike. Although Japan introduced the unfair labor practice system modeled after the Wagner Act in the US, it did not adopt the exclusive representation system.

PRIMARY SOURCE

Labor Union Act (LUA)

(Labor Unions)

Article 2

(1) The term "Labor unions" as used in this Act shall mean those organizations, or federations thereof, formed voluntarily and composed mainly of workers for the main purposes of maintaining and improving working conditions and raising the economic status of the workers; however, this shall not apply to any of the following items:
   (i) which admits to membership of officers; workers in supervisory positions having direct authority with respect to hiring, firing, promotions, or transfers; workers in supervisory positions having access to confidential information relating to the employer's labor relations plans and policies so that their official duties and responsibilities directly conflict with their sincerity and responsibilities as members of the labor union said; and other persons who represent the interests of the employer;
   (ii) which receives the employer's financial assistance in paying the organizations'

operational expenditures, however, that this shall not prevent the employer from permitting workers to confer or negotiate with the employer during working hours without loss of time or wage and shall not apply to the employer's contributions for public welfare funds or welfare and other funds which are actually used for payments to prevent or relieve economic adversity or misfortunes, nor to the giving office of minimum space

(iii) whose purposes are confined to mutual aid service or other welfare service;

(iv) whose purposes are principally political or social movements.

(Treatment of an Organization That Has Been Formed as a Labor Union)

Article 5

(1) Unless the labor union has submitted evidence to the Labor Relations Commission and proved that it is in compliance with Article 2 and paragraph 2 of this Article, the labor union shall not be qualified to participate in the procedures provided in this Act and shall not be granted the remedies provided in this Act, provided, however, that nothing herein shall be construed so as to deny protections for any individual worker pursuant to Article 7, item 1.

(2) The constitution of a labor union shall include the provisions listed in any of the following items:

(i) name;

(ii) the location of its principal office;

(iii) that members of a labor union other than a labor union that is a federation (such other labor union hereinafter referred to as a "local union") shall have the right to participate in all issues or disputes of such labor union and shall have the right to receive equal treatment;

(iv) no one shall be disqualified from union membership in any case on the basis of race, religion, gender, family origin or status;

(v) in the case of a local union, that the officers shall be elected by direct secret vote of the union members, and, in the case of a federation or a labor union having national scope, that the officers shall be elected by direct secret vote either of the members of the local unions or of delegates elected by direct secret vote of the members of the local unions;

(vi) that a general meeting shall be held at least once every year;

(vii) that a financial report showing all sources of revenues and expenditures, the names of main contributors and the current financial status, together with certificate of accuracy by a professionally qualified accounting auditor commissioned by the union members, shall be released to the union members at least once every year;

(viii) that no strike shall be started without a majority decision made by direct secret vote either of the union members or of delegates elected by direct secret vote of the union members;

(ix) in the case of local union, that the constitution shall not be revised unless such revision has received majority support by direct secret vote of the union members, and, in the case of a labor union which is a federation or a labor union which has national scope, the constitution shall not be revised unless such revision has received majority support by direct secret vote either of the members of the local unions or of the delegates elected by direct secret vote of the members of the local unions.

(Unfair Labor Practices)

Article 7

The employer shall not commit the acts listed in any of the following items:

(i) to discharge or otherwise treat in a disadvantageous manner a worker by reason of such worker's being a member of a labor union, having tried to join or organize a labor union, or having performed justifiable acts of a labor union; or to make it a condition of employment that the worker shall not join or shall withdraw from a labor union. However, where a labor union represents a majority of workers employed at a particular factory or workplace, this shall not preclude an employer from concluding a collective agreement which requires, as a condition of employment, that the workers shall be members of such labor union;

(ii) to refuse to bargain collectively with the representatives of the workers employed by the employer without justifiable reasons;

(iii) to control or interfere with the formation or management of a labor union by workers or to give financial assistance in paying the labor union's operational expenditures, provided, however, that this shall not preclude the employer from permitting workers to confer or negotiate with the employer during working hours without loss of time or wage, and this shall not apply to the employer's contributions for public welfare funds or welfare and other funds which are actually used for payments to prevent or relieve economic adversity or misfortunes, nor to the giving of office of minimum space;

(iv) to discharge or otherwise treat in a disadvantageous manner a worker for such worker's having filed a motion with the Labor Relations Commission that the employer has violated the provisions of this Article; for such worker's having requested the Central Labor Relations Commission to review an order issued under the provisions of Article 27–12, paragraph 1; or for such worker's having presented evidence or having spoken at an investigation or hearing conducted by the Labor Relations Commission in regard to such a motion, or in connection with a recommendation of a settlement to those concerned, or at an adjustment of labor disputes as provided for under the Labor Relations Adjustment Act (Act No. 25 of 1946).

Problem 1 discussion – United States

Under the National Labor Relations Act an employer is required to bargain with a representative "designated or selected" by a majority of employees in a unit appropriate for such a purpose. The representative becomes the exclusive representation for all the employees in the unit: the employer must bargain with it, and *only* with it, and in good faith over statutory subjects of bargaining: wages, hours, and working conditions. The employer may no longer deal with employees individually, absent agreement with the union. Nor may it act unilaterally in these matters before exhausting its bargaining obligation.

An employer may, but is not required, to bargain with an organization for only its members – unlike Germany and Japan. However, it may not agree to bargain with a union that lacks majority support as an exclusive bargaining agent even if it believes in good faith that the union actually has majority support. In Problem 1, if the company agreed to a collective agreement with a union that lacked majority support, it would have committed an unfair labor practice and the contract would be of no effect.

As U.S. law has evolved, even if an employer knows that the union has the support of a majority it may refuse to bargain – so long as it commits no unfair practice – and can require a National Labor Relations Board (NLRB)-run election to decide the question of representative status. This can be done by the employer filing a petition for an election if a demand to bargain has been made on it or by doing nothing in the face of the union's demand, which would place the burden on the union to file a petition for an election. Alternatively, an employer can agree to a process to decide the question of representation outside the NLRB, for example, a "card check," a count of those who have signed to indicate support for the union, by a neutral party. However, a union is allowed to picket the employer for recognition, but only for a "reasonable period" not to exceed 30 days without filing a petition.

A union's petition must be supported by at least 30 percent of the employees in the unit petitioned for, usually by signed cards indicating that support. If a petition is filed, the employer can contest the bargaining unit petitioned-for by the union, the cluster of jobs whose incumbents can vote and so be represented.

In the event of a dispute the NLRB will decide what the bargaining unit is, the touchstone being the "community of interests" of the employees. The Board has to decide whether the unit petitioned-for is "an" appropriate unit, not whether some other unit is more appropriate. Commonly, white collar employees are held to lack a sufficient "community of interest" with production workers and would not be petitioned-for in a production unit. In Problem 1, the union's demand would most likely be for a unit of production workers exclusive of office clericals, guards and watchmen (who must be placed in a separate unit), and supervisors (who have no collective bargaining rights). The office clericals can separately be petitioned-for.

The employer is free to campaign vigorously against representation so long as it commits no unfair labor practice. The employee may speak freely so long as it promises no benefit and threatens no reprisal; it can even hold "captive audience" assemblies for that purpose, a practice that would be unlawful in many countries – including Japan and Brazil. The pages of the NLRB's reports are replete with cases that govern campaign behavior. When the line has been crossed, the Board may order a new election or, in egregious cases, actually issue an order to bargain where a union's majority – manifested on the bases of signed support – has been dissipated by the employer's wrongful conduct and a fair election cannot be held.

However, the employer can take a less adversarial stance. The employer can make an agreement with the union to remain neutral on the question of representation, to say nothing at all on the question, or agree not to disparage the union; the union can agree reciprocally not to disparage the company or its management. These "neutrality" agreements are sometimes coupled with "card check" provisions and provision for enforcement outside the NLRB, by arbitration. The parties can take an even more cooperative stance: they can agree on a set of principles or goals they will seek to achieve in bargaining should the union secure a majority, but they may not negotiate an agreement contingent on the union's securing majority support (except in the construction trades). In recent years, unions have secured bargaining status more often outside of resort to the Labor Board.

References and suggested readings

The leading one-volume treatise is ROBERT A. GORMAN AND MATTHEW W. FINKIN, LABOR LAW: ANALYSIS AND ADVOCACY (in press). The NLRB's decision allowing the parties to frame their mutual goals before the employees decide whether to opt for representation was sustained by a federal appeals court. *Montague v. NLRB*, 698 F.3d 307 (6th Cir. 2012). On neutrality (and card check) agreements *see* JAMES BRUDNEY, *Neutrality and Card Check Recognition: Prospects for Changing Paradigms*, 90 IOWA L. REV. 819 (2005).

> Engaging with employee voice and the Works Council ... results in productivity gains that have benefited not only employees but also the firm ... I wonder, absent company values supporting informal employee voice and participation mechanisms at a U.S. company, if such an approach would even [be] considered ... Challenge yourself to look at [the] potential positive benefits a co-determination system might offer.
>
> Director, HR, Industrial Manufacturing Sector

Questions for Discussion – Problem 1

1. Note the very different approaches to effecting the right to collective representation these countries take:
   - In *Brazil*, unions are certified by the government for a specific occupational category across all employers in a geographic area: an employer has no role to play in its employees' selection of a representative and, in fact, its employees may have little or no role either. The employer can be bound by a contract it never negotiated or agreed to be bound by; its employees may be represented by a union they have not joined and which need not have any members in the workplace, even as they are required to pay dues to it.
   - In *Japan*, where unions are overwhelmingly enterprise-based, the employer must bargain with every union that meets the statutory qualifications and that has even a single member in the company; but, it can agree to a collective agreement with the majority union and refuse further to negotiate with the others on those terms – a structure that could be conducive either to a coalition or to marginalizing minority unions even as they attract dissenters and strive to maintain a presence.
   - In *Australia*, the employer must bargain in good faith with each and every workplace representative: a union that has but a single member, even a single employee as a self-representative; the structure contemplates coalition and multi-party bargaining. But the result of the bargain must be put to a vote and is not effective without majority approval.
   - In *Germany*, the law focuses on the representative nature of the union and its capacity for forceful action independent of the

employer. Whether the employer bargains or not is a result of the union's economic power; indeed, lack of power deprives the union of the capacity to contract, which contract may be challenged on that ground by a rival union in the labor courts.

- In the *United States*, the union must secure majority support from the employees in a "bargaining unit" which, if contested, is to conform to the "community of interests" of the employees. Once a union is selected, the law is largely indifferent to the structure of bargaining. A single employer may have to bargain with one or more unions selected by a variety of bargaining units. Several employers can agree to bargain with one or more unions. Such multi-employer units cannot be commanded into being, but, once consensually created, the NLRB makes exit difficult in order to bolster bargaining stability. No law requires that employees subject to the collective agreement have a right to vote on its ratification.

2. Evaluate these approaches from at least three perspectives: (a) How much diversity in employee interests and desires should the employee representative be expected to reconcile in arriving at a set of bargaining proposals or in making compromises and concessions to achieve an agreement? (b) How effective can a representative be if it represents narrower congruent interests in contrast to larger numbers? (c) How can an employer best structure the bargaining relationship for ease of bargaining, to reduce the time, cost, and effort of conducting a multiplicity of bargains? (d) How much diversity of employee interests and desires should the employer be asked to reconcile?

3. In considering 2(b), above, note that in Germany it is possible for a group with a strategic workplace situation – just the pilots of an airline, for example – to break away from an employer sectorial (or even enterprise) bargaining structure, if they have enough independence and power, and force the employer to bargain with them. Is this unworkable? In the U.S., guided by the "community of interests" test, it is possible for just the 31 rental agents of a car agency's 109 employees at a single facility of a multi-facility national company to be a bargaining unit. *DTG Operations, Inc.*, 357 NLRB No. 175 (2011). How would the separate, felt needs of these employees be dealt with in Australia, Brazil, and Japan?

4. Evaluate how much power the employer and the union are able to exert in these different bargaining structures. Is there a trade-off between representative capacity and bargaining power?

5. Consider the role of the state in each of these systems:
   (a) in deciding who the employees' representative is;
   (b) in deciding the enforceability of a collective agreement.
   Should the state be deciding these questions?

6. What is the role of the state if the union need not be responsive to those it represents or if it lacks significant bargaining power? Is it to legislate even more exactingly on terms and conditions of employment, i.e. to elaborate the floor of standards and protections below which the union cannot derogate? Or should the law make the union more responsive? Or should the role of the state be to redress an imbalance in bargaining power? In either case, how would that be accomplished?

7. Return to Problem 1. You have consulted counsel in each country. What is your response to the union's demands in each of these countries? Why?

PROBLEM 2: RESTRUCTURING WORKPLACE OPERATIONS

The company has undertaken a study of its labor costs. This includes a detailed review of each employee's base pay, overtime pay, and periods of time lost to a variety of personal leaves, e.g. for illness, child care, etc. It has run several models of alternative staffing arrangements that look at: changing the mix of full- and part-time employees; lowering the rates of pay and benefits; and changing the scheduling of work, including the use of flextime and home work. Before it acts in any of these matters, must it:

(a) inform its employees, or their representatives, that it is doing so;
(b) share all or some of this information (including information compiled by bids by outsourcing companies and temporary staffing agencies) with its employees or their representatives; if so, must it
(c) consult with its employees' representatives before acting to alter any aspect of the status quo; if so,
(d) for how long (i.e. at what point does that consultation cease); and
(e) may it act thereafter unilaterally to:
  - reduce the wages and/or benefits of current full- and part-time employees;
  - adopt a lower wage and benefit scale for newly hired employees;
  - change the mix of full- to part-time by decreasing the former and increasing the latter;
  - change the work hours?

Note that one course of action that could be considered and, possibly, taken is to terminate a number of incumbent employees and contract for that work to be done either by a domestic contractor or one abroad. This scenario will be taken up, as an aspect of dismissal law, in Problem 10.

Problem 2 discussion – Australia

In terms of information sharing and consultation, Australian law does not have any general laws on these matters. But if any of the employees affected are covered by either an award or an enterprise agreement, there is likely to be some sort of obligation to consult.

All modern awards contain a standard term that obliges employers to notify employees and their representatives of significant workplace changes and then discuss those changes. Section 205 of the Fair Work Act 2009 likewise requires all new enterprise agreements to include a term of this kind. The parties to an agreement can draft a consultation clause of their own, but if they fail to do so, a model term (contained in Schedule 2.3 to the Fair Work Regulations 2009) is taken to be included in the agreement by default. That model term is essentially the same as the standard term found in awards. The requirement does not apply to pre-Fair Work Act agreements, but in practice most union-negotiated agreements do have a provision of this kind.

Applying the model term to these facts, the obligation to consult only arises once there is a "*definite decision* to introduce a major change to production, program, organisation, structure, or technology" (emphasis added), and that change is likely to have a "significant effect" on certain employees. If those requirements are satisfied, as they appear to be here, the employer must first notify the employees, then hold discussions with the employees and any representative (most obviously a union) they may appoint. The discussions must cover the nature of the change, the effect it is likely to have on the employees, and any measures the employer is taking to avert or mitigate any adverse effects on them.

In terms of information, the employer is required to disclose "all relevant information" that bears on those matters. Crucially, however, this does not extend to the release of "confidential or commercially sensitive information" – which in this case almost certainly means that there would be no need to release the details of bids provided by other companies.

The employer's obligation ends when the decision has been notified, and appropriate consultation has taken place. At the very least, the employer must afford a "bona fide opportunity to influence the decision maker" (*Community and Public Sector Union v Vodafone Network Pty Ltd*, Australian Industrial Relations Commission, PR911257, 2001 at [25]). A failure to do so may lead to court proceedings for breach of the relevant award or agreement, the imposition of monetary penalties, and/or an injunction to restrain any further action being taken. But if the procedural requirements are met, the employer is not obliged to change its mind or gain the consent of the workforce, subject to what is said below about the constraints on unilateral variations.

The only thing to add is that if the restructuring ultimately involves the loss of 15 or more jobs, an affected employee (or a union acting on their behalf) can ask FWA to intervene, on the basis that there has been inadequate notification or consultation. This can be done even in the absence of any consultation obligation in an award or agreement. In such a case, FWA can make an order to redress that situation, subject to certain limitations that include not seeking to reinstate an employee whose employment had already ended: Fair Work Act 2009 ss 531–3, 786–8. Such a power has been used on a number of occasions to halt redundancies from being implemented, to ensure that appropriate consultation occurs: see e.g. *Australian Bureau of Statistics v Community and Public Sector Union* [2009] AIRC 476.

Turning to the question of unilateral variations, there are two constraints here. The first is that even if an employer has the capacity to make such changes, it cannot reduce wages or conditions below the minimum entitlements mandated under the NES, an applicable award or enterprise agreement, or any other applicable labour law.

Secondly, an employer cannot generally reduce the wages, conditions or status of an existing employee without their consent, because that will usually amount to a repudiation of the employment contract: see e.g. *Whittaker v Unisys Australia Pty Ltd* [2010] VSC 9. As the High Court of Australia has confirmed in *Visscher v Giudice* [2009] HCA 34, an employee in this situation has the option of either refusing to accept the change and insisting that they remain employed under their original terms, or resigning and suing for wrongful or unfair dismissal.

There may, however, be circumstances where an employer can rely on a provision in an enterprise agreement or employment contract to allow it to make certain changes without that amounting to a breach of the employment contract: for example where a mobility clause permits the employee to be required to change job locations, or where the employer is authorised to make rostering changes.

The employer may also be able to effect a change by seeking to terminate an existing hiring and replacing it with a new hiring on varied terms. But there are costs and risks associated with that course, including the prospects of the employee simply accepting the termination and asking for a payout of their accrued leave entitlements, and possibly indeed suing for unfair dismissal. In practice, while it is common to be able to get away with imposing changes on casual employees (for example, reducing their hours), employees on ongoing or fixed term contracts may be less accommodating – especially if they are unionised.

PRIMARY SOURCES

Fair Work Regulations 2009

Select Legislative Instrument 2009 No. 112 as amended

made under the Fair Work Act 2009

Schedule 2.3 Model consultation term

(regulation 2.09)

Model consultation term

(1) This term applies if:
  (a) the employer has made a definite decision to introduce a major change to production, program, organisation, structure, or technology in relation to its enterprise; and
  (b) the change is likely to have a significant effect on employees of the enterprise.

(2) The employer must notify the relevant employees of the decision to introduce the major change.

(3) The relevant employees may appoint a representative for the purposes of the procedures in this term.

(4) If:
  (a) a relevant employee appoints, or relevant employees appoint, a representative for the purposes of consultation; and
  (b) the employee or employees advise the employer of the identity of the representative;

the employer must recognise the representative.

(5) As soon as practicable after making its decision, the employer must:
  (a) discuss with the relevant employees:
    (i) the introduction of the change; and
    (ii) the effect the change is likely to have on the employees; and
    (iii) measures the employer is taking to avert or mitigate the adverse effect of the change on the employees; and
  (b) for the purposes of the discussion – provide, in writing, to the relevant employees:

(i) all relevant information about the change including the nature of the change proposed; and
(ii) information about the expected effects of the change on the employees; and
(iii) any other matters likely to affect the employees.

(6) However, the employer is not required to disclose confidential or commercially sensitive information to the relevant employees.

(7) The employer must give prompt and genuine consideration to matters raised about the major change by the relevant employees.

(8) If a term in the enterprise agreement provides for a major change to production, program, organisation, structure or technology in relation to the enterprise of the employer, the requirements set out in subclauses (2), (3) and (5) are taken not to apply.

(9) In this term, a major change is *likely to have a significant effect on employees* if it results in:
(a) the termination of the employment of employees; or
(b) major change to the composition, operation or size of the employer's work-force or to the skills required of employees; or
(c) the elimination or diminution of job opportunities (including opportunities for promotion or tenure); or
(d) the alteration of hours of work; or
(e) the need to retrain employees; or
(f) the need to relocate employees to another workplace; or
(g) the restructuring of jobs.

(10) In this term, *relevant employees* means the employees who may be affected by the major change.

References and suggested readings

As to consultation obligations under the Fair Work Act, see ANDREW STEWART, STEWART'S GUIDE TO EMPLOYMENT LAW §§8.31; 16.26–16.29 (4th ed. 2013).

As to the capacity to vary contractual entitlements, see *id. at* §6.9; CAROLYN SAPPIDEEN, PAUL O'GRADY, JOELLEN RILEY & GEOFF WARBURTON, MACKEN'S LAW OF EMPLOYMENT §§9.170–9.230 (7th ed. 2011).

Problem 2 discussion – Brazil

Employers, in the use of their directive authority over employee work, may act unilaterally in order to organize labor conditions. As to this prerogative of acting unilaterally, the question is how far they can go. From an individual perspective, changes may not be introduced in the labor contract if they are prejudicial to the employee's working conditions. Thus, changing for instance, labor hours or payment conditions is unacceptable if the result is prejudicial for the employee, such as lowering the rates of pay and benefits. Whatever may be the results of labor cost analysis, the company has no right, from an individual standpoint, to impose changes on a labor contract.

On the other hand, things are not so simple when put from a collective perspective. As a matter of fact, new labor conditions are often negotiated with labor unions and its outcome may not be a priori perceived as prejudicial (or not) to employees' working conditions (even if they are). For instance, a collective negotiation may approve the creation of a *banco de horas* (bank of hours) which allows for the introduction of a compensatory system for extra hours of work. In such conditions, accordingly to Federal Statute 9.601 (Jan. 21, 1998), extra hours are not accounted for on a daily or weekly basis, but are calculated on a long period term of 120 days. How prejudicial such a measure can be is a question that cannot easily be answered. One would have to examine the working conditions of each and every employee individually to conclude one way or another.

Thus, as the parties are engaged in a collective bargain, on the one hand, one may say they both are primarily interested in the increase of their benefits, but, on the other hand, no one is in a position to anticipate the outcome and whether it will represent an increase of benefits. In between these extremes, two issues may summarize the problem's contour: (1) the requirement of information sharing and consultation; and, (2) the ability to act unilaterally.

As to issue (1), although there is no legal statute stipulating what must be previously disclosed in a collective negotiation, Brazilian labor courts have reaffirmed the obligation to act in good faith and therefore to forward all the information available to enhance the parties' ability to negotiate on an equal basis. Only confidential data may be excluded from the obligation to share information. As to issue (2), employers may not act unilaterally as Brazilian labor courts have reaffirmed their duty to negotiate. Actually, they have repeatedly refused to examine a collective bargaining blockage if proof of a previous negotiation attempt is not provided by the parties.

References and suggested readings

BRASIL, Federal Statute No.9.601, from Jan. 21, 1998, *accessed at* http://www.planalto.gov.br/ccivil_03/LEIS/L9601.htm (last visited: Feb. 14, 2010).

BRASIL, TRIBUNAL REGIONAL DO TRABALHO DA 15ª REGIÃO, DC 309–2009–000–15–00–4, *accessed at*: http://www.trt15.jus.br/voto/padc/2009/000/00033309.rtf (last visited: Feb. 15, 2010).

BRASIL, TRIBUNAL SUPERIOR DO TRABALHO, RODC 309/2009–000–15–00.4, *accessed at*: http://brs02.tst.jus.br/cgi-bin/nph-brs?s1=4889173.nia.&u=/Brs/it01.html&p=1&l=1&d=blnk&f=g&r=1 (last visited: Feb. 15, 2010).

ELINA G. DA FONTE PESSANHA, IVAN ALEMÃO & JOSÉ LUIZ SOARES, TST, Dissídios Coletivos, Demissão Massiva: Novos Desafios para a Justiça do Trabalho, *in* O MUNDO DO TRABALHO – LEITURAS CRÍTICAS DA JURISPRUDÊNCIA DO TST: EM DEFESA DO MUNDO DO TRABALHO (GRIJALBO FERNANDES COUTINHO, HUGO CAVALCANTI MELO FILHO, JORGE LUIZ SOUTO MAIOR & MARCOS NEVE FAVA eds. 2009).

Problem 2 discussion – Germany

According to section 92 para. 1 sentence 1 of the Works Councils Act (*Betriebsverfassungsgesetz*) the employer is obliged to inform the works council comprehensively and in time with regard to measures he intends to take with regard to "staff planning" (*Personalplanung*). "Staff planning" comprises *inter alia* identifying future manpower requirements and ascertaining the need for a possible reduction of the workforce. The employer has to inform the works council as soon as he has entered the stage of concrete steps which he has in mind in this regard. However, if he does no more than "weighing possible options" there is no duty to inform yet (Federal Labor Court 19.06.1984 – 1 ABR 6/83). If the employer breaches his obligations under section 92 of the Works Councils Act he will be fined (section 121 of the Works Council Act). In severe cases the employer may be ordered to abstain from certain actions (section 23 para. 1 sentence 1 of the Works Councils Act).

Under section 92 para. 1 sentence 1 of the Works Councils Act the employer is obliged to share with the works council all relevant information. The works council has to be informed comprehensively even if this amounts to giving the works council the opportunity to get notice of business secrets. The employer has to share all information which forms the basis of his planning (Federal Labor Court 19.06.1984 – 1 ABR 6/83). What is more he has to make available all relevant data (written or otherwise).

According to section 92 para. 1 sentence 2 of the Works Councils Act the employer is obliged to consult with the works council with regard to the nature and extent of intended measures in the area of personnel "staff planning" (in particular, recruitment/reduction of the workforce). Consultation has to take place with the aim of avoiding hardship for the workforce. By way of illustration, the works council has to be consulted with if the employer plans to replace staff by temps or subcontracting work. Consultation ceases if the process of planning has come to an end.

Apart from the fact that wages and benefits, in particular, may be fixed by binding collective agreements, the employer must not amend the content of individual employment contracts unilaterally. He can only terminate the employment relationship and offer new terms at the same time (so-called *Änderungskündigung*: notice of termination pending an amendment of the existing contract). In this case the Act on Dismissal Protection (*Kündigungsschutzgesetz*) applies, however. With regard to a change of work hours, it must be noted in addition that the works council enjoys a co-determination right under section 87 para. 1 no. 2 of the Works Councils Act with regard to the beginning and end of daily work, including breaks and the spreading of working hours over the week. As a consequence the employer must reach an agreement with the works council before. As for the options of recruiting new personnel (part-timers, for instance) and/or getting rid of parts of the existing workforce (full-time employees, for instance), it is noteworthy that both hiring employees and firing them are subject to certain rights of the works council: under section 99 of the Works Councils Act the works council has to be informed if the employer wants to recruit new staff members; in a limited number of cases the works council enjoys in addition a certain power of vetoing the decision of the employer (the so-called right to deny approval or "*Zustimmungsverweigerungsrecht*"). Equally, the works council has to be informed about a decision to dismiss a worker; this right comes with a limited right of the works council to contradict (section 102 of the Works Councils Act, so-called "*Widerspruchsrecht*").

PRIMARY SOURCE

Works Councils Act

Division Three Social matters

Section 87 Right of co-determination

(1) The works council shall have a right of co-determination in the following matters in so far as they are not prescribed by legislation or collective agreement:

1. matters relating to the rules of operation of the establishment and the conduct of employees in the establishment;
2. the commencement and termination of the daily working hours including breaks and the distribution of working hours among the days of the week;
3. any temporary reduction or extension of the hours normally worked in the establishment;
4. the time and place for and the form of payment of remuneration;
5. the establishment of general principles for leave arrangements and the preparation of the leave schedule as well as fixing the time at which the leave is to be taken by individual employees, if no agreement is reached between the employer and the employees concerned;
6. the introduction and use of technical devices designed to monitor the behavior or performance of the employees;
7. arrangements for the prevention of accidents at work and occupational diseases and for the protection of health on the basis of legislation or safety regulations;
8. the form, structuring and administration of social services whose scope is limited to the establishment, company or combine;
9. the assignment of and notice to vacate accommodation that is rented to employees in view of their employment relationship as well as the general fixing of the conditions for the use of such accommodation;
10. questions related to remuneration arrangements in the establishment, including in particular the establishment of principles of remuneration and the introduction and application of new remuneration methods or modification of existing methods;
11. the fixing of job and bonus rates and comparable performance-related remuneration including cash coefficients;
12. principles for suggestion schemes in the establishment;

13. principles governing the performance of group work; group work within the meaning of this provision is defined as a group of employees performing a complex task within the establishment's workflows, which has been assigned to it and is executed in a largely autonomous way.

(2) If no agreement can be reached on a matter covered by the preceding subsection, the conciliation committee shall make a decision. The award of the conciliation committee shall take the place of an agreement between the employer and the works council.

Division Five

STAFF POLICY

Subdivision One

General staff policy

Section 92 Manpower planning

(1) The employer shall inform the works council in full and in good time of matters relating to manpower planning including in particular and future manpower needs and the resulting staff movements and vocational training measures and supply the relevant documentation. He shall consult the works council on the nature and the extent of the action required and means of avoiding hardship.

(2) The works council may make recommendations to the employer relating to the introduction and implementation of manpower planning.

(3) Subsections (1) and (2), above, shall apply, mutatis mutandis, to measures under section 80 (1) Clauses 2a and 2b, in particular, the adoption and implementation of measures to promote equality between women and men.

Section 92a Securing employment

(1) The works council may submit proposals to the employer relating to the security and promotion of employment. These recommendations may refer to, in particular, a flexible design of working hours, the promotion of part-time work and old-age part-time work, new forms of work organization, changes in working methods and working processes, the improvement of worker qualifications, alternatives to the spin-off of operations or outsourcing, as well as the production and investment plan.

(2) The employer shall consult the works council concerning these proposals. If the employer believes that the works council's proposals are inadequate, he shall give reasons for this opinion, and in establishments with more than 100 employees the reasons shall be provided in written form. The employer of the works council may be accompanied by a representative of the Federal Employment Agency in these consultations.

Subdivision Three

Individual staff movements

Section 99 Co-determination in individual staff movements

(1) In companies normally employing more than twenty employees with voting rights the employer shall notify the works council in advance of any recruitment, grading, regrading and transfer, submit it to the appropriate recruitment documents and in particular supply information on the persons concerned; he shall inform the works council of the implications of the measure envisaged, supply it with the necessary supporting documentation and obtain its consent to the measure envisaged. In the case of recruitments and transfers the employer shall in particular supply information on the job and grading envisaged. Members of the works council shall refrain from divulging any information relating to the personal circumstances and private affairs of the employees concerned that has come to their knowledge in connection with the staff movements referred to in the first and second sentences, where such information is of a confidential nature by reason of its implications or contents; the second to fourth sentences of section 79 (1) shall apply, mutatis mutandis.

(2) The works council may refuse its consent in the following cases:
1. if the staff movement would constitute a breach of any Act, ordinance, safety regulation or stipulation of a collective agreement or works agreement, or of a court order or official instruction;
2. if the staff movement would amount to non-observance of a guideline within the meaning of section 95;
3. if there is factual reason to assume that the staff movement is likely to result in the dismissal of or other prejudice to employees of the establishment not warranted by operational or personal reasons; in any cases of permanent recruitment non-consideration of an equally suitable employee on a fixed term contract shall also be considered a prejudice to that employee;
4. if the employee concerned suffers prejudice through the staff movement although this is not warranted by operational or personal reasons;
5. if the vacancy has not been notified in the establishment as required under section 93; or
6. if there is reason based on facts to assume that the applicant or employee envisaged for the staff movement would cause trouble in the establishment through unlawful conduct or gross violation of the principles laid down in section 75 (1), in particular racist or xenophobic activities.

(3) If the works council refuses its consent, it shall notify the employer in writing, giving its reasons, within one week of being informed by the employer. If the works council fails to do so within the said time limit it shall be deemed to have given its consent.

(4) If the works council refuses its consent, the employer may apply to the labour court for a decision in lieu of consent.

Problem 2 discussion – Japan

Two issues are presented here: (1) the requirement for information sharing and consultation; and, (2) the ability to act unilaterally.

As to issue (1), Japanese employers bear a duty to bargain collectively with labor unions. The refusal to bargain without proper reasons constitutes an unfair labor practice (Labor Union Act, Art. 7 No. 2), and the administrative agency known as "*Rodo Iinkai*" (Labor Relations Commission) issues remedial orders against the employer to bargain in good faith (Labor Union Act, Art. 27–12).

However, Japan does not adopt such an exclusive representation system as in the U.S. Therefore there are neither elections to choose an exclusive representative of employees nor the concept of a bargaining unit. Each labor union has full-fledged rights to bargain collectively and go on strike irrespective of the number of members. In order for a labor union to enjoy a right to collective bargaining a majority support of employees is not required in Japan. In a company with 100 employees, for instance, not only a labor union A which organizes 70 employees but also a labor union B which organizes 20 employees as well as a union C with only 2 employees can request the employer to bargain in good faith (plural unionism).

It should be noted that Japan has not established a rule prohibiting unilateral modification of working conditions without collective bargaining. As a result, the existence of labor unions does not automatically mean that the employer must provide information and bargain with them. The duty to bargain and share information becomes effective only when the labor union has requested collective bargaining on mandatory subjects.

The mandatory subjects on which an employer cannot refuse to bargain are viewed as areas that are within the employer's control and that concern terms and conditions of employment, other treatment of union members, and the management of collective labor relations. Matters concerning management and production policies, such as introduction of new machines, restructuring of production processes, relocation of plants, and subcontracting are understood to be mandatory only when they affect the working conditions or other treatment of union members. Therefore, measures envisaged in Problem 2 can be regarded as mandatory subjects so long as these affect the terms and conditions of union members.

However, union density in Japan was 18.5 percent in 2011. Thus four out of five Japanese employees are free of the protection through union rights provided in the Labor Union Act.

Unlike in the EU, Japan does not have regulations on consultation or information sharing through works councils or employee representatives. Thus, Japanese employers without any labor unions are free of the obligation to share information and to consult with employee representatives. However, when an employer plans to adopt unfavorable measures and implement them for all employees, he is de facto required to provide proper information and to consult with employees under the "reasonable modification rule" which will be explained below.

As to issue (2), Japan has not established a strict "impasse" rule like that in the U.S. Thus, the alteration of working conditions before reaching an impasse in collective bargaining does not constitute an unfair labor practice per se. However, there is a risk that such unilateral action could be regarded as unfaithful bargaining.

In Japan, dismissals for economic reasons are strictly restricted. In order to compensate for such rigidity, Japanese law allows employers to unilaterally alter working conditions by "reasonably" modifying "*Shugyo Kisoku*" (work rules or rules of employment). When an employer alters work rules, he or she must consult the majority representative of the employees, but their consent is not necessary. In this sense, employers may unilaterally change work rules. In a 1968 case, the Japanese Supreme Court held that reasonably modified work rules shall have a binding effect on all employees including those who opposed the modification. This case law rule was transposed into Article 10 of the Labor Contract Act in 2007. Therefore, most of the measures listed in (e) (except for the termination of incumbent workers) will be possible by modifying work rules without obtaining individual employees' consent, provided that such modification is regarded as reasonable by the courts.

In determining the reasonableness of the modification of work rules, the courts examine such factors as the need to change working conditions, the appropriateness of the contents of the changed work rules, how the employer negotiated with labor unions and employees, and other circumstances pertaining to the change in work rules (Labor Contract Act, Art. 10). Among these, whether the employer obtained the labor union's consent or endeavored to do so is an important factor in determining reasonableness.

PRIMARY SOURCES

Labor Union Act

(Unfair Labor Practices)

Article 7 The employer shall not commit the acts listed in any of the following items:

(ii) to refuse to bargain collectively with the representatives of the workers employed by the employer without justifiable reasons;

Labor Contract Act

(Change to the Contents of a Labor Contract Based on Rules of Employment)

Article 9.

An employer may not, unless agreement has been reached with a worker, change any of the working conditions that constitute the contents of a labor contract in a manner disadvantageous to the worker by changing the rules of employment; provided, however, that this shall not apply to the cases set forth in the following Article.

Article 10.

In cases where an employer changes the working conditions by changing the rules of employment, if the employer informs the worker of the changed rules of employment, and if the change to the rules of employment is reasonable in light of the extent of the disadvantage to be incurred by the worker, the need for changing the working conditions, the appropriateness of the contents of the changed rules of employment, the status of negotiations with a labor union or the like, or any other circumstances pertaining to the change to the rules of employment, the working conditions that constitute the contents of a labor contract shall be in accordance with such changed rules of employment; provided, however, that this shall not apply to any portion of the labor contract which the worker and the employer had agreed on as being the working conditions that are not to be changed by any change to the rules of employment, except in cases that fall under Article 12.

References and suggested reading

On the general rules governing collective bargaining and modification of terms and conditions of employment, *see* KAZUO SUGENO, JAPANESE EMPLOYMENT AND LABOR LAW (LEO KANOWITZ TRANS., 2002); TAKASHI ARAKI, LABOR AND EMPLOYMENT LAW IN JAPAN (2002); Tadashi Hanami & Fumito Komiya, LABOUR LAW IN JAPAN (2011). On the mechanism for establishing and changing terms and conditions of employment, *see* Takashi Araki, *Japan*, 53

BULL. of COMP. LAB. REL. 135–56 (2004). On labor and employment law on corporate restructuring, *see* Ryuichi Yamakawa, *Japan*, 47 BULL. of COMP. LAB. REL. 103–22 (2003). On the Labor Contract Act regulating reasonable modification of work rules, *see* Ryuichi Yamakawa, *The Enactment of the Labor Contract Act: Its Significance and Future Issues*, 6 JAPAN LABOR REVIEW 4–21 (2009).

Problem 2 discussion – United States

Two issues are presented here: (1) the requirement for information sharing and consultation; and, (2) the ability to act unilaterally.

If the employees are unionized the employer must share with the union at the union's request information that is in the company's possession and that is relevant to the union's function as contract negotiator and administrator; but trade secrets or confidential business information need not be disclosed or may be made subject to special protections. Importantly, only that information that is relevant to the statutory subjects of bargaining need be disclosed. In Problem 2, most of the information compiled by the company would seem to be disclosable and all the actions under consideration – reduction of wages and benefits, reduction of hours, reduction in the number of full-time vis-à-vis part-time employees – would have to be bargained with the union in the absence of a collective agreement. Where there is an agreement it may: (a) fix these terms for the agreement's term, which means that the union may but is not required to renegotiate them during the contract's term; or (b) reserve to management the power to make all or some of these changes. Whether it did so or not would usually be submitted to an arbitrator in the event of a dispute under the collective agreement.

However, only 6 percent of employees eligible for collective representation in the United States are represented; absent a bargaining representative, federal law makes no provision for information sharing or consultation. On the contrary, as will be seen in the discussion of Problem 3, federal law limits an employer's power to create employee consultative bodies or even to deal with those bodies that might arise spontaneously.

Analysis turns next to the potential legal constraints on employer action in the absence of a collective bargaining representative, i.e. for the vast majority of American employees. The basic source of the law of employment, of how terms and conditions of employment are established and, more importantly for our purposes here, modified or abrogated, is state law. The employer might be bound by contracts of employment that limit its ability unilaterally to reduce wages and benefits or hours of work; but such individual contracts are rare. Most employment in the United States is held at will without individual contracts stating terms binding for a period of time: the employee can be discharged at any time and for any lawful reason. As that is so, the employer may reduce wages, non-vested benefits, and hours, without violating any legal right of the incumbents. (However, action taken with the motive of *preventing* the accrual or vesting of a welfare or pension benefit subject to the Employee Retirement Income Security Act (ERISA) would be actionable under that Act.) Consequently, unless a promise has been either made expressly to the individual or contained in a contractually binding policy statement, once the policy change has been clearly announced to the workforce and the employee continues to work with knowledge of the change, for example, a reduction in pay, benefits, or hours, the law assumes there has been legally operative assent. A very few jurisdictions – the District of Columbia, for example – may require a brief period of time to elapse before acceptance can be implied by continuance, i.e. for the employee to make up his or her mind. But, even then, the burden of non-acceptance would rest on the employee, i.e. to continue to work under the changed (reduced) terms or to quit.

References and suggested readings

On the request for the provision of information to a union and the obligation to bargain, *see* ROBERT GORMAN & MATTHEW FINKIN, LABOR LAW ANALYSIS AND ADVOCACY (in press).

On the absence of mechanisms for employee "voice" other than collective bargaining, *see* RICHARD FREEMAN & JOEL ROGERS, WHAT WORKERS WANT (updated ed. 2006) and STEPHEN BEFORT & JOHN BUDD, INVISIBLE HANDS, INVISIBLE OBJECTIVES: BRINGING WORKPLACE LAW AND PUBLIC POLICY INTO FOCUS (2009).

On the capacity of employer policies on wages, benefits, and hours to be legally binding and on the ability of employers unilaterally to modify or abrogate them, *compare* Restatement (Third) Employment Law ch. 2 (2009) *with* MATTHEW W. FINKIN, LEA VANDERVELDE, WILLIAM CORBETT, & STEPHEN F. BEFORT, *Working Group on Chapter 2 of the Proposed Restatement of Employment Law: Employment Contracts*, 13 EMP. RTS. & EMP. POL'Y 93–142 (2009). The District of Columbia decision noted in the text is *Kaufman v. Int'l Bro. of*

Teamsters, 950 A.2d 44 (D.C. Cir. 2008). It is possible for an employer policy legally to bind the employer to afford a specified number of hours of work, but such policies are rare. *See* the discussion in *Garcia v. Frog Island Seafood, Inc.*, 644 F.Supp.2d 696 (E.D.N.C. 2009).

> The challenge for HR in multinational companies is to achieve balance between the company's business needs/strategic objectives, core values (e.g. adherence to ethical standards such as refusal to contract with suppliers using involuntary employees or child laborers) and local/regional legal requirements (e.g. minimum wage and or awards structures) with local workforce expectations (e.g. paid time off) in the different countries. This will not result in "one-size-fits-all", harmonized global policies and practices, but a core set of policies which are executed according to the local regulations and interpreted to meet local cultural expectations.
>
> HR Consultant, Multiple Sectors

> Why would you or the company you work for want to do this, what is the business case?... My most recent experience came from an analysis we completed at a previous company to offshore our collections operations.... There was a clear wage gap between on-shored call center operations and off-shore capabilities across a multiple of countries. However, when you viewed all the dimensions of the problem – DSO rates, collection and recovery metrics, turnover, training requirements and even hours of operation the financials only proved to be slightly ahead and from a customer satisfaction perspective, yes customer satisfaction even in collections, we had a huge hurdle with cultural differences. Our role as HR experts has to be to ensure we help the businesses think through the real business challenges. Taking data points in isolation is a very dangerous proposition and often can lead to poor decisions with lingering ramifications for companies. There absolutely could be key business reasons to consider part-time work, variable production schedules, call center operations, where and how do you hire your workforce ... Our decision was actually to on-shore the work from India and Brazil and put our collection operations in Iowa. Marginally higher compensation, high population of farmers – and their spouses, who wanted steady afternoon/early evening work not for the highest compensation, but for benefits. Our DSO was cut in half improving cash flow to operations 3X and customer satisfaction (Net Promoter Score – NPS) improved 15 points over the next 18 months.
>
> Senior Vice President, HR, Biomedical Sector

> It would be immensely helpful if there were a public clearinghouse to proactively test potential issues of conflict, rather than relying on the regressive, lengthy, and expense of the courts. Although the strength of the co-determination approach in Germany could be considered to be highly restrictive for employers, co-determination should result in much more reasoned and thoughtful decisions. Converse to the freedoms enjoyed (and risked) by the United States, Works Councils essentially protect employers from themselves.
>
> Vice President, HR, Financial Sector

Questions for Discussion – Problem 2

1. Should employees be heard, and, if so, should they have a legally enforceable right to be heard on these decisions? If not, why not? If so, at what point should the obligation to notify ripen: When these employer studies are being commissioned? When they are received? When action is under consideration? When action is authorized?

2. There is a rich literature on whether and how unions and works councils affect profitability and productivity. One student of German works councils argues that, even if there is a negative effect on profitability (which he doubts), there is a positive effect in productivity. If that is so, why don't companies introduce them without a legal mandate? He explains the need for a legal mandate thus:

   > Among these explanations are managerial risk aversion and a possible difference between the short- and long-term effects of works councils. [*Citing* Steffen Mueller, *Works Councils and Firm Profits Revisited*, 49 BRITISH J. INDUS. REL. 27 (2011).] Additionally, managers may oppose the introduction of powerful works councils because managers may trade the expected productivity gains against their own loss in power and managerial prerogatives.

   Steffen Mueller, *Works Councils and Establishment Productivity*, 65 I. L. R. REV. 880, 894 (2012).

   To the extent a legal mandate affects managerial flexibility, consider the degree of flexibility each of these systems afford. This issue should be revisited at the close. *See* Part VIII (C) ("Political Economy: Varieties of Capitalism").

3. Inasmuch as the vast majority of American employers are not unionized most employers can take these actions summarily. Nevertheless, would you advise your company in the U.S. to give notice to the workforce that these decisions were under consideration? If an ad hoc work group forms, and requests the information which the company has compiled, and requests to meet and discuss these decisions, would you advise that the company do so? (It might help to prepare Problem 3, infra, at this point.)

4. There has been much debate in the United States on the "representation gap" – that according to survey data a sizeable majority of American workers want to be represented in a manner that will effectively influence employee policies and aren't. See the Freeman & Rogers study noted in the references to the U.S. entry. Befort and Budd, in a book in the same note, recommend that the Congress adopt a version of the German Works Councils Act. Do you agree; or not?

   In considering that question the student might take note of the fact that

   > there appears to be a significant long-term decline in the number of workplaces with works councils and in the workforce represented by them. Since works councils have a legal mandate to supervise the enforcement of applicable collective agreements, their decline detracts from the efficacy of the collective bargaining regime.

   WOLFGANG STREECK, RE-FORMING CAPITALISM: INSTITUTIONAL CHANGE IN THE GERMAN POLITICAL ECONOMY 40 (2009).

According to the data Prof. Streeck points to, about 46 percent of private sector workers were represented by works councils in Western Germany in 2005, which may be higher than the level of union representation. He notes also that employees had increasingly pressed works councils into making concessionary agreements in derogation of the terms of multi-employer bargains to which the employer was legally bound and which, legally, works councils were not authorized to make:

> Ultimately unions had no choice but to make space for local deviations in industry-level collective agreements, through so-called "opening clauses." In effect, these clauses delegated major bargaining rights to the works councils, which are formally nonunion bodies and legally prohibited from negotiating wages and working hours.

Id. at 41.

5. The European Union's Directive on employee information sharing and consultation was set out at the outset of this Part. Does it provide a desirable, useful – and workable – alternative?

6. In considering question 5, above, it might be useful to consider the role of labor-management consultation in Japan. A 2008 survey of 924 reporting Japanese companies in major industrial groups indicated that 71 percent had joint management–labor consultative systems – 51 percent at unionized companies and 21 percent in companies that had no union. Japan Institute for Labor Policy and Training, LABOR SITUATION IN JAPAN AND ANALYSIS: DETAILED EXPOSITION 2011/2012 (2011) at 60. Some precede collective bargaining and some are set up to solve collective bargaining issues, but some are a form of "participative management, for the purpose of discussing management and productivity issues that are different from the collective bargaining issues." *Id.* at 63. The differences between the two, based on a study by Prof. Kazuo Sugeno, can be displayed in tabular form (see Table II.4 below).

Table II.4 Collective bargaining and joint consultation in Japan

	Collective bargaining	Labor-management joint consultation system
Legal basis	Labor Union Act (Article 28 of the constitution)	Agreement between the parties
Parties in interest	Labor unions, employers or employers' associations	Labor unions – employers or employee meetings
Objective	"Negotiation of working conditions on equal standing (Paragraph 1 of Article 1) Conclusion of collective agreements and other matters (Article 6)"	Participation in management, improvement of production, information sharing, exchange of opinions
Subject matter	Working conditions (the treatment of workers), and other matters (rules on labor-management issues etc.) (paragraph 1 of Article 1, Article 6, Article 16)	Management/production matters (status/direction of management, production plan/ methods, etc.)
Person in charge	Representatives of a labor union or those to whom the authority has been delegated by the labor union, representatives of the employer or those to whom the authority has been delegated by the employer (Article 6)	Agreement between the parties
Deadlock	The right to carry out acts of dispute which are justifiable acts (Article 28) of the Constitution, Paragraph 1, Article 2 of the Labor Union Act, Article 8)	No planned labor dispute actions, the differentiations between "description report" "hearing of opinions" "mutual consultations, agreement"
Legal protection	The duty of the employer to bargain collectively (Article 6, Article 7–2), immunity from prosecution (Paragraph 2 of Article 1), no civil liability (Article 8), bail-out from unfair labor practices (Article 7, Article 27)	Arbitrary procedure between labor and management

Source: Japan Institute for Labor Policy and Training, LABOR SITUATION IN JAPAN AND ANALYSIS: DETAILED EXPOSITION 2011/2012 (2011) at 62 (Table 5–4) (edited).

PROBLEM 3: CONSULTATION ON "ECO-FRIENDLY" ISSUES

A number of employees (perhaps acting through their legally recognized representative) have approached the company claiming that it is not "eco-friendly" or "green" in its use of energy. Must the company respond to their criticism? Must it give the employees or their representative access to data on its energy use? Must it consult with them about its energy use? If they propose alternatives to make the company more eco-friendly – not only in its infrastructure (energy efficient light and transport) and processes (distributing excess heat for use at a local community center and using biodegradable packaging), but in its product design as well – must the company engage with them on their proposals?

Problem 3 discussion – Australia

As noted in relation to Problem 2, there is no general obligation under Australian law to disclose information to employees, or to consult with them. Unlike Problem 2, there is no suggestion here of any "decision" by the company that involves a "significant change" impacting on employees.

The only way in which an obligation to release data of this sort might arise would be if the employees, or their bargaining representative, sought to deal with the issue of energy use in a new enterprise agreement. Section 228 of the Fair Work Act 2009 requires bargaining representatives to comply with certain good faith bargaining requirements when negotiating a proposed enterprise agreement. The requirements include "disclosing relevant information (other than confidential or commercially sensitive information) in a timely manner".

Even if the data is not confidential or commercially sensitive, however, it is not clear that it would be *relevant*. This is because, under s 172, an agreement may only deal with certain "permitted matters". Such matters are generally confined to matters "pertaining" to the employer's relationships with the employees and/or unions to be covered by the proposed agreement. The term "matters pertaining" has a long and unhappy history in Australian labour law. It has been interpreted to mean only matters that *directly* impact on the employment relationship. To satisfy the requirement, the matter in question must be "connected with the relationship between an employer in [their] capacity as an employer and an employee in [their] capacity as an employee in a way which is direct and not merely consequential" (*Re Manufacturing Grocers Employees Federation*; *Ex parte Australian Chamber of Manufactures* (1986) 160 CLR 341 at 353). For example, shop opening hours have been held not to be a matter pertaining to employment, despite their obvious impact on the working hours of retail employees: see *R v Kelly*; *Ex parte Victoria* (1950) 81 CLR 64.

On the face of it, issues of energy use would not satisfy the "matters pertaining" requirement. It is notable that in the Explanatory Memorandum for the Bill that became the Fair Work Act, the drafters of the legislation specifically mentioned "corporate social responsibility" terms, for example relating to climate change, as an example of provisions that would *not* be permitted: see para [673]. If that view prevailed, a clause that related to energy use or efficiency could not be validly included in an enterprise agreement. That would in turn seem to mean that there could be no enforceable obligation to disclose information on the issue, or indeed to respond to any employee proposals on the matter.

PRIMARY SOURCE

Fair Work Act 2009

228 Bargaining representatives must meet the good faith bargaining requirements

(1) The following are the *good faith bargaining requirements* that a bargaining representative for a proposed enterprise agreement must meet:
  - (a) attending, and participating in, meetings at reasonable times;
  - (b) disclosing relevant information (other than confidential or commercially sensitive information) in a timely manner;
  - (c) responding to proposals made by other bargaining representatives for the agreement in a timely manner;
  - (d) giving genuine consideration to the proposals of other bargaining representatives for the agreement, and giving reasons for the bargaining representative's responses to those proposals;
  - (e) refraining from capricious or unfair conduct that undermines freedom of association or collective bargaining;
  - (f) recognising and bargaining with the other bargaining representatives for the agreement.

(2) The good faith bargaining requirements do not require:
   (a) a bargaining representative to make concessions during bargaining for the agreement; or
   (b) a bargaining representative to reach agreement on the terms that are to be included in the agreement.

172 Making an enterprise agreement

Enterprise agreements may be made about permitted matters

(1) An agreement (an *enterprise agreement*) that is about one or more of the following matters (the *permitted matters*) may be made in accordance with this Part:
   (a) matters pertaining to the relationship between an employer that will be covered by the agreement and that employer's employees who will be covered by the agreement;
   (b) matters pertaining to the relationship between the employer or employers, and the employee organisation or employee organisations, that will be covered by the agreement;
   (c) deductions from wages for any purpose authorised by an employee who will be covered by the agreement;
   (d) how the agreement will operate

References and suggested readings

Andrew Stewart, Stewart's Guide to Employment Law §§8.18–19; 8.33–7 (4th ed. 2013).

Problem 3 discussion – Brazil

Employers are under no legal obligation to deal with such a group of employees (or their representative). It follows that employers may simply ignore employees' criticism of their use of energy.

Actually, environmental questions in labor conditions under Brazilian law do not come from employees' conscience, but are directly extracted from the right to a healthy and safe working environment. So, if the criticism of the employer's use of energy is related to working conditions, although still under no legal obligation to deal with this group of employees (or their representative), the employer's reaction may be different as a third party, i.e. Labor Inspection, should become involved.

Such a possibility may occur as the group of employees (or just one of them) may file a complaint in the Labor Inspection Office which is under an obligation to verify if the company is acting accordingly to the *Normas Regulamentadoras* (Regulatory Standards). These are an ensemble of legislation related to health and safety in the workplace edited by the Ministry of Labor and Employment through a tripartite commission composed by government officials and representatives of employers and employees. As of today, there are 35 *Normas Regulamentadoras*. They regulate a wide range of subjects, ranging from the functioning of the *Comissão Interna de Prevenção de Acidentes* (Internal Commission for Accident Prevention) to the use of *Equipamento de Proteção Individual* (Individual Protection Equipment).

As for the problem itself, the company's energy use has to be made according to its *Programa de Prevenção de Riscos Ambientais* – PPRA (Prevention of Environmental Risk Program), whose existence and implementation are required by the *Norma Regulamentadora nº 9* (Regulatory Standard no. 9). The PPRA is a mandatory program that has to be established by every employer in order to preserve employees' health and integrity through anticipation, recognition, evaluation and control of environmental risks in the workplace, never neglecting the protection of natural resources and environmental conditions.

Therefore, if the employees are capable of linking their complaint to health and safety conditions, the company may be compelled to respond to their criticism, especially when Labor Inspection becomes involved.

References and suggested readings

BRASIL, *Norma Regulamentadora nº 9 – Programa de Prevenção de Riscos Ambientais (PPRA)*, MINISTÉRIO DO TRABALHO E EMPREGO, *accessed at* http://www.mte.gov.br/legislacao/normas_regulamentaDORAS/nr_09_at.pdf (last visited Feb. 14, 2010).

On Labor Inspection, see ADALBERTO CARDOSO & TELMA LAGE, *A INSPEÇÃO DO TRABALHO NO BRASIL*, 48 DADOS 451 (2005), accessed at http://redalyc.uaemex.mx/redalyc/pdf/218/21848301.pdf (last visited: Feb. 14, 2010).

Problem 3 discussion – Germany

In 2001, the Works Councils Act was amended partly with a view to strengthening the role works councils can play with regard to issues of environment protection at plant level. According to section 88 no. 1a of the Works Councils Act, works councils and employers are free to conclude works agreements (*Betriebsvereinbarung*) relating to issues of environment protection at plant level.

According to section 89 para. 1 sentence 1 of the Works Councils Act, the works council has to see to it that regulations concerning environment protection at plant level are implemented properly. Questions of energy consumption might fall within this area. According to section 89 para. 2 sentence 2 of the Works Councils Act, the employer is obliged to call the works council in with regard to all inspections and questions relating to issues of environment protection at plant level. In addition the employer is under an obligation to make available all protocols relating to examinations, inspections and conversations regarding environment protection at plant level (section 89 para. 5 of the Works Councils Act). Apart from that the financial committee – which has to be erected in enterprises with a workforce of more than 100 workers (section 106 para. 1 of the Works Councils Act) and whose members are nominated by the works council (section 107 para. 2 sentence 1 of the Works Councils Act) has to be consulted with regard to questions of environment protection at plant level (section 106 para. 3 no. 5a of the Works Councils Act). This consultation right in particular encompasses individual measures of environment protection at plant level, their costs and their consequences for members of the workforce.

According to section 43 para. 2 sentence 3 of the Works Councils Act, the employer has to inform staff at least once per year on the occasion of so-called "employees meetings" (*Betriebsversammlung*) about, among other things, issues of environment protection at the level of the establishment.

If a joint works council has been established – there is an obligation to do so if several works councils exist in an enterprise (section 47 para. 1 of the Works Councils Act) – the employer is obliged to inform workers' representatives regularly (at least once per year) about a couple of issues, matters of environment protection at the enterprise level among them (section 53 para. 2 no. 2 of the Works Councils Act).

Apart from all that, it may be noteworthy that environment protection at the enterprise level may become an issue for discussions at company board level (which consists in larger companies of shareholders' and staff representatives in equal numbers).

PRIMARY SOURCE

Works Councils Act

Division Three

Social Matters

Section 88 Works agreements on a voluntary basis

The following, in particular, may be determined by works agreements:

1. additional measures to prevent accidents at work and health damages;

1a. *measures concerning the establishment's environmental policy* [emphasis added];

2. the establishment of social services whose scope is limited to the establishment, company or combine;

3. measures to promote capital formation;

4. measures to promote the integration of foreign employees and to combat racism and xenophobia in the establishment.

Section 89 Health and safety as well as environmental protection at work

(1) The works council shall endeavor to ensure that the provisions on safety and health at work and accident prevention as well as environmental protection are observed in the establishment. It shall support the competent occupational safety and health authorities, the statutory accident insurance institutions and other relevant bodies in their efforts to eliminate safety and health hazards by offering suggestions, advice and information.

(2) The employer and the bodies referred to in the second sentence of subsection (1) shall be obliged to invite the works council or the members it delegates for that purpose to participate in all inspections and issues relating to safety and health at work or the prevention of accidents and inquiries into accidents. The employer shall also consult the works council concerning all inspections and issues relating to environmental protection in the company, and shall immediately inform it of any conditions imposed and instructions given by the competent bodies relating to

safety and health at work, the prevention of accidents, or environmental protection in the establishment.

(3) For the purposes of this Act, environmental protection in the establishment comprises all personnel and organizational measures as well as all measures relating to the establishment's buildings, rooms, technical equipment, working methods, working processes and work places that serve the protection of the environment.

(4) Members delegated by the works council shall take part in discussions between the employer and the safety delegates within the context of Section 22 (2) of the Seventh Book of the Social Code.

(5) The works council shall receive from the employer the minutes of inquiries, inspections and discussions in respect of which subsections (2) and (4) provide for in its participation.

(6) The employer shall supply the works council with a copy of the accident notification to be signed by the works council under section 193 (5) of the Seventh Book of the Social Code.

Division Four

Financial Matters

Subdivision One

Information on financial matters

Section 106 Financial committee

(1) A finance committee shall be established in all companies that normally have more than 100 permanent employees. It shall be the duty of the finance committee to consult with the employer on financial matters and report to the works council.

(2) The employer shall inform the finance committee in full and in good time of the financial affairs of the company and supply the relevant documentation in so far as there is no risk of disclosing the trade or business secrets of the company and demonstrate the implications for manpower planning.

(3) The following, inter alia, are financial matters covered by this provision:
1. the economic and financial situation of the company;
2. the production and financial situation of the company;
3. the production and investment programmes;
4. rationalisation plans;
5. production techniques and work methods, especially the introduction of new work methods;
5a. *issues concerning the establishment's environment policy* [emphasis added];
6. the reduction of operations in or closure of establishments or parts of establishments;
7. the transfer of establishments or parts of establishments;
8. the amalgamation or split-up of establishments or parts of establishments;
9. changes in the organization or objectives of establishments; and

10. any other circumstances and projects that may materially affect the interests of the employees of the company.

Section 108 Meetings

(1) The finance committee shall meet once a month.

(2) The employer or his representative shall attend the meetings of the finance committee. He may be accompanied by competent employees of the company including members of the executive staff covered by section 5 (3). The participation of experts and their duty to observe professional secrecy shall be governed by section 80 (3) and (4), mutatis mutandis.

(3) The members of the finance committee shall have access to the documents to be submitted under section 106 (2).

(4) The finance committee shall without delay give a full report on each meeting to the works council.

(5) The annual balance sheet shall be explained to the finance committee in conjunction with the works council.

(6) Where the works council or central works council has decided to assign the functions of the finance committee to another committee, subsections (1) to (5) shall apply, mutatis mutandis.

Section 109 Settlement of differences

If despite a request from the finance committee information on financial matters as defined in section 106 is not furnished or not furnished in good time or if the information given is inadequate and if no agreement on the matter is reached between the employer and the works council, the matter shall be decided by the conciliation committee. The award of the conciliation committee shall take the place of an agreement between the employer and the works council. The conciliation committee may call in experts if it needs their evidence to reach a decision; section 80 (4) shall apply, mutatis mutandis. Where the works council or the central works council has decided to assign the functions of the finance committee to another committee, the first sentence shall apply, mutatis mutandis.

Section 110 Information of employees

(1) In companies that normally have more than 1,000 permanent employees, the employer shall report to the staff in writing on the financial situation and progress of the company at least once every calendar quarter after prior coordination with the finance committee or the bodies referred to in section 107 (3) and the works council.

(2) The preceding subsection shall also apply to companies that do not meet the conditions laid down in the preceding subsection but normally have more than twenty permanent employees with voting rights, subject to the proviso that the employees of such companies may also be informed orally. If such company is under

no obligation to set up a finance committee, the employees shall be informed after prior coordination with the works council.

References and suggested readings

Michael E. Meyer & Michael E. Reichel, *Betrieblicher Umweltschutz als Schnittstelle zwischen Arbeitsrecht und Umweltrecht*, Recht der Arbeit (RdA) 101 (2003); Günther Wiese, *Beteiligung des Betriebsrats beim betrieblichen Umweltschutz nach dem Gesetz zur Reform des Betriebsverfassungsgesetzes*, Betriebs-Berater (BB) 674 (2002).

Problem 3 discussion – Japan

In Problem 3, two legal issues are raised under the Japanese labor law: whether the group of workers is regarded as a labor union protected by the Labor Union Act (LUA); and whether the "eco-friendly" or "green" issues are mandatory subjects for collective bargaining.

In order to enjoy protected rights of labor unions, the group of workers must meet the requirements for "labor unions" in the LUA. To become a "qualified union" under the LUA, there are five requirements to be met:

First, the group of workers or the organization must be "composed mainly of workers." (LUA Art. 2) "Workers" in the sense of the LUA are defined in the Act as "those persons who live on their wages, salaries, or other equivalent income, regardless of the kind of occupation." (LUA Art. 3)

Second, the organization must be independent of the employer. The Act requires three specific types of independence. One is that the organization must be "voluntarily" formed by the workers themselves (LUA Art. 2).

Third, the main purpose of the organization must be "maintaining and improving working conditions and raising the economic status of the workers." (LUA Art. 2) Therefore, an organization whose purposes are confined to "mutual aid service or other welfare service" (LUA Art. 2 Proviso No. 3) or whose purposes are "principally political or social movements" (LUA Art. 2 Proviso No. 4) is not a qualified union under the LUA.

Fourth, the group of workers must be "organizations, or federations thereof." (LUA Art. 2) To be deemed an organization, there must be more than two members.

Finally, the organization must establish a union constitution which includes the enumerated items in Article 5 paragraph 2 of the LUA. Most of the enumerated items concern the democratic administration of the internal affairs of the union, such as the equal treatment of union members, and secret ballot elections for union officers or for strike decisions.

Other than the foregoing prerequisites, there are no further requirements. Majority support by the workers is not required, neither is a minimum number of members nor registration with a governmental agency. In short, Japan has few requirements for organizing labor unions.

As to the group of workers in Problem 3, it becomes especially questionable whether it meets the third (organization's purpose) and fifth (union constitution) requirement. If the group of workers is not regarded as a qualified labor union, it cannot seek any remedies against refusal to bargain collectively from an administrative agency (the Labor Relations Commission).

Even if the group of workers is regarded as a qualified labor union under the LUA, whether or not the subjects the group has raised ("eco-friendly" or "green" issues) are within the scope of "mandatory subjects" for collective bargaining should be examined. In Japan, mandatory subjects are generally understood as areas that are within the employer's control *and* that concern working conditions or other treatment of union members (e.g. wages, hours, holidays, health and safety, compensation for work related accidents, vocational training, and personnel matters such as transfer, discipline, dismissal) and the management of collective labor relations (e.g. union shop agreements, rules governing union activities, grants of convenience for union activities, rules and procedures for collective bargaining, labor-management consultations, rules and procedures for dispute acts).

It would be difficult for "eco-friendly" or "green" issues to be deemed a mandatory subject for collective bargaining unless the company plans to introduce measures that affect the working conditions of the workers. However, there are no legal obstacles to Japanese employers discussing these issues with a group of workers on a voluntary basis.

PRIMARY SOURCE

Labor Union Act of 1949

Article 2

The term "Labor unions" as used in this Act shall mean those organizations, or federations thereof, formed voluntarily and composed mainly of workers for the main purposes of maintaining and improving working conditions and raising the economic status of the workers; however, this shall not apply to any of the following items:

(i) which admits to membership of officers; workers in supervisory positions having direct authority with respect to hiring, firing, promotions, or transfers; workers in supervisory positions having access to confidential information relating to the employer's labor relations plans and policies so that their official duties and responsibilities directly conflict with their sincerity and responsibilities as members of the labor union said; and other persons who represent the interests of the employer;

(ii) which receives the employer's financial assistance in paying the organizations' operational expenditures; however, that this shall not prevent the employer from permitting workers to confer or negotiate with the employer during working hours without loss of time or wage and shall not apply to the employer's contributions for public welfare funds or welfare and other funds which are actually used for payments to prevent or relieve economic adversity or misfortunes, nor to the giving office of minimum space;

(iii) whose purposes are confined to mutual aid service or other welfare service;

(iv) whose purposes are principally political or social movements.

Article 5

Unless the labor union has submitted evidence to the Labor Relations Commission and proved that it is in compliance with Article 2 and paragraph 2 of this Article, the labor union shall not be qualified to participate in the procedures provided in this Act and shall not be granted the remedies provided in this Act, provided, however, that nothing herein shall be construed so as to deny protections for any individual worker pursuant to Article 7, item 1.

(2) The constitution of a labor union shall include the provisions listed in any of the following items:
- (i) name;
- (ii) the location of its principal office;
- (iii) that members of a labor union other than a labor union that is a federation (such other labor union hereinafter referred to as a "local union") shall have the right to participate in all issues or disputes of such labor union and shall have the right to receive equal treatment;
- (iv) no one shall be disqualified from union membership in any case on the basis of race, religion, gender, family origin or status;
- (v) in the case of a local union, that the officers shall be elected by direct secret vote

of the union members, and, in the case of a federation or a labor union having national scope, that the officers shall be elected by direct secret vote either of the members of the local unions or of delegates elected by direct secret vote of the members of the local unions;

(vi) that a general meeting shall be held at least once every year;

(vii) that a financial report showing all sources of revenues and expenditures, the names of main contributors and the current financial status, together with certificate of accuracy by a professionally qualified accounting auditor commissioned by the union members, shall be released to the union members at least once every year;

(viii) that no strike shall be started without a majority decision made by direct secret vote either of the union members or of delegates elected by direct secret vote of the union members;

(ix) in the case of local union, that the constitution shall not be revised unless such revision has received majority support by direct secret vote of the union members, and, in the case of a labor union which is a federation or a labor union which has national scope, the constitution shall not be revised unless such revision has received majority support by direct secret vote either of the members of the local unions or of the delegates elected by direct secret vote of the members of the local unions.

Problem 3 discussion – United States

In a unionized workplace an employer must bargain with a union over statutory subjects of collective bargaining: "wages, hours, and working conditions." These are "mandatory" subjects. An employer cannot take unilateral action on these until it has exhausted its bargaining obligation and a union can strike over them. But non-statutory subjects, subjects especially that the United States Supreme Court has identified as going to the "core of entrepreneurial control," are lawful but "permissive," subjects. The Court has said, in a pregnant passage unnecessary to the decision that, "Congress had no expectation that the elected union representative would become an equal partner in the running of the business enterprise ..." *First National Maintenance Corp. v. NLRB*, 452 U.S. 666, 667 (1981). If a company is willing to talk about its product line or product design with a union – and if the union would like to be heard on these matters which bear necessarily on profitability and so indirectly on job availability and wages – the parties are free to agree to do so. Indeed, should they make an agreement on a permissive subject, the agreement would be enforceable. But, the Labor Act does not compel bargaining about such matters.

Thus analysis focuses on what "eco-friendly" or "green" issues the employees wish to raise. In a prescient discussion of the issue almost four decades ago, Professor James Oldham argued for giving the statute broad reach insofar as unions might be motivated to bargain for socially responsible environment policies. The closer the connection to in-plant (or in-office) workplace life, the more obviously the subject would be covered by the Act: in the early 1970s the United Auto Workers persuaded several General Motors plants to replace gasoline powered trucks used in the plant with electric battery operated equipment; today the substitution of energy efficient lighting might well be a "working condition." But, in view of the narrowing of the scope of mandatory bargaining subjects by the United States Supreme Court in decisions subsequent to Oldham's analysis, it is doubtful that the communal (or global) environmental impact of investment decisions would come within the compass of workplace-grounded subjects that would be mandatorily bargainable.

Turning to the non-unionized workplace, it follows from the discussion of Problem 2 that there is no provision in federal law obligating the employer to deal with an ad hoc employee group or committee. Actually, the question presented in the United States is whether the employer is even allowed to do so. (This question would be presented as well were an employer to wish to consult its employees on the issues set out in Problem 2.) The obstacle to the employer's doing so flows from the Labor Act's prohibition of the evil of "company unionism" as it was perceived in the 1930s.

Section 8(a)(2) of the NLRA makes it an "unfair labor practice" for an employer to "dominate" or to 'interfere in the formation or administration" of a "labor organization." A "labor organization" is defined in sweeping terms, "as any organization of any kind, or any agency or employee representation committee or plan, in which employees participate and which exists for the purpose, in whole or in part, of dealing with employers concerning grievances, labor disputes, wages, rates of pay, hours of employment, or conditions of work."

The issue here turns on the "dealing with" clause. If what the workers or their committee wish to discuss does not concern "grievances, labor disputes, wages, rates of pay, hours of employment, or conditions of work" within the meaning of the statute, then even though the group or committee is an organization of *any* kind, and employees participate in it, the employer's dealing with it could invoke no problem of domination or interference – and so no violation of §8(a)(2) – because it would not be dealing with a statutory labor organization.

Three additional points should be mentioned. First, even if the company is "dealing with" a labor organization, such dealing does not necessarily work a violation of the Act: the company must "dominate" or "interfere" in the organization's administration in order for an unfair labor practice to result. So long as the company's dealings with this group are truly arm's-length – the company does not create the body, select its members, set its agenda, and the like – the law would not be violated *even if* the subjects the employees wish to have dealings with the employer about are statutory subjects.

Second, even if the line is transgressed, the law would have practical bite only if a charge of an unfair labor practice is filed with the NLRB. (Any person is free to file a charge, but §8(a)(2) is most often invoked by unions that, seeking to establish exclusive representation status, wish to eliminate any competing center of power.) Were a charge to be filed, a Board agent would be assigned to investigate it and, if it appeared to be well founded, is authorized to settle with the company, in this case merely by having the company cease its course of dealing; indeed, such would be the remedy were the company to refuse to settle and were the matter to be litigated by the Board through its administrative process. In other words, violating §8(a)(2) is relatively costless and, apparently, rather common insofar as high performance work groups' treatment of product quality and other non-statutory issues overlap onto wages, hours, and other statutory working conditions.

Finally, the question may also be posed rather differently: may the company discharge workers, consistent with the NLRA, who publicly criticize the company's environmental policies or actions or seek by concerted activity to change them? Such may be protected under state "whistleblower" laws; but these vary considerably in scope and procedure. In terms of the Labor Act, section 7 protects employees, including employees in non-unionized workplaces, who engage in "concerted activity… for mutual aid or protection" from employer retaliation. But a countervailing consideration obtains here: such activity must address the "employees' interests *as employees*," in the words of the United States Supreme Court. At some point the interests being advanced may become so "attenuated," the Court said, so removed from employee interests as employees, as to lack statutory protection. *Eastex v. NLRB*, 437 U.S. 556 (1978). This is the reverse of the §8(a)(2) issue: if these environmental demands are remote from the employees' interests as employees, if they are being advanced for the communal, even the global good, as distinct from parochial employee-centered concerns, §8(a)(2) would not apply and the employer would be free to deal with them; but, so, too, as such conduct would not be for statutory mutual aid or protection, such speech and other activity in furtherance of these non-parochial interests would not be protected under this statute and the employees could be discharged for having sought to raise them or requesting to be heard about them. For example, where an employee designed a plan for the enterprise's employees to acquire the enterprise by use of the employee stock ownership plan – or ESOP – and was ordered by management to cease his solicitation for it amongst his co-workers, the issue was presented to the Labor Board of whether that order was lawful. It held it was:

> The thrust of the proposal was to cast employees in the role of owners with ultimate corporate control, and thus fundamentally to change how and by whom the corporation would be managed. The current employees would not enjoy any of the envisioned benefits unless and until they, through the ESOP, effectively controlled the corporation. Although Winn [the employee] presented his proposal within the employee-employer relationship, it was designed to change that relationship. The test of whether an employee's activity is protected is not whether it relates to employees' interests generally but whether it relates to "the interests of employees qua employees". Here, the proposal advances employees' interests not as employees but as entrepreneurs, owners and managers. The complaint must be dismissed.

Harrah's Lake Tahoe Resort Casino, 307 N.L.R.B. 182 (1992). Had Mr. Winn persisted and been discharged for violation of the company's order – or, for that matter, for pressing his proposal per se – the discharge would not have been unlawful under the Labor Act: sections 8(a)(1) and (3) prohibit discharge for engaging in statutorily protected speech and his speech was not statutorily protected as too far afield from his and his co-workers' interests "as employees."

References and suggested readings

On the Labor Act, see ROBERT GORMAN & MATTHEW FINKIN, LABOR LAW ANALYSIS AND ADVOCACY (in press). A strong effort was mounted in the 1980s to amend §8(a)(2) to permit broadened (non-collective bargaining) employee consultation. It failed.

Oldham's argument is found in JAMES OLDHAM, *Organized Labor, the Environment, and the Taft-Hartley Act*, 71 U. MICH. L. REV. 935 (1971). He reports in detail on union activity, and inactivity, starting with this 1970 Resolution of the United Auto Workers:

> The unchecked pollution by the automobile and related industries is of direct concern to auto workers not only because they are citizens concerned for their environment but because there is a direct threat to their jobs and their job security. The workers' stake in resolving this problem for society and the nation is compounded by the stake in his own job. We shall raise this issue sharply in 1970 negotiations in discussions with the companies ...

Id. at 970–71.

An argument for a more expansive reading of §7 vis-à-vis environmental concerns has also been made by CYNTHIA ESTLUND, *What Do Workers Want?: Employee Interests, Public Interests, and Freedom of Expression Under the National Labor Relations Act*, 140 U. PA. L. REV. 921, 959 (1992): "The restriction of section 7 protection to activity motivated by economic self-interest rests on an impoverished understanding of what work means to people: it denies that employees have a genuine and legitimate interest in the broader implications of their work." The irony of U.S. labor law here is that to the extent Estlund's argument proves influential, the more, that is, employers must bargain with unions about their environmental policies, the greater is the likelihood that dealing with interested work groups on these issues in the non-union setting would come under shadow of prohibition of §8(a)(2) depending on how these groups were created, function, and are financed.

Questions for Discussion – Problem 3

1. A student of corporate environmental policy in the United States has written that "current environmental regulation works reasonably well to control behavior that creates harmful environmental risks, but it is a blunt and imperfect tool to inspire and motivate creative responses that lead to greener products and processes – and eventually to a more sustainable society. We need additional policy tools to achieve this..." KURT STRASSER, MYTHS AND REALITIES OF BUSINESS ENVIRONMENTALISM: GOOD WORKS, GOOD BUSINESS, OR GREENWASH? 29 (2011). He surveys the international literature on four unilateral corporate approaches: voluntary reporting, voluntary environmental performance standards, negotiated compliance agreements, and environmental managerial systems (EMS). Of these, he finds the latter the more promising – but not without reservations.

   > EMS sets up a system, first to evaluate a company's environmental impacts, and, second, to manage daily operations and long term decisions to reduce them. The management effort is to extend from the top to the bottom, throughout the entire company hierarchy. The management system is an ongoing process that aims at continuous evaluation and improvement. At each stage, the system plans and evaluates, then undertakes to implement the plans, and finally checks to evaluate progress before repeating the sequence-using the "plan, do, check" structure so familiar in modern business management. A core justification for establishing an EMS is that this regularly structured attention to environmental management throughout the whole organization will lead to better environmental performance and ongoing, continuous improvement.

Id. at 24. Absent from this discussion, however, is any mention of a consultative or participative role for unions or employees.

2. Professor Strasser concludes that a failure of EMS is its singular focus on the particular business facility: "Yet, the argument runs, fundamental redesign of products or processes requires sustained creative effort, sustained financial commitment, and willingness to confront the substantial business risks that are presented by the processes. While these must have support within the facility, they also require top-management support at the highest levels in the company." *Id.* at 29–30. Do employees have an interest as employees in the risks the company is considering assuming in an effort to assure or further sustainability? If so, should that interest be represented? If so, how?

3. Return to the European Directive on Information Sharing and Consultation set out at the close to the introduction to this Part. Would it cover this situation?

4. A network of social scientists compile survey data from citizens on a national basis to produce the *World Values Survey*. More will be said about this in Part VIII (D), infra. National views on the environment is a subject of inquiry, producing the data shown in Table II.5 for the countries of interest here. Note that these are four separate questions and, for concision, we have only included selected responses for each question (rather than the full range of possible responses, which would total 100 percent).
   (a) Is the treatment of the environment as a labor law issue consistent with the value the survey data indicate these populations attach to environmental protection?
   (b) Note the contrasting views on the use of increased taxes to prevent environmental pollution, with relatively high support in Australia (66.6 percent) and Japan (53.4 percent) compared with relatively low support (28 percent) in Germany. Do you see these views as consistent with the role of the state in employment matters in these countries or not? If not, why not?

Table II.5 Selected national views on the environment: World Values Survey 2005/2006

	Australia (2005)	Brazil (2006)	Germany (2006)	Japan (2005)	United States (2006)
Environmental problems in the world: Global warming or the greenhouse effect (very serious)*	64.2%	61.1%	49.9%	71.3%	48.5%
Environmental problems in the world: Pollution of rivers, lakes and oceans (very serious)*	79.0%	72.3%	43.6%	57.9%	65.4%
Increase in taxes if used to prevent environmental pollution (strongly agree/ agree)**	66.6%	49.5%	28.0%	53.4%	49.8%
Government should reduce environmental pollution (strongly agree/agree)**	64.6%	81.8%	75.8%	57.7%	66.1%

Notes:
* Four point scale: very serious, somewhat serious, not very serious, not serious at all;
** Five point scale: strongly agree, agree, neither agree or disagree, disagree, strongly disagree.
Sample sizes are: Australia N = 1,238; Brazil N = 1,042; Germany N = 1,408; Japan N = 1,496; United States N = 2,014.

Source: http://www.worldvaluessurvey.org.

PART III

DISCRIMINATION IN EMPLOYMENT

"The principle of equality and prohibition of discrimination in employment ... is based on the legal and moral proposition that workers who are alike should be treated alike." Ruth Ben-Israel, *Equality and the Prohibition of Discrimination in Employment* in COMPARATIVE LABOUR LAW AND INDUSTRIAL RELATIONS IN INDUSTRIALIZED MARKET ECONOMICS 239 (R. Blanpain & C. Engels eds., 7th rev. ed. 1998). We have been reminded, however, that "Persons are never alike in all aspects ... [a] decision needs to be made as to which differences matter in order to ascertain whether persons are truly alike." Dagmar Schiek, Lisa Waddington & Mark Bell, NON-DISCRIMINATION LAW 27 (2007). As these authors point out, groups have often been treated differently, most prominently because of race – or caste – sex, nationality, or religion, which distinctions have been grounded in deeply entrenched social conventions that legitimated such treatment. The commodification of labor mapped on to these conventions giving breathing space for employment policies to track or build upon them. Because disfavored groups could be segregated into less well-paying jobs or paid less for the same work, employers might have an economic basis for discrimination or to indulge co-worker or customer preferences that echo these conventions. *See generally* Gary Becker, THE ECONOMICS OF DISCRIMINATION (2d ed. 1971).

In the political sphere, democratic values found expression in resounding proclamations of equality: in the American Declaration of Independence (1776) ("all men are created equal"), the French Declaration of Human Rights (1789) ("all men are ... equal before the law"), and in numerous national constitutions. But, little or no law reached discriminatory distinctions in private employment until after the Second World War. Interestingly, one of the first subjects of concern was for equal pay for women who did work equal to men. Some radical American trades unions called for this as early as the 1860s; as did socialists in the 1880s. But in terms of law, the Italian Constitution of 1947 gave women workers "the same rights as men, including the right to equal pay for equal work," and the Treaty Establishing the European Economic Community (1957) contained an analogous provision, at France's insistence. (The French government was anxious about Belgian competition in its textile industry due to the wage differential paid to female textile workers in Belgium. Brian Bercusson, EUROPEAN LABOUR LAW 338 (2d ed. 2009).) The United States followed suit in the Equal Pay Act of 1963.

Starting in the 1960s and accelerating ever since, the catalogue of protected classes and prohibited actions has grown significantly – and idiosyncratically. Some categories have become almost universally accepted – race, sex, religion, national origin. Some are achieving growing acceptance – age, disability – or are seeking it, notably sexual orientation. But the protection of those outside these categories is contingent on domestic social and political conditions particular to the jurisdiction as the many differences in coverage between the states of the United States amply evidence. In addition, the nature of proof, the manner of legal vindication, and the remedial schemes vary enormously from jurisdiction to jurisdiction. What follows will examine some – but only some – of these similarities and differences.

In what follows it might pay to attend closely to the categories that each of the countries has legislated as needing legal protection – why these and not others? Why *do* they differ? Whereas Japan protects "social status" from discrimination, none of the other four separate out such a category, though Australia may come close. The Fair Work Act §351(1) disallows adverse action to be taken against an applicant or incumbent employee because of the person's "race, colour, sex, sexual preference, age, physical or mental disability, marital status, family or carer's responsibilities, pregnancy, religion, political opinion, national extraction or social origin." But then Japan does not address age or disability or sexual preference. The U.S. treats the former two by federal law and the third is treated by the laws of some states – some of which may go further to protect "gender identification" – but nowhere does the U.S. protect "social status" or "social origin" directly.

The reader may care to pursue the purpose of these laws: are they grounded in some notion of human rights? Human rights are claimed to be universal, as inherent in the very idea of humanity. If so, how can the right to be free of invidious discrimination be so legally contingent? Are these laws grounded in labor market policy – to maximize a nation's fullest utilization of its human resources? If so, why hasn't the market done that, assuming that employers are driven to maximize the resources they are able to draw on? Should human resource managers harmonize equal opportunity policies across countries despite the fact that some of those who would be singled out for special solicitude could not claim domestic legal protection and might be viewed domestically as rightly to be disfavored?

If the lack of protection reflects some deeply seated cultural norm about the way such persons are regarded and so co-workers push back against the policy – one that does not reflect domestic law – what should (or could) management do? You might care to consider this in conjunction with the discussion of Problem 5.

PROBLEM 4: SHIFT TO PART-TIME WORKERS

Return to your company's concern for its labor costs in Problem 2. It has a complement of warehouse "picker-packers" paid $16/hr. (U.S.) for a 40-hour week, plus benefits. But with unemployment so high, especially among the less skilled, it can hire part-timers to do that work for 24 hours a week (for twice daily peak warehouse "sorts") six days per week at $8.35/hr. Apart from an obligation to bargain with a union if one is in place (discussed in Problem 2), is there any obstacle to its implementation of this policy? Note that the company is neither terminating its full-time picker-packers nor reducing their wages, but it is hiring these lesser paid part-timers for peak hour work (rather than increase overtime for the existing workforce or hire additional, new full-time workers).

Problem 4 discussion – Australia

It is unlikely that this would be lawful in Australia. For a start, for reasons explained in relation to Problem 2, the company could not unilaterally cut existing workers' pay – it could only implement the new policy in relation to new employees.

In any event, the minimum rates of pay set by awards (and indeed typically enterprise agreements) are expressed as hourly rates that apply equally to full-time and part-time employees. Awards and labour statutes in Australia generally entitle part-time employees to a pro rata equivalent of whatever minimum entitlements are created for full-time workers: see for example a sample clause below from a modern award regulating clerical employment.

So the only circumstances in which this strategy could be attempted would be either (a) where the existing full-time employees had contractually agreed "over-award" earnings that were well in excess of the applicable minimum rate, or (b) the jobs in question were award-free (which would usually only mean managers or senior professionals) and the part-time rate complied with the national minimum wage.

Even then, there would still be problems. As in the US, women are far more likely than men to work on a part-time basis, which would open up the possibility of sex discrimination claims if the new workforce were disproportionately female. There is also a power under Part 2–7 of the Fair Work Act 2009 for FWA to make an order ensuring "equal remuneration for work of equal or comparable value". This new power was first exercised in a major test case to improve wages for the mostly female workers in the social and community services sector: see *Equal Remuneration Case* [2011] FWAFB 2700; [2012] FWAFB 1000; [2012] FWAFB 5184.

PRIMARY SOURCES

Clerks – Private Sector Award 2010

11. Part-time employment

11.1 A part-time employee is an employee who is engaged to perform less than the full-time hours at the workplace on a reasonably predictable basis.

11.2 Part-time employees are entitled on a pro rata basis to equivalent pay and conditions to those of full-time employees.

11.7 A part-time employee employed under the provisions of this clause must be paid for ordinary hours worked at the rate of the 1/38th of the weekly rate prescribed for the class of works performed.

Fair Work Act 2009

302 FWA may make an order requiring equal remuneration

Power to make an equal remuneration order

(1) FWA may make any order (an *equal remuneration order*) it considers appropriate to ensure that, for employees to whom the order will apply, there will be equal remuneration for work of equal or comparable value.

Meaning of equal remuneration for work of equal or comparable value

(2) *Equal remuneration for work of equal or comparable value* means equal remuneration for men and women workers for work of equal or comparable value.

Who may apply for an equal remuneration order

(3) FWA may make the equal remuneration order only on application by any of the following:
   (a) an employee to whom the order will apply;
   (b) an employee organisation that is entitled to represent the industrial interests of an employee to whom the order will apply;
   (c) the Sex Discrimination Commissioner.

References and suggested readings

ANDREW STEWART, STEWART'S GUIDE TO EMPLOYMENT LAW §§11.3; 10.16–17 (4th ed. 2013).

Problem 4 discussion – Brazil

Wages cannot be lower than the federal minimum wage, which is established for three different parameters: hour, day and month. Furthermore, through collective bargaining minimum wages can be established for a whole category of workers. A worker's category is voluntarily defined through professional identity and common economic interests. It is a peculiarity of the Brazilian union system that union representation has to be unique for a given area. It follows that a union's legitimacy to negotiate does not come from a union's worker adherence rate, but comes directly from the law, and the outcome of its negotiations must be extended to every worker belonging to the category. In the absence of a minimum wage defined through collective bargaining, State governments are allowed to establish a minimum state wage for each category. However it does not correspond to a uniform State minimum, i.e. it must be established by category.[1]

Article 58-A of the *Consolidação das Leis do Trabalho* (Consolidation of Labor Laws) establishes that a labor contract is considered to be part-time when it does not exceed 25 hours per week. Overtime is strictly forbidden for part-time workers (article 59, §4º, *Consolidação*). Their wage must be proportional to the duration of work in comparison to those performing the same function in a full-time position. The legal reasoning could be summarized by the idea of equal pay for equal work according to the amount of working hours. Defined by article 461 of the *Consolidação*, the equal pay for equal work principle establishes that, regardless of sex, nationality or age, equal pay is assured for equal work in the same municipality, which corresponds to all work done with identical

1 Overtime compensation, not applicable to this problem, is due whenever employees work more than 8 daily hours or 44 weekly hours. Nonetheless, this may not be the case if through collective bargaining or individual agreements, the parties have established the possibility of compensating overtime working hours with reduced working days on other occasions. This is the so-called *banco de horas* (bank of hours) mentioned in Problem 2.

productivity and technical performance by different employees whose time difference in the same function is inferior to two years. It definitely applies to part-time workers, but the hour *ratio* has to be observed. Thus, the answer to the question posed by the problem is straightforward: the company may not implement such wage policy as it goes directly against the legal dispositions of the *Consolidação*.

References and suggested readings

BRASIL, TRIBUNAL SUPERIOR DO TRABALHO, *Súmula 6*, *accessed at* http://www3.tst.jus/br.jurisprudencia/Sumulas_com/Sumulas_Ind_50.html#SUM-6 (last visited: Oct. 2, 2012).

Problem 4 discussion – Germany

Section 4 of the Part-time and Fixed-term Employment Act (*Teilzeit- und Befristungsgesetz*) sets out a far-reaching prohibition of discrimination against part-timers. According to section 4 para. 1 sentence 1 of the Act, a part-timer must not be discriminated against in comparison with a (comparable) person working full time if there is no reason which justifies a differentiation other than the hours worked. According to section 4 para. 1 sentence 2 of the Act, a part-timer can claim remuneration at least to the same extent to which a person working full time would be able to make such a claim (so-called *pro rata temporis* principle); section 4 para. 1 sentence 2 of the Act undoubtedly applies to wages (Federal Labor Court of 16.06.1993 – 4 AZR 317/92). In addition discriminating against part-timers regularly amounts to (indirectly) discriminating against women and as a consequence breaches Article 157 of the Treaty on the Functioning of the European Union. Apart from that it should be noted that questions of "remuneration policy" at plant level form part of the list of issues which according to section 87(1) no. 10 of the Works Councils Act are subject to the mandatory co-determination rights of the works council. That means that the employer has to reach an agreement with the works council if he wants to modify existing remuneration principles, consistent with the law.

The part-timer can indeed claim pay proportional to his working time on the one hand and the working time of a full-timer on the other. Even additional payments, due to, for instance, extremely hard work or shift work, have to be granted "in proportion" if they are dependent on working time. If, on the other hand, an employer reduces a Christmas allowance equally for full- and part-timers (1,000 Euro less for both), he is discriminating against part-timers because at the end of the day they receive less (relatively speaking) than full-timers (Federal Labor Court of 24.05.2000 – 10 AZR 629/99)

References and suggested readings

Excerpt from Maximilian Fuchs, *Germany: Part-time Work – a Bone of Contention, in* EMPLOYMENT POLICY AND THE REGULATION OF PART-TIME WORK IN THE EUROPEAN UNION: A COMPARATIVE ANALYSIS Ch. 5 (Silvana Sciarra, Paul Davies & Mark Freedland eds., 2004) (footnotes omitted).*

4.4 Recent legislation: the Part-Time Work and Fixed-Term Contracts Act

4.4.1 Objectives of the Act

The Promotion of Employment Act discussed in sections 4.1 and 4.1.1 above was repealed on 31 December 2000. The replacement of its regulations came into effect with the Part-Time Work and Fixed-Term Contracts Act (*Teilzeit- und Befristungsgesetz*, or TzBfG) on 1 January 2001. In as far as part-time work is concerned, the new Act implements "Directive 97/81/EC on part-time work". In its presentation of the draft of the Act, the Federal Government gave extensive reasons for the necessity of legal regulation. In its view, all effective instruments for the promotion of employment must be used to achieve prolonged employment security. These also include sharing out the existing workload between more people by means of the reduction of individual working time in the form of part-time work. The quota of part-time jobs could be raised because many full-time employees show a willingness to reduce their number of working hours, a willingness that is constructive with regard to labour market policy. The demand for part-time work is rising steadily. The Government makes reference to the findings of the IAB, the Labour Market Research Institute of the Federal Labour Office, according to which exploitation of this potential demand for part-time work could trigger considerable alleviatory effects on the labour market. The Government claims that those affected have often not been able to regularize their part-time job because such jobs have just not been offered. Legal regulations that enable employees to recognize their part-time job demands could, therefore, make an effective contribution to employment security and the promotion of employment.

The aspect of the "work-life balance" is given great importance and attention in the law-maker's argumentation. To quote from the text:

> Additionally, part-time work has great importance in respect to emancipation and social welfare policies. With a share of 87 percent, women account for the majority of part-time employees... More than half of part-time workers are engaged in part-time jobs because of family or personal reasons. Hence the major reason for reducing the number of working hours is the desire to have more time for the family. Other motives lie in the desire to take part in voluntary activities as well as to pursue non-professional interests. The wish to make use of the time gained by part-time employment for further education is another motivation. The reasons for the latter are on the one hand the possibility of "lifelong learning" and on the other hand to obtain extra qualifications outside the company. Thus the advancement of part-time work not only promotes equal opportunities for men and women and better reconciliation of work and family, it also takes into account the different visions of life that employees have.

Lastly, the legislature turns its attention to the requirements of employers in its presentation of the draft. It is claimed that, as a rule, consideration of the desire for a reduction in working hours also has positive effects for employers, such as higher flexibility and productivity as well as better work quality. In contrast, work regulations that bypass the needs and possibilities of employees can have considerable follow-up costs as a consequence, owing to increased staff turnover or higher absenteeism. With reference to the research of an eminent consultative institution, it is also stressed that the expansion of part-time work need not lead to higher costs. There is no general disadvantage as regards costs for part-time work compared with full-time work. Additional costs for part-time work are often offset by gains in productivity. The average initial costs for the introduction of part-time work are often amortised within a year.

Thus the line of reasoning of the Act shows that the German legislature, in passing the TzBfG, has taken into account all objectives that were shown above to be in discussion in political and social welfare policies, but especially those objectives seen as relevant among the ranks of employees and employers. The following deliberations will be concerned with the question of how these objectives, recognized by the government in its draft, have been considered in the resultant legal regulation.

4.4.2 Content of the new Act

In general it can be said that the TzBfG has largely incorporated the regulations included in the Promotion of Employment Act. A few innovations are due to the fact that the legislature was obliged to conform to "Directive 97/81/EC on part-time work". In part it wanted to realize ideas of a more far-reaching nature.

Fundamentally, section 2 TzBfG retains the existing definition of a part-time employee, choosing for the basis of its regulation the deviation from the regular weekly working hours of a comparable full-time employee. Also section 2 TzBfG now models its basis for comparison on Clause 3(2) of Directive 97/81/EC.

The creation of the ban on discrimination in section 4 TzBfG also adheres to the former legal provision. To this end, its being modeled on Directive 97/81/EC has led to clarity and precision to avoid legal disputes. A part-time employee may not be treated less favourably than a comparable full-time employee unless a concrete reason justifies different treatment. The law-maker has also put into practice the *pro-rata-temporis* principle recommended in the Directive. Accordingly, a part-time employee is entitled to pay or other divisible form of remuneration of at least the same amount as a comparable full-time employee receives for the same time. In accordance with the Directive, nor may parties to collective agreements diverge from the ban on discrimination to the disadvantage of the employee. This had already been ruled by the Federal Labor Court, however, in the past.

The ban on discrimination is strengthened – again in conjunction with the European Directive – in that section 5 TzBfG rules that an employer may not put an employee at a disadvantage because the latter makes a claim based on this Act. A further guarantee for equality of treatment between full-time and part-time employees is ensured by the prohibition of dismissal in section 11 TzBfG: termination of employment is not binding in the case of an employee's refusal to change from full-time to part-time employment or vice versa.

Really new in the TzBfG are those regulations in which the law-maker was at pains to implement the programme for promotion of part-time work to be found in Directive 97/81/EC. In detail this involves the following. Initially the concern was to create transparency in conjunction with Clause 5(3)(e). Extensive information from employer and employee representatives regarding the possibilities of part-time employment in the company is a prerequisite for the increase of part-time work. Section 7 TzBfG thus includes the obligation on an employer to advertise vacancies also as part-time positions, should this be compatible with the position. Apart from this, an employer is obliged to give an employee information concerning relevant vacancies in the company or group when the employee has expressed the wish to make a change in the duration or scheduling of working hours that have been agreed by contract. Additionally, the employer is obliged to give the employees' representatives any information concerning part-time opportunities in the company or group, especially existing or planned part-time opportunities and the conversion of part-time into full-time positions or vice versa.

Moreover, the legislature based its regulations for the promotion of part-time work on the following arguments. In order to exploit to the full the employment potential that arises from the expansion of part-time work, measures are necessary which, in compliance with recommendations in the Part-Time Directive, ensure that employee applications for a change from full-time to part-time employment are taken into account as far as possible. The concerns here are, firstly, to enable a clear expansion of part-time work and, secondly, to safeguard the legitimate organisational and planning interests of the employer. The presumption of the law-maker is that employer and employee will normally come to an agreement regarding the reduction of working hours. Directive 97/81/EC also makes the assumption that the development of part-time work will take place on a voluntary basis and in consensus between employer and employee.

The German legislature has adopted a more far-reaching position than that of the concept of voluntary agreement. It has included in section 8 TzBfG the individual right of an employee to a reduction in the working hours agreed by contract. This right had been much disputed during the deliberations in Parliament. Its introduction was fiercely contended, especially on the part of the employers and their organisations. It was claimed that such a right would compromise a company's freedom of choice in staff placements to too great an extent and that in the long term it would not have a beneficial effect on the labour market. The additional administrative work often involved in the introduction of part-time work, which would put a strain on small and medium-sized enterprises especially, was stressed.

The law-maker did not regard these objections as legitimate. Independently of the survey carried out by the McKinsey consultants already mentioned above, which presumes initial short-term increase in productivity, the following arguments were of interest for the law-maker when allowing an individual right to part-time employment. The wording of the arguments for the Act reads as follows:

> In Germany, according to the analysis of the IAB, the wishes of full-time and part-time employees are moving towards a reduction in weekly working hours of the order of between five and nine hours. The large majority of full-time employees (approx. 30 per cent) want a reduction in the working week of about eight hours. A similar conclusion was reached in a survey carried out for the EU and Norway (1999) by the European Foundation for the Improvement of Living and Working Conditions, which found that only approx. 15 per cent of the employees questioned wanted a reduction in the working week of 15 or more hours. A reduction of less than five hours was wanted by only 7 per cent. On average, the employees questioned preferred a reduction in working hours of about five hours. A survey carried out by the Institute for Research into Social Equality (ISO) for the Ministry of Labour and Social Welfare of the Land Nordrhein-Westfalen (1999) came to the following conclusions – which correspond to the above-mentioned findings – that the majority of full-time employees who express a wish for a reduction in working hours are not in fact looking for a part-time job but rather a reduction of 12, in their weekly hours, to 27 hours spread over a three or four day week. With this in mind, and to enable the realisation of the desire for a reduction in working hours, the law-maker allows employees to plan their weekly working hours individually. The planned regulations enable the meaningful use, with regard to labour market policy, of the existing potential for a redistribution of working hours as well as enabling a drastic increase in the effect of part-time work from an employment policy point of view.

The law-maker has hereby acknowledged the precedence of individual employee interests over those of the employer. This does not mean, however, that the interests of the employer have not been taken into account in the concrete formulation of the right. The regulation of the right that is expounded in the subsequent passage is, rather more, a compromise between the interests of the employees and those of the employers. The right of an employee to a reduction in working hours that have been agreed by contract does not take effect until six months after conclusion of the contract. The employee must claim the reduction in his working hours and also state the extent of the reduction three months before it begins, including informing the employer of the desired distribution of working hours (section 8 para. 2 TzBfG).

That in principle the German law-maker is also interested in a voluntary concept for the introduction of part-time employment can be seen in the provision of section 8 para. 3 TzBfG. This provision provides for a period of negotiation between employer and employee. Both parties are required to discuss the employee's request with a view to reaching an agreement. Only in the case of failure to reach such an agreement is the employer obliged, according to section 8 para. 4 TzBfG, to agree to the desired reduction in working hours and to arrange their distribution accordingly. This, however, comes into force only in so far as there are no internal company reasons to hinder it. The intention with this regulation was to take the employer's interests into account. The internal company reasons that can impeded the employee's right include the following particular cases: the reduction of the working hours concerned adversely affects the company organization, the work process or safety aspects considerably, or comparatively high costs are incurred by the employer because of the introduction of part-time work. Further reasons for refusal can be determined by collective agreement. The objections of the employer to an employee's desire for a reduction in or redistribution of his working hours must be given in writing, at the latest, one month before the desired start. Otherwise the request made by the employee to the employer comes into force.

The argument brought forward by employers during the discussions in Parliament, namely that the introduction of part-time employment would especially burden small and medium-sized companies with great problems, has been given partial consideration by the law-maker. Section 8 para. 7 TzBfG rules that the right to a reduction in working hours is effective only in companies that generally have more than fifteen employees.

The TzBfG also regulates the return of a part-time employee to a full-time position. This topic is also mentioned in Clause 5(3)(b and c) of the Part-Time Directive. Accordingly, section 9 TzBfG rules than an employer must give preferential consideration to a request by a part-time employee for an extension of his contractually agreed working hours when filling a compatible vacancy requiring the same skills, unless urgent internal company reasons or the wishes of another part-time employee stand in the way of such a decision.

The intention with the ruling in section 10 TzBfG – again in concurrence with Directive 97/81/EC – was to recognise the request of part-time employees for training and further education: the employer must ensure that part-time workers also have the opportunity to participate in training courses and further education schemes in order to promote their professional development and mobility, in so far as internal company reasons do not stand in the way.

In so far as it includes regulations that promote part-time work, the new Act has been warmly welcomed by academic lawyers. However, opinions vary greatly where the principle of the individual right of an employee to a part-time position is concerned. Most authors express objections to the introduction of this right. Their arguments are divided into two categories. According to the first, the subjective right of an employee to a reduction in working hours results in serious disadvantages for the company organization, disadvantages that lead to higher costs. Whether or not the new regulation will have any beneficial effect from an employment policy point of view is doubtful: if at all, the effect could only be very modest. The second category of argumentation applied by critics is of a constitutional nature. It is maintained that the right to part-time work curtails the employer's right of ownership. It is even pointed out in the reasons for this that the BAG has already recognized the employer's freedom to organize his own company where duration and scheduling of working hours are concerned. In a recent judgment, however, the Federal Labor Court saw no violation of this entrepreneurial right by Section 8 TzBfG.

Problem 4 discussion – Japan

Until the 2007 revision of the Part-time Work Act (PTWA), Japan did not have any statutory regulations on prohibition of unfavorable treatment of part-time workers. However, the 2007 revision introduced a prohibition on discriminatory treatment against part-time workers under strict conditions.

The ban on discrimination concerning wages, occupational training and welfare facilities by reason of being part-time workers applies only when the following three conditions are fulfilled. First, the content of the part-time worker's job, including the level of responsibilities for the job, must be the same as that of ordinary or full-timer workers employed in the same establishment (same job content). Second, the part-time contract must be for indefinite period or, if its period is definite, the contract must be reasonably deemed as indistinct from an indefinite period contract because it has been repeatedly renewed (same contract period). Third, the changes in the job contents and assignment of the part-time worker are likely to be made in the same range as for *ordinary workers*. When a part-time worker meets these three requirements, he or she is regarded as "part-time worker equivalent to ordinary workers" (same personnel management).

Non-discriminatory regulation normally requires equal treatment for equal work. However, the PTWA not only requires the same job content between part-time and full-time workers, but also requires such further prerequisites as the same contract period and same personnel management. As a result, there are said to be very few among Japanese part-time workers who fulfill these stringent requirements (so-called "part-time worker equivalent to ordinary workers").

Secondly, however, the revised PTWA introduced unique regulations on "balanced treatment" between part-time and ordinary (full-time) workers concerning wages, occupational training, and welfare facilities (PTWA Arts. 9

to 11). The balanced treatment regulation applies not only to so-called "part-time worker equivalent to ordinary workers," but also to other part-time workers who fail to meet the said three requirements. The balanced treatment regulations in the PTWA, however, remain the duty to "endeavor" or the duty "to give due consideration" to balanced treatment. In order to implement these unique moral duties, the Act imposes a legal duty on employers to explain the factors considered in making decisions on the matters required for balanced treatment upon part-time workers' request (PTWA Art 13). Whether such unique procedural regulations are effective or not remains to be seen.

In short, when the part-time worker is not regarded as "equivalent to ordinary workers," Japanese employers are legally allowed to pay a lower wage but, upon the part-time worker's request, they must explain what factors are considered to determine wages lower than those of ordinary workers. The worker's satisfaction with the explanation is not required. Thus, when the worker is not satisfied with the employer's explanation, he or she may bring the case to the conciliation procedures at the local office of the Ministry of Health, Labor and Welfare, but such dissatisfaction with the explanation in itself does not give rise to any legal responsibilities.

References and suggested reading

Michiyo Morozumi, *Balanced Treatment and Bans on Discrimination – Significance and Issues of the Revised Part-Time Work Act*, 6 JAPAN LAB. REV. 39–55 (2009).

Table III.1 sets out the change in the distribution of type of employment in Japan 1987–2010.

Table III.1 Changes in types of employment (%) in Japan

	1987	1994	1999	2003	2007	2010
Total	100.0	100.0	100.0	100.0	100.0	100.0
Regular employees	84.0	77.2	72.5	65.4	62.2	61.3
Non-regular employees	16.0	22.8	27.5	34.6	37.8	38.7
Contract employees	0.9	1.7	2.3	3.7	4.6	5.9
Transferred employees	1.2	1.4	1.3	1.5	1.2	1.5
Dispatched workers	0.6	0.7	1.1	2.0	4.7	3.0
Temporary employees	2.6	4.4	1.8	0.8	0.6	0.7
Part-time employees	9.9	13.7	20.3	23.0	22.5	22.9
Others	0.9	1.0	0.7	3.4	4.3	4.7

Source: Hodaka Maeura, *The Mechanism Behind the Increase in Non-Regular Employment: Case Study of the Supermarket Company A*, 9 JAPAN LAB. REV. 124 (2012) (Table 1 at p. 125, from government reports).

The case illustrates the substitution of part-time for (existing) full-time workers as a cost reduction measure, which is problematic under Japanese law. The author does not discuss whether at some point the functional upskilling that comes with experience will create a legal question around whether the part-time workers have become equivalent to ordinary workers.

Problem 4 discussion – United States

In the United States, the employer must observe the federal and applicable state minimum hourly wage; the latter is sometimes higher than the former. And should more than 40 hours be worked in a work week, federal and applicable state law for overtime compensation would have to be observed. But, legally, there need be no equality between full- and part-time wage rates.

Unlike race or sex, part-time employment status is not a suspect category for the purposes of antidiscrimination in employment law. Nor, unlike some countries, does the United States require "comparable pay for comparable work." However, the federal Equal Pay Act of 1963 requires that in any "establishment" (as defined by the federal Fair Labor Standards Act) "equal pay" be paid for "equal work" regardless of sex. At first blush, a company that pays a higher rate of pay for a full-time male worker performing the same tasks, requiring equal skill and ability than it does for a part-time female employee, might be subject to challenge on that basis. But, one of the Act's defenses is the observance of a "differential other than sex." An Interpretive Bulletin of the U.S. Department of Labor, which administered the Equal Pay Act at the time, opined that, "No violation of the equal pay standards would result, if,... the difference in working time is the basis for the pay differential, and the [part-time] pay is applied uniformly to both men and women." 29 C.F.R. § 800.150 (1980). Importantly, this defense does not address an employer policy or practice of shunting women disproportionally into part-time positions: that would be unlawful under Title VII of the federal Civil Rights Act of 1964 as well as cognate state law.

References and suggested reading

Basic texts in employment discrimination law are SUSAN OMILIAN & JEAN KEMP, SEX-BASED EMPLOYMENT DISCRIMINATION (available on Westlaw) (updated Sept. 2009) and HAROLD LEWIS & ELIZABETH NORMAN,

EMPLOYMENT DISCRIMINATION LAW AND PRACTICE (2d ed. 2004). There has been a shift from full-time to part-time work especially in service jobs – retailing (wholesale and retail) and hospitality and leisure. Since 2006, a million full-time jobs in retailing have been eliminated and 500,000 part-time jobs created. About twice as many part-timers in these sectors would prefer full-time work to part-time work generally. http://www.nytimes.com/interactive/2012/10/28/business/parttime.html?ref=business (Oct. 28, 2012). *See also* Francois Carré & Chris Tilly, "Work Hours in Retail: Room for Improvement," W.E. Upjohn Inst. For Employment Research Policy Paper No. 2012–012. (There are about 18.6 million workers in retailing.) Two features critically characterize the part-time workforce in these sectors. First is the difference in compensation, set out in Figure III.1.

Figure III.1 Difference in compensation full-time/part-time (U.S. services)

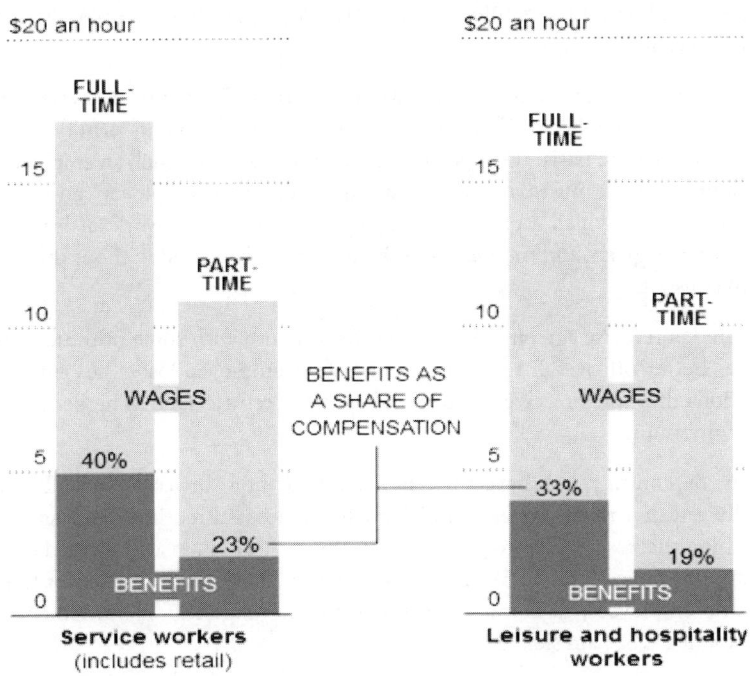

Source: Bureau of Labor Statistics (June, 2012).

Second is control over the number of hours assigned and when they will be worked. Many companies use sophisticated computer software to predict need and assign hours on a weekly or even daily basis. One program used at a fast food operation will take a slow-down in noontime orders to reduce the hours given an employee assigned 9:00 am to 2:00 pm by 15 minutes. This software reduced labor cost by 4–5 percent, amounting to over a million dollars a year.

The risk of uncertainty in income and scheduling for work is thus shifted to the part-time employee.†

A note on the casualization of work

The law in the United States allows employers to shift on to employees the cost of casualization: unpredictability in income; and unpredictability in the schedule of work, with a resulting inability to plan around work time for family and personal needs. How would our comparison countries deal with such a policy?

In *Australia* the legal situation is a little complicated. As Professor Stewart explains:

> In Australia, the awards that set minimum conditions for the great majority of non-managerial employees draw an important distinction between "casual" (temporary) employees and part-time employees (or "permanent part-time" employees as they are sometimes called).
>
> Part-time employees are those who work less than 38 hours per week and have "reasonably predictable hours". They receive the same entitlements as full-time employees, but on a pro rata basis. Awards typically require that when such an employee is hired their hours of work must be agreed in writing. While the employer can subsequently alter the times at which a part-time employee is rostered to work, at least 48 hours' notice must be given, and the *number* of hours cannot be varied without the employee's written consent.
>
> Registered enterprise agreements can relax or dispense with some of these restrictions, but the "better off overall test" means that if an employee loses the benefit of such protections they must receive some other benefit in return, such as higher pay than the award minimum.
>
> Casuals, by contrast, can have their hours varied more or less at will. But they are typically entitled to be rostered and paid for at least three hours on any one shift (something that also applies to part-time employees). They are also entitled to a loading or premium (typically now 25 percent) on top of the basic wage rate set for full-time or part-time employees, to compensate for not being eligible for entitlements such as recreation leave or paid sick leave.
>
> Around one in every four Australian employees now work as a casual, even though many have permanent jobs in all but name and can often work for years in such "temporary" positions. This suits many employers, who like the perception that they can hire, fire and vary hours at will – even if in fact they do not ever do that! It also suits many employees, who are happy to take the higher rates of pay rather than the leave

† As this goes to press the *Wall Street Journal* reports that a significant number of employers of low-wage workers, notably hotels, restaurants, and retailers, expect to shift from full-time to part-time workers to avoid the cost or penalties for providing medical insurance required for full-time workers under the federal Affordable Care Act. *Wall Street Journal (Online)*, (Nov. 5, 2012).

entitlements. But for some, casual status is not at all voluntary, and that has generated great debate in recent years about the issue of security of employment.

The law in *Brazil* is as yet unsettled. As Professor Fragale explains:

> The legality of an unpredictable scale of working hours is the basis of a big discussion related to McDonald's working procedures. They use a mobile working schedule that does not allow the employee to know way ahead when he/she is going to be working and how much he/she will be making in terms of salary. There are decisions saying that this is not possible as it becomes too much of a burden on the employee and others assuming that there is no illegality on that as the minimum hour payment [minimum wage] would be respected.

Germany, as one would expect, has dealt with the issue in precise detail. As Professor Waas explains:

> Under section 14 of the Act on Part-Time and Fixed-Term Contracts an employer and an employee may enter into a so-called "on call-agreement" (*Abrufarbeit*) which means that the employee must provide his or her service according to what is required. Such agreement is permitted if a couple of legal requirements are met. In particular, the parties must fix a certain weekly and daily workload (section 15(1) sentence 3). If there is no explicit agreement on daily working hours an agreement is deemed to be reached according to which the employee has a right to work for a period of at least three consecutive hours (section 12(1) sentence 4). What is more, the employee is obliged to work only if the employer informs him or her at least four days in advance about what is required and when (section 14(2) of the Act). The statutory requirements may be disposed of on the basis of collective agreements (section 14(3) of the Act).

And Professor Araki has explained the law in *Japan*:

> Labor Standards Act, Art. 15, orders an employer to clarify for his employees the starting time and ending time of working hours in writing at the time of hire. Art. 89, LSA, also requires an employer to specify the starting time and ending time of working hours in the work rules in advance. These regulations apply to part-timers. However, if part-timers themselves want individually differentiated scheduled hours, it is understood that work rules may stipulate basic scheduled hours and entrust the concrete allocation of working hours to individual employment contracts.
>
> Where an employer does not specify any working hours in advance and orders the next day's work hours the day before, this would be regarded as being contrary to Art. 89, LSA, which is intended to accommodate employees allowing them to know their working hours in advance and make their own life schedule. But temporary agency workers hired on a daily basis are subject to day by day specification of work hours. As for very short working hours, Japan does not have any regulation on minimum remuneration. Thus, if scheduled working hours on a certain date is one hour, the employer need not pay more than one hour. Such a short work hour agreement is not regulated in Japan.

> Why [would] a company … stray from uniform treatment of employees in the first place? In the case of paying part-timers less, the reason would be purely economic: to save money. Although there would be obvious payroll savings initially, in the long-term it [could] be economically disadvantageous for companies to pay employees a lower hourly rate than full-time employees in a comparable job. Economic supply and demand principles would suggest that reducing wages would decrease a company's ability to attract and retain quality employees. Why wouldn't a company pay the same for part-time vs. full-time employees? The payroll costs saved would not seem to outweigh the cost of limiting its candidate selection pool. Furthermore, there could be other economic advantages gained even if the wage rates were equalized, such as increased flexibility in scheduling and increased productivity. [On the other hand,] the implication that sex discrimination is occurring because of the disproportionate amount of women filling part-time positions versus men is [a] reason for companies to avoid adversely impacting this protected group.
>
> Director, HR, Food and Beverage Sector

> … I have seen some employers use part-time work (with lower part-time pay) as a method for screening and selecting the right employees to "promote" to full time with full time pay and benefits. Normally the part-time work was done through a temp staffing agency as a trial period. Then, when the employee had satisfied an acceptable level of performance, he or she was offered to come on board at full pay and full time status. There are not a lot of labor savings [realized] because temp staffing agencies have a significant up-charge rate.
>
> Vice President, HR, Electrical Manufacturing Sector

> … it would be interesting to review the impact of part-time workers (by choice) [on] families [with respect to] societal issues such as divorce rates, teen pregnancy, juvenile delinquency and health/stress-related illnesses.
>
> Manager, Talent Acquisition, Service Sector

Questions for Discussion – Problem 4

1. As the discussion on German law evidences, the law there is enmeshed in a fabric of European law deeply concerned about "atypical" workers –

those who are not regular, permanent employees – of which cohort part-timers are a significant category. As the late Brian Bercusson explained:

> It has become necessary to determine which elements of the contract of employment should be emphasized for different social purposes. This debate has been influenced less by labour lawyers than by economists and industrial relations experts. In the labour law literature, the issue of 'new forms of employment' is situated in the context of a debate in which the focus of attention tends to be on the distinction between typical and atypical employment. The literature focuses on the implications for labour and social security law of legal relations which deviate from the standard model.
>
> The industrial relations literature places the issue of new forms of employment in the context of the debate over labour market flexibility. In the economic literature, 'new forms of employment' is part of the more general debate on segmentation of the labour market. Each of these formulations by different disciplines includes the issue of "new forms of employment" as a component of a broader problematic. The question as to strategies of the actors on new forms of employment will be answered differently depending on whether the legislator addresses the problem as one of typical/atypical employment, labour market flexibility or labour market segmentation.

Brian Bercusson, EUROPEAN LABOUR LAW 362–3 (2d ed. 2009) (emphasis in original). Northern European states had disproportionately high numbers of part-time workers, while southern European states had disproportionately high numbers of non-permanent workers. The European Union's treatment of these was intended to deal with "social dumping." *Id.* at 368.

2. What aspects of part-time and non-permanent work are most relevant or salient when viewed as a legal issue, as compared to those aspects of part-time work that are most relevant or salient when viewed from an economic or industrial/employment relations perspective? Consider aspects such as pay level, type of work, impact on full-time workers, composition of the part-time workers, training, workplace safety, and other factors.

3. Anti-discrimination in employment laws is usually directed at invidious discrimination on the basis of some immutable characteristic – national origin, race, sex (which, though not immutable, is still rather difficult to change) – or a status that may be subjected to stereotypical disadvantage, such as age or religion. In the U.S. the taking of part-time work is seen as purely market-mediated behavior, of the employee's free choice. In Europe – but not there alone, as we have seen – it is considered a basis for

wrongful discrimination. How to explain this rather sharp difference in perspective?

4. All the contributions note the possibility of job segregation as potentially actionable on sex discrimination grounds. This opens up an issue legally too complex to be treated in this survey: of how the issues of proof of "indirect discrimination" (in European parlance) or "disparate impact" (in American parlance) are treated. Nevertheless, the following tables may open a window on the differences in legal treatment these contributions reveal. Table III.2 displays the distribution by sex in nonstandard work in the U.S. in 2005 – the last year for which these data are available.

Table III.2 Nonstandard workers in the U.S. workforce, 2005

	All	Women	Men
Nonstandard workers	30.6%	35.2%	26.5%
Regular part-time	13.2	19.0	7.9
Direct hire temporaries	2.1	2.3	2.0
Temp agency	0.9	1.0	0.8
Regular self-employed	4.4	5.1	3.8
Independent contractor (self-employed)	6.5	4.6	8.2
Independent contractor (wage & salary)	1.0	1.0	1.0
On-call/day laborers	2.0	2.0	2.0
Contract company employees	0.5	0.4	0.7
Standard workers	69.4%	64.8%	73.5%
All	100.0%	100.0%	100.0%

Source: LAWRENCE MISHEL, JARED BERNSTEIN & HEIDI SCHIERHOLZ, THE STATE OF WORKING AMERICA, 2008/2009, Table 4.7 at 253 (2009).

Table III.3 compares the distribution of women in part-time employment with our comparative cohort. Note that definitions of part time are not directly comparable with Table III.2, but are comparable within Table III.3 (at least for all but Brazil, which may or may not be comparable across countries, but is within Brazil for men and women).

Table III.3 Part-time employment rates by gender, 2009

Part Time	Male Rate	Female Part Time Rate
Australia	12%	38%
Brazil	6%	18%
Germany	8%	37%
Japan	10%	34%
United States	9%	29%

Sources: For data on Australia, Germany, Japan, and U.S.: U.S. Bureau of Labor Statistics, "Charting International Labor Comparisions" (August, 2011, p. 21). For Brazil: Pesquisa Nacional por Amostras de Domicílio (PNAD) 2008 [2008 National Household Sample Survey] conducted by Instituto Brasileiro de Geografia e Estatística (IBGE).

PROBLEM 5: REQUEST TO PRAY THREE TIMES A DAY

About 5 percent of the company's workforce are of the Muslim faith. They have requested (or demanded) that the work schedule be adjusted to permit them adequate time to pray during work time. (Islam requires the faithful to pray five times a day. It is likely that this will require three "prayer breaks" during a normal shift, but the time consumed in prayer is only a matter of a few minutes.) May the Company reject their demand? What if the work process is continuous and there is an insufficient number of "relief" workers to fill in for 5 percent of the workforce even for such brief periods? What if other workers object because they aren't given equal time off work?

Problem 5 discussion – Australia

Section 351 of the Fair Work Act 2009, applicable to companies in all States and Territories, prohibits an employer from taking adverse action against an employee because of (among other things) their "religion". (It is unclear whether that term extends to cover both religious beliefs and activities associated with that belief, though presumably it does.) Adverse action is defined by s 324(1) for this purpose to include discriminating between the employee and other employees. The prohibition is breached even if the alleged reason (in this case, religion) is just *one* of the reasons for taking the action in question (s 360). Furthermore, an employer is presumed to have taken action for an alleged reason unless they prove otherwise (s 361).

Religious discrimination in relation to employment is also prohibited by general anti-discrimination laws in all States and Territories except New South Wales and South Australia. Those laws are typically expressed to cover both religious belief and religious activity. Discrimination is defined to cover both direct and indirect forms of discrimination.

Three jurisdictions go further. Western Australia specifically prohibits an employer from refusing an employee permission to perform a "necessary or desirable" religious practice during working hours, where such performance would be "reasonable having regard to the circumstances of the employment" and would not subject the employer to any detriment. Equal Opportunity Act 1984 (WA) s 54(3). There are broadly similar provisions in the Australian Capital Territory and the Northern Territory: see Discrimination Act 1991 (ACT) s 11; Anti-Discrimination Act 1992 (NT) s 31(3). Hence this problem would need to be addressed in terms of the "reasonableness" of seeking prayer breaks, and the question of "detriment" to the employer.

In other jurisdictions, two broad issues would need to be considered. The first is whether the employer is actually "discriminating" against the Muslim employees. It is worth emphasising that, with certain exceptions (such as those mentioned above), Australian anti-discrimination laws do not impose a positive duty on employers to make reasonable adjustments to accommodate employees with particular characteristics. Rather, there is a prohibition on differential treatment. Hence so long as the company can show that it would reject requests from non-Muslim employees for breaks of a similar length, it could defend any action for unlawful discrimination. But if, for instance, the company routinely allowed employees to take "smokos" (a short break to smoke a cigarette, typically now something that involves going out into the open air), that would make such an argument much harder to sustain.

In *McIntosh v TAFE Tasmania* [2003] TASADT 14, the applicant, a teacher who was a practising Muslim, complained (among other things) about his employer's refusal to provide him with a dedicated prayer room. The Tasmanian Anti-Discrimination Tribunal rejected his complaint, on the basis that he had not shown that he had been treated differently from an employee of any other religion who may have asked for such a facility.

A second possible defence would be to argue that the action in question (in this case, refusing prayer breaks) has been taken because of the "inherent requirements" of the job in question. This defence is recognised in s 351(2)(b) of the Fair Work Act. There are equivalent provisions in the relevant State and Territory laws, though these typically refer to "genuine occupational requirements". The problem here would be to establish that it was the nature of the employee's *job* that required a refusal of prayer breaks, as opposed to the impact of those breaks on the employer's preferred system of work.

PRIMARY SOURCE

Fair Work Act 2009 (Cth) ss 351(1)–(2), 342(1) (infra)

Fair Work Act 2009

351 Discrimination

(1) An employer must not take adverse action against a person who is an employee, or prospective employee, of the employer because of the person's race, colour, sex, sexual preference, age, physical or mental disability, marital status, family or carer's responsibilities, pregnancy, religion, political opinion, national extraction or social origin.

Note: This subsection is a civil remedy provision (see Part 4-1).

(2) However, subsection (1) does not apply to action that is:
- (a) not unlawful under any anti-discrimination law in force in the place where the action is taken; or
- (b) taken because of the inherent requirements of the particular position concerned; or
- (c) if the action is taken against a staff member of an institution conducted in accordance with the doctrines, tenets, beliefs or teachings of a particular religion or creed – taken:
  - (i) in good faith; and
  - (ii) to avoid injury to the religious susceptibilities of adherents of that religion or creed.

342 Meaning of adverse action

The following table sets out circumstances in which a person takes *adverse action* against another person.

Table III.4 Meaning of adverse action

Item	Column 1 *Adverse action* is taken by …	Column 2 if …
1	an employer against an employee	the employer: (a) dismisses the employee; or (b) injures the employee in his or her employment; or (c) alters the position of the employee to the employee's prejudice; or (d) discriminates between the employee and other employees of the employer.

Item	Column 1 *Adverse action* is taken by ...	Column 2 if ...
2	a prospective employer against a prospective employee	the prospective employer: (a) refuses to employ the prospective employee; or (b) discriminates against the prospective employee in the terms or conditions on which the prospective employer offers to employ the prospective employee.

References and suggested readings

ANDREW STEWART, STEWART'S GUIDE TO EMPLOYMENT LAW ch. 14 (4th ed. 2013). NEIL REES, KATHERINE LINDSAY & SIMON RICE, AUSTRALIAN ANTI-DISCRIMINATION LAW: TEXT, CASE AND MATERIALS 374–8 (2008).

Problem 5 discussion – Brazil

Religion at the workplace has not really been an issue for Brazilian labor regulation. Whenever it has emerged as a problem, it was to reaffirm the impossibility of any discrimination on such grounds. Lately, the scope of the discussion has widened as three new different aspects have been integrated into the problem: (a) discussion over religious holidays which are not recognized as "official" ones, (b) increasing religious proselytism at the workplace of expanding new religions, and (c) the entrepreneurial organization of these same new religions.

The idea of "official" religion holidays in a laical State may seem a paradox, but is not incomprehensible when examined through the Brazilian historical lens. In the nineteenth century Roman Catholicism was the official State religion and according to the 2000 demographic census, three-quarters of the Brazilian population declared themselves to be catholic. Federal law has thus established as national holidays the Celebration Day of Our Lady of *Aparecida* (October 12), All Souls Day (November 2), and Christmas (December 25). The problem emerges when employees from different faiths demand their religious holidays to be treated alike. Every employer deals with such demand as it best suits its human resources policy as long as it does not result in discriminatory conduct. For instance, its answer must be the same if demands are forwarded by different faiths. As for the Catholic holidays, these are established by federal law and so do not color the employer's actions.

The increasing proselytism at the workplace is a consequence of the growing importance of new religions in Brazilian society. Recent years have witnessed a growing religious mobility, with an impressive number of conversions. Actually, data from the 2000 demographic census indicates that over the last 20 years the Catholic presence in the Brazilian population declined from 90 percent to 75 percent. New religions impose new obligations and they will no doubt have an impact on the workplace. Recently, the Regional Labor Court of São Paulo was called on to decide whether it was lawful to terminate on a justified basis a labor contract of an employee who, after religion conversion, started to miss work on every Saturday. The court ruled against the employee, indicating that freedom of religion does not constitute a free pass to impose changes on the original conditions of the labor contract. In a similar way, freedom of religion cannot be transformed into a burden on employers or to introduce disruptive practices in the workplace. Of course, the foregoing concerns secular employments only, not employment by confessional institutions.

Finally, as to the problem itself, it is difficult to imagine a workforce in Brazil whose composition would include a 5 percent presence of Muslims (the 2000 demographic census identified fewer than 28,000 Muslims in the country). But it is clear that religious demands may not cause discriminatory treatment in the workplace: all should be treated alike.

References and suggested readings

BRASIL, TRIBUNAL REGIONAL DO TRABALHO DA 2ª REGIÃO, RO 00213200747202001, *accessed at* http://gsa.trtsp.jus.br/search?q=cache:eptGmuF_Db4J:trtcons.trtsp.jus.br/cgi-bin/db2www/aconet.mac/main%3Fselacordao%3D20090883203%26a%3Dabc+religi%C3%A3o+s%C3%A1bado&site=Acordaos&client=trt2Acordao&lr=lang_pt&access=p&ie=UTF-8&output=xml_no_dtd&proxystylesheet=trt2Acordao&oe=UTF-8 (last visited Feb. 17, 2010).

On religious diversity in Brazil, see César Romero Jacob, *A diversificação religiosa*, 18 ESTUDOS AVANÇADOS [ONLINE] 9 (2004), *accessed at* http://www.scielo.br/pdf/ea/v18n52/a02v1852.pdf (last visited: Feb. 17, 2010).

On the Muslim presence in Brazil, see Silvia Maria Montenegro, *Identidades muçulmanas no Brasil: entre o arabismo e a islamização*, 2 LUSOTOPIE 59 (2002), *accessed at* http://www.lusotopie.sciencespobordeaux.fr/montenegro.pdf (last visited: Feb. 17, 2010).

Problem 5 discussion – Germany

One of the basic rights protected by the German Constitution (*Grundgesetz*) is the freedom of religion. It not only protects the right to choose one's religion but also the right to exercise it. Praying is one of the most essential parts of this right. In general, a private employer has to take this right into consideration when making employment decisions. However, it is natural that this right has boundaries. If it conflicts with an employer's legitimate interests, one has to balance between the two rights. The employer has a legitimate interest in organizing his work process in a way that avoids work stoppages as far as possible.

Dealing with a case similar to the one described in this problem, the Higher Labor Court (LAG) in Hamm decided that an employer may reject the demand for prayer breaks *only* if such breaks interfere with a smooth work process. Although the right to pray was deemed to be very important, the court argued that the employer's interest in avoiding work stoppages outweighs the employees' rights. However, if the requested prayer breaks don't interfere with the work process, the employer has no right to reject them. The company may therefore reject the employees' demand, but only if the requested prayer breaks would impede the work process. This may well be the case in this problem as 5 percent of the workforce is not an insignificant number of workers and three prayer breaks during a normal shift could cause frequent work stoppages depending on the amount of time involved and the specific job tasks the workers perform.

However, the situation may be different if the employer distinguishes between religions, for example, allowing employees of the Roman Catholic religion to take prayer breaks but not employees of the Muslim faith. The German General Equal Treatment Act (*Allgemeines Gleichbehandlungsgesetz*) prohibits, among other things, discrimination on the basis of religion. A company policy distinguishing between Catholics and Muslims regarding prayer breaks is direct discrimination. This is lawful only if the employer can justify it. This is highly unlikely as it is hard to see why the religion shall qualify as an occupational requirement, which alone would be able to justify such discrimination according to section 8 para. 1 *Allgemeines Gleichbehandlungsgesetz*. Difference of treatment on the basis of any of the grounds defined in §1 is lawful where, by reason of the nature of the particular occupational activities concerned or of the context in which they are carried out, such a characteristic constitutes a genuine and determining occupational requirement, provided that the objective is legitimate and the requirement is proportionate.

References and suggested readings

Achim Seifert, *Religious Expression in the Workplace: The Case of the Federal Republic of Germany*, 30 COMP. LAB. L. & POL'Y J. 529 (2009):

General Principles of the New Anti-discrimination Legislation

This shadowy existence of anti-discrimination law in Germany only ended recently as a result of the rapid development of European anti-discrimination law and its transposition into German law in the General Act on Equal Treatment [*Allgemeines Gleichbehandlungsgesetz* – abbr. AGG] from August 2006.

As far as discriminations on the ground of religious belief are concerned, Directive 2000/78/EC from November 27, 2000, establishing a General Framework for Equal Treatment in Employment and Occupation, for the first time in EU-law laid down a legal framework for combating discriminations in the workplace. It is not an exaggeration to say that the Directive overshadowed by far the relevance of article 3 GG. The Directive has been transposed by the Federal Republic of Germany – after a heated political debate and with a delay of several years – with the AGG. Only a few words on the core elements of this new anti-discrimination legislation will be necessary in the present context.

Sections 1 and 7, in conjunction with section 3, paragraphs 1–2 *AGG* prohibit direct as well as indirect discriminations on the ground of religious belief. Furthermore, section 3, paragraph 4 AGG considers harassments related to the religious belief of a worker as discrimination. The same applies to instructions to discriminate against persons on any of the grounds prohibited by the AGG (section 3, paragraph 5 AGG). The prohibition of discriminations on the ground of religious belief covers – as the prohibition of discrimination on the other grounds enumerated in section 1 *AGG* – *inter alia* the conditions for access to employment, employment and working conditions, and pay (section 2, paragraph 1 AGG). Although section 2, paragraph 4 AGG explicitly provides that the Act on Dismissal Protection [*Kündigungsschutzgesetz*] should only apply for dismissals, the Federal Labor Court has recently ruled, that dismissals also must respect the prohibition of discriminations enshrined in the AGG.

Direct discriminations on the ground of religion or belief are forbidden in general. Section 8, paragraph 1 AGG, however, considers unequal treatment not to be a discrimination where, by reason of the nature of the particular occupational activities concerned or of the context in which they are carried out, such a characteristic constitutes a genuine and determining occupational requirement, provided that the objective is legitimate and the requirement is proportionate. In a modern society, however, there will be only very few cases in which the religion of the worker is a legitimate occupational requirement under section 8, paragraph 1 AGG.

In addition, employers are not only obliged to abstain from discriminations in the sense of the AGG. They also have a prevention duty (section 12, paragraph 1 AGG): They have to guard against discriminations of their workers by taking the necessary measures. The employer fulfills this prevention duty by providing a training for his personnel in the anti-discrimination legislation (section 12, paragraph 2 AGG).

The AGG provides several sanctions for discriminations on the ground of religious belief. Leaving aside the right of the victim to complain (section 13 AGG), the victim of a harassment is entitled to refuse to perform his work without losing his remuneration (section 14 AGG). Furthermore, the victim can claim from the employer who has discriminated compensation of material damage (section 15, paragraph 1 AGG) as well as immaterial damage (section 15, paragraph 2 AGG); if the discrimination concerns a recruitment, the compensation for immaterial damage is limited to three months' salary when the victim has not been the best qualified candidate and would not have been recruited without the discrimination.

So far, there is no case law of the ECJ and of German labor courts on discrimination on the ground of religions or belief. However, all cases decided by the Courts before the coming into force of the AGG and referring to religious expression in the workplace have to be reconsidered in the light of the provisions of the AGG and of Directive 2000/78/EC. As the requirements of the Directive are more severe compared to those of the constitutional principle of equal treatment under article 3, paragraph 3 GG, the impact of the Directive cannot be underestimated. We will come back to this point when discussing some areas of conflict.

Working Time Interruption for Prayers

Another conflict between the working time schedule and religious freedom of workers can arise from Muslim workers' demands to interrupt the work for a prayer during the working time. In 2002, the Labor Court of Appeal of Hamm had to decide such a case, but only in a procedure that concerned a demand for an interlocutory injunction: The plaintiff requested from his employer a working time interruption of three minutes between 6 and 8 a.m. for his morning prayer but the employer refused. Nonetheless, the plaintiff made his prayer without the authorization of his superior and received several warning notices by the employer. In the subsequent lawsuit, he demanded that the employer remove the warning notices. The Labor Court of Appeal of Hamm dismissed the lawsuit with the argument that the plaintiff could not claim the demanded working time interruptions for his morning prayer from the employer. The Court conceded that the prayer is covered by the constitutional right of religious freedom (article 4 GG) and that, in principle, the employer has the duty to take this right into consideration.

However, the plaintiff could not demonstrate that the protection of his religious freedom prevails over operational requirements protected by the employer's right of free enterprise (article 12, paragraph 1, article 14 GG).

Until now, the ruling of the Labor Court of Appeal of Hamm is the only labor court decision dealing with this problem. Although this problem might occur in many companies, employers have not faced it by creating works agreements with their works councils or company agreements with a trade union. However, it can be expected that the question will continue to occupy the labor courts in the future.

Work Performance and the Respect of Ramadan

A specific problem for Muslim workers can be in respect of the fasting month of Ramadan. The strict observance of these religious rules might conflict with the duty to work and might make necessary work interruptions for Muslim workers or their temporary transfer to other workplaces. So far, the labor courts have not had to decide upon the employer's duty to be considerate of these religious interests of workers. There is no doubt that the employer has the duty, resulting from section 241, paragraph 2 BGB in conjunction with article 4 GG to take into consideration these religious duties of Muslim workers as far as operational requirements are not conflicting. In practice, these problems seem to be settled in the companies in an uncomplicated way by giving vacations to these workers or by using the flexibility of working time schemes existing in many companies.

Conclusions

As has been pointed out, religious expression in the workplace is an increasingly relevant issue in German labor law. At the beginning, it was basically an issue that concerned the balancing of worker protection by state labor law and the constitutional autonomy of religious societies under article 137, paragraph 3 of the Constitution of Weimar privileging in particular the Christian churches; as a result, a specific "labor law of Churches" [*Kirchenarbeitsrecht*] has been established recognizing a far-reaching loyalty duty of workers employed in church institutions. However, the increasing relevance of non-Christian religions in German society, in particular the growing presence of the Islam, going back to a heavy immigration during the post-war decades, has shifted the attention to how labor law has to cope with the challenges arising from this social process. In this respect, religious diversity and immigration are strongly linked issues in the German debate.

So far, German law has not developed a coherent concept coping with the various conflicts that arise nowadays from religious expression in the workplace and equally recognizing the different religious communities existing in Germany. The overall picture is rather contradictory. There is still preferential treatment of the traditionally predominant Christian churches. One important example is the specific labor law of the churches that has "clericalized" the employment relationships of workers in church institutions to a certain extent: The core element is their right to determine the character of the service in the churches according to their dogmata and to define accordingly the loyalty duty of their workers (section 9 AGG). In spite of the religiously neutral character of this provision, non-Christian communities, such as the Islam will have difficulties obtaining this status because of their believers' missing affiliation required by that article. Another example is the way various Federal States are presently dealing with the headscarf problem in the public sector: Although religious neutrality is recognized as a fundamental constitutional principle, the so-called neutrality acts of some of the Federal States emphasize the Christian and occidental tradition as being admitted to the public sphere.

On the other hand, there are serious attempts in the jurisdiction of the labor courts to also protect religious freedom of workers belonging to non-Christian religious communities. The Federal Labor Court's headscarf decision of 2002 is one definitive example in this context. Perhaps this process towards religious pluralism based on an equal recognition of the existing religions will be hastened by one "dark horse" that should not be under-estimated in this context: The impact of European anti-discrimination law on German labor law. It remains to be seen to what extent the future jurisdiction of the ECJ regarding the prohibition of discriminations on the ground of religious belief under Directive 2000/78/EC will have an impact on religious expression at the workplace in German law.

References and suggested readings

Landesarbeitsgericht Jan. 18, 2002, NEUE ZEITSCHRIFT FÜR ARBEITSRECHT (NZA) 675, 2002; Landesarbeitsgericht Feb. 2, 2002, NEUE ZEITSCHRIFT FÜR ARBEITSRECHT (NZA) 1090, 2002; MÜNCHENER KOMMENTAR ZUM ARBEITSRECHT, §3 AGG, Rn. 49 (5. Aufl. 2007); MÜNCHENER KOMMENTAR ZUM ARBEITSRECHT, §616 BGB, Rn. 46; BECK'SCHER ONLINE-KOMMENTAR, Art. 4 GG, Rn. 76 (Stand 2009); KÜTTNER, PERSONALBUCH 2009 Rn. 6. (16. Aufl. 2009), reference: "Arbeitsverweigerung aus Gewissensgründen."

Problem 5 discussion – Japan

The Labor Standards Act (LSA) Article 3 reads "An employer shall not engage in discriminatory treatment with respect to wages, working hours or other working conditions by reason of the nationality, creed or social status of any worker." "Creed" is interpreted as including a person's thought, belief and religious and political creed. Therefore, discriminatory treatment by reason of religion is prohibited, with criminal and civil penalties under the LSA.

As long as the employer gives one break during a shift uniformly to all employees, it does not give rise to violation of Article 3 because such uniform treatment does not constitute a prohibited "discriminatory" treatment. Legal problems would arise if Muslim employees were to take praying breaks during the shift although the work rules or employment contracts do not allow such breaks, and the employer disciplines them. The Muslim employees may contend that such disciplinary actions are null and void because they violate the prohibition of discriminatory treatment under Article 3 of the LSA.

However, it would be difficult for such an allegation to be supported by the courts because the disciplinary action would be deemed as arising not by reason of religion but because the actions were violating work rules and disturbing the workplace order. If the work rules and contracts which do not give three breaks during the shift should be interpreted as being against public policy and order, the employer could not discipline the Muslim employees because their actions to take three breaks would no more violate the valid work rules. However, it seems that current Japanese courts will not take such interpretation.

PRIMARY SOURCE

Labor Standards Act

Article 3

An employer shall not engage in discriminatory treatment with respect to wages, working hours or other working conditions by reason of the nationality, creed or social status of any worker.

Problem 5 discussion – United States

Title VII of the U.S. Civil Rights Act of 1964 was amended in 1972 to expand and clarify the Act's prohibition of discrimination on grounds of religion. It did so by adding a definitional section that coupled the definition to its operational effect:

The term "religion" includes all aspects of religious observance and practice, as well as belief, unless an employer demonstrates that the firm is unable to reasonably accommodate to an employee's or prospective employee's religious observance or practice without undue hardship on the conduct of the employer's business. Title VII is not preemptive of state law and there is a web of cognate state and even local laws requiring religious accommodation.

There is no doubt that these Muslim employees' demands meet the threshold test of being genuinely grounded in religious belief and practice. The question is whether the employer can accommodate them without "undue hardship," which has been read as applying not only to the employer's business but to the imposition of undue hardship on other of its employees. Further, "undue hardship" has been construed by the United States Supreme Court as anything that imposes more than a *de minimis* burden. *Trans World Airlines* v. *Hardison*, 432 U.S. 63 (1977).

In this case, the lack of "fill-in" workers could be remedied by hiring them, but such a cost would appear to be more than *de minimis*. Non-Muslim workers might be denied break time in order to fill in for their Muslim co-workers, but that additional work assignment would also appear to impose a more than *de minimis* burden on them. Are there other courses of accommodation available? As is the case with all other countries in this cohort, distinctions between religions in time off for religions purposes would be prohibited.

References and suggested readings

The federal case law is assembled by Andrew M. Campbell, Annotation, *What Constitutes Employer's Reasonable Accommodation of Employee's Religious Preferences Under Title VII of Civil Rights Act of 1964*, 134 A.L.R. FED. 1 (2008). The state and local law is assembled by Marjorie A. Shields, Annotation, *Necessity of and What Constitutes, Employer's Reasonable Accommodation of Employee's Religious Preference Under State Law*, 107 A.L.R. 5th 623 (2008).

A collection of papers on countries not represented here on *Religious Expression in the Workplace* appears in 30 Comp. Lab. L. & Pol'y J. No. 3 (2009). The essay on French law by the late François Gaudu stands in sharp contrast to the others and to the laws under review here.

Efforts to impose more than the *de minimis* rule are discussed in a law student note, *A Struggle of Biblical Proportions: The Campaign to Enact Workplace Religious Freedom Act of 2003*, 16 U. FLA. J.L. & PUB. POL'Y 579 (2005).

Return to the considerations discussed in the introductory to this part. One obvious distinction that explains differences in the scope of antidiscrimination law is the degree of diversity the population reflects. Set out in Tables III.5 and III.6 are data concerning the religious composition of the populations of the countries under study and – as a crude proxy for ethnic diversity – the percentage of foreign-born residents.

Table III.5 Religious distribution of populations

Australia (2006)	%
Christian	63.8
Buddhist	2.1
Muslim	1.7
Other	2.4
Unspecified	11.3
None	18.7
Brazil (2010)	
Roman Catholic	64.4
Evangelical	22.0
Other	5.6
None	8.0
Germany (2008)	
Protestant	30
Roman Catholic	30
Muslim	not provided
Other	not provided
None	not provided
Japan (2008)	
Shinto	52
Buddhist	42
Christian	1
Other or none	5

United States (2008)	
Christian	75.8
Other religions	3.8
None or not given	15.0

Sources:

Australia: Central Intelligence Agency, THE WORLD FACT BOOK 43 (2011).

Brazil: Censo Demográfico (2010) Table 1.9.1. This source is quite detailed and indicates a Jewish population of about 100,000; Buddhists of over 240,000; and 35,000 Muslims.

Germany: Statistiches Bundesamt – https://www.destatis.de/EN/FactsFigures/SocietyState/Population/CurrentPopulation/Table. Although the Turkish Muslim population is quite large, it is not represented by an officially recognized religious body which could supply figures. There is such a body for the Jewish population which reports just over 100,000 adherents.

Japan: Cultural Affairs Dept., Agency for Cultural Affairs. N.B. many Japanese adhere to both Shintoism and Buddhism.

United States: U.S. Census Bureau, Statistical Abstract of the U.S. Table 75 (2012). Though small in percentage, the figures indicate the following numbers of adherents:

Jewish	8,880,000
Muslim	2,700,000
Buddhist	1,300,000
Hindu	580,000
Wiccan	340,000
Pagan	340,000

Table III.6 Foreign-born residents

Country	Foreign-born (Absolute number & percent of population)	Major Sources	
Australia			
(2010)	6,000,000	U.K.	1,190,000
	(27%)	China	540,000
		India	340,000
Brazil			
(2000)*	650,000	Portugal	212,000
	(0.3%)	Japan	67,000
Germany			
(2011)	5,660,00	EU	4,380,000
	(7%)	Turkey	1,100,000

Country	Foreign-born (Absolute number & percent of population)	Major Sources	
Japan			
(2009)	2,200,000	China	680,000
	(1.7%)	Korea	578,000
		Brazil	267,000
United States			
(2010)	40,000,000	Mexico	1,160,000
	(13%)	China	200,000

* Latest available statistics.

Sources: Australia: Australian Bureau of Statistics, Year Book Australia, 2012.
Brazil: OECD, Latin America Economic Outlook 2010.
Germany: Statistisches Bundesampt, Central Register of Foreigners (2011).
Japan: Japan Bureau of Statistics, Registered Foreigners by Nationality (2010).
United States: U.S. Census Bureau, The Newly Arrived Foreign-Born Population of the United States: 2010 .

The concept of "official" religious holidays came up in the Brazil readings. This reminded me of a situation that arose at my company two years ago when in an effort to provide more flexibility and consideration of religious observances of non-Christian faiths, we decided to remove the company holiday of Good Friday, and replace it with a "Flex Day" also known as a "Floating Holiday". Employees were communicated to about the change and the rationale and told that they could choose to use this Flex Day on any day that they choose … including Good Friday. It was surprising to see the wide range of reaction that we received from the employees. The non-Christian employees were very thankful and appreciative. And a nice surprise was that many of our African-American employees wrote notes of appreciation because they planned to use this day to observe Martin Luther King Junior Day (which our company at the time did not observe as a company holiday). However two groups were not pleased with this decision. First, Christians who for years had taken this day off, now felt pressure to come to work since it was not a company holiday. Secondly, the Finance and Manufacturing managers who need to accrue correct labor dollars and plan for certain level of productivity did not like how this flexibility impacted their planning requirements … [W]hile there are laws that protect certain basic rights, the cultural norms and expectations within a country continue to drive employers to adjust their own policies and practices to meet the needs of the growing diverse population, but not without implications to the "majority".

Vice President, HR, Electrical Manufacturing Sector

[B]eing Danish, [my company] ... tends ... to look at issues through the eyes of a Dane ... Expatriates like myself are creating and bringing change to the workplace and encouraging them to look at issues differently. For example Diversity is a non-issue in Denmark, and where it is discussed it is done so from the perspective of woman in the workplace. Our immigration has tended to be people from Africa and Turkey, so Muslim religion is emerging. Our newspapers talk about the building of mosques, we are not prepared and address our issues in the press. In the workplace, rules are fairly clear and reflect Danish background. We will face these challenges in the near term. We have considered our footprint in the places where we operate and have discussed our values and beliefs in the open, we recognize that one approach, even a Danish approach will not work everywhere and are beginning to look for ways to influence and create change in workplaces.

Head of Compensation and Benefits, Shipping/Natural Resources Sector

For eleven years I headed the HR function for a market research company in the US, seven European countries, including Germany, and India. We provided market research services and had small call centers in each country. Our work product was not continuous, except in the call centers where we received calls continuously during the day. In Europe, we had over 2000 employees who came from a diverse set of cultures and religions. As we quickly grew our operations in Europe, we began to have questions from managers in all countries regarding religious breaks and prayer sessions during the day. The President of our European operations requested a legal analysis on what our rights were in each country to deal with these situations so managers could then decide how they wanted to respond.

I was able to influence the President of Europe and our CEO that we needed to look at this issue first as a business issue, second as an employee relations issue, and lastly as a legal issue. I also felt it was important to address this issue through our corporate values which had been developed with the participation of the President of Europe and the CEO.

We addressed the issue in the following manner:

(1) From a business stand point we were a service company providing data, analytics, and information so our customers could make better decisions. The work was not continuous and in most cases people started and stopped work based on their work load although there were a core set of hours. In the call centers we always staffed to ensure we can cover people's lunch hours and breaks. The executive team agreed that except in emergencies our business would not be adversely affected by allowing people to take a prayer or religious break during the day. They could do so before they started work, during a break, or during lunch. We also provided private rooms so employees had privacy.

(2) Because our compensation was only at the 50th percentile of our labor markets, our HR strategy was to create a positive flexible work environment that retained people who could earn more compensation at competitors or comparable firms. Allowing people to take short prayer breaks fit in to our overall HR strategy. We also allowed people smoking breaks, lactation rooms for mothers, and allowed employees to visit their children in nearby day care centers during a break once a day.

(3) Because we operated in nine different countries, diversity and the appreciation of different cultures was a core value to our firm. If we were going to state that diversity was a core value it was hard to see us deny employees whether Muslim, Catholic or any other religion, the right to conduct prayer during the day regardless of the legal requirements in each country.

As a result of this philosophy we continuously had lower turnover compared to other service firms in the seven European countries, and high employee engagement scores. In most cases employees did not abuse the time we gave them whether it was for prayer or to visiting their child in a local day care center. Employees understood that if they abused the flexibility we provided to them, they could potentially have the flexibility reduced.

Selection of managers and training were key components of successfully implementing this HR strategy. When we hired managers from the outside we focused on the type of work environments they were coming from and whether they had the ability to manage people's results and not necessarily how many hours they worked. For internal promotions to supervisory positions, we often put employees through an assessment on how they would handle these types of situations.

From a management training perspective, we started every management training session with a review of our core values, our overall HR strategy as described above, and a video of our CEO who discussed our approach and philosophy to people. It was important that managers understood why we permitted so much flexibility in the workplace, and how this would help us retain employees who were not paid at the top of the market. The majority of the training focused on case studies and roll playing on how to handle cultural differences, requests from employees, what to do when there were abuses. We also had lectures on the different cultures and religions within our countries and would recognize all holidays on our website and in the various work sites.

In summary, I believe the strategy we created in our company was the correct one for our situation. We were a large service business, where except in our call centers, work was not continuous. In our call centers managers had the flexibility to provide employees with short breaks where they could do anything they wanted whether praying, visiting their child at a nearby day care center or to take a smoking break. Employees valued this type of environment and it allowed us to retain people even though we did not pay as well as some competitors.

Like anything else in business, this philosophy could not work without the strong commitment of the CEO and senior leaders.

Senior Vice President, HR, Information Technology Sector

Although the burden of proof falls on employers to show undue hardship, it has been my experience that making accommodations for multicultural groups tends to spill over into other areas and creates a more satisfied workforce.

Manager, Talent Acquisition, Service Sector

Questions for Discussion – Problem 5

1. As the introduction to this part observed, the claim for protection against invidious discrimination is often grounded in terms of human rights. As Hugh Collins has observed: "The modern idea of human rights building on historical antecedents in natural law theory, proclaims that all human beings should be accorded certain fundamental rights by virtue of their humanity. These human rights are universal and imperative, with a special moral weight that normally overrides other considerations." HUGH COLLINS, *Theories of Rights as Justifications for Labour Law* in THE IDEA OF LABOUR LAW 136, 140 (Guy Davidov & Brian Langille eds. 2011). As we have seen, however, the aspects of humanity worthy of protection vary from parsimonious in Japan (with separate statutory treatment on grounds of sex to be discussed in the next problem), to a rather more robust catalogue in Australia: "race, colour, sex, sexual preference, age,

physical or mental disability, marital status, family or carer's responsibilities, pregnancy, religion, political opinion, national extraction or social origin." If the anti-discrimination principle is a universal human right, what explains this difference?

2. Should human resource managers harmonize non-discrimination policies across countries despite the fact that some of these categories could not claim domestic legal protection? If so, how would you define discrimination in a harmonized policy? If there was a harmonized policy that failed to provide protection for a particular group (and that was not illegal), but that disturbed some deeply seated cultural norm about the way such persons are regarded, and if workers pushed back against the company's policy – what should management do? (For example, let's say that your policy did not encompass Roma in Germany, but there was a push back in the workplace around the way some co-workers and supervisors treated people from Roma families.) In deciding that the following observation may be apt:

   > As nations contend with the growing assertiveness of such claims [for religious accommodation] on the polity, each state must struggle to apply its underlying church-state regime to the domain of labor law, find a way to define "religion" that corresponds to the lived reality of religious communities, and cope with religious traditions that make much stronger demands on individual believers than dominant faith communities. For societies that have considered themselves as culturally and religiously unitary, states for whom immigration is considered a problem rather than a resource, this will be no small challenge.

   Kenneth Wald, *Religion in the Workplace: A Social Science Perspective*, 30 COMP. LAB. L. & POL'Y J. 471, 483 (2009). If you do not think that there should be a single harmonized policy, how would you defend restricting a particular form of discrimination in one country, but not in another? What could be the complications from just stating that different countries have different laws?

3. Instead of being grounded in a human right, might the non-discrimination principle be grounded in labor market policy, that is, to maximize the fullest utilization of human resources and to enhance human capability? If so, why hasn't the market done that, assuming that employers wish to maximize the resources they are able to draw on?

4. Note that Australia insulates "social origin" from disparate treatment and Japan does so for "social status," but at neither the federal nor the state level does the United States have any cognate category. Since Meiji times, Japan has struggled with the integration of members of former outcast

communities – at the time labeled with strongly pejorative terms, eta and hinin, and, in modern times, burakumin – who are ethnically Japanese – identified with the hereditary performance of low status occupations, e.g. tanner, executioner, and whose ancestry may only be ascertainable (if uncertainly) by place of residence. As a student of this group, which has a well-organized anti-discrimination organization, explains:

> The fact that discrimination against burakumin is considered discrimination at all in the present is completely predicated upon the idea that this action is socially and morally reprehensible. Yet the idea that "discrimination" against certain groups in society is wrong is a relatively new idea in Japan, at least in legal terms. The law that granted eta equality in "status" (mibun) was only promulgated in 1871, and barely fifty years before that, the Tokugawa shogunate was actually warning eta and hinin groups through state legislation not to perform acts that went beyond their particular status limitations. There would seem to be, therefore, significant changes in institutional and social perceptions of what constitutes a marginalizing act in Japan ...

TIMOTHY AMOS, EMBODYING DIFFERENCE: THE MAKING OF BURAKUMIN IN MODERN JAPAN 95 (2011).

It might be well to think about distinctions we make among different groups of employees today that seem perfectly ordinary to us, that might, over the coming decades, come to be seen as a form of "discrimination" in the future. Cf. William Corbett, *What Is in Gina's Genes? The Curious Case of the Mutant-Hybrid Employment Law*, 64 OKLA. L. REV. 1 (2011) (on genetic discrimination law).

5. A group of social scientists produce the World Values Survey which will be discussed in greater detail in Part VIII (D), infra. The 2005/2006 survey put the following question to which the respondents in the five sample countries responded: "When jobs are scarce, employers should give priority to [the respondent's nation's] people over immigrants."

   Should human resource managers harmonize non-discrimination policies across countries despite the fact that some of these categories could not claim domestic legal protection? If the lack of protection reflects some deeply seated cultural norm about the way such persons are regarded, and if co-workers push back against the company's policy – one that does not reflect domestic law – what should management do?

Figure III.2 Nation preference in job allocation

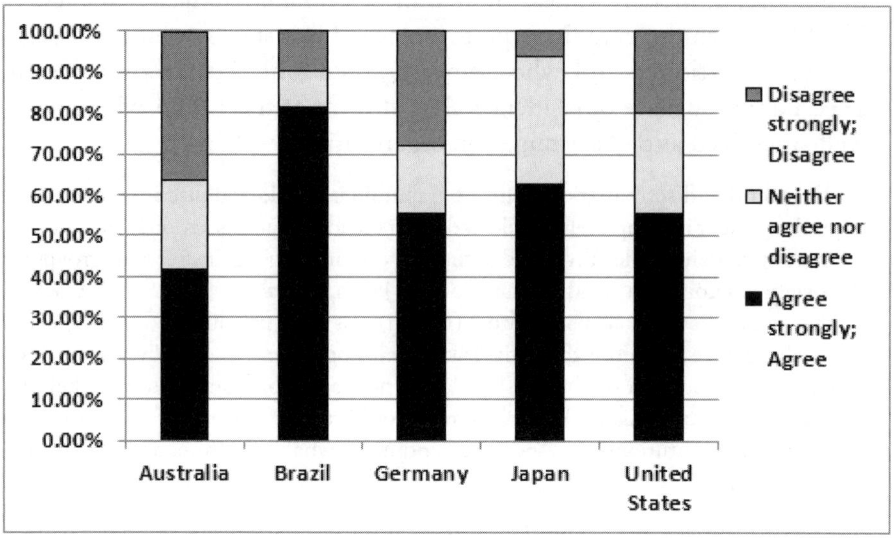

Source: World Values Survey (see Part VIII (D), infra).

PROBLEM 6: HIRING A WOMAN WHO IS PREGNANT

A job applicant volunteers without any prompting that she is in her second month of pregnancy. She has applied for a key planning job on a major project. The interviewer has explained that the position will require the employee to devote considerable time and effort, and, possibly, travel to remote locations, for the next 12 months. The applicant, who is otherwise extremely well qualified, has responded that she believes any problems can satisfactorily be dealt with. May she be rejected?

Problem 6 discussion – Australia

The prohibition on employment discrimination in s 351 of the Fair Work Act 2009, discussed (and extracted) in relation to Problem 5, also covers refusing to hire a prospective employee on the ground of "pregnancy". To be unlawful, that need only be *one* of the grounds for refusing to hire the applicant. Each of the State and Territory anti-discrimination laws has a similar prohibition. So too does the federal Sex Discrimination Act 1984, the relevant provisions in which are set out below.

There have been a number of decisions dealing with direct discrimination against pregnant workers – though generally in the context of existing employees complaining about their treatment on returning from maternity leave, rather than pregnant job applicants. It has been accepted in these cases that it is appropriate to compare the employer's treatment of the pregnant worker with the way in which they have or would have treated a non-pregnant worker in similar circumstances: see e.g. *Thomson v Orica Australia Pty Ltd* (2002) 116 IR 186; *Sterling Commerce (Australia) Pty Ltd v Iliff* (2008) 173 IR 378. Hence in this case the company would need to establish that non-pregnant applicants would likewise be denied a job because of their lack of availability for the whole year. As Branson J observed in *Commonwealth v Evans* [2004] FCA 654 at [71]: "it is not illegitimate for an employer, all other things being equal and provided indirect discrimination is avoided, to favour for re-employment an employee who takes limited leave over an employee who regularly takes a lot of leave, albeit that it is leave to which he or she is entitled."

Although there does not appear to be any case law in point, the job applicant here could presumably attempt to complain of indirect discrimination (for example, under s 7(2) of the Sex Discrimination Act 1984), on the basis that the employer was seeking to impose a facially neutral requirement – year-round availability – that would disadvantage pregnant job applicants. In that case, the company would seek to rely on the standard defense in such cases (see e.g. s 7B of the Sex Discrimination Act) that the requirement was reasonable in the circumstances.

It is worth emphasizing that in any proceedings brought under s 351 of the Fair Work Act, the onus would be on the employer to prove that they did not take "adverse action" against the plaintiff because of her pregnancy: see e.g. *Ucchino v Acorp Pty Ltd* [2012] FMCA 9 (though this again was a case involving an existing employee, rather than a job applicant).

For completeness, it should be noted that under the National Employment Standards (NES), an employee does not become entitled to (unpaid) parental leave until they have served at least one year: Fair Work Act 2009 s 67. Hence there could be no complaint here of the employer violating s 340 of the Act by taking adverse action against a job applicant because of their intention to exercise a "workplace right" (i.e. take parental leave).

PRIMARY SOURCES

Fair Work Act 2009 (Cth) ss 351(1)–(2), 342(1) (see Problem 5)

Sex Discrimination Act 1984 (Cth) ss 14(1), 7, 7B–7C (infra)

Sex Discrimination Act 1984

14 Discrimination in employment or in superannuation

(1) It is unlawful for an employer to discriminate against a person on the ground of the person's sex, marital status, pregnancy or potential pregnancy, breastfeeding or family responsibilities:
   (a) in the arrangements made for the purpose of determining who should be offered employment;
   (b) in determining who should be offered employment; or
   (c) in the terms or conditions on which employment is offered.

7 Discrimination on the ground of pregnancy or potential pregnancy

(1) For the purposes of this Act, a person (the *discriminator*) discriminates against a woman (the *aggrieved woman*) on the ground of the aggrieved woman's pregnancy or potential pregnancy if, because of:
   (a) the aggrieved woman's pregnancy or potential pregnancy; or
   (b) a characteristic that appertains generally to women who are pregnant or potentially pregnant; or
   (c) a characteristic that is generally imputed to women who are pregnant or potentially pregnant;

the discriminator treats the aggrieved woman less favourably than, in circumstances that are the same or are not materially different, the discriminator treats or would treat someone who is not pregnant or potentially pregnant.

(2) For the purposes of this Act, a person (the *discriminator*) discriminates against a woman (the *aggrieved woman*) on the ground of the aggrieved woman's pregnancy or potential pregnancy if the discriminator imposes, or proposes to impose, a condition, requirement or practice that has, or is likely to have, the effect of disadvantaging women who are also pregnant or potentially pregnant.

(3) This section has effect subject to sections 7B and 7D.

7B Indirect discrimination: reasonableness test

(1) A person does not discriminate against another person by imposing, or proposing to impose, a condition, requirement or practice that has, or is likely to have, the disadvantaging effect mentioned in subsection 5(2), 6(2) or 7(2) or 7AA(2) or section 7A if the condition, requirement or practice is reasonable in the circumstances.

(2) The matters to be taken into account in deciding whether a condition, requirement or practice is reasonable in the circumstances include:

(a) the nature and extent of the disadvantage resulting from the imposition, or proposed imposition, of the condition, requirement or practice; and
(b) the feasibility of overcoming or mitigating the disadvantage; and
(c) whether the disadvantage is proportionate to the result sought by the person who imposes, or proposes to impose, the condition, requirement or practice.

7C Burden of proof

In a proceeding under this Act, the burden of proving that an act does not constitute discrimination because of section 7B lies on the person who did the act.

References and suggested readings

ANDREW STEWART, STEWART'S GUIDE TO EMPLOYMENT LAW ch. 14 (4th ed. 2013).

NEIL REES, KATHERINE LINDSAY & SIMON RICE, AUSTRALIAN ANTI-DISCRIMINATION LAW: TEXT, CASE AND MATERIALS 224–6; 374 (2008).

Australian Human Rights Commission, FEDERAL DISCRIMINATION LAW, ch 4.2.4 *accessed at* http://www.humanrights.gov.au/our-work/legal/federal-discrimination-law-2011.

As to the specific question of how "comparators" are constructed for the purpose of anti-discrimination laws, *see e.g.* Belinda Smith, *From* Wardley *to* Purvis: *How Far has Australian Anti-Discrimination Law Come in 30 Years?*, 21 AUSTL J LAB L 3 (2008).

Problem 6 discussion – Brazil

Introduced in the *Consolidação* in May 1999 to prevent discrimination against women in the labor market, article 373-A forbids employers to: (I) post or publish a job advertisement with references to gender, age, color or marital status, unless the nature of the activity to be undertaken publicly and notoriously so requires; (II) refuse to employ, promote or justify a dismissal because of sex, age, race, marital status or pregnancy status, unless the nature of the activity is publicly recognized as incompatible; (III) consider sex, age, color or family situation as a determining variable for purposes of pay, training and career opportunities; (IV) demand certificate or examination of any nature, for proof of sterility or pregnancy, at admission or job retention; (V) block access, or adopt subjective criteria for granting the registration or approval procedures, in private companies, based on gender, age, race, marital status or pregnancy status; and, (VI) to do intimate searches on female employees.

This article apparently leaves no room for discussion as employers are not allowed to refuse hire due to a pregnancy condition. However, the door gets slightly open as one tries to define what should be considered "publicly recognized in the activity's nature as incompatible to the pregnancy condition." It is difficult to imagine that the circumstantial demand of all efforts' devotion constitutes an incompatibility related to the nature of the activity. But, unfortunately, case law on the matter is scarce. Most of the case law is related to the protection of pregnancy during a labor contract. This is due to the fact that the Brazilian Constitution (article 10, II, "b", of the Constitutional Transitory Dispositions Act) makes the *dismissal* of pregnant women unlawful from the confirmation of conception to five months after birth, except if the dismissal is due to an employee's fault.

Apropos of dismissal, where there is a texture of law, the jurisprudence of the Tribunal Superior do Trabalho, expressed through its Súmula 244, has established that (I) an employer's lack of knowledge of the pregnancy condition does not constitute an exculpatory condition as to the obligation to pay indemnities for the period, i.e. such protection does not require employees to notify employers about their pregnancy condition and if they are wrongfully dismissed in the meantime employers are supposed to pay salaries and all other benefits for the entire period of protection; (II) the reintegration of the employee on the job can be determined if litigation occurs during the protection period; and (III) the pregnancy protection is not applicable if dismissal is related to the conclusion of the experience period of the labor contract, which under Brazilian law cannot exceed 90 days.

References and suggested readings

BRASIL, TRIBUNAL SUPERIOR DO TRABALHO, *Súmula 244, accessed at* http://www.tst.jus.br//Cmjpn/livro_pdf_atual.pdf (last visited Feb. 17, 2010).

Problem 6 discussion – Germany

The German General Equal Treatment Act, *Allgemeines Gleichbehandlungsgesetz*, prohibits, among other things, discrimination on the basis of sex. Direct discrimination based on sex occurs not only if a person is discriminated against because of being a woman for example, but also if a woman receives less favorable treatment because of pregnancy or maternity; Section 3 para. 3 (2) *Allgemeines Gleichbehandlungsgesetz.*

Rejecting the applicant because she is pregnant constitutes, therefore, direct discrimination. Although section 8 para. 1 *Allgemeines Gleichbehandlungsgesetz*[2] provides an opportunity to justify direct discrimination because of occupational requirements, one has to assume that a court would hold the rejection of the applicant in this problem to be unlawful. As the European Court of Justice (4.10.2001 – C-109/00, NJW 2002, 123) has decided, the employer is *not* allowed to terminate a time-limited employment contract based on the employee's pregnancy even if the employee conceals her pregnancy in the job interview and even if she is unfit to work for most of the contract's duration. If a termination of the contract is unlawful, it would also be unlawful not to hire her only because of her pregnancy. The applicant discriminated against may claim material damages and damages for pain and suffering, but it is questionable if she can be ordered to be hired because such is not expressly provided for in section 15 *Allgemeines Gleichbehandlungsgesetz.*[3]

This jurisprudence is questionable as it takes only the interests of the employee into account and ignores vital and legitimate employer interests. Some German

---

2 "Difference of treatment on the basis of any of the grounds defined in § 1 is lawful where, by reason of the nature of the particular occupational activities concerned or of the context in which they are carried out, such a ground constitutes a genuine and determining occupational requirement, provided that the objective is legitimate and the requirement is proportionate."

3 Reads in parts as follows:

> (1) The employer is obligated to compensate employees for any damages resulting from a violation of the prohibition of discrimination, unless the employer is not liable for the breach of duty.
> (2) The affected employee may demand reasonable compensation in the form of monetary damages for any non-economic losses.
> (6) A violation by the employer […] does not give rise to any claim for employment […].

scholars argue that the employer may reject a pregnant woman applying for a *time-limited* employment if it is foreseeable that she will be unfit for work for most of the time. However, there can be no doubt that the rejection of an applicant based on her pregnancy would be unlawful if the job offered is *not* time-limited.

References and suggested readings

For a general overview, see Bernd Waas, *New Developments in Employment Discrimination Law: Germany*, 68 BULL. COMP. LAB. REL. 69 (2008). More specifically regarding the above, see ECJ 10.2001 – C-109/00, NEUE JURISTISCHE WOCHENSCHRIFT (NJW) 123 (2002; BAG 6.2.2003 Neue Zeitschrift für Arbeitsrecht (NZA) 848 (2003), Ulrich Pallasch, *Diskriminierungsverbot wegen Schwangerschaft bei der Einstellung*, NEUE ZEITSCHRIFT FÜR ARBEITSRECHT (NZA) 306 (2007); Gerlind Wisskirchen/Alexander Bissels, *Das Fragerecht des Arbeitgebers bei Einstellung unter Berücksichtingung des AGG*, NEUE ZEITSCHRIFT FÜR ARBEITSRECHT (NZA) 169 (2007).

Problem 6 discussion – Japan

Article 65 of the Labor Standards Act (LSA) prescribes maternity leave. When a woman who is expected to give birth within 6 weeks requests leave from work, the employer shall not make her work. After the childbirth, an employer is *prohibited* to have the woman work within 8 weeks without any request from her.

Therefore, when the employer knows at the hiring that the applicant is pregnant and cannot perform the expected task, it seems that the employer can legally refuse to hire her, but no actual cases have been litigated on this. However, once the employer has hired the applicant and knows about her pregnancy thereafter, it would be prohibited from discharging her by reason of her pregnancy under the Equal Employment Opportunity Act (EEOA). Article 9 of the EEOA prohibits dismissals and other unfavorable treatment by reason of the female worker's being pregnant, giving birth, requesting or taking maternity leave prescribed in the LSA, Article 65, and thus such dismissals are null and void.

Then, is it allowed to ask the applicant whether she is pregnant or not at a hiring interview? The Supreme Court in the *Mitsubishi Jushi* case emphasized employers' freedom of hiring stemming from the Constitutional freedom of doing business and of executing contracts, and held that a company's refusal to hire by reason of an applicant's beliefs and creed cannot be automatically condemned as illegal. As to the bans on discriminatory treatment by reason of creed in Article 3, Labor Standards Act (discussed in Problem 4), the Supreme Court held that this regulation refers to post-hiring working conditions but does not regulate hiring itself. In connection with the freedom of hiring, the Supreme Court also held that investigating an applicant's beliefs and creed in the hiring process is permissible because a refusal to hire on account of beliefs or creed was not itself unlawful.

If the *Mitsubishi Jushi* ruling on freedom of hiring and investigation could still apply to Problem 6, the employer would be allowed to ask about the applicant's pregnancy. However, the Supreme Court admits that the employer's freedom to hire can be restricted by statutory regulations. When the *Mitsubishi Jushi* case was handed down in 1973 there were no regulations on sex and pregnancy discrimination. The EEOA was enacted in 1985 and strengthened by 1997 and 2006 revisions. Under the developed statutory regulations against discrimination, it is highly questionable whether the Supreme Court ruling emphasizing employer's freedom to hire can be maintained. In a case involving hiring discrimination by reason of union membership in 2003 (Supreme Court, *JR Hokkaido* case, Dec. 15, 2003), however, the Supreme Court once again emphasized employers' freedom of hiring and dismissed the contention that the employer had violated the Labor Union Act prohibiting unfavorable treatment of workers by reason of union membership. The decision has been severely criticized by scholars, however.

Therefore, the extent to which an employer is permitted to investigate an applicant's pregnancy at the hiring stage still remains an open question in Japan. As regards the problem, of course, the employee volunteered that information without being asked.

PRIMARY SOURCES

Labor Standards Act

Article 3

An employer shall not engage in discriminatory treatment with respect to wages, working hours or other working conditions by reason of the nationality, creed or social status of any worker.

Article 65

(1) In the event that a woman who is expected to give birth within 6 weeks (or within 14 weeks in the case of multiple fetuses) requests leave from work, the employer shall not make her work.

(2) An employer shall not have a woman work within 8 weeks after childbirth; provided, however, that this shall not prevent an employer from having such a woman work, if she has so requested, after 6 weeks have passed since childbirth, in activities which a doctor has approved as having no adverse effect on her.

(3) In the event that a pregnant woman has so requested, an employer shall transfer her to other light activities.

Equal Employment Opportunity Act

Article 9

(1) Employers shall not stipulate marriage, pregnancy or childbirth as a reason for retirement of women workers.

(2) Employers shall not dismiss women workers for marriage.

(3) Employers shall not dismiss or give disadvantageous treatment to women workers by reason of pregnancy, childbirth, or for requesting absence from work as prescribed in Article 65, paragraph 1, of the Labor Standards Act (Act No. 49 of 1947) or having taken absence from work as prescribed in the same Article, paragraph 1 or 2, of the same act, or by other reasons relating to pregnancy, childbirth as provided by Ordinance of the Ministry of Health, Labor and Welfare.

(4) Dismissal of women workers who are pregnant or in the first year after childbirth shall be void. However, this shall not apply in the event that the employers prove that dismissals are not by reasons prescribed in the preceding paragraph.

References and suggested readings

Hiroya Nakakubo, *"Phase III" of the Japanese Equal Employment Opportunity Act*, 4 JAPAN LAB. REV. 9–28 (2007); Michiyo Morozumi, *Special Protection, Equality, and Beyond: Working Life and Parenthood under Japanese Labor Law*, 27 COMP. LAB. L. & POL'Y J. 513 (2006).

Problem 6 discussion – United States

Title VII of the U.S. Civil Rights Act of 1964 was amended in 1978 by the Pregnancy Discrimination Act (PDA) to include, as sex discrimination, employer action taken "on the basis of pregnancy, childbirth, or related medical conditions." (The amendment legislated against a narrow construction given by the U.S. Supreme Court to the meaning of "sex" allowing employers to exclude pregnancy from their health benefits.) It would surely *seem* to be the case that a refusal to hire an applicant *because* she is pregnant – or to discharge her shortly thereafter when her condition is revealed (if she has not volunteered that information) – would violate the law; and, by close parsing of the text it does, *if* the ground of action is pregnancy per se. See *EEOC v. High Speed Enterprise, Inc.*, 833 F.Supp.2d 1153 (D.Ariz. 2011).

Interestingly, there is very little decisional law on this point. In what may be by default the leading case, decided by the United States Court of Appeals for the Eighth Circuit in 1983, *Marafino v. St. Louis Cnty. Cir. Ct.*, 707 F.2d 1005 (8th Cir. 1983), a state court refused to hire a staff attorney who, due to her pregnancy, "planned to take a leave of absence within a few months of beginning work." She was refused hire because of concern about the harmful effect of an interruption in service during her training period. Terming it "a very close case," the court of appeals sustained the lower court's conclusion that the applicant was denied appointment not because of her pregnancy but because of the immediate prospect of her taking leave. This line of reasoning was taken up 15 years later by the United States Court of Appeals for the Seventh Circuit in the discharge of a newly hired staff member whom the employer learned was pregnant and planning to take a pregnancy leave at a time when she would be needed most. *Marshall v. Am. Hosp. Ass'n*, 157 F.3d 250 (7th Cir. 1993). Other sex-neutral grounds for discharge were offered and accepted by the lower court as motivating the action; but the Court of Appeals addressed this scenario as an independent ground and, as such, not constituting discrimination on the basis of pregnancy:

> As previously noted, the PDA "requires the employer to ignore an employee's pregnancy, but … not her absence from work, unless the employer overlooks the comparable absences of non-pregnant employees." … Marshall [the employee] makes no showing

> that AHA [the employer] terminated her because of her pregnancy rather than because she was planning an extended absence during the busiest time of her first year as an Associate Director. Marshall presents no evidence that a non-pregnant, probationary employee who was going to be on extended leave in the months immediately preceding the annual conference would not have been terminated.

From the *Marafino* case legal commentators have abstracted the rule to be that an employer can deny a pregnant applicant a job if the employer can show it would refuse to hire anyone, male or female, who required a similar leave fast upon starting work; i.e. that a neutral, evenly applied rule would have disqualified all applicants.

It might be useful to note here that in 1993 Congress enacted the Family and Medical Leave Act (FMLA). It requires covered employers to afford eligible employees up to 12 weeks of unpaid leave a year for medical conditions including childbirth; and it forbids retaliation against employees for having availed themselves of the Act's benefit. But, in order to be eligible for FMLA leave the employee must have been in the company's employ for at least a 12 month period and to have worked at least 1,250 hours in that period. However, no provision is made prohibiting a refusal to hire in order to avoid the accrual of that statutory benefit.

References and suggested readings

For a snapshot of the law today, *see* Thomas Bernard & Adrienne Rapp, *Pregnant Employees, Working Mothers, and the Workplace – Legislation, Social Change and Where We Are Today*, 22 J. L. & HEALTH 197 (2009).

When I first started 12 years ago, I could count on my two hands the number of female Outside Sales Associates employed out of the 100+ total. Our culture has changed and we now have 33% female Sales Associates. With that shift has come the introduction of scenarios akin to what was presented in Problem 6. A few things have helped me to persuade hiring managers to be more agreeable to considering pregnant applicants, or to persuade existing managers to be more patient when they discover that one of their Sales Associates is pregnant. Keep in mind that their primary concern is that our industry is extremely competitive, and that building relationships with customers is key to growing sales. Any absence or change in sales representation leads to increased exposure to lost business. In the recent past, we have had two female applicants disclose their pregnancy status in their interviews. The first happened to be a successful sales employee at one of our competitors. This set the stage for us to hire her and allow her an unpaid 6-week LOA during her first year (note that we do not allow a LOA of undetermined length for any

> employee within their first year, regardless of reason for leave). This time flew by, and she has since proven to be an incredible asset to the company. Our actions have helped to reinforce with this employee, as well as other employees, that we are fair and compassionate... The more we have had existing employees become pregnant, leave the workforce for up to 12 weeks, and then return to work as productive appreciative employees, the more this perspective is reinforced.
>
> Director, HR, Food and Beverage Sector

> [H]aving the pregnancy conversation with an applicant early on in the interview process can be somewhat tricky, particularly if the applicant is not showing or if [she is] inquiring because [she is] "planning" to become pregnant. My advice to my hiring managers has always been to treat questions or comments like those as if they were related to any other medical event, whether it is planned or unplanned. If health benefits and short term disability are available on day one, and a new male employee breaks his leg or requires a medical procedure and is out for 4 to 6 weeks six months into his position, it is unlikely he would be terminated from his job. His responsibilities would roll over to another employee.
>
> Manager, Talent Acquisition, Service Sector

> Another situation we have had is one in which the applicant does not state that they need a LOA, but they are visibly pregnant. Here, I have cautioned the hiring manager about making assumptions, taking into consideration the nature of pregnancy. Even if the applicant stated clearly that they were requesting 12 weeks of leave, who is to say whether or not that leave will come to fruition? We have had, unfortunately, several employee pregnancies that have not reached full-term. The applicant may not even want to take more than several weeks off, or may be considering adoption. A reminder that we cannot treat that applicant any differently because of her pregnancy, and encouragement to remain flexible, led to our hiring the applicant described in this situation.
>
> Director, HR, Food and Beverage Sector

Questions for Discussion – Problem 6

1. In the scenario Problem 6 lays out, Brazil and Germany emerge as most protective of the woman's choice to work, or, *per contra*, least sensitive to the claim of managerial need; Japan the least protective; and Australia and

the U.S. as straddling a balancing test so long as the employer's policy is not discriminatorily applied. It would seem that in Germany and Brazil your company cannot refuse to hire. But in Japan it could. Would you advise your Japanese office to reject the applicant? What would your advice be in Australia and the U.S.? Why?

2. Even though Brazil and Germany would prohibit a refusal to hire based on pregnancy, the underlying reasons are different. What are the situations in which these underlying differences would result in different treatment of pregnant women in Brazil and Germany? For example, would pregnant women be treated differently in Germany and Brazil if the work is time bound? Are there any other ways in which the underlying rationale in the two countries would produce different outcomes for pregnant women?
3. In thinking about Question 2, above, you might also consider the following from the World Values Survey (2005/6), to be discussed in greater detail in Part VIII (D), infra. Figure III.3 presents the response to the statement "When jobs are scarce, men should have more right to a job than women."

Figure III.3 National preference in job allocation by sex

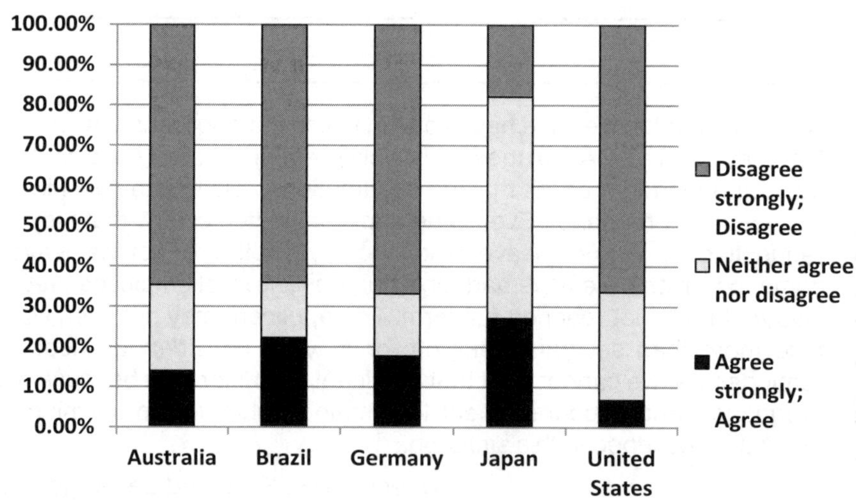

4. All economically advanced democracies struggle with the accommodation of work life and family life. Many countries require paid maternity leave; some extend that benefit to fathers as well. (Federal law in the United States does not require paid leave for child care, nor does it require paid sick leave. A few states, notably California, and some cities have taken steps in this direction. See Mark Schuster, Paul Chung & Katherine

Vestal, *Children with Health Issues*, 21 THE FUTURE OF CHILDREN 91 (2011) (symposium on "Work and Family").) However, the thrust of most of these policies is less an effort to reformulate social norms regarding parenting than to reduce barriers for female entry and participation in the labor market. See generally, LABOUR LAW, WORK, AND FAMILY (Joanne Conaghan & Kerry Rittich eds. 2005). If the International Labor Organization (ILO) wanted to establish an international standard around the rights of pregnant women in the workplace, how would you word the part of such a standard that deals with hiring such that it could be acceptable to policy makers in all five of these countries?

PART IV

PRIVACY, DIGNITY, AND AUTONOMY

Privacy, dignity, and autonomy may be defined differently across cultures and are manifested in the law in ways that reveal deep underlying assumptions about people, work, organizations, and markets. Consequently, multinational managers find them particularly challenging.

"Autonomy" seems pretty clear conceptually: a right of self-determination, a freedom from control by others. As much cannot be said for "privacy" or even "dignity." There is a rich texture of philosophical as well as anthropological and historical discussion of what we conceive of when we speak of "privacy" – and the conceptual wellspring grounding it, human dignity. Some of the historical context is discussed in Matthew Finkin, *Menschenbild*: *The Conception of the Employee as a Person in Western Law*, 23 COMP. LAB. L. & POL'Y J. 577, 590–91 (2002) (references omitted):

> The word "privacy" did not come into common English usage until the 16th century, a time of enormous economic development, domestically and internationally, both commercial and proto-industrial, and of urbanization. The two may not be unrelated. Ferdinand Schoeman has argued that the practice of privacy
>
>> evolves only when there is a high degree of social and economic specialization, when this specialization liberates individuals from dependence on any group, and where social welfare and security come to depend as much on individual intiative as on cultural rigidity.
>
> This has been challenged ... not so much on the historical record, which seems indubitable, as on the conclusion to be drawn to the extent it might discount an innate human need. It is argued, that is, that social structure conditions only the probability of the "emergency of privacy or autonomy as a social norm," not the innateness of the human desire for respect of it.

Along with a great many other nations, the countries under study here all recognize that employees have a right of privacy (and dignity and autonomy) that they can assert against their employers to *some degree* – robustly in Germany (and in Europe more generally), much less so in the United States, and even less in Japan. The above article argues that the U.S. situation can be explained by the conjunction of two circumstances: the lack of a well-developed legal concept – anything like the German concept of *Persönlichkeit*, which will be explored below – and a commitment to the market, to the commodification of labor in which privacy and autonomy (and, perhaps, even dignity) are merely working conditions capable of being bargained away in return for the job. Some see in this an aspect of the common law tradition. As Michael Ford has observed of the United Kingdom:

> To a degree the common law continues to see the labour relationship through... nineteenth century spectacles, with the consequence that management's right, derived from property ownership or the private law of contract, to dictate what happens on its premises or in the course of the labour relationship is not easily reconciled with workers' rights to private spaces at work. Legal recognition of a right to privacy hardly overwrites this doctrine. On one conception of privacy, property rights simply trump privacy rights; on another, privacy rights cannot be waived and are resistant to what is "agreed" in the contract.

Michael Ford, *Two Conceptions of Worker Privacy*, 31 INDUS. L.J. 135, 137–8 (2002) (footnote omitted).

In Japan, the English word "privacy" defied translation – an English borrowing supplies a Japanese neologism – given the strong communal roots of Japanese society in which the various strata of society traditionally possessed obligations, not rights. The transition from a pre-modern to an industrial economy did not radically change this way of thinking. "Japanese corporations," one observer has explained, "are more like communities than a group of individuals bound by contractual relationships." Ikuko Sunaoshi, *The Legal Reformation of Disclosure of Personal Information of Employees or Prospective Employees to Employers or Prospective Employers in Japan*, 21 COMP. LAB. L. & POL'Y J. 745, 746 (2000). As she explains,

> Intracompany personal relations are marked by the socialization that one would find in a community rather than in a contractual relationship. Therefore, the mutual acquisition of personal information is viewed as indispensable to the forging of amicable relationships. Persons who refuse to divulge such information are given negative evaluations. Relationships of trust are often built through frank discussions between managers and their subordinates, which often take place over drinks after working hours. In fact, managers are expected to acquire an intimate knowledge of their subordinates. The absence of respect for employees' personal information reflects this situation.

Id. at 746–7.

We have encountered this aspect of Japanese corporate culture and law in the course of Problem 5, in the fact that a Japanese employer is permitted to screen applicants for creedal and other forms of conformity – including union membership – at the port of entry to the firm, the legal prohibition of discrimination becoming applicable only after the person has been hired.

The problems in this Part probe the culturally freighted question of whether, and the extent to which, a person's autonomy, privacy, and even dignity is subject to exchange. In perhaps no area is the law quite so diverse and so much in the course of change.

References and suggested readings

On Privacy: the literature in philosophy, anthropology, and law is substantial. Some helpful introductory readings include PRIVACY & PERSONALITY (J. Roland Pennock & John W. Chapman eds. 1971); FERDINAND SCHOEMAN, PRIVACY AND SOCIAL FREEDOM (1992); ELIZABETH NEILL, RITES OF PRIVACY AND THE PRIVACY TRADE (2001); DANIEL SOLOVE, UNDERSTANDING PRIVACY (2008); and BEATE RÖSSLER, DER WERT DES PRIVATEN (2001). On the comparative law of privacy some helpful sources are: GLOBAL EMPLOYEE PRIVACY & DATA SECURITY LAW (Miriam Wugmeister & Christine Lyon eds., 2d ed. 2011); REASONABLE EXPECTATIONS OF PRIVACY? ELEVEN COUNTRY REPORTS ON CAMERA SURVEILLANCE AND WORKPLACE PRIVACY (Sjaak Nouwt, Berend de Vries & Corien Prins eds. 2005); COLIN BENNETT & CHARLES RAAB, THE GOVERNANCE OF PRIVACY: POLICY INSTRUMENTS IN GLOBAL PERSPECTIVE (2003).

On Dignity: For an introduction to the debate on whether "dignity" has any meaning *compare* MICHAEL ROSEN, DIGNITY: ITS HISTORY AND MEANING (2012) *with* GEORGE KATEB, HUMAN DIGNITY (2011). *See also* ANDREW SAYER, WHY THINGS MATTER TO PEOPLE Ch. 6 (2011) (from the perspective of social science) and ERIN DALY, DIGNITY RIGHTS (2013) (from the perspective of comparative constitutional law).

A note on the concept of personality

The responses on German law to the problems posed in this Part speak of the infringement or potential infringement of an applicant or an employee's "right of personality." Personality is a literal translation of the German *Persönlichkeit*, and it is customarily translated as such. But there really is no cognate concept in English. The student may get a better, if only, perhaps, an intuitive sense of it by its historical development:

> The standard account given by German historians begins in earnest in the eighteenth century, in the work of moral philosophers building on or resonating against theories of natural law in an effort to develop a conception of the inherent and inalienable attributes of personality; *i.e.*, in the work especially of Donellus (1527–91) and Grotius (1583–1645) in the early modern period, followed by Pufendorf (1632–94), and later by Christian Wolff (1679–1754) ... These many threads came together in the eighteenth century, in a time that has come to be called "The Enlightenment." Christian Wolff's

influence found expression in the Prussian Civil Code, the *Allgemeines Landrecht* (ALR) of 1794. But the most celebrated German *philosophe* of the Enlightenment was Immanuel Kant (1729–1804) whose influence was felt in the Austrian Civil Code, the *Allegemeines Bürcherliches Gesetzbuch* (ABGB) of 1811, especially in Section 16 which provided that, "*Every man has innate rights accorded directly by the enlightened law of reason and is thus to be considered a person.*" [Emphasis added.] However, the ALR was never treated as a definitive source of law and section 16 of the ABGB quickly became a dead letter; what the right to be considered a person meant lay dormant.

By the third quarter of the nineteenth century, a reaction had set in led by Friedrich von Savigny and adherents of the Historical School. Strong efforts were mounted by Otto von Gierke, Karl Gareis, Joseph Kohler, and others to fashion a general right of personality (*allgemeines Persönlichkeitsrecht)*, which, in 1931, H.C. Gutteridge summarized thusly:

> [T]he law must be such as to protect the individual to the fullest extent in the exercise of his faculties in every conceivable direction. The individual is therefore entitled to complain of any unauthorized interference, not merely with his person or his property or his reputation, but also with the social, intellectual and economic activities, opportunities and amenities, which combine to form the sum total of his existence. In short, any willful and unauthorized incursion by others into the private life of an individual is *prima facie* to be regarded as an actionable wrong.

Even as he penned this description, Gutteridge was quick to note that the general right of personality had not been accepted as such by the German courts. As Reinhard Zimmermann has pointed out, given the text and legislative history of the German Civil Code, *Bürgerliches Gesetzbuch* (BGB) of 1900, "recognition of a general right to the protection of a person's individual sphere of life would have constituted an unprecedented and impermissible rebellion against the law." Nevertheless, in Gutteridge's estimation, the force of the theory was by "no means spent"; it "may still exercise a potent influence" in the future.

In the period that followed, 1933–1945, that was not to be… It was in reaction to the Nazi period that the German judiciary created the general right of personality abstracted from the post-war constitution's commitment to Enlightenment values and applied as legal norms that permeate even private contractual relations …

Matthew Finkin, *Some Further Thoughts on the Usefulness of Comparativism in the Law of Employee Privacy*, 14 EMPLOYEE RTS & EMP. POL'Y J. 11, 30–31 (2010) (references omitted).

References and suggested readings

In addition to the sources cited in the above article general legal overviews are supplied by Hans Stoll, *The General Right to Personality in German Law: An Outline of its Development and Present Significance* in PROTECTING PRIVACY Ch. 2 (Basil Markesenis ed. 1999) and, in comparative context, John Neethling, *Personality Rights* in ELGAR ENCYCLOPEDIA OF COMPARATIVE LAW Ch. 53 (Jan Smits ed., 2d ed. 2012).

PROBLEM 7: BACKGROUND CHECKS

May an employer require as a condition of application for a job that the employee consent to a background check for criminal records?

Problem 7 discussion – Australia

Criminal record checks are not as common in Australia as in the US, but their use has increased in recent years. Naylor et al. (see below) report a sevenfold increase in requests to the Australian Federal Police between 1997 and 2007.

There is no general legislation or common law principle in Australia that would restrict an employer from conducting a background check, or indeed requiring a job applicant's consent to such a check. However in four jurisdictions there are laws that expressly restrict the use to which such information may be put. Tasmania and the Northern Territory both prohibit discrimination on the basis of an "irrelevant" criminal record: Anti-Discrimination Act 1998 (Tas) s 16(q); Anti-Discrimination Act 1992 (NT) s 19(q). A record is deemed to be irrelevant when it does not show a conviction, or where the conviction has been overturned or is now considered "spent", or where it is "not directly relevant to the situation in which the discrimination arises". Western Australia and the Australian Capital Territory simply prohibit discrimination on the basis of a spent conviction: Spent Convictions Act 1988 (WA) s 18; Discrimination Act 1991 (ACT) s 7(1)(o). Most other jurisdictions, while not specifically prohibiting such discrimination, do restrict access to information about spent convictions and stipulate that the persons concerned may legitimately refuse to mention them if asked about any criminal record: see e.g. Spent Convictions Act 2009 (SA).

There is also the possibility in all jurisdictions that a job applicant of Aboriginal background might complain that a compulsory criminal records check amounted to indirect discrimination on the ground of race. This is because, as Naylor et al. note in the article referred to below, indigenous Australians are disproportionately represented amongst those who have been convicted of criminal offences.

References and suggested readings

Bronwyn Naylor, Moira Paterson & Marilyn Pittard, *In the Shadow of a Criminal Record: Proposing a Just Model of Criminal Record Employment Checks*, 32 MELB. U.L.R. 171 (2008) (providing a detailed account of the law).

NEIL REES, KATHERINE LINDSAY & SIMON RICE, AUSTRALIAN ANTI-DISCRIMINATION LAW: TEXT, CASE AND MATERIALS 359–61 (2008).

Problem 7 discussion – Brazil

Due to the development of information technologies, background check can be easily done. As a matter of fact, many proclaim that privacy is dead and no one is exempt from seeing their private life disclosed through a simple keyboard touch. Information disclosed through participation on social networks on the web is available to each and every one. As it is clear that personal data cannot be used to discriminate in the hiring process (and throughout the course of the work relationship), the problem lies thus in the use made by employers of such information. Do they use it to avoid the hiring of previously convicted candidates? Do they use it to better place or to define job suitability for possible candidates? Do they ask for it due to legal obligation or voluntarily?

When examined by the *Tribunal Superior do Trabalho*, the demand for background checks has been subject to very different rulings depending on the case circumstances and on the chamber deciding on the matter. For instance, the Fifth Chamber has decided that these demands were to be considered an offense to the human dignity principle and should necessarily be perceived as grounds for a discriminatory action (TST-RR-98.912/2004–014–09–40.3). The Sixth Chamber has however decided that it does not constitute unlawful conduct, when the background check is required by law, such as is the case for private security services (TST-RR-1557/2004–020–05–00.7). The Fourth Chamber, on the other hand, has decided that a background check for criminal records is constitutionally guaranteed by the right of petition and may legally be conducted by any employer as long as it does not constitute the basis for a discriminatory practice, but may not be conducted by a third party hired by the employer as this would constitute a violation of privacy rights (TST-RR-98903/2005–014–09–00.9).

As one may perceive from the rulings mentioned above, employee consent, whether written or not, does not seem to be an issue in the matter. The problem presents thus two facets: (a) the employer's capacity to act unilaterally, and (b) the use of a third party to conduct the background check. As for the former, two possibilities may be foreseen: (a.1) the background check is an employer's option, or (a.2) is required by law. Despite the strictest rulings from the *Tribunal Superior do Trabalho*, the second scenario does not seem unlawful. As for the first scenario, eventual unlawful conduct may derive from the use of the information – especially if it is a discriminatory one – and not necessarily from the background check itself. As for the latter, problems may relate to the use of protected data and privacy rights.

Actually, in the Brazilian context the major problem related to background check does not concern criminal records, but deals with the background check on labor litigation. In fact, as the ensemble of Brazilian Labor Jurisdictions' examinations since 1994 represents a caseload of more than two million suits every year, some employers started to demand a certificate proving that employees' candidates did not have a previous history of litigation. As a consequence, employees who used to litigate over their previous labor contracts ended up with fewer work opportunities. Background checks are used here as a means to prevent future litigation. Courts have addressed the issue, indicating such conduct is discriminatory and in order to avoid such conduct, some courts have eliminated the possibility of doing a suit follow-up on their website through employees' names.

References and suggested readings

BRASIL, TRIBUNAL SUPERIOR DO TRABALHO, RR-98.912/2004–014–09–40.3, *accessed at* http://brs02.tst.jus.br/cgi-bin/nph-brs?s1=4318160.nia.&u=/Brs/it01.html&p=1&l=1&d=blnk&f=g&r=1 (last visited Feb. 17, 2010).

BRASIL, TRIBUNAL SUPERIOR DO TRABALHO, RR-1.557/2004–020–05–00.7, *accessed at* http://brs02.tst.jus.br/cgi-bin/nph-brs?s1=4760771.nia.&u=/Brs/it01.html&p=1&l=1&d=blnk&f=g&r=1 and http://brs02.tst.jus.br/cgi-bin/nph-brs?s1=4849549.nia.&u=/Brs/it01.html&p=1&l=1&d=blnk&f=g&r=1 (last visited Feb. 17, 2010).

BRASIL, TRIBUNAL SUPERIOR DO TRABALHO, RR-98.903/2005–014–09–00.9, *accessed at* http://brs02.tst.jus.br/cgi-bin/nph-brs?s1=4419865.nia.&u=/Brs/it01.html&p=1&l=1&d=blnk&f=g&r=1 (last visited Feb. 17, 2010).

On Brazilian labor caseload, see BRASIL, TRIBUNAL SUPERIOR DO TRABALHO, *Movimentação processual por ano (desde 1941), accessed at* http:// www. tst.jus.br/mov-procesual/justica-do-trabalho (last visited Oct. 2, 2012).

Problem 7 discussion – Germany

As in the United States, German employers are often interested in gathering as much information as possible about the job applicant's potential criminal record. From the German perspective two main questions arise in this context:

(1) If the employer asks a job applicant about his criminal record during the job interview, does the applicant have a right to lie in order not to worsen his chances of being hired?
(2) May the employer ask a former employer of the job applicant about his or her criminal record?

Question 1 In order to protect the applicant's right of personality an employer may ask him questions only if he has a legitimate interest that outweighs the employee's personality rights. The German labor courts have developed a catalogue of questions that are unlawful; some of these questions are unlawful in general, in particular questions about private matters (e.g. about the applicant's family background or plans to marry), whereas the lawfulness of other questions depends upon the specific situation. If the question is unlawful, the applicant has not only the right to refuse the answer, but also the "right to lie". This is based on the idea that otherwise the applicant would either be "forced" to disclose information he would like to keep confidential or would run the risk of not being hired because he refused to answer a question the employer might deem important for the hiring decision. If the employee responds to an unlawful question with a lie, the employer can't void the employment contract. But, if the employee unlawfully lies in response to a legitimate question, the employer may later void the contract and, in some situations, even claim damages.

In order to protect the applicant's right of personality he may lie to an employer's question about his criminal record if one or both of the two following requirements are fulfilled: (a) The previous conviction was deleted in the "Federal Central Register of previous convictions" (*Bundeszentralregister*) that records all criminal acts, but only for a limited period of time, depending on the sentence. (b) The previous conviction was based on a type of crime that has no relationship to the job he is seeking. Therefore, an applicant for a position as cashier must not lie in response to a question regarding previous offences against property, whereas he may lie in respect to a conviction for driving under the influence of alcohol. Vice versa, an applicant for a position as a chauffeur has to tell the truth about an earlier conviction for drink driving, but has no duty to disclose that he was once convicted of stealing from a supermarket.

Question 2 In an early case the German Federal Labor Court (*Bundesarbeitsgericht*) decided that the employer may ask a former employer about the applicant even without the latter's consent (BAG 18. 12. 1984 NJW 1986, 341 et seq.). However, it is doubtful that the court would decide the same way today, as since 1984 the German data privacy laws were changed significantly. The disclosure of private information is legal only if this is either allowed by statutory law (which is not the case in the present context) or if the applicant has consented in advance. The employer may require the applicant's consent only if a direct question about the applicant's criminal record is legal. Therefore, the same rules apply as those laid down above.

References and suggested readings

BAG Nov. 10, 1995 NEUE ZEITSCHRIFT FüR ARBEITSRECHT (NZA) 371 (1996); HOHENSTATT & STAMER, *Background Checks von Bewerbers in Deutschland: Was ist erlaubt?* NEUE ZEITSCHRIFT FüR ARBEITSRECHT (NZA) 1065 (2006); WISSKIRCHEN & BISSELS, Das Fragerecht des Arbeitsgebers bei Einstellung unter Berücksichtigung des AGG, NEUE ZEITSCHRIFT FüR ARBEITSRECHT (NZA) 169 (2007); THÜSING/LAMBRICH, *Das Fragerecht des Arbeitgebers – aktuelle Probleme zu einem klassischen Thema*, Betriebs-Berater (BB) 1146 (2002); STAUDINGER, RICHARDI & FISCHINGER, BÜRGERLICHES GESETZBUCH, § 611 BGB, Rn. 190 et seq.

Problem 7 discussion – Japan

Japan does not have specific statutory regulations on collecting details of an applicant's criminal record and case law admits employers' freedom to investigate applicants' personality, including belief and creed. According to the current case law, it seems that the employer is allowed to request that applicants submit information on criminal records, and also to consent to background check for criminal records. Such respect for the employer's freedom of hiring relates to the Japanese long-term employment system.

First, the prevalence of the long-term employment relationship under which the employer's right to dismiss is significantly restricted because of the courts' severe scrutiny of the abusive exercise of rights and the correspondingly high level of security regular workers enjoy, has made employers cautious in selecting job seekers not only as to whether the person can provide normal service but also as to whether he/she is suitable to continue in a long-term relationship as a member of the corporate community until mandatory retirement age. Such considerations led the Supreme Court decision on the *Mitsubishi Jushi* case (Supreme Court, Grand Bench (Dec. 12, 1973), 27 *Minshu* 1536) to interpret the employer's wide freedom of hiring to include a refusal to hire based upon thoughts and creed, and also a wide freedom to investigate the individual's beliefs and creed. In the *Mitsubishi Jushi* case, the employer refused to hire a person as a regular worker upon completion of the probationary period on the grounds that he made a false statement with regard to his experience of political activities on his personal statement which was submitted to the company at the time of the recruiting examination, and that the making of the false statement itself disqualified him as a managerial candidate.

The court faced the question as to whether the company's refusal runs counter to the Constitutional provisions of equality under the law (Constitution Art. 14) and freedom of thought and conscience (Constitution Art. 19), as well as the prohibition on discrimination in working conditions on account of creed under the Labor Standards Act (LSA Art. 3). The Supreme Court held that the human rights provisions of the Constitution do not apply directly to relations between private individuals and that Article 3 of the Labor Standards Act refers to post-hiring working conditions but does not regulate hiring itself. Emphasizing that the Constitution guarantees companies' freedom to do business and to execute contracts guaranteed by Articles 22 and 29 of the Constitution, the Supreme Court ruled that even if a company refused to employ a person with a certain belief or creed on account of such characteristics, the failure to hire cannot automatically be condemned as illegal.

In connection with the freedom of hiring, this case raised the question of whether a company was permitted to investigate an applicant's beliefs or creed in the hiring process. The Supreme Court held the view that it was not illegal to do so because even actual refusal to hire on account of beliefs or creed was itself not unlawful.

In light of the Supreme Court ruling in the *Mitsubishi Jushi* case stressing that "employment relations in a company … call for mutual trust in the context of a continuous human relationship, and it is all the more so in a society like Japan where lifetime employment is an established fact of life …," long-term employment practices seem to influence the Court's interpretation of the employer's freedom to hire. Under the long-term employment practices, a regular worker, once employed, cannot be dismissed without a compelling reason, such as serious misconduct. Therefore, the Court perhaps thought employers should be free to investigate a candidate's personality *before* concluding a regular employment contract, so as to ascertain whether they could start such long-term relations.

Faced with information technology developments and abusive handling of personal data, it was thought necessary to establish rules concerning the proper handling of personal information. At the same time, it was recognized that there was a need to make domestic regulations on data handling compatible with international norms. In particular, the EU directive on personal data which restricts transfer of personal data to a third country where personal data protection is not sufficient had a big impact. Thus, the 2003 Personal Information Protection Act (PIPA) was enacted as the first legislation that provides comprehensive personal information protection, including in the private sector. Corresponding to the eight principles (collection limitation, data quality, purpose specification, use limitation, security safeguards, openness, individual participation, and accountability) of the 1985 OECD guidelines, the PIPA introduces various regulations for the proper treatment of personal information.

Although the Act does not specifically aim to regulate employment relations, corporations which process workers' personal data such as name and birth date which can identify individuals, and which use the personal data for business purposes, including personnel management within the corporation, are subject to the PIPA regulations when the number of personal data records is more than 5,000. Therefore large corporations are required to abide by the PIPA regulations such as use limitation (Art. 16), notice of the purpose for collecting information (Art. 18), safe administration measures (Art. 20), transfer limitation to third parties (Art. 23), disclosure to the principal (Art. 25), correction (Art. 26) and suspension of data use (Art. 27), etc.

Thus, in larger companies, those with more than 5,000 employees, applicants must be informed of the purpose for collecting criminal records and the collected criminal records must be treated properly. However, collecting criminal records itself is not regulated.

As to the collection of personal information in employment relations, the Ministry of Labor publicized the Code of Practice of Workers' Personal Data Protection (CPWPDP) in 2000. Among other things, the CPWPDP establishes rules concerning the collection of personal data: namely, personal data should in principle be collected directly from the person himself. Data collected exceeding the collection purpose must not be used. The CPWPDP also prohibits the collection of certain categories of data: (1) information related to race, ethnicity, social status, family origin, legal domicile, and birthplace, as well as thought, creed and belief; (2) union membership or information on union activities; and (3) medical personal data. Criminal records are not listed here. Furthermore, the CPWPDP is not legally binding but encourages employers to establish rules concerning workers' personal data protection modeled on the CPWPDP.

In sum, Japanese employers enjoy wide freedom to collect information about applicants and no statutory regulations exist on collecting applicants' criminal records except for informing applicants' regarding the purpose of collection. Thus Problem 6 is answered in the affirmative in Japan.

PRIMARY SOURCES

Constitution

Article 14:

All of the people are equal under the law and there shall be no discrimination in political, economic or social relations because of race creed, sex, social status or family origin.

Article 19:

Freedom of thought and conscience shall not be violated.

Labor Standards Act

Article 3:

An employer shall not engage in discriminatory treatment with respect to wages, working hours or other working conditions by reason of the nationality, creed or social status of any worker.

References and suggested readings

Takashi Araki, *Personal Information and Privacy Protection of Employees and Japan's Employment System*, 8 JOURNAL OF THE JAPAN-NETHERLANDS INSTITUTE 167 (2005).

Problem 7 discussion – United States

The growth of inexpensive information technology has made the conduct of background checks on applicants widespread in the United States – almost ubiquitous. A major area of such checking is an applicant's criminal history. In fact, for some jobs a criminal background check is a statutory requirement. The status of criminal records is governed by a complex legal fabric primarily of state law. The complexity is compounded by the fact that the term "criminal records" sweeps in an enormous amount of information, including arrests, offense reports, indictments, convictions, deferred prosecutions, deferred sentences, postconviction information, and expungement provisions, for each of which category separate treatment may be accorded by law or administrative regulation.

Three questions arise in this context: whether the company must secure the consent of the applicant to conduct a criminal background check; whether release of the information to the company is constrained by such a requirement; and, implicitly, what use may be made of the information.

On the first, if the prospective employer uses a company that provides such services to conduct the check (a "consumer reporting agency" in the terminology of the federal Fair Credit Reporting Act (FCRA)), a strict set of obligations applies, including requiring the written consent of the applicant. However, the FCRA does not apply to checks run by the prospective employer's own employees. Some states, notably California, have extended the requirement of written consent to employer-conducted background checks, however.

On the second, many states require criminal record checks for certain specified employments. Some require the written consent of the person concerned to allow disclosure of the record, place a limit on the timeliness of the information to be released, restrict information as to exonerated persons or expunged or sealed records, or forbid disclosure of arrest records. A few states require notice to the subject of the inquiry that his or her criminal records have been supplied and limit the jobs for which those records can be requested. Under the FCRA, a conviction that is more than seven years old may not be reported to the credit reporting agency unless the job involved pays $75,000 per annum or more.

On the third, a few states have legislated with respect to an employer's use of criminal records in the hiring process, for example, to forbid a refusal to hire for an employee's failure to provide information regarding an arrest not resulting in conviction or, a more broadly, to forbid discrimination in employment on grounds of prior convictions unrelated to the position.

The use of criminal records is also regulated, if indirectly, by federal anti-discrimination in employment law to the extent such reliance has a statistically disproportionate impact on a statutorily protected class, commonly on the grounds of race or national origin, subject to a defense of legitimate business necessity. Where that impact can be shown regarding *arrest* records it is virtually impossible for the employer to make out a satisfactory defense of "business necessity." The law is more nuanced concerning the use of criminal *convictions*, however. This has been the subject of recent review by the Equal Employment Opportunity Commission, Enforcement Guidance No. 915.002 (April 25, 2012).

It should be noted that the law seems to work at cross-purposes: on the one hand, federal (and cognate state) antidiscrimination policies tend to discourage reliance on criminal records in the hiring process: arrest records almost completely and conviction records on an individualized basis. (And a few states encourage rehabilitation by making reliance on a conviction unrelated to the job specifically forbidden as, for example, does New York.) On the other hand, the law of negligent hiring, which imposes liability on an employer for hiring a person whom the employer should have known to have had certain propensities, especially for violence, encourages examination of criminal histories as at least a defensive measure to reduce the risk of liability. Inasmuch as the United States currently incarcerates about 1.4 percent of the labor market – at about 1.8 million inmates – the number of people whose future employability is potentially affected by their criminal histories is not inconsequential.

References and suggested readings

The summary provided above is taken from MATTHEW FINKIN, PRIVACY IN EMPLOYMENT LAW Ch. 5 (9th ed.) (in press), where the legal references are supplied.

Dealing with the larger context see David Solove & Chris Jay Hoofnagle, *A Model Regime of Privacy Protection*, 2006 ILL. L. REV. 357 (especially at 357–76 on background checks) and Maurice Ensellem & Debbie Mickamal, *The New Challenge of Employment in the Area of Criminal Background Checks*, *in* THE GLOVES-OFF ECONOMY Ch. 8 (Annette Bernhardt et al. eds., 2008).

The question for me as a CHRO is what should a multinational company (MNC) policy be on [the issue of criminal background checks] given the laws of countries may differ. In 2002, I faced this issue, and my company was located in seven European countries, including Germany. We made the decision to implement criminal background checks in all seven countries, and did so successfully. Here is how we did it:

(1) We believed we had an obligation to our shareholders to protect our assets, and employees. Therefore, even if our policy possibly would not stand up in a court, we were willing to take a chance.
(2) We had a narrow focus on our background checks. We had a lot of financial positions, and we had a lot of women working for us. Thus, we were most concerned about financial crimes and crimes against women. We were not interested in other convictions like drunk driving or bankruptcy (we were interested, but the lawyers made us have a narrow focus).
(3) We were able to negotiate background checks with the German works council at our location. They were very receptive to accepting this policy as long as we did not have a policy for existing employees. They

were sensitive to our issues in the recruitment stage and our wanting to avoid future problems with a new hire. Maybe we got lucky with our specific works council leader.

(4) In Europe our recruiters went out of their way to tell applicants about our background checks early in the process so that they would more likely drop out and we did not waste each other's time.

(5) We did have time limits in certain countries and they varied based on a country's law. Thus, we would not use a conviction against someone 20 years earlier and they had a clean record since.

In sum: we had a narrowly focused background check policy in all seven countries, and were willing to take on a challenge to the policy in court because we felt it was important to protect our shareholder and employees. We were not interested in implementing a blanket criminal background policy like we had in the USA where any conviction could result in turning away an applicant because we knew we would have serious legal issues with it in Europe.

Senior Vice President, HR, Information Technology Sector

Questions for Discussion – Problem 7

1. Ikuko Sunaoshi's article cited in the introduction to this part points out that case law in Japan has been concerned with the termination of an employee whose criminal record is learned of only after he or she has been hired. In anticipation of Part V, infra, the student may well consider whether an employee who (a) lied in response to a question about his or her criminal record or (b) failed to volunteer that information should be dismissed. (In Germany and Japan, if there is no connection between the criminal conduct and the job, a dismissal – in Japan, in the second scenario (b) – would be wrongful.) If a dismissal would be lawful on the ground alone of a want of truthfulness – or forthcomingness – where there is no connection between the criminal conduct and the incumbent's ability to perform, would you dismiss? If your decision would depend on the circumstances, what would these be?

2. In Australia and the U.S. – and, possibly, Brazil – the law is concerned that systematic encounters with the criminal justice system by members of a protected class, that is, on grounds of race or ethnicity, might have negative consequences for the individual class member. German law is so

tailored that this need not be a concern. But Japanese law seems to be unconcerned with the issue. From what you have read, why would that be so of Japan?

PROBLEM 8: VIDEO CAMERAS AND MONITORING IN THE WORKPLACE

May the company do any of the following:

1. install video cameras openly to monitor the parking lot;
2. install a hidden video camera in the ceiling above an employee's desk when the employee is suspected of theft, to see if she is stealing;
3. install a biomonitoring system, i.e. handprint identification, to record entrance and exit from the facility;
4. retrieve and read an employee's email stored in the employer's system;
5. require random testing for controlled substances, especially marijuana and cocaine;
6. require employees to provide the company with access to their social network websites?

Problem 8 discussion – Australia

Surveillance

There is no general law dealing with workplace privacy in Australia. There is a federal Privacy Act 1988, which applies to businesses dealing with health information or distributing personal information for gain, and to all other businesses that turn over at least A$3 million each year. But it is primarily concerned with the procedures for dealing with personal information that an organisation has collected, rather than the methods used for obtaining that information. Furthermore, there is currently an exemption for any act or practice directly related to an "employee record".

Each State and Territory has its own laws dealing with surveillance. Those laws are capable of applying to employers otherwise subject to the Fair Work Act 2009: see s 27(2)(m). There are only two jurisdictions with comprehensive statutes on surveillance. New South Wales, Australia's most populous State, has the Workplace Surveillance Act 2005 (NSW); while there is also now a Workplace Privacy Act 2011 in the Australian Capital Territory (ACT). The first, third and fourth forms of surveillance listed in the problem would be lawful under these Acts, provided the workforce was given written notice in advance. The covert surveillance of the suspected employee would require special permission from a magistrate.

In Victoria, Part 2A of the Surveillance Devices Act 1999 (Vic) also deals with workplace surveillance, but only to the extent of restricting surveillance of private areas such as bathrooms or change rooms. Hence outside New South Wales and the ACT, there would be no statutory constraints on the forms of surveillance listed in the problem. (There has been some suggestion that the federal Telecommunications (Interception and Access) Act 1979 applies to employer monitoring of emails, but this does not appear to have been tested in litigation.)

Assuming that the question of surveillance is not dealt with in an enterprise agreement at the relevant workplace, that leaves the common law. There has been some suggestion of the development of a tort of invasion of privacy in Australia, but recent court decisions have cast doubt on this development: see for example *Giller v Procopets* (2008) 79 IPR 489.

More generally, it has been suggested that employers are under an implied duty not to damage or destroy the element of "trust and confidence" in the employment relationship. This is now firmly accepted by the British courts, where it is often now described as a duty of good faith and fair dealing. Such a duty might well have something to say about permissible forms of surveillance – especially covert surveillance. But while there are Australian judgments that support the existence of the duty (see e.g. *Barker v Commonwealth Bank of Australia* [2012] FCA 942), other decisions have either rejected the idea, or questioned whether there is scope to imply such a term in an employment relationship already regulated (as many are) by awards and/or enterprise agreements: see e.g. *Dye v Commonwealth Securities Ltd* [2012]; *South Australia v McDonald* (2009) 104 SASR 344.

Random drug testing

It is unclear whether employees have an implied duty to submit to testing. Whether a direction to do so would be regarded as lawful and reasonable, in the absence of any express obligation, might well depend on the nature of the employment: see *Anderson v Sullivan* (1997) 78 FCR 380, where it was held that a federal police officer suspected of having consumed drugs could be required to provide a urine sample. It would also be relevant to consider whether the employer could justify the testing by reference to its occupational health and safety obligations. One way to avoid such issues is to seek to introduce testing arrangements by agreement. In practice, it is common for this to be the subject of negotiation (and indeed disputation) in unionised workplaces: see e.g.

Endeavour Energy v Communications, Electrical, Electronics, Energy Information, Postal Plumbing and Allied Services Union of Australia, NSW Divisional Branch [2012] FWAFB 4998.

Directing employees to provide access to social networking sites

As a matter of common law, employees are under an implied contractual obligation to comply with any "lawful and reasonable" directions from their employer: *R v Darling Island Stevedore & Lighterage Co Ltd; Ex p Halliday and Sullivan* (1938) 60 CLR 601 at 621–2. The question is how far an employer's authority can legitimately extend into an employee's private life.

In a much-quoted judgment in *Rose v Telstra Corp Ltd* (1998) 45 AILR ¶3–966, then Vice-President Ross of the Australian Industrial Relations Commission suggested that an employer may seek to control or regulate "out of hours conduct" only when the conduct is likely to cause serious damage to the employment relationship or the employer's interests, or is incompatible with the employee's performance of their duties. Likewise, in *McManus v Scott-Charlton* (1996) 70 FCR 16 at 28, Finn J referred to conduct that "can be shown to have significant and adverse effects in the workplace – because of its impact on workplace relations, on the productivity of others, or on the effective conduct of the employer's business".

From that perspective, it is unlikely that an instruction to be given access to an employee's social networking sites would be considered lawful, unless (for example) there was evidence to suggest that the employee was using those sites to harass a co-worker or to vilify the employer. Defamatory or threatening posts have been found to provide valid grounds for dismissal: see e.g. *Dover-Ray v Real Insurance Pty Ltd* [2010] FWA 8544; *O'Keefe v Williams Muir's Pty Ltd* [2011] FWA 5311. But mere "grumbling" about work or management may not be something that the employer can legitimately seek to control, even if the employee uses strong or offensive language: see e.g. *Linfox Australia Pty Ltd v Stutsel* [2012] FWAFB 7097.

An employee dismissed for failing to comply with an unlawful instruction would have good prospects of success in an action for wrongful or unfair dismissal.

On the other hand, it is possible that an employer might legitimately stipulate that an employee may only use the employer's equipment to gain access to social networking sites at work (e.g. during breaks), if the employee agrees to the employer having similar access.

References and suggested readings

P.J. Holland, A.M.D. Pyman & J. Teicher, *Negotiating the Contested Terrain of Drug Testing in the Australian Workplace*, 47 J. INDUS. REL. 326 (2005).

ANDREW STEWART, STEWART'S GUIDE TO EMPLOYMENT LAW §§ 12.6; 12.13; 13.24–5; 13.27 (4th ed. 2013) (excerpt follows).

12.6 Behaviour away from work

There are circumstances in which behaviour outside the workplace can breach an employment contract. Some contracts – for example, in professional sports – expressly impose restrictions on an employee's private conduct. But even in the absence of such a provision, misconduct away from work can be treated as a breach of duty, provided it has a sufficient connection to the employment. Examples have included:

- assaulting a foreman at a hotel where workers gathered to drink after work – *Re Transfield* (1974);
- a bank worker being found guilty of credit card fraud – *Hussein v Westpac* (1995);
- an academic having a sexual relationship with a student – *Orr v University of Tasmania* (1957);
- a manager allegedly sexually assaulting a more junior employee, while socialising after a training course – *Civil Service Association of WA v Director General* (2002);
- an employee having an affair with his employer's wife, as revenge for what the employee believed to have been a previous affair with his own wife – *Wall v Westcott* (1982);
- an employee of a company publicly committed to the promotion of "responsible drinking" being caught drink driving – *Kolodjashnij v Lion Nathan* (2010).

In each of these cases, the conduct either called into question the employee's fitness to perform their duties, or was capable of harming the reputation or efficient management of the employer's business or organisation.

By contrast, in *Rose v Telstra* (1998) it was held that an employee could not be dismissed for assaulting a colleague during a fight after work. The person assaulted here was not a supervisor and the incident was not considered to affect the employer in any way. In *Moreton Bay College v Teys* (2008), a school principal's clandestine affair with the mother of a pupil was likewise regarded as having no bearing on the performance of his duties.

In *Streeter v Telstra* (2008), an employee was sacked following an incident in which she offended a co-worker by her conduct following an after-work function. What was found to warrant her dismissal was not the incident itself, but her lack of honesty when questioned about it. It was considered that, in light of the co-worker's complaint, management had a legitimate interest in seeking an explanation from her – even though the activities concerned were conceded to be of an 'inherently personal nature'.

One issue currently generating a deal of discussion, not to mention litigation, is the extent to which an employer can legitimately control or sanction postings by workers on social networking sites such as Facebook or Twitter. These allow what may be thought to be private observations to be disseminated (sometimes inadvertently) to a wide audience.

In *Dover-Ray v Real Insurance* (2010), an employee used a MySpace blog to accuse her employer of bias and corruption after management rejected her complaint of sexual harassment by a co-worker. Although the posting was limited to her "friends", they included work colleagues. That fact, together with the damage her allegations might cause to the company, was sufficient to create a valid reason for her dismissal. It was also relevant that she had not made the comments in the heat of the moment and then deleted them, but left them up on the site for several weeks despite requests to remove them. By contrast in *Fitzgerald v Smith* (2010) a "grumble" about an employee's treatment posted on Facebook was not regarded as sufficiently serious to warrant dismissal. The comments did not identify the employer, who in any event did not react at the time but only raised the issue with the employee after her dismissal. Clearly, however, employees need to take care in what they say on such sites.

. . .

12.13 Testing and surveillance

In some instances, employers may wish to test employees for drug or alcohol use. This tends to be a contentious issue, especially if the testing is to be conducted randomly, or the method of testing is invasive: see eg *Shell Refining v CFMEU* (2009). From a legal perspective, it is unclear whether an employee has an implied duty to submit to testing. Whether a direction to do so would be regarded as lawful and reasonable, in the absence of any express obligation, might well depend on the nature of the employment: see *Anderson v Sullivan* (1997). It would also be relevant to consider whether the employer could justify the testing by reference to its occupational health and safety obligations. One way to avoid such issues is to seek to introduce testing arrangements by agreement: see eg *Caltex v Australian Institute of Marine and Power Engineers* (2009). Alternatively, an employer may incorporate a requirement to comply with testing procedures into the express terms of an employment contract.

Any test results obtained by an employer will generally need to be kept confidential. They may also be subject to the requirements of privacy legislation. Those issues, together with the legality of workplace surveillance, are considered separately in the next chapter.

As for the use of polygraph testing, it is banned outright in New South Wales: see *Lie Detectors Act* 1983. In other States, whether an employee suspected of wrongdoing could be required to submit to such testing might again depend on a court's view of their contractual obligations.

. . .

Confidentiality and Privacy: The Employer's Obligations

13.24 Common law duties

An employer may be bound by a duty of confidence, as much as an employee: see eg *Prout v British Gas* (1992). This will most obviously apply in relation to any personal information about an employee that may come into the employer's possession. That may happen, for example, through medical assessments, or any screening of e-mails or internet usage at work. At common law, a duty of confidence may arise in relation to information that is "improperly or surreptitiously acquired", as much as information that is voluntarily disclosed: *ABC v Lenah Game Meats* (2001) at 224, 271–2, 289.

It is possible too that any misuse of such information, such as supplying contact details to a telemarketer, would also be a breach of the implied duty of fair and reasonable treatment discussed in Chapter 12. The same could be said of various forms of covert surveillance of workers, except where this is done in accordance with the legislation outlined below.

It is even possible that the Australian common law might recognise a tort of invasion of privacy. The possibility of such a development was left open by the High Court in *ABC v Lenah Game Meats*. In the wake of that decision, some lower courts have been prepared to impose liability for unreasonable intrusions into a person's privacy: see eg *Doe v ABC* (2007). But higher courts have either rejected the idea, or at least cast doubt on the need for such a tort: see eg *Kalaba v Commonwealth* (2004); *Giller v Procopets* (2008).

13.25 The Privacy Act

The federal *Privacy Act* 1988 requires organisations to observe certain privacy principles when collecting, storing and using "personal information" – that is, information or opinions about a named or identifiable person. Among other things, individuals must be given a reasonable opportunity to access and correct information about them, subject to certain exceptions. There are also special provisions in relation to "sensitive" information. This includes information as to a person's race, their political, religious or philosophical beliefs, their sexual preference, any criminal record they may have, and their health. The Act applies to the Commonwealth public sector, to businesses dealing with health information or distributing personal information for gain, and to all other businesses that turn over at least $3 million each year.

Importantly, there is an exemption for any act or practice that is "directly related" to an employee record. An "employee record" is defined for this purpose to mean "a record of personal information relating to the employment of the employee". It includes information about the employee's health, the terms of their employment, their training, and the termination of their employment. The exemption does not, however, apply to information about contractors or unsuccessful job applicants. Nor can it protect an employer who does something that is not directly related to the employment relationship, even if the information concerned is contained in an employment record: see eg *C v Commonwealth Agency* (2005).

Where a person can identify a breach of the Act's requirements, they can lodge a complaint with the Privacy Commissioner (who since November 2010 has operated as part of the new Office of the Australian Information Commissioner). The Commissioner has the power either to issue a restraining order or to award compensation to the complainant. In practice, such complaints are often resolved by conciliation: see eg *T v Commonwealth Agency* (2009). But any orders made can be enforced in the Federal Court or Federal Magistrates Court. Alternatively, those courts can be approached directly to grant an injunction restraining a breach of the Act: see eg *Yousif v Commonwealth Bank* (2010). An employee may also seek to rely on a breach of the Act to establish the unlawfulness of a direction or practice that intrudes into their personal life: see eg *Griffiths v Rose* (2011), although in that case it was found not to be inconsistent with the Act to monitor the use of an employer-supplied laptop, where the employee had been warned this could happen.

In 2008, the Australian Law Reform Commission has recently completed a review of the Privacy Act. Its recommendations include that the legislation be made national in operation, apply to businesses of all size, and contain stronger penalties for non-compliance. The Commission has also proposed that the employee records exemption be abolished, with protection only for confidential "evaluative material", such as references. However, the federal government has not yet announced any response (whether positive or negative) to any of these particular proposals.

. . .

13.27 Workplace surveillance: statutory controls

The extent to which employers may conduct surveillance of employees at work differs widely around Australia. It is a matter that is generally left to State or Territory laws, which can validly apply to national system employers: see FW Act 2009 s 27(2)(m).

There are restrictions in all jurisdictions on the use of "listening devices" to monitor or record private conversations without consent: see eg *Listening and Surveillance Devices Act* 1972 (SA). But these do not cover other possible forms of private surveillance in the workplace, including the use of video cameras with no microphone or the sound turned off.

New South Wales is the only State to have comprehensive legislation on the subject. The *Workplace Surveillance Act* 2005 regulates surveillance by video cameras, through computers, and also by the use of tracking devices. It requires employees to be notified of any of these forms of surveillance, except where covert surveillance is authorised by a magistrate for the purpose of determining any involvement in unlawful activities. There are outright prohibitions on surveillance of change rooms or bathrooms, as well as any surveillance of employees while away from work. There are also limitations on the extent to which employers can block e-mails or internet access.

In Victoria, Part 2A of the *Surveillance Devices Act* 1999 also deals with workplace surveillance, but only to the extent of restricting surveillance of private areas such as bathrooms or change rooms.

Problem 8 discussion – Brazil

Brazilian legislation dealing with the impact of new technologies in the workplace has in the past focused on its overall impact on employment. On the whole, one may say that jobs were to be protected from technology. Questions of privacy, especially regarding individual labor contracts, were not (and still are not) a part of the legislative agenda. Yet, as new technologies are redesigning most work processes, problems come up and eventually end up in the labor courts. However, as they have concerned mostly individual and isolated cases, the caseload is still sparse and extremely fragmented. As for employers, even if they are cautious in their actions, they have up to now enjoyed a lot of latitude, with the most important barrier being the constitutional rights of privacy. Once one puts all these ingredients together, this is the resulting framework: lack of legislation, scarce jurisprudence and lots of latitude for employers' actions which may eventually be restrained by a diffuse constitutional right of privacy. Now, each of the six itemized problem possibilities may be examined.

Open video surveillance

Nowadays, cameras are everywhere. They have invaded public areas and can be found on streets and roads, parking lots, elevators, buses, private clubs, and many working spaces. Yet, they have not been the object of legal regulation. There is no doubt that a company may install as a safety measure video cameras that openly monitor the parking lot. As there is no expectation of privacy on the parking lot and the surveillance would be random, no waiver or consent from employees would be necessary.

Hidden video surveillance

While it is true that an employee has no expectation of privacy at his/her working desk, the use of hidden video surveillance – especially due to suspicion of theft – may be easily challenged in court as it may represent unequal treatment of employees. Furthermore, if hidden video surveillance does not confirm the suspicion of theft and the employee becomes aware of its previous use, there is no doubt that the company could face litigation based on tort law.

Biometric monitoring

Biometric data (especially fingerprints and iridology) has so far been used without raising any questions of privacy to control entrance and exit hours of work, i.e. it is used as an updated version of the blue-collar worker punching card. Curiously, questions raised on the matter focus on the accuracy of the hours registered as many employees argue that employers use technology to manipulate their registers and as a consequence to avoid overtime payment. Biometric monitoring by subcutaneous chips, on the one hand, is clearly unacceptable as it would constitute an infringement of the constitutional principle of human dignity and, on the other hand, seems so unrealistic that it has not been considered a real possibility in the juridical academic literature.

Retrieval of stored employee email

Labor courts have been hesitant on the matter, deciding either way according to the circumstances of each and every case. It is true that most courts have already upheld that email communications are similar to other ways of correspondence and therefore enjoy the same constitutional protection. Yet, when used in the work environment, this protection has been clearly mitigated. Consequently, employers may retrieve and read an employee's email stored in the employer's system, but to enhance the lawfulness of such action notification should be considered.

Random drug testing

If in a random drunk driving test performed on the streets by police officers, Brazilians have the right to refuse to be tested, what about in the workplace? Considering that refusal may be offered to public authority, it is hard to imagine that employers may require workers to be tested for controlled substances. Actually, due to privacy protection, random drug testing can only be demanded by employers when they are legally mandatory. Besides such a test cannot be performed by the employer.

Social network websites

Social network websites have been used to increase a company's knowledge of its reputation and/or the satisfaction of its employees. However, gathering such information cannot require employees to provide access to their social network websites and must rely on free access just as everyone else may do. Actually, most employers do not allow employees to access their social network websites from the work computer as it is perceived to be an extremely time-consuming activity and a threat to the company's web safety.

References and suggested readings

Roberto Fragale Filho & Joaquim Leonel de Rezende Alvim, *Information Technology and Worker's Privacy: the Brazilian Law*, 23 COMP. LAB. L. & POL'Y J. 281 (2005).

Problem 8 discussion – Germany

Section 87 para. 1 no. 6 of the Works Councils Act enshrines far-reaching co-determination rights for works councils with regard to the "introduction and application of technical equipment that aims at monitoring the behavior or performance of workers". Installing video cameras at the workplace clearly qualifies as the "introduction and application of technical equipment" within this meaning. If the cameras are installed at a parking lot, section 87 para. 1 no. 6 might apply as far as the aim is to monitor the behavior of the workers. Applying section 87 para. 1 no. 6 implies that the employer has to reach a consensus with the works council. If no agreement can be reached, an arbitration board will decide (section 87 para. 2 of the Works Constitution Act). The agreement between employer and works council regularly takes the legal form of a works agreement (*Betriebsvereinbarung*). Such works agreements have normative effects and are legally binding on all members of the work force (section 77 para. 4 sentence 1 of the Works Councils Act). In concluding a works agreement, the parties have to honor the right of workers to privacy which is protected by section 75 para. 2 of the Works Constitution, but also forms a fundamental right guaranteed by Articles 2 para. 1 and 1 para. 1 of the German Constitution, the Basic Law (*Grundgesetz*). The Federal Labor Court has made it clear that interference with workers' privacy must be justified by equally worthy interests of the employer. A proportionality test is applied in this regard. The upshot is that inroads into workers' privacy on the legal basis of a works agreement are lawful only if they are adequate, necessary and reasonable in the light of the interests brought forward by the employer (Federal Labor Court of 29.06.2004 – 1 ABR 21/03). Whether installing a video camera passes the proportionality test is dependent on the intensity of interference with workers' privacy. This essentially means that it is dependent on the number of staff involved, the length of monitoring and whether or not workers themselves have given a reason for the measure (Federal Labor Court of 26.08.2008 – 1 ABR 16/07).

In addition, section 6b of the Federal Data Protection Act (*Bundesdatenschutzgesetz*) must be taken into account when installing video cameras where the place is open to the public. Section 6b among other things requires the employer to be able to refer to substantiated (concrete) purposes justifying the measure. In applying these criteria, the Federal Labor Court has for instance decided that it is not admissible to put workers under the permanent pressure of being monitored (Federal Labor Court of 14.12.2004 – 1 ABR 34/03). Installing hidden video cameras may on the other hand be legitimate if there is no other realistic means of counteracting theft (Federal Labor Court 07.10.1987 – 5 AZR 116/86 and, more recently, Federal Labor Court of 21.06.2012 – 2 AZR 153/11).

Measures aimed at recording entrance and exit from the facility are subject to the co-determination right laid down in section 87 para. 1 no. 1 of the Works Councils Act regarding the rules on work rules and workers' behavior. Again, the employer must reach agreement with the works council.

The issue of retrieving and reading an employee's email stored in the employer's system touches upon the co-determination right fixed in section 87 para. 1 no. 6 of the Works Councils Act. This implies that installing technical systems with the purpose of getting access to the email of staff is not possible without having reached an agreement with the works council. Apart from that, essentially the same rules apply to retrieving and reading an employee's email which apply to overhearing telephone conversations. The latter, however, must in principle be regarded as a violation of privacy (Federal Labor Court of 23.04.2009 – 6 AZR 189/08) and can only be justified under exceptional circumstances. Finally, the provisions (section 88, in particular) of the Telecommunications Act (*Telekommunikationsgesetz*) have to be respected, which protect privacy of telecommunications, a right which is also guaranteed under the German Constitution (Article 10 of the Basic Law). In addition to that, the legal restrictions laid down in the Federal Data Protection Act (for instance, section 3a fixing an "*ultima ratio*" principle with regard to collecting personal data) have to be taken into account. As a rule of thumb, it can be said that in most cases the employer might be restricted to controlling the number and extent of emails only and not allowed to control content.

Medical examinations are admissible only if there are worthy interests of the employer justifying them. Because such examinations are mostly far-reaching the courts are rigid in this regard (Federal Labor Court of 12.09.1999 – 2 AZR

55/99 – according to which there is generally no duty of the employee to consent to examinations aiming at revealing whether he is drug- or alcohol-dependent). Drug-testing of job applicants was one of the issues in proceedings concerning an "ethical codex" established by Wal Mart. In its ruling the State Labor Court Düsseldorf (of 12.12.2005 – 10 TaBV 46/05) emphasized the fact that such rules are to a considerable extent subject to the co-determination rights fixed in section 87 para. 1 of the Works Councils Act. The court did not have to decide upon the lawfulness of the codex as far as drug-testing was concerned because Wal Mart in a court agreement quickly acknowledged the said co-determination rights after the deliverance of the ruling of the court of first instance (Labor Court Wuppertal of 15.06.2005 – 5 BV 20/05) which had emphasized these rights, sections 95 and 87(1) no. 1 of the Works Councils Act.

Requiring employees to provide the company with access to their social network websites would qualify as a breach of the employer's duty to respect the privacy of employees. Again it should be noted that privacy forms a (non-disposable) fundamental right which is guaranteed by the Constitution.

PRIMARY SOURCE

Directive 95/46 EC, the "Data Protection" Directive, infra.

References and suggested readings

Detlef Grimm & Jennifer Schiefer, *Videoüberwachung am Arbeitsplatz*, RECHT DER ARBEIT (RdA) 329 (2009); Volker Vogt, *Compliance und Investigations – Zehn Fragen aus Sicht der arbeitsrechtlichen Praxis*, NEUE JURISTISCHE WOCHENSCHRIFT (NJW) 3755 (2009); Andrea Raffler & Peter Hellich, *Unterwelchen Voraussetzungen ist die Überwachung von Arbeitnehmer-e-mails zulässig?*, NEUE ZEITSCHRIFT FÜR ARBEITSRECHT (NZA) 862 (1997); Michael Kort, *Ethik-Richtlinienim Spannungsfeldz wischen US-amerikanischer Compliance und deutschem Konzernbetriebsverfassungsrecht*, NEUE JURISTISCHE WOCHENSCHRIFT (NJW) 129 (2009); Frank Braun & René Hoppe, *Arbeitnehmer-E-Mails: Vertrauen ist gut – Kontrolle ist schlecht – Auswirkungen der neuesten Rechtsprechung des BVerfG auf das Arbeitsverhältnis*, MULT MEDIA UND RECHT – ZEITSCHRIFT FÜR INFORMATIONS-, TELEKOMMUNIKATIONS- UND MEDIENRECHT (MMR) 80 (2010).

http://beck-online.beck.de/?vpath=bibdata\zeits\njw\2009\cont\njw.2009.129.1.htm&pos=2&hlwords=wal%c3%90mart%c3%90arbeitnehmer – FN1#FN1.

Problem 8 discussion – Japan

As discussed in Problem 7, the Personal Information Protection Act of 2003 (PIPA) provides personal data protection, including for employees. However, video monitoring and biomonitoring are not specifically covered by the PIPA. Although the Ministry of Health, Labor and Welfare issued guidelines on proper treatment of personal data in 2004, these remain administrative guidelines without legally enforceable effect. Therefore, the legal issues raised by video monitoring, blood testing, HIV testing, health check, and monitoring of emails in Japan concern whether these measures constitute illegal acts or torts that infringe on individuals' personal rights or privacy.

In the past, employers' collection of health information about their employees was generally allowed or, rather, encouraged. This is because Japanese employers owe a duty to care for their employees' safety and health as an ancillary duty of employment contracts in personnel management. In order to properly implement this duty to care, employers need information about the health conditions of employees.

In accordance with the enhancement of awareness of individuals' privacy and personal rights, collecting data about employees' health conditions started to be questioned. For instance, the Tokyo Metropolitan Police Department conducted the HIV antibody test as part of the recruitment process. Applicants agreed to a blood test as part of a general health check, but was not informed that the blood was also used for the HIV antibody test. The court held that conducting the HIV antibody test without obtaining the applicant's consent was an illegal act and constituted a tort (*Tokyo Metropolitan Police Department HIV Testing* case, Tokyo District Court May 28, 2003, Rodo Hanrei No. 852 p. 11). In another case in which the company conducted a hepatitis B test without obtaining the employee's consent, the company was held liable for damages caused by the infringement of the employee's privacy (*B Finance Corporation* case, Tokyo District Court, June 20, 2003, Rodo Hanrei No. 854 p. 5).

Compared to the above-mentioned collection of health information about individuals through blood testing, video monitoring and biomonitoring are less invasive in their manner. Thus these forms of monitoring would not be held to be illegal acts so long as the employer demonstrates objective reasons necessitating such monitoring, such as to prevent crimes in the parking lot or to maintain workplace order.

As for monitoring emails and investigating personal belongings, there are several cases where these issues have been discussed. First, if the employer establishes a right to monitor or investigate emails for personal belongings, they will not cause any problems of infringement on privacy in principle. Where no such employer's right has been established in the employment contract, in the forms submitted by the employee to utilize the corporate PC, or in the work rules, courts will compare employees' interests in respect for privacy and the employer's need to monitor emails. Currently courts tend to prioritize employers' interest over employees' privacy.

Problem 8 discussion – United States

These questions implicate a complex web of federal and state law in the United States that nevertheless allow for a wide range of discretion. Each should be taken in turn. But before doing so, it should be stressed that the United States has nothing akin to the European Union's Data Protection Directive nor any general legal concept of "informational self-determination."

Inasmuch as being subject to such monitoring is a working condition, if the employees are collectively represented the company has to bargain with the union on this subject – but the company may bargain, in good faith, to retain its managerial prerogative over all aspects of the technology's deployment and use. This is so as well for the use of hidden videos, use of biometric systems of identification, access to email, drug testing, and – though there are no cases as yet – access to employees' social networks. What follows will assume that the affected employees are not unionized.

Open video monitoring. No positive law at the federal or state level deals with the introduction or use of video monitoring of work areas. The test for liability under the tort of invasion of privacy – of "wrongful intrusion into seclusion" – requires first that the employee has a "reasonable expectation of privacy," and second, that the means of intrusion be unreasonably offensive. Video monitoring of open work areas fails to meet either of those requirements.

Hidden video surveillance. A few jurisdictions prohibit video surveillance of restrooms or changing areas by statute; but otherwise there is no positive law. The legal approach rests on the law of tort as outlined above. Generally speaking, an employee has no more reasonable expectation that her desk will not be subject to hidden video surveillance than she has in an open work area. However, surveillance of some specially situated areas – for example, a nurse's station where employee/patients may be subject to medical examination – would be subject to a reasonable expectation of privacy.

Biometric monitoring. There is little positive law: Colorado, Illinois, and Texas have legislated with respect to the collection, use, storage, and destruction of biometric data. But there are no restrictions on the deployment of these technologies in the workplace. Nor is there any common law development as yet.

Retrieval of stored employee email. This area is governed by the federal Electronic Communications Privacy Act (ECPA) and cognate state statutes. The law distinguishes between the "interception" of an electronic communication, one in transmission, and retrieval from electronic storage. Generally speaking, interception requires the consent of the employee, but sufficiently conspicuous notice of interception has been held to warrant consent. (Two states have legislated to require notice be posted in the workplace or displayed on the employee's computer screen.) There is no federal statutory constraint on the employer's ability to retrieve and read messages stored in its *own* system. Absent an assurance to the employee or to the workforce that that would not be done or would be subject to other self-imposed constraint, an employer is free to retrieve and read employee email. In terms of tort law, there is a division of authority along positivist and realist lines. According to the former, if the employer has made it clear that it has reserved the right to monitor and the employee was aware of that reservation, the employee can have no reasonable expectation of privacy in her communications via the employer's system or even in her use of her own private email account accessed through the employer's system. According to the latter, however, whether the employee has a reasonable expectation of privacy turns on the "operational realities" of the workplace. If, despite an employer policy to the contrary, the employer's behavior could and did lead the employee reasonably to expect that her communications would not be read, monitoring could work an actionable invasion of privacy.

Random drug testing. Three states limit an employer's ability to require drug testing of incumbent employees to safety sensitive positions – Alaska, Massachusetts, and West Virginia. In all other states the employer is free to require random drug testing for any or all jobs. (Employees in the interstate transportation industry are subject to exacting federal drug testing requirements and rules.) About half the states have legislated concerning the *manner* in which testing may be conducted, for example, requiring the use of a confirming test by a certified laboratory and the like, and about the consequences of a positive test, for example, disallowing discharge in lieu of completion of a drug assistance program for a first offense, etc. Otherwise, there are no limits on the employer's power to impose such a regime.

Social network sites. There are no common law constraints on an employer's ability to require access. Eight states thus far – Colorado, Illinois, Maryland, Michigan, Nevada, Oregon, Utah, and Washington – have legislated to forbid employers to require or request access to social media of applicants or employees. Insofar as an employer might retaliate against an employee for a message that is in aid or in anticipation of employee concerted activity authority for mutual aid or protection under the National Labor Relations Act, the employer will have committed an unfair labor practice. *See* NLRB General Counsel Memorandum OM 12–59 (May 30, 2012).

References and suggested readings

The law is surveyed by MATTHEW FINKIN, PRIVACY IN EMPLOYMENT LAW (4th ed.) (in press). Each of these areas has generated a good deal of discussion.

Video monitoring and hidden surveillance: The American Management Association's (AMA's) 2007 Electronic Monitoring & Surveillance Survey indicates that almost 48 percent of the companies surveyed use video monitoring to counter theft, violence, or sabotage. This compares with 51 percent in 2005, but only 33 percent in 2001. Seven percent of employers videotape selected categories of employees in their job performance, compared with 10 percent in 2005; 6 percent in 2006 videotaped all employees. In 2007, 78 percent of employers notified employees of antitheft video surveillance, and 89 percent of employers notified employees of job performance video monitoring. Video workplace monitoring has been used by employers to prove misconduct and has been relied on to deny unemployment compensation benefits.

Biometric monitoring: The use of tracking devices has generated considerable concern among nurses. *See* United American Nurses, AFL-CIO, *UAN Nurse Tracking Survey Results* (Nov. 2009). The types of tracking reported by the nurses' union are shown in Table IV.1.

Table IV.1 UAN tracking responses

Type of tracking	Percentage reporting Use
Swipe Cards	75.9%
Bar Code [on drugs]	35.6%
Infrared Tracking Badge	17.2%
Radio Frequency Tracking Device (RFID)	17.2%
Biometric Technology	12.6%
A Global Positioning Tracking (GPS) system	11.5%
I don't know	13.8%

Retrieval of email: A fuller picture is shown by the prevalence of electronic monitoring in general.

Monitoring of employee email. The American Management Association has surveyed employer practices. Its latest report, up to 2007, revealed the following as the sample reporting.

Table IV.2 U.S. employer monitoring practices, 2001–2007

	2001	2005	2007
Recording and review of telephone conversations	11.9%	19%	16%
Storage and review of voice mail messages	7.8%	15%	9%
Storage and review of computer files	36.1%	50%	43%
Storage and review of email messages	46.5%	55%	N/A
Monitoring internet connections	62.8%	76%	66%
Telephone use (time spent, numbers called)	43.3%	51%	45%
Computer use (time logged on, keystroke counts, etc.)	18.9%	36%	45%

Source: 2001, 2005, and 2007 AMA Survey: Workplace Monitoring & Surveillance.

A June, 2009, survey conducted by Proofpoint, Inc., a provider of email security and data loss prevention services, indicated that 38 percent of the companies surveyed employ staff to read or analyze employee email.

Drug testing: A 2007 U.S. governmental survey indicated that about 30 percent of full-time workers were subject to random drug testing in their workplaces – about 32 million workers.

Social networking: Table IV.3 shows the findings of a survey conducted by Cross-tab for Microsoft regarding companies' use of different types of internet sites when researching applicants.

Table IV.3 Percentage of recruiters and human resources professionals who use different types of internet sites when researching applicants

Search engines	78%
Social networking sites	63%
Photo and video sharing sites	59%
Professional and business networking sites	57%
Personal websites	48%
Blogs	46%
News sharing sites (e.g. Twitter)	41%
Online forums and communities	34%
Virtual world sites	32%
Websites that aggregate personal information	32%
Online gaming sites	27%
Professional background-checking services	27%
Classifieds and auction sites	25%
None of these	2%

Source: Cross-tab, Online Reputation in a Connected World (Jan. 2010), at 8.

A note on "Data Protection"

In 1995, the European Union promulgated what has come to be called the "Data Protection Directive." Actually, it doesn't protect data. It requires Member States to adopt laws protecting privacy rights arising out of data collected, filed, compiled, collated or disseminated about persons – "natural persons" – human beings. Because of the prohibition on the transmission of covered data from an EU Member State to a foreign state whose laws do not afford an "adequate level of protection" as measured by European standards, the Data Protection Directive has proven highly influential worldwide. States as diverse as Morocco (where French companies have opened customer call-in centers), Israel, and Hong Kong have adopted laws to meet the EU's transferability standard. Japan has as well, but only in a law applicable to companies with more than 5,000 employees, i.e. those more likely to receive such information from abroad.

The United States does not meet the European test of adequacy. However, the EU decided that its standards would be satisfied if an individual enterprise gives a legally binding assurance of compliance. Toward that end a "safe harbor" agreement was made to be administered by the Commerce Department and enforced by the Federal Trade Commission. The provisions of the safe harbor and a list of its signatories are found on the Commerce Department's website: http://export.gov/SafeHarbor/. Set out below is an edited text of Directive 95/46 EC.

DIRECTIVE 95/46 EC

CHAPTER I – GENERAL PROVISIONS

Article 1

Object of the Directive

1. In accordance with this Directive, Member States shall protect the fundamental rights and freedoms of natural persons, and in particular their right to privacy with respect to the processing of personal data.

Article 2

Definitions

For the purposes of this Directive:

(a) "personal data" shall mean any information relating to an identified or identifiable natural person ("data subject"); an identifiable person is one who can be identified, directly or indirectly, in particular by reference to an identification number or to one or more factors specific to his physical, physiological, mental, economic, cultural or social identity;

(b) "processing of personal data" ("processing") shall mean any operation or set of operations which is performed upon personal data, whether or not by automatic means, such as collection, recording, organization, storage, adaptation or alteration, retrieval, consultation, use, disclosure by transmission, dissemination or otherwise making available, alignment or combination, blocking, erasure or destruction;

(c) "personal data filing system" ("filing system") shall mean any structured set of personal data which are accessible according to specific criteria, whether centralized, decentralized or dispersed on a functional or geographical basis;

(d) "controller" shall mean the natural or legal person, public authority, agency or any other body which alone or jointly with others determines the purposes and means of the processing of personal data; where the purposes and means of processing are determined by national or Community laws or regulations, the controller or the specific criteria for his nomination may be designated by national or Community law;

(e) "processor" shall mean a natural or legal person, public authority, agency or any other body which possesses personal data on behalf of the controller;

(f) "third party" shall mean any natural or legal person, public authority, agency or any other body other than the data subject, the controller, the processor and the persons who, under the direct authority of the controller or the processor, are authorized to process the data;

(g) "recipient" shall mean a natural or legal person, public authority, agency or any other body to whom data are disclosed, whether a third party or not; however, authorities which may receive data in the framework of a particular inquiry shall not be regarded as recipients;

(h) "the data subject's consent" shall mean any freely given specific and informed indication of his wishes by which the data subject signifies his agreement to personal data relating to him being processed.

Article 3

Scope

1. This Directive shall apply to the processing of personal data wholly or partly by automatic means, and to the processing otherwise than by automatic means of personal data which form part of a filing system or are intended to form part of a filing system.

SECTION 1

PRINCIPLES RELATING TO DATA QUALITY

Article 6

1. Member States shall provide that personal data must be:

(a) processed fairly and lawfully;

(b) collected for specified, explicit and legitimate purposes and not further processed in a way incompatible with those purposes …

(c) adequate, relevant and not excessive in relation to the purposes for which they are collected and/or further processed;

(d) accurate and, where necessary, kept up to date; every reasonable step must be taken to ensure that data which are inaccurate or incomplete, having regard to the purposes for which they were collected or for which they are further processed, are erased or rectified;

(e) kept in a form which permits identification of data subjects for no longer than is necessary for the purposes for which the data were collected or for which they are further processed ...

SECTION II

CRITERIA FOR MAKING DATA PROCESSING LEGITIMATE

Article 7

Member States shall provide that personal data may be processed only if:

(a) the data subject has unambiguously given his consent; or

(b) processing is necessary for the performance of a contract to which the data subject is party or in order to take steps at the request of the data subject prior to entering into a contract; or

(c) processing is necessary for compliance with a legal obligation to which the controller is subject; or

(d) processing is necessary in order to protect the vital interests of the data subject; or

(e) processing is necessary for the performance of a task carried out in the public interest or in the exercise of official authority vested in the controller or in a third party to whom the data are disclosed; or

(f) processing is necessary for the purposes of the legitimate interests pursued by the controller or by the third party or parties to whom the data are disclosed, except where such interests are overridden by the interests for fundamental rights and freedoms of the data subject which require protection under Article 1 (1).

SECTION III

SPECIAL CATEGORIES OF PROCESSING

Article 8

The processing of special categories of data

1. Member States shall prohibit the processing of personal data revealing racial or ethnic origin, political opinions, religious or philosophical beliefs, trade-union membership, and the processing of data concerning health or sex life.

2. Paragraph 1 shall not apply where:
   (a) the data subject has given his explicit consent to the processing of those data, except where the laws of the Member State provide that the prohibition referred to in paragraph 1 may not be lifted by the data subject's giving his consent; or
   (b) processing is necessary for the purposes of carrying out the obligations and specific rights of the controller in the field of employment law in so far as it is authorized by national law providing for adequate safeguards; or

(c) processing is necessary to protect the vital interests of the data subject or of another person where the data subject is physically or legally incapable of giving his consent; or
(d) processing is carried out in the course of its legitimate activities with appropriate guarantees by a foundation, association or any other non-profit-seeking body with a political, philosophical, religious or trade-union aim and on condition that the processing relates solely to the members of the body or to persons who have regular contact with it in connection with its purposes and that the data are not disclosed to a third party without the consent of the data subjects; or
(e) the processing relates to data which are manifestly made public by the data subject or is necessary for the establishment, exercise or defence of legal claims.

SECTION IV

INFORMATION TO BE GIVEN TO THE DATA SUBJECT

Article 10

Information in cases of collection of data from the data subject

Member States shall provide that the controller or his representative must provide a data subject from whom data relating to himself are collected with at least the following information, except where he already has it:

(a) the identity of the controller and of his representative, if any;

(b) the purposes of the processing for which the data are intended;

(c) any further information such as
- the recipients or categories of recipients of the data,
- where replies to the questions are obligatory or voluntary, as well as the possible consequences of failure to reply,
- the existence of the right of access to and the right to rectify the data concerning him

in so far as such further information is necessary, having regard to the specific circumstances in which the data are collected, to guarantee fair processing in respect of the data subject.

Article 11

Information where the data have not been obtained from the data subject

1. Where the data have not been obtained from the data subject, Member States shall provide that the controller or his representative must at the time of undertaking the recording of personal data or if a disclosure to a third party is envisaged, no later than the time when the data are first disclosed provide the data subject with at least the following information, except where he already has it:
   (a) the identity of the controller and of his representative, if any;
   (b) the purposes of the processing;
   (c) any further information such as

- the categories of data concerned,
- the recipients or categories of recipients,
- the existence of the right of access to and the right to rectify the data concerning him

in so far as such further information is necessary, having regard to the specific circumstances in which the data are processed, to guarantee fair processing in respect of the data subject.

SECTION V

THE DATA SUBJECT'S RIGHT OF ACCESS TO DATA

Article 12

Right of access

Member States shall guarantee every data subject the right to obtain from the controller:

(a) without constraint at reasonable intervals and without excessive delay or expense:
  - confirmation as to whether or not data relating to him are being processed and information at least as to the purposes of the processing, the categories of data concerned, and the recipients or categories of recipients to whom the data are disclosed,
  - communication to him in an intelligible form of the data undergoing processing and of any available information as to their source,
  - knowledge of the logic involved in any automatic processing of data concerning him at least in the case of the automated decisions referred to in Article 15 (1);

(b) as appropriate the rectification, erasure or blocking of data the processing of which does not comply with the provisions of this Directive, in particular because of the incomplete or inaccurate nature of the data;

(c) notification to third parties to whom the data have been disclosed of any rectification, erasure or blocking carried out in compliance with (b), unless this proves impossible or involves a disproportionate effort.

Article 14

The data subject's right to object

Article 15

Automated individual decisions

1. Member States shall grant the right to every person not to be subject to a decision which produces legal effects concerning him or significantly affects him and which is based solely on automated processing of data intended to evaluate certain personal aspects relating to him, such as his performance at work, creditworthiness, reliability, conduct, etc.

2. Subject to the other Articles of this Directive, Member States shall provide that a person may be subjected to a decision of the kind referred to in paragraph 1 if that decision:
   (a) is taken in the course of the entering into or performance of a contract, provided the request for the entering into or the performance of the contract, lodged by the data subject, has been satisfied or that there are suitable measures to safeguard his legitimate interests, such as arrangements allowing him to put his point of view; or
   (b) is authorized by a law which also lays down measures to safeguard the data subject's legitimate interests.

SECTION VIII

CONFIDENTIALITY AND SECURITY OF PROCESSING

Article 16

Confidentiality of processing

Any person acting under the authority of the controller or of the processor, including the processor himself, who has access to personal data must not process them except on instructions from the controller, unless he is required to do so by law.

Article 17

Security of processing

1. Member States shall provide that the controller must implement appropriate technical and organizational measures to protect personal data against accidental or unlawful destruction or accidental loss, alteration, unauthorized disclosure or access, in particular where the processing involves the transmission of data over a network, and against all other unlawful forms of processing.

CHAPTER III – JUDICIAL REMEDIES, LIABILITY AND SANCTIONS

Article 22

Remedies

Without prejudice to any administrative remedy for which provision may be made, inter alia before the supervisory authority referred to in Article 28, prior to referral to the judicial authority, Member States shall provide for the right of every person to a judicial remedy for any breach of the rights guaranteed him by the national law applicable to the processing in question.

Article 23

Liability

1. Member States shall provide that any person who has suffered damage as a result of an unlawful processing operation or of any act incompatible with the national provisions adopted pursuant to this Directive is entitled to receive compensation from the controller for the damage suffered.

2. The controller may be exempted from this liability, in whole or in part, if he proves that he is not responsible for the event giving rise to the damage.

CHAPTER IV – TRANSFER OF PERSONAL DATA TO THIRD COUNTRIES

Article 25

Principles

1. The Member States shall provide that the transfer to a third country of personal data which are undergoing processing or are intended for processing after transfer may take place only if, without prejudice to compliance with the national provisions adopted pursuant to the other provisions of this Directive, the third country in question ensures an adequate level of protection.
2. The adequacy of the level of protection afforded by a third country shall be assessed in the light of all the circumstances surrounding a data transfer operation or set of data transfer operations; particular consideration shall be given to the nature of the data, the purpose and duration of the proposed processing operation or operations, the country of origin and country of final destination, the rules of law, both general and sectoral, in force in the third country in question and the professional rules and security measures which are complied with in that country.

As this book goes to press the European Commission has proposed revisions, via a General Data Protection Regulation, dealing with the processing of employment related data. General Data Protection Regulation, COM (2012) 0011-C7–6025/2012–2012/0011 ((01)), on which a Rapporteur of the Committee on Employment and Social Affairs of the European Parliament commented on August 11, 2012

> I can imagine all kinds of scenarios where employers who are engaged in the six things listed in problem seven (video monitoring the parking lot and employees' desks, biomonitoring, monitoring social networks, reading private emails, etc.) would uncover all kinds of personal and private things about their employees. Relationships between co-workers, drug habits, non-disclosed sexual preference issues, illegal activities outside of work, health issues, the list is endless. My question is: Are we prepared for all of the unintended information of a confidential nature that would accidentally come to the employer's awareness? The potential for liability claims if the information is mishandled or misused would appear to be limitless.
>
> Manager, HR, Automotive Sector

I briefly served as the HR Manager at a large, unionized bottling and distribution facility early in my career. Stories swirled during my tenure of the history of the plant, in which a suspected drug dealing ring had been operating out of the facility. Management investigated the issue, but couldn't come up with any hard evidence that it was happening. Through the investigation, reports had been received that drug deals were happening in the locker room, but management could not catch anyone in the act. It was becoming an even more serious distraction in the workplace as co-workers bickered about "ratting out" each other, threats of violence had been made, racial tensions soared, and worker/management relations were strained. To address these serious concerns, the HR Manager at the time had approved the secret installation of a video camera in the locker room. It was pointed away from the bathing and lavatory facilities, towards the changing area. Through the use of this secret video footage, several drug transactions were caught on camera, and the drug dealers were terminated. Unfortunately, this is not the end of the story. The method by which the drug dealers were caught later leaked out to the workforce. Union leaders were outraged. Employees felt that there was a violation of their privacy by being secretly videotaped, which was particularly sensitive since it took place in an area in which many workers would change clothes. The local media was alerted. A CNN camera crew arrived in the parking lot one day. The company received highly negative publicity for its actions, even though the choice to install a hidden camera was a last resort, to address serious workplace issues. A public apology was issued. Although the collective bargaining agreement did not directly address the use of technology in the workplace, management agreed to not use hidden cameras again without informing union leadership. I entered the facility nearly 4 years later, but the event was still a topic of conversation. It was frequently used as an example of management betraying the trust of the workforce. Although the act was legal, was within the scope of management rights per the collective bargaining agreement, and served to prevent a felony crime, it had a lasting negative impact upon the facility and the workforce. I would suggest that any legal ability of management to enact measures which could be viewed as a narrowing of employees' privacy should be very thoughtfully considered. Although certain such acts may be legal, they could potentially result in far-reaching negative consequences.

Vice President, HR, Financial Sector

[C]ompanies, as they begin to press globally, try to mix and match their approach. For example in the case of our company, we have some policies that are completely localized while others are globalized push downs of home-company practices. Neither works very well – the first is met with

> frustration from corporate and the latter are not routinely accepted without a fight due to "legal concerns."
>
> Director, HR, Industrial Manufacturing Sector

Questions for Discussion – Problem 8

1. For each of the five countries, consider each of the things the company would like to do and indicate: does it infringe upon an employee's privacy in that country? If not, why not – because (a) there is no privacy interest at stake, or (b) because the employee freely bargained it away, or (c) because the employer's interest necessarily controls? If the latter, what is the interest? Is there a conflict of interest?

2. If there is a conflict between the employer and the employee on any of these privacy issues due to the employer's actions in Problem 8, should the conflict be resolved ultimately by the employer? If not, should the conflict be resolved by some third party? If the latter, what would that be: a works council? An arbitrator? An administrative agency? A judge? What are the advantages and disadvantages of each?

3. Note that for the most part, it would be a tort in the U.S. for an employer to intrude in an area in which an employee has a "reasonable expectation of privacy" by means that are "unreasonably offensive," but that the employer's business interest in effecting the intrusion is often taken by the courts to go to the reasonableness of it. In New South Wales, an employer would have to appear before a magistrate, albeit ex parte, and satisfy him or her of the need for and reasonableness of the surveillance, to be conducted under terms to be decided by the magistrate. From what appears, the law there makes no distinction between an intrusion by a public center of power which, in the U.S., would require much the same showing if conducted by the police, and an intrusion by a private center of power. Why might this be the case and what are the implications for employers?

4. In Brazil, we saw that citizens can refuse a police request to take a breathalyzer test – suggesting that it might also be clear that workers can refuse such a test by the employer. Given this reality and the other information provided, what would you recommend as an employer policy for maintaining a workplace that is free of drug and alcohol abuse?

5. If, under German law, requiring applicants to supply access to their social media is unlawful, how do you explain the results of the Cross-tab survey set out in the U.S. report (see Table IV.4)?

Table IV.4 Types of online reputational information that influenced decisions to reject a candidate

	U.S.	U.K.	Ger.	France
Concerns about the candidate's lifestyle	58%	45%	42%	32%
Inappropriate comments and text written by the candidate	56%	57%	78%	58%
Unsuitable photos, videos, and information	55%	51%	44%	42%
Inappropriate comments to text written by friends and relatives	43%	35%	14%	11%
Comments criticizing previous employers, co-workers, or clients	40%	40%	28%	37%
Inappropriate comments or text written by colleagues or work acquaintances	40%	37%	17%	21%
Membership in certain groups and networks	35%	33%	36%	37%
Discovered that information the candidate shared was false	30%	36%	42%	47%
Poor communication skills displayed online	27%	41%	17%	42%
Concern about the candidate's financial background	16%	18%	11%	0%

Source: Cross-tab, Online Reputation in a Connected World (Jan. 2010), at 9.

PROBLEM 9: DATING POLICY

To avoid possible problems of sexual harassment the company would like to adopt an absolute prohibition on co-workers "dating or becoming romantically involved" with one another. May it do so?

Problem 9 discussion – Australia

This raises the same issue as discussed in Problem 8 – the scope of the employer's capacity to issue "lawful and reasonable" directions that affect an employee's private life. In the absence of prior consent by employees, it is unlikely that a blanket direction of this kind would be considered lawful.

References and suggested readings

ANDREW STEWART, STEWART'S GUIDE TO EMPLOYMENT LAW §12.6 (4th ed. 2013) (see Problem 8, supra).

Problem 9 discussion – Brazil

Although there is no legal regulation in Brazil that would prevent an employer from adopting such a policy, if courts were called on to examine its legality they would most probably perceive it as extremely intrusive into employees' private lives and therefore rule it as offensive to human dignity, which is constitutionally protected. As a consequence, any action taken on this basis would most probably be considered void. However, as there is neither legal regulation nor any case law on the matter, employers are not precluded from adopting such a policy which may be useful in clarifying what can (and cannot) be done in the workplace. As a matter of fact, even though there are no figures as to how many

Brazilian employers adopt such codes of conduct, they are not foreign to the Brazilian labor scene. While they are a valuable tool for clarifying what an employer thinks about romance in the workplace, they are not capable of eliminating the chances of an affair between co-workers and they do not constitute a free pass to avoiding possible problems of sexual harassment.

If the setting of a rule would suffice to avoid sexual harassment, might Brazilian employers go one step further and establish a policy that employees may socialize as colleagues in the workplace but may not become friends outside? In doing so, employers would supposedly ensure that every worker would be eligible to testify as a witness in a labor dispute. Why so? Because whenever an employee is called to testify in a labor suit, to ascertain neutrality as to the litigation outcome two questions are usually asked by labor judges: "have you any interest in the outcome of this litigation?", and "are you a friend or an enemy of any of the parties involved?" The former, although easily answered by a negative reply, has generated an enormous caseload over what interest means, especially for witnesses who are also litigating against their old employer. Jurisprudence from the *Tribunal Superior do Trabalho* has consolidated the idea that such a situation cannot necessarily be interpreted as an interest in the litigation outcome. On the other hand, there is no case law on the latter which usually generates some hesitation and gets a dubious response: "we were friends at work". Obviously, such an answer assumes that friendship at work is not like friendship outside the workplace. "We were (are) colleagues at work" would thus be a good translation for such an answer. Now, can conviviality be stopped at the workplace's entrance and life be separated into two different moments: in the workplace and outside it?

References and suggested readings

BRASIL, TRIBUNAL SUPERIOR DO TRABALHO, *Súmula 357, accessed at* http://www3.tst.jus.br/jurisprudencia/Sumulas_com_indice/Sumulas_Inc_351_400.html#SUM-357 (last visited Oct. 2, 2012).

Problem 9 discussion – Germany

The German Constitution (*Grundgesetz*) protects, among other things, human dignity and the right of personality. Both have to be observed in the employment relationship, too. As the Düsseldorf Higher Labor Court decided, one of the most important parts of these rights is the freedom to choose one's friends and, even more, boy- or girlfriend. This is not only true for leisure time but also for time spent at work, in particular since most employees spend a substantial part of their time at work. Therefore the unobstructed opportunity to enter into friendship relationships is crucial for the development of the employee's personality.

In the specific case decided by the Düsseldorf Higher Labor Court, the company's policy forbade dating between employees only if one of them may influence the working conditions of the other, for example, dating between the boss and his secretary. Although the court acknowledged that dating between such persons may cause problems within the workforce, it nonetheless declared the policy as void because of violation of the employees' human dignity and right of personality. It held that the employer is allowed to intervene only if and when specific problems arise because of such a relationship.

The strict rejection of such a company policy by the court may be explained by the fact that such policies were totally unknown in Germany. Taking the employer's side, one may argue that the decision makes it more difficult to prevent sexual harassment. However, there are other methods to accomplish that or, at least, to make it more difficult for potential harassers (e.g. establishing an efficient in-house complaint procedure); therefore, such a company policy can't be justified as it is not in accordance with the principle of proportionality. As the Federal Labor Court has not had to address this question yet, all has not been said and done – however, it is likely that it would come to the same conclusion as the Düsseldorf Higher Labor Court.

References and suggested readings

Landesarbeitsgericht Nov. 14, 2005, 10 TaBV 46/05, NEUE ZEITSCHRIFT FÜR ARBEITSRECHT [NZA] 81, 2006; Bittmann & Lenze, DER BETRIEB 165

(2006); Deinert & Kolle, ARBEIT UND RECHT (AuR) 177 (2006); Schneider, ARBEITSRECHT IM BETRIEB 10 (2006).

Problem 9 discussion – Japan

There is no statutory regulation in Japan that would limit the employer's ability to adopt a "no fraternization" rule. In Japan, however, a company has long been regarded as a community and employees have been regarded as members of such a community. Therefore, it has been a celebrated event when a man and woman working for the same company got acquainted, fell in love and got married. In the past, workplaces were indeed important places where young people met their prospective spouses. Thus, a prohibition on co-workers' dating was and still is not common in Japanese companies so long as the co-workers are single.

If one of the couple is a single and the other married, or if both are married, their relationship might develop into adultery, which is illegal under Japanese law. Such an illegal relationship can be deemed to be prohibited misconduct, disturbing workplace order and harming a company's good reputation, which is subject to disciplinary action. However, courts tend not easily to endorse disciplinary measures when an intimate relationship outside working hours has had no actual adverse impact on work performance or on order in the workplace.

In Japan, cases involving sexual harassment have increased in recent years and companies are often held liable for not having properly prevented their worker from harassing co-workers. Thus, it would not be surprising if some companies were to adopt a "no fraternization" rule. However, courts will severely examine a company's disciplinary actions that treat an employee who dates his or her co-worker in the same vein as adultery. If their relationship did not cause any harm to their performance or to workplace order in reality, courts will nullify the disciplinary actions.

References and suggested readings

For sexual harassment in Japan, see Ryuichi Yamakawa, *We've Only Just Begun: The Law of Sexual Harassment in Japan*, 22 HASTINGS INT'L. & COMP. L. R. 523–65 (1999).

Workplace order and discipline in Japan is overviewed in SUGENO KAZUO, JAPANESE EMPLOYMENT AND LABOR LAW 419–34 (2002) and in TAKASHI ARAKI, LABOR AND EMPLOYMENT LAW IN JAPAN 149–58 (2002).

Problem 9 discussion – United States

There is no federal law in the United States that would limit the employer's ability to adopt a "no fraternization" rule and a decade-old survey indicates that about 12 percent of companies responding had such a policy. United Parcel had such a policy, as a manager with over 20 years' service learned when he was discharged for having married a co-worker. *Ellis v. United Parcel Service, Inc.*, 523 F.3d 823 (7th Cir. 2008). However, a non-fraternization policy cannot be so broadly framed as to trample on the statutory right of employees to interact with co-workers and others – with employees of contractors or with customers – in furtherance of mutual aid or protection. *Guardsmark, LLC v. NLRB*, 475 F.3d 369 (D.C. Cir. 2007).

Three states – California, Colorado, and North Dakota – prohibit retaliation for engaging in any lawful off-duty activity that has no adverse workplace impact and, presumably, dating would be such an activity. A number of states forbid discrimination on the basis of "marital status," but there is a lively dispute on whether that prohibition extends to the person of the spouse in contrast to the status of being married. Were the UPS manager to have been dismissed in one of the jurisdictions extending protection to the person of the spouse – the states of Washington, Hawaii, and, perhaps, Minnesota – the UPS manager might have had a claim; but those marital status laws would not reach other romantic relationships.

Most U.S. states have recognized that there is a right to privacy; a few by statute, but most by a common law tort. But, oxymoronic as it sounds, the common law of the "right to privacy" does not extend to the protection of one's private life.

References and suggested readings

The law is surveyed in MATTHEW FINKIN, PRIVACY IN EMPLOYMENT LAW (4th ed.) (in press).

Plenary employer prerogative over employee private life is defended as a managerial prerogative by Robert Howie & Lawrence Shapiro, *Lifestyle Discrimination Statutes: A Dangerous Erosion of At-Will Employment, a Passing Fad, or Both?*, 31 EMP. REL. L. J. 21 (2005), replied to by Matthew Finkin, *Life Away From Work*, 66 LA. L. REV. 945 (2006).

Questions for Discussion – Problem 9

1. It is clear that you may not apply this policy prohibiting co-worker dating in Germany. It would most likely not be enforceable in Australia and would be dubious in Japan. But you could apply it in Brazil and the U.S. Assuming the company insisted on having the policy wherever it was likely to be effective, would you try to enforce it in Brazil and the U.S.? In Japan? If yes, why, and if no, why not?

2. In the Ellis case, discussed in the U.S. report, the dismissed employee's romantic relationship was with an employee in another department for which Mr. Ellis had no responsibility or working relationship. But the policy banned all co-worker dating irrespective of these considerations. Would you advise your company to adapt such a policy in the U.S.?

3. If you were a local manager in Australia, Germany, or Japan, what policies would you recommend in each country as an alternative to the prohibition on dating so as to assure top corporate management that their underlying concerns about avoiding sexual harassment litigation would be addressed? (Note: Develop a policy that respects privacy law in each of these countries, while still mitigating the risk of inappropriate behaviors and litigation.)

4. We saw that romantic relationships among single co-workers in Japan are accepted and even celebrated, while adulterous relationships are illegal under the law and seen as potentially damaging to workplace operations and the reputation of the employer. Assume you are working for a Japanese multinational company that wants to honor the principles that

underlie these policies. Identify one or more underlying principles from this Japanese circumstance that you would recommend in the form of a policy for use in any one of the other four countries? Can you craft a policy that would be lawful and effective in all five countries?

A note on dignity: the case of captive audition

As the introduction to this part explained, the idea of dignity is rooted deeply in European natural law thought and flowered in the eighteenth century. It embodies the idea that every person has within himself or herself a core or kernel of humanity that is deserving of respect; and that all persons share in this equally. Moreover, a wrong against the person can be worked not only by an involuntary infringement, but also by a consented-to or bargained-for infringement: that *some* dignity-depriving actions cannot be consented to as the person would be reduced in his or her humanity, would be less of a person. For example, slavery would be seen as a dignitary wrong whether the person is enslaved involuntarily or sells himself or herself into that condition.

As noted earlier, this conception of dignity is philosophically contested, but it finds resonance in the employment setting, at least existentially, and in law. The installation of a hidden video surveillance device to capture misbehavior, for example, was held excessive by an American court with these words: "The status of being an employee does not carry with it the elimination of personal dignity." *Richards v. County of Los Angeles*, 775 F.Supp.2d 1176, 1184 (C.D. Cal. 2011).

In the United States, employers may speak freely to employees against unionization so long as they neither threaten reprisal nor promise a benefit. 29 U.S.C. §158(c). For over a half century, the National Labor Relations Board has held that an employer's assembly of its workforce or work groups on paid time to hear the company's anti-union message – a "captive audience speech" – is lawful under the Labor Act. *But see, 2 Sisters Food Group, Inc.,* 357 N.L.R.B. No. 168 (2011) (Member Becker, dissenting). Nor does the Act require the company to give equal time to union organizers. *Livingston Shirt Corp.*, 107 N.L.R.B. 400 (1953). In other words, the Labor Act's only concern in the deployment of this device in an anti-union campaign is as a matter of industrial relations policy, not human dignity.

However, captive audition has been thought to infringe on dignity in just the sense discussed above. "Few shafts could strike with more on-target insult at the very manhood of humanity," wrote Professor Charles L. Black, "than its degradation into a collective *object* of speech, powerless to escape, powerless to answer." "[C]oerced and unreplying attention to the words of another is known immemorially as an individual badge of servility." Charles Black, *He Cannot But Hear: The Plight of the Captive Auditor*, 53 COLUM. L. REV. 960, 966, 967 (1953) (emphasis in original). Cf. ANDREW SAYER, WHY THINGS MATTER TO PEOPLE 197 (2011): "Not being at liberty to speak one's mind ... affronts ... our dignity."

Could an employer compel its employees to listen to a presentation of its views on unionization in Australia, Brazil, Germany, or Japan? Do other countries view captive audition differently – either as a matter of labor policy or as a matter of human dignity?

The question was put to Professor Andrew Stewart. Like the United States, Australia would see the issue as one of industrial relations, but to somewhat different effect:

> [N]ow that the Fair Work Act 2009 provides for the making of a "majority support determination" that compels an employer to engage in collective bargaining (see my notes to Problems 1 and 2), it is certainly possible we could see employers trying to use this tactic to influence any ballot to establish majority support. Alternatively (and this is more likely to arise in practice), an employer could call a meeting of employees to seek to persuade them to vote for an enterprise agreement that is being proposed by the employer, but opposed by one or more union representatives.
>
> As in the US, there would be nothing unlawful as such in a captive audience speech. But the employer would need to be careful not to do anything to misrepresent the nature or scope of an employee's right to express support for collective bargaining or to approve or reject a proposed agreement, or to misrepresent the consequences of exercising such a "workplace right." That would be a breach of section 345 of the Fair Work Act. Section 343 likewise prohibits any coercion in relation to the exercise of workplace rights.
>
> On the other hand, while a union would not have a right of equal time as such, any accredited union official is entitled under section 484 of the Fair Work Act to gain entry to a workplace for the purpose of holding discussions with any workers who wish to attend and whom the union in question is entitled to represent under its rules. Those workers may be actual or merely potential members. Such discussions – which could clearly include an attempt to rebut or indeed preempt any arguments put by the employer about a proposed enterprise agreement – must be held during mealtimes or other breaks (s 490(2)), in any room or area reasonably nominated by the employer (s 492).

In Brazil and Germany, the issue has not arisen because employers do not give captive audience speeches, but the law would speak to it if employers made that effort. In Japan, the issue has arisen as Japanese employers regularly hold morning assemblies and the like – and, given Japan's plural union structure, the employer may well prefer one over another and would like to express that preference; and the issue has been litigated. In all of these, the issue has been seen as of one less of industrial relations than of individual liberty – or dignity.

Brazilian law has been treated by Roberto Fragale Filho and Ronaldo Lobão, *Captive Audience Speech in the Brazilian Labor Law*, 29 COMP. LAB. L. & POL'Y J. 341 (2008). They opine that the employer

> does not buy the possibility to sustain any kind of speech or do whatever pleases him/her. In fact, it is irrelevant if the so-called speech is of an anti-union nature or of a broader character, such as a political one… [E]mployers are entitled to free speech but they cannot stretch their prerogative to impose on workers the burden of listening to whatever they want… Captive audience speeches must then be related to the workplace and it is not so unusual to have this kind of situation related, for example, to a safer work environment… On the other hand, speeches advocating a certain political choice or emphasizing the disastrous consequences of unions' activities seem to be unacceptable.

Id. at 346.

German law has been discussed by Christoph Gyo, *Legitimacy of Captive Audiences in Germany*, 29 COMP. LAB. L. & POL'Y J. 119 (2008). He explains:

> In the case of captive audiences, constitutional rights of both the employer and the employee are affected. On the part of the employer these are the right of free expression accordant to Article 5 GG [the German Constitution], the right of occupational freedom accordant to Article 12 GG and the right of ownership accordant to Article 14 GG. On the employees' part the constitutional rights involved are the freedom of personality accordant to Article 2 paragraph 1 GG and the right of freedom of association according to Article 9 paragraph 3 GG. These constitutional provisions are only violated if the scope of protection is affected without being justified.
>
> …
>
> A speech of the employer to his employees about his personal opinion on unionization, politics, and social policies, as an expression of his opinion belongs to the scope of protection of this constitutional provision and certainly this scope of protection would be affected if these kinds of speeches were prohibited. However, Article 5 paragraph 2 GG allows the limitation of the scope of protection among others by general laws. General laws pursuant to Article 5 paragraph 2 GG are laws that are not directed against the expression of opinion itself but intend to serve the protection of a comprehensive legally protected interest… Article 5 paragraph 1 GG does not allow an employer to force his speech on others against their will.
>
> …
>
> Even though there are no specific laws governing captive audience speeches in Germany, the possibilities of an employer to address his employees are limited. If the

> employer wants to address issues typically addressed in American captive audiences, there is virtually no chance of doing so legally.

Id. at 122, 127 (footnote omitted).

Japanese law has been explained by Hisashi Okuno, *Captive Audience Speeches in Japan: Freedom of Speech of Employers v. Workers' Rights and Freedoms*, 29 COMP. LAB. L. & POL'Y J. 129 (2008), in the context of political and religious messages as well as messages on unionization:

> The courts and the Labor Commissions as well as most legal commentators view the legality of these "captive" meetings negatively. Although freedom of speech is guaranteed by the Constitution, the workers' right to organize, freedom of thought and conscience, as well as the freedom of religion are also guaranteed by the Constitution. The workers' right to organize encompasses the right to form and manage a union by themselves, free from the employer's influence. Similarly, the freedom of thought and conscience and freedom of religion include freedom from imposition of certain ideas and religious beliefs. These rights and freedoms work as counterbalances to and limitations of the freedom of expression that employers enjoy. Because of their coercive nature, "captive audience speeches" on anti-union, political, or religious matters seriously infringe on these rights and freedoms and are therefore viewed negatively. In Japan, employers' anti-union speeches as well as political or religious speeches are discussed and dealt with not only from the viewpoint of the freedom of expression of the employer, but also from the viewpoint of the right and freedom that workers enjoy, all of which are guaranteed by the Constitution.

Id. at 145.

Comments and Questions for Discussion

1. Is Charles Black correct? Is captive audition an infringement on human dignity? Cf. Caroline Mala Corbin, *The First Amendment Right Against Compelled Listening*, 89 B.U.L. REV. 939 (2009) (reviewing constitutional law applicable to state action forbidding captive audition).

2. Return to Problem 1. Assume the company disfavors union representation and would like to assemble its employees to express its views. The company may not be able to do this in Brazil, Germany or Japan; but it could in the U.S. without affording the union equal time. It could do so in Australia as well, but employers have to allow union access to the workforce whether or not the employer holds a captive audience speech.

Would you advise the company to hold such meetings in the U.S.? In Australia? Would you allow employees who disagree with the company's message to express their disagreement in the meeting?

PART V

WRONGFUL DISCHARGE

Involuntary termination from employment can be a serious, even catastrophic event, especially for long-serving employees. There is a loss of income and, possibly, critical benefits that are dependent on employment; as time goes by without employment there may be an erosion or loss of critical skills as well. In addition, there can be serious psychological and social consequences from a loss of status and self-respect – in some cases, a sense of having been treated arbitrarily or abused – and a lack of connectedness with what had been a work group. In communities, displaced workers represent lost purchasing power, increased social service needs, and, when many workers are displaced, a risk to the viability of the community. Being responsible for such social displacement weighs heavy on most managers, but the many externalities have led to various forms of regulation of involuntary termination.

Despite, or perhaps due to, the emotional intensity of job loss, the terminology (in English) conveys varying degrees of severity – from being laid off, to being displaced, to being declared redundant, to being discharged, to being severed, to being terminated. There are also numerous euphemisms, including "position elimination," "cutbacks," "workforce reduction," "reduction in force or RIF," "downsizing," "delayering," "right sizing," "smartsizing," "re-engineering," "repurposing," "reorientation," "realignment," "retrenchment," "managed attrition," "thinning the herd," and "shoot the stragglers." Sadly, the various terms and euphemisms can be met with resistance and even violent behavior. Not surprisingly, then, all developed countries have developed ways to deal with claims of wrongful dismissal. However, as we will see through a look at the five countries, there is a range of very different ways of doing so. The conventional economic wisdom is that higher termination costs deter job formation; that higher termination costs associated with exiting the market deter companies from entering the market. *See generally*, EMPLOYMENT SECURITY AND LABOR MARKET BEHAVIOR: INTERDISCIPLINARY APPROACHES AND INTERNATIONAL EVIDENCE (Christophe Buechtemann ed. 1993). As usual, the precise effects must look to the details of each system. *See* Stefano Liebman, *Evaluate Labor Law: Dismissal Rules*, Bocconi University Legal Studies Research Paper No. 43 (2008).

Rather than explain these differences up front, the differences become evident in more detailed and instructive ways from a close engagement with the ensuing problems. These will distinguish, as all these laws do, between a large-scale displacement of employees for economic or other reasons not based on considerations personal to the employee on the one hand, and, on the other, a discharge that is based upon such considerations. But first, prefatory to that close engagement, set out in Table V.1 are the reactions of corporate CEOs to the question of how they perceive the flexibility they have over hiring and firing in our five country sample.

Table V.1 Hiring and firing practices

United States	5.0
Brazil	3.3
Australia	3.2
Germany	3.1
Japan	2.8

Note: CEOs were asked "How would you characterize the hiring and firing of workers in your country?" (1 = impeded by regulations; 7 = flexibly determined by employers). Weighted average for 2011–12 is shown (mean for 144 nations is 3.9).

Source: World Economic Forum, Executive Opinion Survey, Global Competitiveness Report 2012–2013.

A note on wrongful discharge litigation

The countries surveyed here take different paths as to whether and in what manner employees may vindicate a right not to be dismissed wrongly; in access, expedition, and cost. They also reflect rather different experiences in terms of the frequency with which resort is made to the legal process. The data in some cases is difficult, if not impossible, to come by. What is set out in Table V.2 is a crude effort to get *some* sense of the shape of these institutions. And so some words of caution are necessary.

In Australia, statutory claims of wrongful ('unfair') dismissal are now heard by Fair Work Australia, the Fair Work Act expanding the cohort of those able to assert that right to about 6.7 million employees. Employment discrimination claims are treated separately, such that a complaint must first be made to the human rights commission, after which resort the employee can sue under State or Territorial law. The statistics on discrimination litigation are not available; thus, the figure given in Table V.2 understates the total amount of wrongful dismissal litigation.

Brazil and Germany maintain labor court systems to which an employee may have resort, inexpensively and without legal representation, on a wide variety of issues. Both courts are required to conciliate the dispute as a condition precedent to adjudication. Thus, the figures given in Table V.2 for the number of complaints of wrongful dismissal filed do not account for the settlement rate which, in Germany, is generally about a third of the cases filed up front, i.e. within three months of the filing.

Japan maintains a system of informational outreach on labor rights, proceeding to consultation and conciliation, applicable to individual employment problems and disputes. In 2008, over a million "consultations" were conducted, about 23 percent – over 230,000 – on "employment status" issues. *See* Japan Institute for Labor Policy and Training (JILPT), LABOR SITUATION IN JAPAN AND ANALYSIS: 2009/2010 at 104– 5 (2009). An employee who desires formal legal redress has a choice between proceeding directly to the district court or going to a labor tribunal of the court – akin to a labor court – from which he or she has further resort to the district court if dissatisfied with the labor tribunal's disposition. In 2008, a little over 3,700 labor cases were filed in the Japanese courts, but of those only 719 concerned a "declaration of status," mostly concerning dismissal. As with the data for Australia, this does not include discrimination claims, which, in Japan, tend to be few.

The United States poses an even more complicated problem. As there is no federal wrongful dismissal law, wrongful dismissal has to be brought under some other head: discharge for activity protected by the Labor Act under §8(a)(3), of which the employee must complain exclusively to the National Labor Relations Board (NLRB); discharge as the result of unlawful discrimination, of which the employee must first complain to the Equal Employment Opportunity Commission (EEOC), and which could then be heard in an individual lawsuit brought in federal or state court; discharge in violation of any number of state laws, which would have to be resolved by litigation, commonly in a state court; discharge allegedly not for "just cause" under a collective bargaining agreement, which would be subject to a union/management grievance procedure in which resort may be had to arbitration at the union's discretion (*labor arbitration*); and, in the non-unionized sector, the employee might be governed by an employer arbitration policy in which almost all legal claims would have to be heard (*employment arbitration*).

There are almost no statistics on the operation of these employment arbitration systems. Labor arbitrators are selected through a variety of listing agencies – of which the Federal Mediation and Conciliation Service (FMCS) is only one – or chosen directly by the parties. The data regarding state-level individual employment litigation is difficult, if not impossible, to gather. There is data on the number of charges of violation of §8(a)(3) brought to the NLRB and of discriminatory complaints brought to the EEOC, but these sweep in much in addition to dismissal. FMCS does record the issue before the arbitrators who hear cases through its selection system; but, again, this is a snapshot of only a segment of the labor arbitration scene.

In sum, there is ample evidence that several hundred thousand workplace complaints are lodged by American employees every year – of discriminatory action of all kinds, pension or benefits claims, worker compensation claims, unemployment insurance claims, and more. But the estimate set out in Table V.2 – and it *is* a crude estimate – deals only with cases involving wrongful dismissal pressed to litigation (including those later disposed of on motions). As such, it is surely a *conservative minimum*. We should not be surprised if the actual figure, including employment arbitrations for which we have no data, might be double this estimate or more. Even were that to be so, however, it would not significantly change the relative situation of the United States vis-à-vis the comparison states.

Table V.2 Litigation: individual discharge complaints filed for adjudication (2007/2008)

Country	Number of cases	Cases per 1,000 workers
Australia (wrongful dismissal only, Fair Work Australia (2009–10))	13,983	1.24
Brazil (all labor court complaints)	1,824,661	20.09
Germany (wrongful dismissal only)	176,112	4.23
Japan (declaration of status only)	719	0.01
U.S. (wrongful dismissal)	20,000+ (see note below)	0.13+

Sources:

Australia: Towards more Productive and Equitable Workforces: An Evaluation of the Fair Work Legislation 215 (2012).

Brazil: Labor Court statistics supplied by Roberto Fragale.

Germany: Günter Grötmann-Hofling, *Die Arbeitsgerichtsbarkeit 2008 im Licht der Statistik*, AuR (2010) 113, 116.

Japan: JILPT 2009 Report, supra, at 110–11.

United States: NLRB Annual Report 2009, table 2 at p. 94; EEOC Statistics: http://wwwl.eeoc.gov/eeoc/statistics/enforcement/litigation.cfm?renderforprint=1 (9/23/2012); FMCS, 2011 Annual

Report at p. 12; Employment Discrimination (2009): complaints filed with EEOC: 93,277; federal anti-discrimination in employment lawsuits filed: 15,654;
NLRB §8(a)(3) (2009): Charges filed: 6,496; complaints issued (*all* charges): 9.7% (presumably about 650 §(a)(3) complaints); total hearings (of *all* § 8(a)(3) complaints): 162;
Wrongful Discharge under Collective Bargaining Agreements: FMCS Arbitration (2007): arbitrators appointed: 6,465; cases heard: 2,067; Wrongful discharges heard: 762.

PROBLEM 10: OUTSOURCING ABROAD

Return to the labor cost analysis in Problem 2. The company has decided that it would be more cost effective to terminate its customer service workers, who constitute 50 of the 400 employees employed at this facility, and outsource the work abroad. Are there any limits on its ability to do so other than information sharing and consultation obligations?

Problem 10 discussion – Australia

There are no laws in Australia that preclude a company from deciding to outsource its labour needs. Even if a union sought to negotiate restrictions on outsourcing, these could not validly be included in an enterprise agreement registered under the Fair Work Act 2009. As explained in relation to Problem 2, such an agreement can generally only deal with matters "pertaining" to the employer's relationships with the employees and/or unions covered by the agreement. There is High Court authority to the effect that a prohibition on the contracting out of labour is not a matter *directly* pertaining to employment relations: *R v Commonwealth Industrial Court*; *Ex parte Cocks* (1968) 121 CLR 313. Nor could a union organise industrial action in protest against an outsourcing decision, since under Part 3–3 of the Act industrial action may only lawfully be taken or organised in support of a new enterprise agreement, after the expiry of any existing agreement.

The reason for the outsourcing is presumably to relocate the jobs in question to a country with lower labour standards than Australia. While the Fair Work Act can in some circumstances apply to employees who work outside Australia, it does not generally cover employment relationships that are formed overseas: see Fair Work Regulations 2009 reg 1.15F and the definitions of "Australian employer" and "Australian-based employee" in s 35 of the Fair Work Act (see infra).

There is, however, one potential cost to the outsourcing. In most cases, an employer that terminates the employment of a group of staff as part of an outsourcing exercise will be required to give each employee notice of termination, and also make a severance payment calculated according to the length of their service with the company. The latter obligation arises because the dismissals are by way of *redundancy* – that is, the employer no longer wishes the job to be performed (or at least, not by anyone the employer is directly hiring).

The minimum obligations in this respect are set out in ss 117 and 119 of the Fair Work Act (infra). For example, an employee aged under 45 with 5 years' service would be entitled to at least 4 weeks' notice, plus 10 weeks' severance pay. The employees can either be required to work out their notice period, or be terminated immediately and paid out their notice. In many cases, union-negotiated agreements set redundancy entitlements that are more generous than the statutory minima. They may allow up to 4 (or even more) weeks' pay per year of service and cap out at anything up to 52 weeks' pay or higher.

Employees also have to be paid out for accrued annual leave entitlements: see s 90(2) of the Fair Work Act. In addition, employees with 10 or more years of service (and sometimes less) will be entitled to be paid out for untaken long service leave under State or Territory legislation. (That entitlement explains why the statutory scale of redundancy pay in s 119(2) actually falls after an employee reaches 10 years of service.)

PRIMARY SOURCES

Fair Work Regulations 2009 reg 1.15F (infra).

Fair Work Act 2009 (Cth) ss 35, 117, 119, 120, 121(1), 123(1)–(2) (infra).

Fair Work Regulations 2009

1.15F Extension of Act beyond the exclusive economic zone and the continental shelf

(2) For subsection 34 (3) of the [Fair Work] Act, the provisions of the Act mentioned in the following table, and the rest of the Act so far as it relates to those provisions, are extended to:
  (a) an Australian employer in relation to the employer's Australian-based employees; and
  (b) an Australian-based employee in relation to the employee's employer if the same enterprise agreement applies to both of them;

in relation to all of the area outside the outer limits of the exclusive economic zone and the continental shelf.

Item	Provision of the Act
1	Part 2–1 – core provisions for Chapter 2
2	Part 2–2 – the National Employment Standards
3	Part 2–3 – modern awards
4	Part 2–6 – minimum wages
5	Part 2–7 – equal remuneration
6	Part 2–8 – transfer of business
7	Part 2–9 – other terms and conditions of employment

Fair Work Act 2009

35 Meanings of Australian employer and Australian-based employee

(1) An *Australian employer* is an employer that:
   (a) is a trading corporation formed within the limits of the Commonwealth (within the meaning of paragraph 51(xx) of the Constitution); or
   (b) is a financial corporation formed within the limits of the Commonwealth (within the meaning of paragraph 51(xx) of the Constitution); or
   (c) is the Commonwealth; or
   (d) is a Commonwealth authority; or
   (e) is a body corporate incorporated in a Territory; or
   (f) carries on in Australia, in the exclusive economic zone or in the waters above the continental shelf an activity (whether of a commercial, governmental or other nature), and whose central management and control is in Australia; or
   (g) is prescribed by the regulations.

(2) An *Australian-based employee* is an employee:
   (a) whose primary place of work is in Australia; or
   (b) who is employed by an Australian employer (whether the employee is located in Australia or elsewhere); or
   (c) who is prescribed by the regulations.

(3) However, paragraph (2)(b) does not apply to an employee who is engaged outside Australia and the external Territories to perform duties outside Australia and the external Territories.

Division 11 – Notice of termination and redundancy pay

117 Requirement for notice of termination or payment in lieu

Notice specifying day of termination

(1) An employer must not terminate an employee's employment unless the employer has given the employee written notice of the day of the termination (which cannot be before the day the notice is given).

Note 1: Section 123 describes situations in which this section does not apply.

Note 2: Sections 28A and 29 of the *Acts Interpretation Act 1901* provide how a notice may be given. In particular, the notice may be given to an employee by:

(a) delivering it personally; or
(b) leaving it at the employee's last known address; or
(c) sending it by prepaid post to the employee's last known address.

Amount of notice or payment in lieu of notice

(2) The employer must not terminate the employee's employment unless:
(a) the time between giving the notice and the day of the termination is at least the period (the *minimum period of notice*) worked out under subsection (3); or
(b) the employer has paid to the employee (or to another person on the employee's behalf) payment in lieu of notice of at least the amount the employer would have been liable to pay to the employee (or to another person on the employee's behalf) at the full rate of pay for the hours the employee would have worked had the employment continued until the end of the minimum period of notice.

(3) Work out the minimum period of notice as follows:
(a) first, work out the period using the following table:

Period

	Employee's period of continuous service with the employer at the end of the day the notice is given	Period
1	Not more than 1 year	1 week
2	More than 1 year but not more than 3 years	2 weeks
3	More than 3 years but not more than 5 years	3 weeks
4	More than 5 years	4 weeks

(b) then increase the period by 1 week if the employee is over 45 years old and has completed at least 2 years of continuous service with the employer at the end of the day the notice is given.

119 Redundancy pay

Entitlement to redundancy pay

(1) An employee is entitled to be paid redundancy pay by the employer if the employee's employment is terminated:
(a) at the employer's initiative because the employer no longer requires the job done by the employee to be done by anyone, except where this is due to the ordinary and customary turnover of labour; or
(b) because of the insolvency or bankruptcy of the employer.

Note: Sections 121, 122 and 123 describe situations in which the employee does not have this entitlement.

Amount of redundancy pay

(2) The amount of the redundancy pay equals the total amount payable to the employee for the redundancy pay period worked out using the following table at the employee's base rate of pay for his or her ordinary hours of work:

Redundancy pay period

	Employee's period of continuous service with the employer on termination	Redundancy pay period
1	At least 1 year but less than 2 years	4 weeks
2	At least 2 years but less than 3 years	6 weeks
3	At least 3 years but less than 4 years	7 weeks
4	At least 4 years but less than 5 years	8 weeks
5	At least 5 years but less than 6 years	10 weeks
6	At least 6 years but less than 7 years	11 weeks
7	At least 7 years but less than 8 years	13 weeks
8	At least 8 years but less than 9 years	14 weeks
9	At least 9 years but less than 10 years	16 weeks
10	At least 10 years	12 weeks

120 Variation of redundancy pay for other employment or incapacity to pay

(1) This section applies if:
  (a) an employee is entitled to be paid an amount of redundancy pay by the employer because of section 119; and
  (b) the employer:
    (i) obtains other acceptable employment for the employee; or
    (ii) cannot pay the amount.

(2) On application by the employer, FWA may determine that the amount of redundancy pay is reduced to a specified amount (which may be nil) that FWA considers appropriate.

(3) The amount of redundancy pay to which the employee is entitled under section 119 is the reduced amount specified in the determination.

121 Exclusions from obligation to pay redundancy pay

(1) Section 119 does not apply to the termination of an employee's employment if, immediately before the time of the termination, or at the time when the person was given notice of the termination as described in subsection 117(1) (whichever happened first):
  (a) the employee's period of continuous service with the employer is less than 12 months; or
  (b) the employer is a small business employer.

123 Limits on scope of this Division

Employees not covered by this Division

(1) This Division does not apply to any of the following employees:
  (a) an employee employed for a specified period of time, for a specified task, or for the duration of a specified season;

(b) an employee whose employment is terminated because of serious misconduct;
(c) a casual employee;
(d) an employee (other than an apprentice) to whom a training arrangement applies and whose employment is for a specified period of time or is, for any reason, limited to the duration of the training arrangement;
(e) an employee prescribed by the regulations as an employee to whom this Division does not apply.

(2) Paragraph (1)(a) does not prevent this Division from applying to an employee if a substantial reason for employing the employee as described in that paragraph was to avoid the application of this Division.

References and suggested readings

ANDREW STEWART, STEWART'S GUIDE TO EMPLOYMENT LAW §§2.29; 8.37; 16.25–8 (4th ed. 2013).

Problem 10 discussion – Brazil

Outsourcing is admitted by law in Brazil in a few circumstances, mostly in private security and maintenance and cleaning services. Nonetheless, an environment of extremely fragmented work has provoked the *Tribunal Superior do Trabalho* to examine whether legal protection could be extended to new and different areas. Its answer so far has consisted in the creation of a not-always very clear distinction between activities-end and activities-means. Outsourcing would only be permitted for the latter, as such matters are not immediately linked to the company's main and direct purpose. For instance, according to such reasoning, outsourcing of call centers which are usually related to customer services – an activity-means – could be authorized by the labor higher court. The problem here lies in the definition of activities-end and activities-means. These categories are so diffuse and hard to define that characterization becomes extremely discretionary: is the manufacturing of brakes an end or a means for the making of an automobile? What about the manufacturing of tires? An answer cannot easily be given.

On the other hand, as a way to moderate the impact of outsourcing, the *Tribunal Superior do Trabalho* has also created a new category of liability for companies outsourcing some of their activities: it is the so-called subsidiary responsibility. It means that companies outsourcing services, even when done lawfully, are not exempt from responsibility in the event of noncompliance with labor obligations by the outsourced company towards its employees. There is an enormous case law in the matter and many still argue that courts have gone so far as to assume legislative prerogatives. Controversy over its applicability to public administration due to federal regulation (*Lei Federal* nº 8.666/1993) is still pending in the *Supremo Tribunal Federal* (Brazilian Supreme Court). Lately, telecommunications companies have also challenged the subsidiary responsibility, arguing that the *Lei Geral das Telecomunicações* (Telecommunications Act) allows them to outsource services without any distinction between activities-end and activities-means. This issue continues to be widely debated.

In contrast to North-American and French experience, where companies have been able to outsource services to India and French-speaking Africa, outsourcing abroad is still largely unknown in Brazil. So far, technology has made possible the outsourcing of some services to different States within the country (such as Bahia and Minas Gerais), but not abroad. One may wonder what would happen to subsidiary responsibility when outsourcing abroad becomes a reality in Brazil: how to hold companies accountable for whatever happens abroad or whether these claims must be submitted to other national jurisdictions.

References and suggested readings

Lei No. 9.472, 1997 (Braz.) *accessed at* http://www.planalto.gov.br/ccivil/leis/L9472.htm (last visited Feb. 19, 2010).

Lei No. 8.666 (Federal Statute nº 8.666) 1993 (Braz.) *accessed at* http://www.planalto.gov.br/ccivil_03/LEIS/L8666cons.html (last visited Feb. 19, 2010).

On the distinction between activities-end and activities-means, see: BRASIL. TRIBUNAL SUPERIOR DO TRABALHO, Súmula 331, *accessed at* http://www3.tst.jus.br/jurisprudencia/Sumulas_com_indice/Sumulas_Ind_301_350.html#SUM-331 (last visited Oct. 2, 2012).

Karen Artur, *O Tribunal Superior do Trabalho e novas noções do contrato de trabalho: o caso da terceirização*. Paper presented at the V WORKSHOP EMPRESA, EMPRESÁRIOS E SOCIEDADE: O MUNDO EMPRESARIAL E A QUESTÃO SOCIAL, Porto Alegre, May 2–5, 2006, PUCRS *accessed at* http://www.fee.tche.br/5workshop/pdf/gt01_karen.pdf (last visited Feb. 19, 2010).

KAREN ARTUR, O TST FRENTE À TERCEIRIZAÇÃO (2007).

Roberto Fragale Filho, *As transformações do trabalho e seu impacto no conceito de subordinação jurídica*. 2 REVISTA DA ABET 121 (2002) *accessed at* http://www.ea.ufrgs.br/graduacao/disciplinas/adm01156/NOVAS%20FORMAS%20DE%20TRABALHO%20E%20LEGISLA%E2%82%AC%C3%87O.doc (last visited Feb. 19, 2010).

Problem 10 discussion – Germany

Termination of the contracts of incumbent (part-time or full time) workers may as such amount to a "modification of business operations" (*Betriebsänderung*) within the meaning of section 111 of the Works Councils Act, triggering rights of the works council to a "compromise of interests" (*Interessenausgleich*) according to section 112 para. 1 sentence 1 of the Works Councils Act – an essentially deliberate agreement on the "whether", "when" and "how" of the "modification of business operations" – and a "social plan" (*Sozialplan*) according to section 112 para. 1 sentence 2 of the Works Councils Act which aims at compensation for possible hardship caused by such "modification of business operations" and resembles a special form of redundancy program. If employer and works council fail to agree on a "social plan", an arbitration board will decide (section 112 para. 4 of the Works Councils Act). It should be noted, however, that the employer in such cases can be forced into a "social plan" only if the thresholds fixed in section 112a of the Works Councils Act are surpassed. This means, for instance, that in establishments with a regular workforce of 500 at least 10 per cent (but in addition at least 60 people) must be dismissed on operational reasons.

As an administrative matter, the employer has to notify the agency of employment about the imminent changes in the workforce if he plans to dismiss 10 per cent of the workforce or more than 25 people in establishments with a regular workforce of between 60 and fewer than 500 employees (section 17 para. 1 of the Act on Dismissal Protection). Before the expiration of a period of one month after notification, the resulting dismissals will become effective only after approval by the agency (section 18 para. 1 of the Acts on Dismissal

Protection). In addition the agency may decide in individual cases that dismissals will not become effective before expiration of a period of two months (section 18 para. 2 of the Act on Dismissal Protection).

PRIMARY SOURCES

Works Councils Act

Section 111 Alterations

In establishments that normally have more than twenty employees with voting rights the employer shall inform the works council in full and in good time of any proposed alterations which may entail substantial prejudice to the staff or a large sector thereof and consult the works council on the proposed alterations. In establishments that have more than 300 employees, the works council may retain a consultant to support it; section 80 (4) shall apply, mutatis mutandis, the foregoing shall be without prejudice to section 80 (3). The following shall be considered as alterations for the purposes of the first sentence above:

1. reduction of operations in or closure of the whole or important departments of the establishment;
2. transfer of the whole or important departments of the establishment;
3. the amalgamation with other establishments or split-up of establishments;
4. important changes in the organization, purpose or plant of the establishment;
5. introduction of entirely new work methods and production processes.

Section 112 Reconciliation of interests in the case of alterations; social compensation plan

(1) If the employer and the works council reach an agreement to reconcile their interests in connection with the proposed alterations, the said agreement shall be recorded in writing and signed by the employer and the works council. The foregoing shall also apply to an agreement on full or part compensation for any financial prejudice sustained by staff as a result of the proposed alterations (social compensation plan). The social compensation plan shall have the effect of a works agreement. Section 77 (3) shall not apply to the social compensation plan.

(2) If no reconciliation of interests can be achieved in connection with the proposed alterations or if no agreement is reached on the social compensation plan, the employer or the works council may apply to the Executive Board of the Federal Employment Agency for mediation, the Board may entrust other staff members of the Federal Employment Agency with this task. If mediation is not applied for or the attempt at mediation is unsuccessful, the employer or the works council may submit the case to the conciliation committee. The chairman of the conciliation committee may request a member of the Executive Board of the Federal Employment Agency or a staff member of the Federal Employment Agency appointed by the Board to take part in the proceedings.

(3) The employer and the works council shall submit proposals to the conciliation committee for the settlement of differences on the reconciliation of interests and the social compensation plan. The conciliation committee shall attempt to reconcile the parties. If an agreement is reached, it shall be recorded in writing and signed by the parties and the chairman.

(4) If no agreement is reached on the social compensation plan, the conciliation committee shall make a decision on the drawing up of a social compensation plan. The award of the conciliation committee shall take the place of an agreement between the employer and the works council.

(5) When making a decision in pursuance of subsection (4), the conciliation committee shall take into account the social interests of the employees concerned while taking care that its decision does not place an unreasonable financial burden on the company. In doing so and within the framework of equitable discretion, the conciliation committee shall be guided by the following principles, in particular:

1. When compensating in full or part any financial prejudices sustained, in particular by a reduction in income, the lapse of additional benefits or loss of entitlements to company pensions, removal costs or increased travelling costs, it shall provide for payments which generally make allowances for the circumstances of the individual case.
2. It shall take into account the prospects of the employees concerned on the labour market. It shall exclude from payments employees who may continue to work in reasonable employment in the same establishment or in another establishment of the company or of a company belonging to the combine, but refuse said continued employment; the possibility of continued employment at another location shall not alone be sufficient grounds for claiming unreasonableness.

2a. In particular, it shall duly consider the support schemes aimed at avoiding unemployment provided for in Book Three of the Social Code.

3. When calculating the total amount of the social compensation plan payments, it shall take care that the continuance of the company or the jobs remaining after the implementation of the alterations is not jeopardised.

Section 112a Enforceable social compensation plan in the event of staff cutbacks, establishment of new businesses

. . .

Section 113 Indemnities

(1) If the employer fails to comply with an agreement on the reconciliation of interests in connection with the alterations proposed without any compelling reasons to do so, the employees who are dismissed as a result of such non-compliance may bring an action in the labour court requesting that the employer should be condemned to pay indemnities; section 10 of the Protection against Dismissal Act shall apply, mutatis mutandis.

(2) If employees sustain other financial prejudice as a result of a non-compliance covered by subsection (1), the employer shall make good such prejudice for a period not exceeding twelve months.

(3) Subsections (1) and (2) shall apply, mutatis mutandis, where the employer carries out any proposed alterations within the meaning of section 111 without having attempted to reach an agreement with the works council on a reconciliation of interests and such action results in dismissals or other financial prejudice to employees.

Problem 10 discussion – Japan

Japan has established a case law *rule* on economic dismissals which has been called the "four requirement rule for economic dismissals." The four requirements are:

(1) there must be a business-based need to resort to a reduction of personnel;
(2) dismissals must be the last resort to cope with the economic difficulties and thus the employer must take every possible measure to avoid adjustment dismissals. Before resorting to dismissals, employers are required to take other measures such as reduction in overtime, reduction in regular hiring or mid-term recruitment, implementation of transfers (*haiten*) or 'farming out' (*shukko*) with respect to redundant workers, non-renewal of fixed-term contracts or contracts of part-timers, and solicitation of voluntary retirement;
(3) the selection of those workers to be dismissed must be made on an objective and reasonable basis; and
(4) the employer is required to take proper procedures to explain the necessity of the dismissal, its timing, scale and method to the labor union or worker group if no union exists, and consult them regarding dismissals in good faith.

Traditionally, the validity of economic dismissals has been determined on the basis of whether these four requirements are met or not. If one of the four requirements is not satisfied, the dismissal has been regarded as an abuse of the right to dismiss. However, since 2000, several district courts have significantly changed the interpretation of the "four requirements." According to these courts, what the court should determine is whether or not a dismissal is abusive, because there are no solid legal grounds for insisting that all four requirements must be satisfied for economic dismissals. Therefore, the so-called "four requirements" are nothing but "four factors" to analyze abusiveness. According to their interpretation, if one of the four "factors" (for example, consultation with a union) is not met, such an economic dismissal can be held legal and valid by taking all other factors surrounding the dismissals into consideration.

Therefore, the legal framework for determining the validity of dismissals for economic reasons has been relaxed. However, there is no clear evidence that the new framework (a four-factor rule) has made economic dismissals easier than before. Even under the four-factor rule, it is generally understood that Japanese courts still severely restrict economic dismissals.

Apart from the scrutiny of the abusiveness of economic dismissals by the courts, the employer owes an administrative duty to report to the Minister of the Health, Labor and Welfare on the massive employment change by the Employment Measures Act (Art. 27). According to the bylaw, dismissals or separation of more than 30 employees are regarded as a massive employment change. Violation of this reporting is sanctioned by criminal penalty (Art. 38 para. 1 no. 1).

Problem 10 discussion – United States

Unionized workplaces Section 8(a)(5) of the National Labor Relations Act requires the employer to bargain in good faith about wages, hours, and working conditions. A decision on the continued availability of work can, obviously, be a working condition. The United States Supreme Court has drawn a distinction between subcontracting, which decision is mandatorily bargainable, and a partial closure, which is not. *Compare Fibreboard Paper Pdts. Corp. v. NLRB*, 379 U.S. 203 (1964) (subcontracting) *with First Nat'l Maintenance Corp. v. NLRB*, 452 U.S. 666 (1981) (partial closure).

The *relocation* of work done by the employees represented by a union falls in between these two poles and the NLRB has adopted a complex amalgam of the

Supreme Court's reasoning distinguishing the two. Basically, if the decision to relocate the *same* work is driven by labor costs, the employer must bargain with the union about the decision unless it proves that doing so would have been futile – that the union was either not in a position to or would not have made a cost concession that would have caused the employee to retain the work in the bargaining unit. *See United Food & Commercial Workers, Local 150-A v. NLRB* (*Dubuque Packaging Co.*), 1 F.3d 24 (D.C. Cir. 1993). Because the Board's remedial power could extend to a restoration of the work pending good faith bargaining, employers are well advised to bargain about economically driven work relocation. But, if an impasse is reached – absent a contractual work presentation agreement which is lawful in the United States – the employer may implement its decision.

Apart from the question of whether the decision to relocate the work is mandatorily bargainable, there is no doubt that an employer is obligated to bargain with the union about the effects of the decision on affected members of the bargaining unit. The idea of "effects" bargaining bears a strong similarity to the German obligation to negotiate a "social plan" with the works council except, importantly, that effects bargaining can occur after the decision is made and even implemented, whereas the process in Germany is precedent to the relocation. Perhaps more importantly, among the consequences of disagreement in the U.S. is the possibility of a strike – by out-of-work employees – whereas in Germany the consequence of disagreement is mandatory arbitration (for which cost the employer must pay).

All workplaces. Whether unionized or not, the federal Worker Adjustment and Retraining Notification Act (WARN) requires 60 days' notice to affected employees of a plant closing or "mass layoff" subject to several exempting conditions. (Some state laws track the federal law but require greater notice.) A mass layoff is defined as a reduction in force that results in an employment loss at a single site of employment during a 30-day period of at least 33 percent of the full-time workforce and at least 50 full-time employees, or of at least 500 full-time employees. In Problem 10, 50 employees will be terminated; but as that represents 12.5 percent of 400 employed at this site, it does not constitute a "mass layoff" for the purposes of the WARN Act and so no notice need be afforded under federal law.

PRIMARY SOURCE

Worker Adjustment and Retraining Notification Act

29 U.S.C. §2101–2108

§2101(a) Definitions

As used in this chapter:

(1) the term "employer" means any business enterprise that employs –
  (A) 100 or more employees, excluding part-time employees; or
  (B) 100 or more employees who in the aggregate work at least 4,000 hours per week (exclusive of hours of overtime);

(2) the term "plant closing" means the permanent or temporary shutdown of a single site of employment or one or more facilities or operating units within a single site of employment, if the shutdown results in an employment loss at the single site of employment during any 30-day period for 50 or more employees excluding any part-time employees;

(3) the term "mass layoff" means a reduction in force which:
  (A) is not the result of a plant closing; and
  (B) results in an employment loss at the single site of employment during any 30-day period for:
    (i)(I) at least 33 percent of the employees (excluding any part-time employees); and
    (II) at least 50 employees (excluding any part-time employees); or
    (ii) at least 500 employees (excluding any part-time employees);

§2102. Notice required before plant closings and mass layoffs

(a) Notice to employees, state dislocated worker units, and local governments

An employer shall not order a plant closing or mass layoff until the end of a 60-day period after the employer serves written notice of such an order –

(1) to each representative of the affected employees as of the time of the notice or if there is no such representative at that time, to each affected employee; and

(2) to the State dislocated worker unit or office… and the chief elected official of the unit of local government within which such closing or layoff is to occur.

(b) Reduction of notification period

(1) An employer may order the shutdown of a single site of employment before the conclusion of the 60-day period if as of the time that notice would have been required the employer was actively seeking capital or business which, if obtained, would have enabled the employer to avoid or postpone the shutdown and the employer reasonably and in good faith believed that giving the notice required would have precluded the employer from obtaining the needed capital or business.

(2) (A) An employer may order a plant closing or mass layoff before the conclusion of the 60-day period if the closing or mass layoff is caused by business circumstances that were not reasonably foreseeable as of the time that notice would have been required.

(3) An employer relying on this subsection shall give as much notice as is practicable and at that time shall give a brief statement of the basis for reducing the notification period.

(c) Extension of layoff period

§2103. Exemptions

This chapter shall not apply to a plant closing or mass layoff if –

(1) the closing is of a temporary facility or the closing or layoff is the result of the completion of a particular project or undertaking, and the affected employees were hired with the understanding that their employment was limited to the duration of the facility or the project or undertaking; or

. . .

§ 2104. Administration and enforcement of requirements

(a) Civil actions against employers

(1) Any employer who orders a plant closing or mass layoff in violation of section 2102 of this title shall be liable to each aggrieved employee who suffers an employment loss as a result of such closing or layoff for –
    (A) Back pay for each day of violation at a rate of compensation not less than the higher of:
        (i) The average regular rate received by such employee during the last 3 years of the employee's employment; or
        (ii) The final regular rate received by such employee; and [benefits] ...

. . .

(1) If an employer which has violated this chapter proves to the satisfaction of the court that the act or omission that violated this chapter was in good faith and that the employer had reasonable grounds for believing that the act or omission was not a violation of this chapter the court may, in its discretion, reduce the amount of the liability or penalty provided for in this section ...

References and suggested readings

See generally WILLIAM BAUMOL, ALAN BLINDER & EDWARD WOLFF, DOWNSIZING IN AMERICA: REALITY, CAUSES, AND CONSEQUENCES (2003). On the WARN Act, *see* S. Nord & Y. Ting, *The Impact of Advance Notice of Plant Closings on Earnings and the Probability of Unemployment*, 44 INDUS. & LAB. REL. REV. 681 (1991). On how closely the WARN Act is parsed, see *Ellis v. DHL Express (USA)* (United States District Court for the Northern District of Illinois 2009), 158 Lab. Cas. [CCH] ¶ 10, 123 (Dec. 9, 2009).

It is hard for us in the U.S. to see the possible advantages of a less flexible employment system such as Germany's. It is possible that employers who are required to keep employees around during a recession are better poised to ramp up production at the slightest hint of an economic upswing, so I would expect that Germany might have a faster recovery than the U.S. During this recession, I've read a number of articles in business magazines warning against cutting too many jobs or closing too many plants for this same reason – once the recovery comes, companies need to be ready. I think culture comes into play in the desire for stability – are people in the country risk-takers or risk-averse? I would guess that Americans are more risk-takers than Germans and are willing to accept a slower recovery with a bigger upside, while Germans would perhaps prefer a more stable environment with shallower lows and shorter highs.

Manager, international Benefits and Compensation,
Consumer Goods Sector

The single greatest implication [of the]... problems on co-determination and consultation... [is] your obligation [as an HR manager]... to ensure [the]... predominantly " Western GM's" we all work for understand the implications [of decisions] beyond the market space and revenue opportunity in global expansion.

Senior Vice President, HR, Biomedical Sector

[I]t is not all altruistic that companies provide... severance agreements. In exchange for the severance benefits, the employee must sign an agreement waiving all rights of discrimination suits such as age discrimination. There are further steps that a company takes to ensure lawsuits are avoided. These include Older Workers' Protection assessments and other adverse impact analysis for terminated people over the age of 40 or minority employees.

Vice President, HR, Electrical Manufacturing Sector

At my company we just let go 5 percent of my workforce. We used [standard] criteria, competencies, behaviors, forced ranking, matched up to future skills needed, etc. We went through this process not to protect ourselves, but to make sure we cut the right 100 employees and kept the employees who could drive the business. We could care less about people suing us or making sure we could justify a dismissal. We wanted to do what was right for the business and keep the best people. If we did not have this process then managers would have picked their friends etc. That is what most human beings do. They pick the people they like even for non-job related reasons.

Senior Vice President, HR, Information Technology Sector

Questions for Discussion – Problem 10

1. Compare how swift and expensive – or inexpensive – it would be to relocate this work from each of these countries (from the perspective of financial consequences and transaction costs, as indicated under the law).

2. Return to the Australian essay in Problem 2. Although a "work preservation" provision prohibiting the relocation of work would not be enforceable – as it would be in the U.S. – unlike the non-unionized U.S. employer, all Australian employers must give notice to employees of a decision to introduce a major change in program or organization that is likely to have a significant effect on employees and consult with their representative chosen for that specific purpose. See Model Consultation Term, supra, in Problem 2. There is no obligation to consult affected employees in the U.S. Might employees have anything to add to the quality of the decision as a company considers work relocation?

3. A unionized U.S employer has to bargain about the "effects" of a relocation decision. A German employer must negotiate a "social plan" with the works council. Dr Fischinger has translated a "Social Compensation Plan" between a company and its works council not atypical in its provisions, set out below. In addition, the authors are indebted to Lawrence Casazza, Esq., of Vedder Price in Chicago, Illinois, a prominent law firm on the management side, who has supplied a similar "Closure Agreement" for the U.S., a not atypical consequence of "effects" bargaining in the United States. These are set out directly below.
   a. How do these two agreements differ in terms of how the affected employees are treated?
   b. If this social plan is normative in the sense that it represents something close to what an arbitration would produce were the company and the works council to fail to reach agreement, to what extent would these likely consequences of market exit play a role in your company's decision to locate a facility in Germany?

c. Extend the same question regarding the consequences of exit relocation from Australia, Brazil, and Japan. You may return to the statistics set out in the Introduction on the nature of U.S. firms operating in these countries in 2008. If exit costs deter location, how do you explain the extent of U.S. market participation?

d. Germany is commonly thought of as being drenched in legalism, while the U.S. is thought of as far more loose and flexible. Consider these two texts from that perspective. What explains the difference in detail and tone?

CLOSURE AGREEMENT [U.S.]

This Closure Agreement ("Agreement") is made and entered into by and between ________________ ("the Company") through its duly authorized representatives, and ________________ for itself and on behalf of its members ("the Union"), through its authorized representatives.

WHEREAS, the Company has operated the _________ facility ("the Facility");

WHEREAS, certain employees of the Facility have been represented by the Union for purposes of collective bargaining;

WHEREAS, for good and legitimate business reasons explained to the Union for purposes of collective bargaining;

WHEREAS, the Company notified the Union of its tentative decision, and both parties negotiated in good faith over the decision and its impact on employees; and

WHEREAS, the Company and the Union wish to reach an agreement for an orderly closure of the facility.

NOW THEREFORE, the Company and the Union hereby agree as follows:

1. **Unanimous Recommendation:**

   The Union's Negotiating Committee unanimously recommends that employees ratify this Agreement.

2. **Incorporation of Recitals**

   The recitals set forth above are part of this agreement and considered a material part of this Agreement.

3. **Notice of Closing**

...

4. **Projected Closure Date**

...

5. **Maintenance of Existing Agreement**

Except as otherwise set forth in this Agreement, the parties' Collective Bargaining Agreement shall remain in full force and effect, including terms regarding pay, benefits, and other terms and conditions of employment, through the date all bargaining unit employees are laid off. The Agreement shall so apply if bargaining unit operations resume in ______ on or before ________, ____. Where this Agreement and the Collective Bargaining Agreement are in conflict, the terms set out in this Agreement will govern.

6. **Cooperation in Shut-Down**

The Union and all bargaining unit employees will use their best efforts to ensure that there is an orderly winding down of operations, transfer of equipment, and closure of the Facility. There shall be no strikes, sabotage, work stoppages, work slowdowns, picketing, protests, or other interruption or interference with operations and closure of the facility.

7. **Order of layoffs**

All layoffs shall be by Company seniority, with the least senior employee laid off first, as provided in the Collective Bargaining Agreement.

8. **Vacation Pay**

The Company will pay employees all accrued but unused _____ vacation pay (earned in ______) to which they are entitled under the parties' Collective Bargaining Agreement within seven (7) business days of an employee's final layoff from employment or within seven (7) business days if the employee was already laid off. The Company will pay ____ vacation pay (earned in ____ prior to layoff) within seven (7) days after the employee returns his or her release and any period to revoke agreement expires.

9. **Retention and Severance Payment**

(a) Eligibility: In order to be eligible for any of the benefits described under this Section 9, an employee must remain an employee in good standing at the time he or she is permanently laid off by the Company. An employee who retires, resigns, accepts an offer of transfer or otherwise ceases to be employed for any reason prior to that date or is subject to discharge for good cause that is not reversed in arbitration shall not receive any of the additional benefits described below. An employee must also execute a Separation Agreement in the form set forth in Exhibit A, and fulfill all conditions and requirements of that Separation Agreement. In the event a fully executed Separation Agreement is not returned to the Company within forty-five (45) calendar days of the date the employee received it, the employee shall be deemed to have rejected it and the employee shall not receive the benefits described in this Agreement. A copy of the Separation Agreement shall be tendered to each employee no later than the date of his or her layoff, or if the employee is laid off before this Agreement is ratified, within seven (7) calendar days.

(b) Separation Payments: Employees who fulfill the conditions of this Agreement will receive the following severance pay: $___ per full year of seniority recognized by the Company with no cap on the number of years of service, even if they later retire. All payments will be subject to applicable state and federal withholding and other deductions required by law...

(c) Continuation of Group Medial Medical Payments: The Company will continue medical and dental insurance to the end of the calendar month following the month that a bargaining unit employee is laid off. For example, if an employee is laid off on November 1, insurance will be maintained through December 31. Employees will be responsible for their share of premium contributions as provided in the collective bargaining agreement during this period, and must submit payment in full within the first ten (10) days of the month to be eligible. Eligible employees also shall be offered and have the right to continue medical and dental insurance coverage under the Consolidated Omnibus Budget Reconciliation Act (COBRA) for up to 18 months after the last date of regular employment, which is the qualifying event for COBRA purposes. Such employees must provide a completed COBRA election form to the Company for entitlement to COBRA to become effective. During the 18 months after the date of regular employment, eligible bargaining unit employees may continue coverage under COBRA by paying the full COBRA premiums. The Company's obligation to provide such medical/dental coverage ends automatically upon the occurrence of any event that causes the eligible employee's entitlement to COBRA continuation to cease.

(d) If any employee elects COBRA coverage for coverage after this period (up to eighteen (18) months), the Company shall reimburse each employee for the first month of the COBRA premium, less the share of the premium that the employee would have paid prior to his or her layoff as provided in the Collective Bargaining Agreement.

...

(e) Unemployment Compensation: The Company agrees not to contest unemployment benefits for an employee who remains in good standing on the date he or she is permanently laid off and not to allocate severance monies to any particular week.

10. **Hiring Opportunities in ______, ___**

For one (1) year following the date of ratification of this Agreement, the Company shall provide the Union notice of any job openings at ______________ in _______, ________ that would otherwise be advertised to individuals who are not currently employed at ________ and while work continues in _______, shall post notices of such openings at the Facility. Employees from the Facility will have the opportunity to apply for any such jobs as new employees of the Company.

11. **Letters of Reference**

The Company shall provide each laid off employee, upon request, a letter of reference stating the positions held (in the last five (5) years), that the employee performed his/her job in a satisfactory manner (as long as employee was in good standing on his or her last work day), that his/her employment was terminated due to a plant closing/relocation, the dates of employment, and the last wage rate.

. . .

17. **Release and Waiver**

. . .

18. **Discontinuation of Bargaining Unit**

    Following the layoff of employees and closure of the Facility, the parties agree that the collective bargaining unit represented by the Union in ______ will cease to exist and the parties' prior collective bargaining agreements, including all side letters, understandings, or other enforceable obligations, will terminate. At that point, the parties' collective bargaining relationship will end, except with respect to disputes concerning compliance with this Agreement, or unless bargaining unit operations resume on or before __________, _____.

19. **Severability**. In the event that any of the provisions of this Agreement shall be held to be invalid or unenforceable, the remaining provisions shall nevertheless continue to be valid and enforceable as though the invalid or unenforceable parts had not been included.

20. **Full Agreement**. This Agreement contains the full and complete agreements and understandings arrived at by the parties, and are not subject to modification or interpretation by reason of any oral statements, discussions or agreements of any kind, whether or not made contemporaneously with the negotiation and execution of this Agreement.

Signed this _____ day of ____________, _____.

FOR THE UNION: FOR THE COMPANY:

_________________ _______________________

Social Compensation Plan [Germany]

Between
the B-GmbH,
represented by its board of directors
(in the following: "the company")
and
the works council,
represented by its chairman
(in the following: "the works council")

A. Area of application

I. This social compensation plan applies to all employees that are in a not terminated employment relationship with the company at 10/1/2012. It does not apply to executive staff.

II. This social compensation plan applies to all personal measures described in the reconciliation of interest agreement of 5/9/2012.

B. Transfer

I. Qualification measures

1. If an employee is transferred or if his field of activity and if his skills and knowledge is not sufficient to perform his new tasks he is entitled to the necessary qualification measures. If necessary such a qualification measure may take up to six months.
2. The employer pays the costs of such qualification measures.
3. In principle such qualification measures will take place during working hours. The employer has to pay the regular wage.

II. Information about the new place of work

1. The employee that is transferred to another location may inform himself on this location about his future place of work and the apartment/housing situation.
2. In order to do so the employee is entitled to up to three days for paid special leave.

III. Relocation payments

If the employee relocates because of the transfer he is entitled to the following benefits:

1. One monthly gross income as basic compensation.
2. Costs for newspaper advertisements/broker's fees up to € 2,500.
3. Shipping costs up to € 3,000.
4. Commuting expenses for two home journeys a month in case of a separation from the family (up to 12 months).

IV. Benefits in case of higher commuting expenses

Employees whose way to work is prolonged by the transfer are entitled to a compensation for 12 months.

V. Wage protection

1. If possible the wage classification shall not be affected by the transfer.
2. If a downgrading is inevitable the employee is entitled to the wage difference for 18 months.

C. Termination

I. Lump sum payment

1. Employees whose employment relationship is terminated for business reasons because of measures described in section A II are entitled to a lump sum payment.

2. Not entitled to a lump sum payment are:
   - employees that were terminated for reasons in their person or their behavior,
   - employees whose time-limited employment relationship ends,
   - employees who worked less than six months for the company at the time of the termination,
   - employees that leave before the end of the cancelation period due to a breach of contract.

3. Basic amount

   The lump sum payment's basic amount is calculated by the following formula…

4. Lowest and highest amount

   The lump sum payment's basic amount minimum for full-time employee is € 5,000. The highest amount possible is € 50,000.

5. Additional payments

   In addition to the basic amount employees are entitled to a supplement:
   - for each child in need of maintenance: € 2,000
   - if the employee is severely disabled: € 300 for each 10 % degree of disability (section 68 p.p. Code of Social Law IX)
   - employees that are older than 50 years: € 15,000
   - employees that would have celebrated their 25th company anniversary within one year after the termination of the employment relationship: € 2,000

II. Premature leave

On request of the employee the company will consent to a premature leave before the end of the cancelation period as long as this does not conflict with the company's business interests.

III. Part-time employees

Part-time employees are entitled to a lump sum payment on a pro-rata basis.

D. General provisions

I. Taxes; maturity

1. All benefits of this social compensation plan are gross benefits. Taxes have to be paid by the employee.

2. The lump sum payment claims are due with the expiration of the cancelation period.

3. Lump sum payment claims are inheritable.

II. Letter of reference

On request each employee receives a detailed letter of reference.

III. Cut-off period

All rights stemming from this social compensation plan have to be claimed in writing within six months after their due date. After expiration of this period they cannot be claimed anymore.

IV. Safeguarding

In case that any of the provisions of this social compensation plan is invalid the validity of the rest shall not be affected. The invalid clause has to be replaced by a provision that comes as close as possible to the parties' will.

V. Coming into effect

This social compensation plan will come into effect on 10/1/2012.

As an addendum to the foregoing – and as a preface to the note that follows – it might be well to get some sense of the comparative average cost of legally mandated severance pay in the countries under study. These are set out in Table V.3.

Table V.3 Redundancy costs in weeks of salary, 2011

Country	Weeks
United States	0
Japan	4
Australia	12
Brazil	13
Germany	22

Source: World Bank/International Finance Corporation, Doing Business 2012: Doing Business in a More Transparent World; authors' calculations.

Attention next turns away from economically or technologically driven decisions that affect the availability of the job for groups of employees to individual conduct which implicates the country's law on wrongful dismissal. Before these are reached it might be helpful to get some sense of the shape of these systems. In considering the following it returns to the "Note on Wrongful Dismissal Litigation" on pages 226–229.

PROBLEM 11: 54-YEAR-OLD "UNDERPERFORMING" SALESMAN

Mr. X is a 54-year-old salesman who has been with the company for 18 years. He does not have a contract of employment for a fixed term. For the first decade of his service he performed superlatively, always exceeding his sales quotas and, for five years in a row, was in the "golden circle" of high achievers. His performance began to decline about six years ago. For the past four years he has fallen below the median sales level in the department and was the lowest in the department, well below his quota, last year. Accordingly, starting last year, he was counseled verbally, has been given written quarterly evaluations that have highlighted his poor performance, and was told last quarter that his failure to bring his sales above the median will result in discharge. His sales this quota are still below the median. May he be dismissed?

Problem 11 discussion – Australia

As Mr. X serves for an indefinite duration, he must be given notice of termination. If no period of notice is expressly stipulated in his contract, the common law will imply an entitlement to "reasonable" notice: *Byrne v Australian Airlines Ltd* (1995) 185 CLR 410 at 429. What constitutes reasonable notice depends on a range of factors, including length of service, degree of responsibility and potential difficulty in finding other work: see e.g. *Lau v Bob Jane T-Marts Pty Ltd* [2004] VSC 69 at [64]–[66]. Given Mr. X's age and seniority, anywhere up to six months might be expected, especially if he had significant managerial responsibilities: see e.g. *Singleton v Trancomm Financial Planning Services Pty Ltd* [1996] IRCA 343.

At an absolute minimum, Mr. X would be entitled to five weeks' notice, regardless of any shorter period stipulated in his contract: see s 117 of the Fair Work Act 2009, extracted in relation to Problem 10.

As a matter of common law, there is no requirement for an employer to have good cause for failing to renew a fixed term contract, or for exercising a power to terminate on notice. However, Mr. X may seek to bring a claim for unfair dismissal under Part 3–2 of the Fair Work Act, selected provisions from which are set out below. His eligibility to bring a claim will depend on whether he can establish *either* that he is covered by an award, or alternatively that his guaranteed annual remuneration is less than the "high income threshold" (currently A$123,300). Many sales staff in Australia are covered by awards, though by no means all. There are, for example, modern awards in relation to commercial travellers, financial planners and real estate agents.

If he is eligible to bring a claim, he must convince the FWA member that hears his complaint that he has been treated harshly, unjustly or unreasonably. As s 387 suggests, however, the company should be able to defend any complaint if (a) it has a legitimate problem with his performance, (b) it has counselled him and given him an opportunity to improve, and (c) it has afforded him an opportunity to have his say before making a final decision to dismiss.

If Mr. X did succeed in an unfair dismissal claim, he could in theory be reinstated, though that remedy is rare in practice – especially where trust and confidence have broken down with the relevant manager(s). It is more likely that he would be awarded compensation of up to six months' remuneration. The precise figure would depend in particular on how quickly he was able (or could be expected to be able) to find an alternative source of income.

Finally, there is the possibility of an age discrimination claim, either under s 351 of the Fair Work Act, or the federal Age Discrimination Act 2004, or under an applicable State or Territory anti-discrimination law. In each case, the company would seek to establish that age had played no part in the way its performance expectations were either framed or applied in this case.

PRIMARY SOURCES

Fair Work Act 2009 (Cth) s 117 (see Problem 10).

Byrne v Australian Airlines Ltd (1995) 185 CLR 410 at 429.

Lau v Bob Jane T-Marts Pty Ltd [2004] VSC 69 at [64]–[66].

Fair Work Act 2009 (Cth) ss 382, 383, 385, 387, 390–392 (infra).

Fair Work Act 2009 (Cth) s 351 (see Problem 5).

Byrne v Australian Airlines Ltd (1995) 185 CLR 410 at 429

Brennan CJ, Dawson and Toohey JJ:

> In the absence of anything to the contrary … at common law a contract of employment for no set term is to be regarded as containing an implied term that the employer give reasonable notice of termination except in circumstances justifying summary dismissal.

Lau v Bob Jane T-Marts Pty Ltd [2004] VSC 69 at [64]–[66]

Osborn J (footnotes omitted):

[64] In *Rankin v Marine Power International Pty Ltd* Gillard J stated:

> "In determining what is a reasonable period in respect to an employee, it must be steadily borne in mind what the primary purpose of giving a period of notice is. It is to enable the employee to obtain new employment of a similar nature. Some types of employment are readily available, whilst others are not. Those who are at the top or near the top of their chosen fields, invariably have very few opportunities to obtain similar employment and hence, the period of notice is usually many months to in excess of a year."

[65] In *Quinn v Jack Chia (Australia) Ltd* Ashley J stated the relevant principles governing the notion of reasonable notice as follows:

> "It was common ground that the content of 'reasonable notice' is to be determined as at the date when notice is given, not when the contract is entered into. In this context matters occurring antecedently to the making of and in the course of the performance of the contract up to the date of termination are not irrelevant.
>
> Macken et al, *Law of Employment*, pp. 157–8, lists certain pertinent considerations. Thus, for example: the duration of the hiring; industry practice; the seniority of the position held; the importance of the position held; the size of the salary; the worker's age; the worker's length of service; what the worker gave up to come to the present employer; the worker's prospective pension or other rights."

[66] The most recent addition of the text to which Ashley J refers states at p. 171 that in addition to the duration of the hiring and industry practice, other relevant job related factors include the "high grade" of the appointment; the importance of the position; the size of the salary; and the nature of the employment. Relevant factors which pertain to the employee include: the length of service of the employee; the professional standing of the employee; the employee's age; the employee's qualifications and experience; her or his degree of job mobility; the expected period of time it would take the employee

to obtain alternative employment; the period it was likely, apart from the dismissal, that the employee would have continued in the employment; what the employee gave up to come to the present employer; and the employee's prospective pension or other rights.

Fair Work Act 2009

382 When a person is protected from unfair dismissal

A person is *protected from unfair dismissal* at a time if, at that time:

(a) the person is an employee who has completed a period of employment with his or her employer of at least the minimum employment period; and

(b) one or more of the following apply:
  (i) a modern award covers the person;
  (ii) an enterprise agreement applies to the person in relation to the employment;
  (iii) the sum of the person's annual rate of earnings, and such other amounts (if any) worked out in relation to the person in accordance with the regulations, is less than the high income threshold.

[Note: In accordance with reg 2.13 of the Fair Work Regulations 2009, the high income threshold is currently A$123,300. It will increase on 1 July each year in accordance with an indexing formula.]

383 Meaning of minimum employment period

The *minimum employment period* is:

(a) if the employer is not a small business employer – 6 months ending at the earlier of the following times:
  (i) the time when the person is given notice of the dismissal;
  (ii) immediately before the dismissal; or</sub-list>

(b) if the employer is a small business employer – one year ending at that time.

[Note: A "small business employer" is defined by s 23 to mean an employer with less than 15 employees.]

385 What is an unfair dismissal

A person has been *unfairly dismissed* if FWA is satisfied that:

(a) the person has been dismissed; and

(b) the dismissal was harsh, unjust or unreasonable; and

(c) the dismissal was not consistent with the Small Business Fair Dismissal Code; and

(d) the dismissal was not a case of genuine redundancy.

387 Criteria for considering harshness etc.

In considering whether it is satisfied that a dismissal was harsh, unjust or unreasonable, FWA must take into account:

(a) whether there was a valid reason for the dismissal related to the person's capacity or conduct (including its effect on the safety and welfare of other employees); and

(b) whether the person was notified of that reason; and

(c) whether the person was given an opportunity to respond to any reason related to the capacity or conduct of the person; and

(d) any unreasonable refusal by the employer to allow the person to have a support person present to assist at any discussions relating to dismissal; and

(e) if the dismissal related to unsatisfactory performance by the person – whether the person had been warned about that unsatisfactory performance before the dismissal; and

(f) the degree to which the size of the employer's enterprise would be likely to impact on the procedures followed in effecting the dismissal; and

(g) the degree to which the absence of dedicated human resource management specialists or expertise in the enterprise would be likely to impact on the procedures followed in effecting the dismissal; and

(h) any other matters that FWA considers relevant.

390 When FWA may order remedy for unfair dismissal

(1) Subject to subsection (3), FWA may order a person's reinstatement, or the payment of compensation to a person, if:
   (a) FWA is satisfied that the person was protected from unfair dismissal (see Division 2) at the time of being dismissed; and
   (b) the person has been unfairly dismissed (see Division 3).

(2) FWA may make the order only if the person has made an application under section 394.

(3) FWA must not order the payment of compensation to the person unless:
   (a) FWA is satisfied that reinstatement of the person is inappropriate; and
   (b) FWA considers an order for payment of compensation is appropriate in all the circumstances of the case.

Note: Division 5 deals with procedural matters such as applications for remedies.

391 Remedy – reinstatement etc.

Reinstatement

(1) An order for a person's reinstatement must be an order that the person's employer at the time of the dismissal reinstate the person by:
   (a) reappointing the person to the position in which the person was employed immediately before the dismissal; or
   (b) appointing the person to another position on terms and conditions no less favourable than those on which the person was employed immediately before the dismissal.

(1A) If:
   (a) the position in which the person was employed immediately before the dismissal is no longer a position with the person's employer at the time of the dismissal; and
   (b) that position, or an equivalent position, is a position with an associated entity of the employer;

the order under subsection (1) may be an order to the associated entity to:
   (c) appoint the person to the position in which the person was employed immediately before the dismissal; or
   (d) appoint the person to another position on terms and conditions no less favourable than those on which the person was employed immediately before the dismissal.

Order to maintain continuity

(2) If FWA makes an order under subsection (1) and considers it appropriate to do so, FWA may also make any order that FWA considers appropriate to maintain the following:
   (a) the continuity of the person's employment;
   (b) the period of the person's continuous service with the employer, or (if subsection (1A) applies) the associated entity.

Order to restore lost pay

(3) If FWA makes an order under subsection (1) and considers it appropriate to do so, FWA may also make any order that FWA considers appropriate to cause the employer to pay to the person an amount for the remuneration lost, or likely to have been lost, by the person because of the dismissal.

(4) In determining an amount for the purposes of an order under subsection (3), FWA must take into account:
   (a) the amount of any remuneration earned by the person from employment or other work during the period between the dismissal and the making of the order for reinstatement; and
   (b) the amount of any remuneration reasonably likely to be so earned by the person during the period between the making of the order for reinstatement and the actual reinstatement.

392 Remedy – compensation

Compensation

(1) An order for the payment of compensation to a person must be an order that the person's employer at the time of the dismissal pay compensation to the person in lieu of reinstatement.

Criteria for deciding amounts

(2) In determining an amount for the purposes of an order under subsection (1), FWA must take into account all the circumstances of the case including:
   (a) the effect of the order on the viability of the employer's enterprise; and
   (b) the length of the person's service with the employer; and
   (c) the remuneration that the person would have received, or would have been likely to receive, if the person had not been dismissed; and
   (d) the efforts of the person (if any) to mitigate the loss suffered by the person because of the dismissal; and
   (e) the amount of any remuneration earned by the person from employment or other work during the period between the dismissal and the making of the order for compensation; and
   (f) the amount of any income reasonably likely to be so earned by the person during the period between the making of the order for compensation and the actual compensation; and
   (g) any other matter that FWA considers relevant.

Misconduct reduces amount

(3) If FWA is satisfied that misconduct of a person contributed to the employer's decision to dismiss the person, FWA must reduce the amount it would otherwise order under subsection (1) by an appropriate amount on account of the misconduct.

Shock, distress etc. disregarded

(4) The amount ordered by FWA to be paid to a person under subsection (1) must not include a component by way of compensation for shock, distress or humiliation, or other analogous hurt, caused to the person by the manner of the person's dismissal.

Compensation cap

(5) The amount ordered by FWA to be paid to a person under subsection (1) must not exceed the lesser of:
   (a) the amount worked out under subsection (6); and
   (b) half the amount of the high income threshold immediately before the dismissal.

(6) The amount is the total of the following amounts:
   (a) the total amount of remuneration:
      (i) received by the person; or
      (ii) to which the person was entitled;

(whichever is higher) for any period of employment with the employer during the 26 weeks immediately before the dismissal; and

(b) if the employee was on leave without pay or without full pay while so employed during any part of that period – the amount of remuneration taken to have been received by the employee for the period of leave in accordance with the regulations.

References and suggested readings

ANDREW STEWART, STEWART'S GUIDE TO EMPLOYMENT LAW Chs. 16–17 (4th ed. 2013).

Problem 11 discussion – Brazil

Brazilian legal regulation for unfair dismissals has undergone three different phases, one after the other, contributing to the weakening of protection against dismissal. In the first period, which runs from the publication of the *Consolidação das Leis do Trabalho* (1943) to the Federal Statute nº 5.107 (1966), an employee with 10 years tenure was fully protected against unfair dismissal. That is, he could not be dismissed unless he committed a significant fault recognized in a judicial procedure. Employees whose tenure amounted to less than 10 years were entitled to receive an indemnification corresponding to one month's salary for each year or fraction above six months of work. A second period began with the approval of Federal Statute nº 5.107, which introduced, without outlawing the old one, a new dismissal protection system called *Fundo de Garantia de Tempo de Serviço* (FGTS) (Length of Service Guarantee Fund). Throughout the employment relation, the employer was supposed to contribute to monthly deposits equivalent to 8 percent of the employee's salary to a dismissal fund, which could be withdrawn by the employee once he was dismissed, with an additional indemnification for wrongful dismissal paid by the employer corresponding to 10 percent of the fund's total savings. The third phase begins with the Federal Constitution of 1988, which outlawed the first dismissal protection system and raised up to 40 percent the additional indemnification of the FGTS.

The problem illustrates one of the major criticisms leveled against the old 10-year tenure system: once the cap of 10 years was overcome, employees, who could not be easily dismissed, too frequently were alleged to have become indolent. While there was (is) no empirical evidence of such working capacity "decline," management complaints grew and were finally dealt with by the introduction of the FGTS system. In the late 1990s, criticism arose as to the cost imposed by the FGTS regime on unfair dismissals. However, as none of the governmental initiatives went through, the system still revolves around the FGTS regime and its additional indemnification of 40 percent. Employers may thus terminate labor contracts at-will as long as, on the one hand, employees are not protected by some special guarantee of job security which may come from federal statute or conventional agreements, and employers, on the other hand, are willing to pay the costs of a dismissal.

Because the 40 percent indemnity is triggered by a finding of wrongful dismissal, the costs may be lower if the dismissal is due to a just cause. This is specified as being one of the following situations listed in article 482 of *Consolidação das Leis do Trabalho*:

(a) dishonesty;
(b) misconduct or bad behavior;
(c) habitual engagement by the employee in commercial transactions on his or her own account or for another without his or her employer's permission, if this involves competition with the undertaking in which he or she is employed or is prejudicial to the performance of his or her work;
(d) a sentence passed on the employee by a criminal court without suspension of the execution of the penalty;
(e) idleness of the employee in the performance of his or her duties;
(f) habitual drunkenness or drunkenness while on duty;
(g) disclosure of a secret of the undertaking;
(h) breach of discipline or insubordination;
(i) desertion of post;
(j) any act detrimental to the honor or good repute of another which is committed during employment, or an assault under the same conditions, except in case of legitimate self-defense or defense of another;
(k) any act detrimental to the honor or good repute of, or an assault against, the employer or a superior, except in case of legitimate self-defense or defense of another; or
(l) habitual indulgence in games of chance.

Lack of productivity might be considered as covered by idleness. However, jurisprudence from the *Tribunal Superior do Trabalho* has established that idleness is negligent conduct expressed through unjustified absences, repeated lateness, lack of zeal and unequivocal unwillingness to work. As a consequence, lack of productivity by itself has rarely been associated with just cause and in order to do so it must be followed by some other characteristic giving cause.

A further dimension may be added to the problem once one takes into account Mr. X's age. Although there is no federal law specifying when someone should be considered "old" at work, if dismissal is due to Mr. X's age it would constitute a discriminatory act as provided in Federal Statute nº 9.029/1995. The problem lies in the burden of proof as it is up to Mr. X to demonstrate that his dismissal was due to his age and therefore may be considered discriminatory.

Finally, many collective agreements stipulate a special job guarantee for employees within two years of retirement. If Mr. X is covered by such an agreement and if he met that condition, his dismissal would be void.

References and suggested readings

On the *Fundo de Garantia de Tempo de Serviço* (Length of Service Guarantee Fund), see its actual regulation: Lei nº 8.036/1990 (Federal Statute nº 8.036) 1990 (Braz.), *accessed at* http://www.planalto.gov.br/ccivil_03/LEIS/L8036consol.html (last visited Feb. 20, 2010); see also: BRASIL. CAIXA ECONÔMICA FEDERAL. Fundo de Garantia de Tempo de Serviço: ações e resultados (2005), *accessed at* http://downloads.caixa.gov.br/_arquivos/fgts/relatoriosacoes/RELATORIO_RESULTADOS_FGTS_2005.PDF (last visited Feb. 20, 2010).

Problem 11 discussion – Germany

Dismissal of older persons is often expressly prohibited or at least restricted by collective agreements the employer may be bound by (as a partner to the agreement or, which is mostly the case, as a member of the employers' association that concluded the agreement). As far as statutory law is concerned, according to section 1 para. 1 sentence 1 of the Act on Dismissal Protection a worker can be dismissed on personal, behavioral grounds or for business reasons if the resulting dismissal is "socially justified". (Old) age as such does not form a personal reason (Federal Labor Court of 28.09.1961 – 2 AZR 428/60). Poor performance, even if due to old age, may, however, constitute a behavioral reason. A dismissal based on the behavior of the employee, on the other hand, requires that the employee willfully fails to exhaust his individual work potential (Federal Labor Court of 11.12.2003 – 2 AZR 667/02). Consequently, in cases where performance still could be improved a warning may be necessary. In addition, it may be necessary to allow the worker concerned some time to improve his performance. Apart from that, there is sufficient reason for dismissal only if performance is less than two thirds of the median (Federal Labor Court of 11.12.2003 – 2 AZR 667/02). If performance is not quantifiable, justification of a dismissal is dependent on the nature, weight and consequences of the failing performance.

In practice it is very difficult for employers to prove sufficiently poor performance (Federal Labor Court of 17.01.2008 – 2 AZR 536/06). The onus on the employer with regard to dismissing "low performers" (for one reason or another the English term is used in Germany in this regard) is heavy (see Federal Labor Court of 27.11.2008 – 2 AZR 675/07, 17.01.2008 – 2 AZR 536/06). Apart from that, a dismissal may be doomed to failure because it either cannot be regarded as the "*ultima ratio*" – the according principle requires the employer to offer any other possible employment under amended terms before terminating employment altogether – or does not pass the "balancing-of-interests test" – which requires a case-by-case weighing of the interests of the employer in terminating the employment against the interest of the employee in retaining it.

References and suggested readings

Wolf Hunold, *Subjektiv determinierte Leistungspflicht des Mitarbeiters und Konkretisierung von Arbeitsanweisungen und Abmahnungen*, NEUE ZEITSCHRIFT FÜR ARBEITSRECHT (NZA) 930 (2009).

Problem 11 discussion – Japan

In Japan, the Labor Contract Act restricts employers' abusive exercise of the right to dismiss. Article 16 of the Labor Contract Acts prescribes that "a dismissal shall, if it lacks objectively reasonable grounds and is not considered to be appropriate in general societal terms, be treated as an abuse of right and be invalid." If the discharged employee brings the case to the court, therefore, the employer is de facto required to demonstrate that there were objectively reasonable grounds to discharge him and that the dismissal is not too harsh and appropriate viewed from the general societal terms. This rule restricting abusive dismissals has sustained Japan's well-known life-time or long-term employment practice.

Japan does not have age discrimination in employment law. Thus Mr. X cannot contest his discharge on that ground as such. However, because of the above-mentioned prohibition of an abusive exercise of the right to dismiss, Mr. X may contend that the discharge is too harsh and socially inappropriate.

Japanese courts have applied the abusive dismissal rule very strictly. In the famous *Kochi Broadcasting Company* case (Supreme Court, Jan. 31, 1977), a newsreader overslept and failed to deliver the morning news at 6:00 a.m., not only once, but twice within a two-week period. The Kochi Broadcasting Company dismissed the newsreader. However, the Supreme Court nullified the dismissal because the failures were not caused by malice but by negligence, the employee apologized, and a co-worker in charge of new manuscripts who had also overslept was not dismissed but simply reprimanded. Given this context, the Supreme Court reasoned, the dismissal could be regarded as too harsh, unreasonable and socially inappropriate.

In the given case, the reason for discharge was not the employee's misconduct but his poor performance for the last four years and no improvement after the warning. Whether the Japanese courts deem such a poor performance sufficient to legally dismiss the employee is questionable. There can be three arguments.

One argument for Mr. X would be as follows. In Japan, standard employees with an indefinite period contract are generally hired as a member of the company. At the hiring, employees' types of work are not specified. Japanese employers hire new recruits for their potential to develop professional abilities in the course of on-the-job training and periodical transfer programs. Once employment relations have been entered into, it is employers' responsibility to fully develop their employees' potential. The employer should have provided a proper program to improve Mr. X's performance before dismissing him. Simply warning him of his poor performance is not sufficient for the discharge to be deemed socially appropriate.

A counter-argument against Mr. X would be as follows. The argument for Mr. X can be applied to the typical lifetime employment employees who were hired as new recruits fresh from school. For such new recruits, employers might have responsibilities to develop their ability. However, Mr. X was hired as a mid-career employee when he was 36-years-old. He was hired for his expected performance. Thus if he failed to perform as expected, the dismissal should be deemed to be based on reasonable grounds and socially appropriate.

The third argument would be as follows. It is certainly unreasonable to compel the employer to maintain Mr. X's employment with seniority-based high remuneration. However, under the restriction of abusive dismissal rule, employers are required to make an effort to avoid dismissals by adopting measures such as transferring him to another section or adjusting his remuneration in line with his poor performance. Japanese law allows employers to take such alternatives in order to maintain employment. Therefore, a discharge without attempting these alternatives would be regarded as an abusive dismissal.

Although all three arguments are possible, the current Japanese courts would likely take the third argument and still be reluctant to admit the legality of Mr. X's discharge.

PRIMARY SOURCE

Labor Contract Act

Article 16.

A dismissal shall, if it lacks objectively reasonable grounds and is not considered to be appropriate in general societal terms, be treated as an abuse of right and be invalid.

TAKASHI ARAKI, JAPANESE EMPLOYMENT AND LABOR LAW, 27–8 (2002) (footnotes omitted):

> The case law governing dismissals has several unique features from a comparative perspective. The first feature is that Japanese case law more severely restricts economic dismissals than other developed countries. Since the economic dismissals are allowed only as a last resort under the case law and Japanese employment practices provide many alternatives, employers are forced to exhaust time-consuming procedures to avoid economic dismissals. Faced with global competition where speed is vitally important in management strategy, such requirements have become a heavy burden for Japanese employers. This is perhaps another consideration behind the recent courts' relaxed interpretation of the "four requirements."
>
> The second feature of the case law rule is its very protective remedies. In many countries, unjust dismissals result in payment for damages. In contrast, under the abuse of the right to dismiss theory in Japan, the employer is obliged not only to pay wages during the whole period of dismissal but also to reinstate the dismissed employee, as the

dismissal is null and void. As a result, if a dismissal is abusive, the employer cannot terminate the employment relations with the worker no matter how much the employer pays the worker.

However, after a prolonged litigation, it is naturally difficult for both the employer and the worker to restore normal employment relations not only because the human relations between them have deteriorated, but also the workplace circumstances have changed and the worker's skills have become outdated. Therefore, it is not surprising that most reinstated workers leave the company within a few years after the dismissal litigation. Thus, some academics advocate introducing a monetary remedy for unjust dismissals while allowing the dissolution of the employment relations.

The third feature relates to the effectiveness of the case law rule. While no statute requires just cause for dismissal, case law requires it. This situation lacks transparency and has led some foreign-affiliated firms as well as Japanese small and medium sized enterprises to believe that just cause is not required under Japanese law. These firms then find themselves subject to a ruling that a dismissal without just cause was illegal.

More problematic is the cost of litigation. In order to take advantage of the case law protection against unjust dismissal, a dismissed worker must bring the case to court. Unlike European Countries, Japan has no special court for labor-related cases. Therefore, all employment-related cases must be filed in ordinary courts. In Japan, it is not easy for individuals to litigate, partly due to the high cost of judicial procedures in terms of money and time, and perhaps, partly due to socio-cultural and psychological hesitancy over litigation. In fact, the number of labor cases is extremely small compared to other developed countries.

References and suggested readings

For the dismissal regulations in Japan, see KAZUO SUGENO (Leo Kanowitz trans.), JAPANESE LABOR AND EMPLOYMENT LAW 473–91 (2002); TAKASHI ARAKI, LABOR AND EMPLOYMENT LAW IN JAPAN 23–8 (2002); Takashi Araki, *Changing Employment Security in Japan Revisited*, LIBER AMICORUM REINHOLD FAHLBECK 25–41 (2005).

Problem 11 discussion – United States

As explained earlier, the United States continues to adhere to the at-will rule: absent a contractual commitment to job security, an employee, even one of very long service, can be dismissed without the employer having to prove just cause. As the thumbnail sketch of U.S. law noted, Montana and Puerto Rico do have wrongful dismissal laws, very different in operation, but we shall assume that Mr. X was not employed there. In addition, Alaska has implied a "covenant of good faith and fair dealing" as part of an at-will employment relationship. In Alaska employers must "treat like employees alike and act in a manner that a reasonable person would regard as fair." *Mitchell v. Teck Cominco Alaska, Inc.*, 193 P.3d 751 (2008). Mr. X might have a ground to contest his termination on either of these grounds: if other salespersons with similar deficiencies were treated more leniently; or, if he could get before a jury on the question of whether the employer acted reasonably and fairly. But, again, we will assume this case does not arise in Alaska.

In this case, however, Mr. X is 54 years of age, well within the class protected by the federal Age Discrimination in Employment Act (ADEA) which protects employees over the age of 40 from dismissal on grounds of age. But, unlike the classes protected by Title VII of the Civil Rights Act – race, sex, religion, and national origin – the U.S. Supreme Court has held that an ADEA employee-plaintiff must prove that age is the "but-for" cause of the employee's discharge.

The employee may proceed by direct evidence of wrongful motivation or by inference, by proving that he was a member of the protected class, was performing up to his employer's legitimate expectations, was terminated, and the job either held open or given to a younger person. If the employer articulates a legitimate reason for termination the employee must prove the proferred ground was pretextual.

In this case, the question is whether Mr. X was performing up to his employer's legitimate expectation. He may challenge his sales quota as having been manipulated ("rigged") to get rid of him or, to sustain an inference of age discrimination, as excessive or unreasonable by comparison with the quotas set for younger but equally situated sales personnel. From what appears it seems doubtful that Mr. X could make out a successful case: nothing indicates the quota was unachievable or unreasonable as compared to any other similarly situated younger salesman and his employer's efforts to improve his performance belie any age-based hostile motivation – unless those efforts can be shown to have been manipulated for the purpose of creating only an appearance of good faith.

The law (Alaska apart) does not require the employer to remediate Mr. X, to work with him to improve his performance. Had it done so for other, younger salesmen but declined to do so for him, the company could be called upon to justify that differential treatment. But nothing in the facts suggests that this was so. In sum, there would appear to be no obvious legal obstacle to Mr. X's discharge.

Would our underachieving salesman be able to receive unemployment compensation benefits? Perhaps yes, perhaps no. Under most unemployment compensation systems an employee who is terminated for "just cause" – usually a high standard of willful misconduct, negligence or the like – cannot receive benefits. The issue was presented in the discharge of a salesman whose performance in his first three and a half years made him one of the company's top performers but who, in his final two months, made only two sales. He attributed this to his health problems and the weak economy. The company countered that its other salespeople who performed well had to contend with the same economic conditions. He was given coaching and credited by his coach with having a "strong work ethic," but his coach also believed he lacked confidence in the company's product. The state's unemployment compensation agency held that he was entitled to the benefit: an employee terminated for reasons beyond his control would not have been discharged for just cause; and the agency stressed the employee's declining health as a reason for his lack of performance. On appeal the administrative decision was sustained but the court noted that the agency could reasonably have concluded to the contrary on the record before it. *Prosper Team, Inc., v. Dept. of Workforce Services*, 256 P.3d 246 (Utah App. 2011).

References and suggested readings

The U.S. Supreme Court decision referred to is *Gross v. FBL Fin. Servs., Inc.*, 557 U.S. 167, (2009). It is a controversial decision and legislation has been introduced to amend the law to repudiate the "but-for" approach to age discrimination. A useful decision applying this framework to the termination of a salesmen in 2005 who had been the company's highest achiever the previous year is *Senske v. Sybase, Inc.*, 2009 U.S. App. LEXIS 26254 (7th Cir. 2009). In *Woodward v. Emulex Corp.*, 854 F.Supp.2d 149 (D. Mass. 2012), the court granted summary judgment to an employer sued by a terminated salesman for age discrimination. The salesman had been among the company's best, but for reasons, which he attributed to managerial misjudgments not within his control, his sales fell and he and two others were discharged. The court noted that, before the court, the employer admitted "that it may have made a mistake in terminating one of its most productive salesmen." Nevertheless, the court found the evidence of age discrimination inadequate to go to trial even though the plaintiff had alleged that other, younger salesmen with lesser sales volumes were retained. Ordinarily one would think that allegation would present a material issue of fact requiring a trial. The case illustrates the very high threshold required for an age discrimination case.

The question of Mr. X poses a challenging situation for any employer. Unfortunately, it is a very realistic situation that many of us have encountered... As with many of the questions that we have encountered, what can be done within the scope of the law may differ from what may be normatively acceptable ... The "at-will" relationship coupled with the risk of establishing a practice limits activities that are commonly found in other countries that may actually provide a benefit both to the employee and the employer. A broad based assumption that because performance metrics are not met an employer must take punitive action can actually be a short sighted strategy. Germany, Japan, and Brazil offer an alternative perspective to consider: Just because an employee may not effectively sustain performance over time, it does not mean that they are without value to the firm. The nature of the type of position the employee is in may endow them with "firm" or "industry" specific knowledge. The employer is faced with two cost-benefit analyses to consider: (1) the cost of replacing this knowledge vs. the benefit of holding strict performance expectations and (2) the cost of reduced firm/industry level expertise vs. the benefit of utilizing the existing employee in knowledge transfer activities. It would seem that the alternative perspective creates a reasonable point of consideration – seeking ways to continue to capitalize on existing knowledge or abilities in alternative or reduced roles.

Director, HR, Industrial Manufacturing Sector

In manufacturing when you have an under-performing process or piece of equipment how many tools do we throw at improvement? Let's consider a few: (1) six sigma; (2) Value Stream Mapping; (3) Maintenance Engineering; (4) automation; (5) moving less productive equipment to a backup line and the list goes on ... Contrast that to an employment problem – how often do we really legitimately apply the same set (they are valid in some cases I think) of tools or number of attempts to resolve a people performance issue? We might too often fall into the trap of train, counsel, written warning, terminate. While we fully admit the cost to replace equipment is/can be prohibitively expensive (even though we have accounting tricks to spread it out) I'm not sure we recognize the same issue with people? What really does it cost to replace Mr. X's application/firm/industry specific knowledge and contacts?

Director, HR, Industrial Manufacturing Sector

What I like about problem 11 is the challenge of turning the situation around and the fact that I think we've all probably experienced a problem similar to this in our professional lives. In the general sense of a high performing organization (no matter where they reside), you have to wonder where management has been the last six years. Here was a star! Someone who was the highest of achievers for five years and received recognition for that as a member of the "golden circle". He's been on a six year slide and all that's been done is verbally counsel him, given him poor performance evaluations ... and told that he'll be discharged if he doesn't move his sales above the median. Why has management been a no show in addressing this performance issue? It's clear there is a major problem here and it's management's job to do a thorough assessment to try and get to the root cause. The organization has a commitment to this employee who has served them at the highest level in the past and to protect an eighteen-year investment that they've made. My assumption is that to bring in someone to replace this person's years of knowledge would be considerable. How could management let the employee walk out the door without putting together an assessment of what the true problem is? When will management learn that "verbally counseling" someone and documenting poor performance is unlikely to change much of anything?

Vice President, Employee Relations, Health Care Sector

Could the fact that Mr. X was allowed to have declining performance over a four year period say more about the culture and employment laws in European countries than management? At my former employer I met a lot of Mr. Xs in Germany and France who were allowed to become dead wood or poor performers because their management were so influenced by the employment laws. The German and French managers felt their hands were tied by employment laws and that they could never fire Mr. X. As a result, Mr. X was allowed to continue to perform poorly in a role not suited for him where maybe he could have been thriving for another company! This is what happens when management acts like a victim and says we can take no action because it is too hard to fire someone. So what do they do, they allow his skills and performance to erode and make him less marketable at an older age.

Senior Vice President, HR, Information Technology Sector

I was CHRO for a U.S. ... company located in seven European countries, Australia, and Japan. We provided [market data to firms and] our new Chairman & CEO developed a new strategy [to sell analytics as well]. This change in strategy would require much different skill sets for our commercial sales and account management employees. In the past, pure sales and relationship management skills were the main requirements. Going forward, sales and account managers would require ... analyz[ing] the data, and then based on what the data showed make recommendations to the clients on how to solve their business issues. While we initially provided our employees with significant analytics and industry training, we quickly found that no amount of training would provide many of them with the analytical thinking or industry knowledge to be successful. In order to execute the business strategy we would be forced to change our sales and account managers by acquiring new these skills in the market place and transitioning out those sales and account managers who could not perform the new role. Worker dismissal laws in many western European countries like Germany make it difficult for firms who need new skills to execute a change in strategy. While the same can be said for Japan, with their paternalistic no dismissal law, at least in Japan there is flexibility to reduce compensation or change job responsibilities. Unless worker dismissal laws in Germany and other like western European nations are modified to better deal with these situations, countries like Germany will continue to be unattractive for new investments by service, software, or consulting type firms.

Senior Vice President, HR, Information Technology Sector

The concept of "at will" in the U.S. has perplexed most HR professionals at one time or another ... while we use the phrase "employment at will" for justification in terminating an employee or outsourcing, it is rare that such a termination would not be challenged by an employee.

Vice President, HR, Electrical Manufacturing Sector

[T]he role of HR is to advise and influence management to do what is best for the business, rather than the overarching political or humanistic viewpoint. Many people think what is best for the business may be bad for employees. This is not the case at all and gets to the point that the interests of the employer and employees are not opposed. If I am an employee at Mr. X's company, I want poor performers dismissed if they are not performing. Why? Because they are a drag on the business which affects my own job security. Having said this, I want the employer to treat Mr. X with dignity and reward him with severance for his 18 yrs. of service. Within the last 30 days, we dismissed 5 percent of the employees in my company. They were working on a major tech transformation for the last three years and the project was over. While we had hope we would still be growing to keep them on, the recession has hurt top line growth. We had a choice, keep them on, have a zero bonus pool in 2010 and 2011 or save $20M annually in costs. For 95 percent of the employees having a bonus pool and a strong company is in their interests. The 95 percent have applauded (based on a pulse survey we just did) our actions. Thus, in problem 9 or 10, dismissing employees like Mr. X or 50 employees through outsourcing may be both in employees and the employer's interests.

Senior Vice President, HR, Information Technology Sector

Based on my experience, I would have to say that we are not truly an "at-will" nation. For example, our current employee handbook clearly states that employment at our company is "at will," meaning the employment may be terminated at any time by the employee or the company for any reason, or no reason, with or without cause, and with or without advance notice. However, in practice, in case of collective dismissal situations not subject to the WARN Act requirements, our company goes through a rather extensive review of its employee data to ensure no negative impact on any protected groups in order to minimize the legal exposure on discrimination cases. In reality, our company rarely (if not ever) terminates someone for no reason either collectively or individually.

Director, HR, Electronics Sector

[T]he "at will" doctrine is as strong as ever. It may not seem like it is in a mass layoff, but on an individual basis, it is as strong as ever. We can fire any one we want as long as we have not discriminated against them. Outside of a layoff, we always let go 5 percent of the lowest performers. We do so quickly and easily in the U.S. In Europe, we cannot do this quickly, easily, and at a low cost. This is why I know the "at will" doctrine is strong… in Germany, France , or Italy it would [take] 12–15 months longer, at three times the cost, and you would have had to share your confidential data with the German works counsel. In France you would have had to present your redundancy plan to French officials.

Senior Vice President, HR, Information Technology Sector

Questions for Discussion – Problem 11

1. In Australia, Germany, and Japan, declaring the dismissal as null and void or a reinstatement are potential resolutions or remedies to a wrongful dismissal, though in Germany the usual remedy is a lump sum payment based on longevity. (In Germany, the remedy would not be "reinstatement" as a wrongful dismissal would be null from the beginning.) In Brazil, the employer must pay a 40 percent surcharge on the employee's length of service fund. In the U.S., absent an independent actionable ground such as age, the employee can be dismissed with impunity.

2. Would you dismiss Mr. X in any of these five countries? If yes, why? If not, what would you do – and why? If in one but not another, again, what would justify that different treatment?

3. Inasmuch as the salesman's position in the United States was held on an at-will basis he could have been dismissed for any reason not otherwise unlawful, including a belief that he lacked confidence in the product he was selling whether or not his sales record was at the team's average or even well above it. Cf. *Woodward v. Emulex Corp.*, 854 F.Supp.2d 149, 151–2 (D. Mass. 2012). Consider whether that would be an allowable ground of discharge in Australia, Brazil, Germany, or Japan.

4. In Japan, the expectation of the courts is that the employer would find a new assignment for Mr. X, which would likely be at a lower wage but maintain employment (often in a supplier organization owned by the same Keiretsu or conglomerate). In which of the other four countries would you be able to do this and would you do so?

5. Which of the five countries do you see as the most restrictive in a case such as this, and why?

6. What insights or assumptions can you derive about the way older workers are viewed in each of these five societies, just by looking as the way this case would be handled? Under which system would you most prefer to work when you are the same age as Mr. X, and why?

PROBLEM 12: CRITICAL BLOG COMMENTS POSTED BY AN EMPLOYEE

Ms. X works in the company's accounting department. She maintains a website on which she puts her observations on political and social events, opinions, and ruminations. The website is not password protected: anyone who has or has access to a computer can read it. One posting claims that her company, whose name was given but not the fact that she was employed by it, has been dumping waste in violation of environmental law. A second posting concerned a recent corporate decision, i.e. the company laid off a number of engineers in its R&D department. The layoff drew comment in the business press. Ms. X wrote that, as an employee, she believed the company was "killing off the 'seed corn' of the future," that management "has no good ability to run the business." Can the company discharge Ms. X?

Problem 12 discussion - Australia

The Australian common law provides no particular protection for whistle-blowers, except to the extent that a court will not enforce an employee's duty of confidentiality where they are seeking to disclose some sort of "iniquity" or wrongdoing on the part of the employer. A court may in that situation refuse to grant an injunction restraining publication of such information: see e.g. *Lion Laboratories Ltd v Evans* [1984] 2 All ER 417. Note that Australia has only limited constitutional protection for freedom of expression, as explained in the extract set out below from Ronald McCallum & Andrew Stewart, *Employee Loyalty in Australia*, 20 COMP. LAB. L. & POL'Y. J. 155 (1999).

As for publicly disparaging one's employer, this is generally treated as a breach of the employee's implied duty of "fidelity" (loyalty), and as grounds for summary dismissal: see e.g. *RW Jaksch & Associates Pty Ltd v Hawks* [2005] VSCA 307.

Most States do have statutes to protect whistleblowers from retaliatory treatment. But with the exception of the Whistleblowers Protection Act 1993 in South Australia, these do not apply to private sector employers: *see* the summary in McCallum & Stewart, supra. Since that article was written, Part 9.4AAA of the Corporations Act 2001 has been enacted. It protects employees (and others) who disclose information about what they suspect on reasonable grounds to be a contravention of the corporations legislation. But that would not apply here. (*See* Problem 13, infra.)

One other possibility would be for Ms. X, assuming she were eligible, to lodge a complaint of unfair dismissal under Part 3–2 of the Fair Work Act 2009. As explained in relation to Problem 11, the prospects of such a claim would hinge on FWA's assessment of the validity of the reason for the dismissal, together with the procedure adopted by the company (for example, whether she had been given an opportunity to explain her conduct), as well as her previous record.

PRIMARY SOURCES

Fair Work Act 2009 (Cth) ss 382, 383, 385, 387, 390–92 (see Problem 11).

Ronald McCallum & Andrew Stewart, *Employee Loyalty in Australia*, 20 COMP. LAB. L. & POL'Y. J. 155, 163, 173–9 (1999):

> Unlike the Constitution of the United States or the Canadian Charter of Rights and Freedoms, neither the Australian Constitution[32] nor any of its State counterparts contain a bill of rights setting out a list of specific rights and freedoms. In particular, there is no express guarantee of freedom of speech. In the 1990s, however, the High Court of Australia has developed a constitutional doctrine which recognises an implied right of freedom of expression in relation to "political" matters.[33] This doctrine is grounded in the necessity of citizens in a democracy having the right to communicate with one another about the operation of the political processes of government,[34] and has a clear potential to impact upon labour law.[35] Its very first application was to strike down a federal provision penalising criticism of the Australian Industrial Relations Commission;[36] and more recently it has been used to invalidate Western Australian

32 The Australian Constitution was enacted into law by the British Parliament: Commonwealth of Australia Constitution Act (U.K. 1900).

33 For a discussion of the most recent High Court decisions on this doctrine, see Twomey, *Dead Ducks and Endangered Political Communication: Levy v. State of Victoria and Lange v. Australian Broadcasting Corporation*, 19 SYD. L. REV. 76 (1997).

34 *See* T. BLACKSHIELD AND G. WILLIAMS, AUSTRALIAN CONSTITUTIONAL LAW AND THEORY 1059–1131 (2d ed. 1998).

35 *See* Doyle, *The Industrial/Political Dichotomy: The Impact of the Freedom of Communication Cases on Industrial Law*, 8 Austl. J. Lab. L. 91 (1995).

36 Nationwide News Pty Ltd. v. Wills, 177 C.L.R. 1 (Austl. 1992).

legislation purporting to control political expenditure by unions.[37] With respect to employee loyalty, it is not difficult to envisage similar arguments being directed at statutory restrictions on public servants in particular, in terms of the comments they may make or the political activities in which they can engage.

* * *

III. Disparaging the Employer

In a 1981 study of employee comment in Australia, the author noted that there were few Australian decisions concerning employee speech.[87] In part, this may be because Australia is a less litigious society than, say, the United States or Canada, and also because until relatively recently the high levels of trade union membership may have dampened employer resolve to retaliate through the taking of legal action. It was also the case that before 1981 remedies for unfair terminations were limited in most jurisdictions, and this meant that it was both difficult and impracticable in most circumstances to challenge terminations which resulted from adverse employee speech. Whatever the reasons for this past scarcity, it is clear that the ability of employees to make comments is becoming an issue of some significance. The Australian workforce of the 1990s – especially at the managerial and professional levels – is highly educated, and many of these articulate persons are to be found within the structures of large employing corporations, which often have transnational operations. The widespread availability of both e-mail and the internet have facilitated communications by making it easier for employees to air their views both within and outside the employing body. What would have been regarded as impermissible comment one or two decades ago may now be viewed as appropriate and reasonable – and vice versa. All these factors show that the issue of employee speech is a volatile one in Australia.

In this portion of our survey, we shall begin by examining the limits of comment within the walls of the employing enterprise before turning our attention to external employee comment. Protective legislation for whistleblowers will then be discussed.

A. Employee Comments Within the Enterprise

It would appear that Australian law gives greater latitude to adverse comments by employees when they are made to superiors within the confines of the employing entity, as against comments which are made to outsiders such as the media. In a recent case which came before the Industrial Relations Court of Australia, for example, an employee brought successful proceedings challenging the validity of his termination. During the hearing he sent two faxes to the president of the employer's parent company in Finland, in which it was alleged that the employer's staff had possibly breached

37 Registrar v. Communications, Elec., Electronic, Energy, Information, Postal, Plumbing and Allied Services Union of Austl. (W. Austl.), 44 Austl. Indus. L.R. para. 13–145 (W. Austl. Indus. Rel. Comm'n 1998). *But see* Communications, Elec., Electronic, Energy, Information, Postal, Plumbing and Allied Services Union of Austl. v. Laing, 159 A.L.R. 73 (Fed. Ct. 1998) (implied limitation not infringed by order to cease unlawful industrial action taken by way of political protest).

87 McCarry, *The Contract of Employment and Freedom of Speech*, 9 SYD. L. REV. 133 (1981). In what follows, we are indebted to this piece.

Australian regulations. The employer argued that this conduct showed that reinstatement should not be ordered. As none of the staff who were named would be working closely with the employee, the argument was rejected. On review, the reinstatement order was upheld.[88] According to Chief Justice Wilcox:

> An employee of a company is entitled to draw the attention of a senior officer of the company to matters that the employee perceives to be irregular or poorly handled, without thereby being treated as unfit for continued or further employment. It is in the interests of the company itself for managers, at all levels, to accept this entitlement; otherwise junior officers will feel inhibited about calling attention to matters that ought to be investigated and perhaps rectified. It is, of course, important that the allegations be made in the right way and to the right person. It would be wrong for an employee to make public allegations damaging to the employer's business and reputation; at least, not unless the employee was satisfied they were accurate and there was an overriding public duty to do so.[89]

B. External Comment and the Defence of Justified Disclosure

In a 1946 decision,[90] the Commonwealth Court of Conciliation and Arbitration upheld the dismissal of a worker who had written an article about his working conditions for an Australian Labor Party newspaper.[91] Given changes to society, we suggest that this fifty year old precedent would not be good law today. From the judgment of Chief Justice Wilcox quoted above, it would appear that the law will now allow some latitude for straightforward comment, provided it is not malicious. However there are obviously limits to this freedom …

It is clear, on the other hand, that where an employee honestly reports possible employer illegalities to the proper authorities, this will not be a breach of the implied term of good faith and fidelity. In *Associated Dominions Assurance Society v. Andrew*[93] the accountant of the Assurance Society wrote to a government department and spoke with a member of the Australian Parliament concerning some returns which the Assurance Society had furnished to the government. The Supreme Court held that there was insufficient evidence to warrant dismissal. However, Chief Justice Jordan commented that where an innocent employee became a party to a deliberate employer breach of the law, "the employer's duty as a citizen and his [sic] interest in exculpating himself from a possible charge of being an accomplice, might well over-ride any duty he would otherwise owe to his employer not to disclose to outsiders details of his employer's business."[94]

…

88 Nokia Communications Pty Ltd. v. Davis (Indus. Rel. Ct. Austl. Oct. 10 1996).

89 *Id.* The quotation was taken from the report of the case at <http://www.austlii.edu.au>.

90 Federated Ship Painters and Dockers Union of Austl. v. Cockatoo Docks & Eng'g Co. Pty Ltd., 57 C.A.R. 137 (C'wth Ct. Conc'n & Arb'n 1946).

91 The report of this decision is brief, but it does appear that the judge regarded some of the allegations as unfounded.

93 49 N.S.W. St. R. 351 (1949).

94 *Id.* at 353.

Whatever the precise formulation for the defence of justified disclosure, however, it is now established that the scope of the relevant disclosure is a crucial factor in determining the success of the defence. As a general rule, disclosure must be to the "proper authorities."[107] Who these are will depend on the nature and significance of the information. Prima facie, wrongdoing or matters of public danger should be disclosed to the appropriate official or semi-official bodies: the police in the case of criminal conduct,[108] public health authorities in instances of medical danger,[109] and so on. Occasionally, however, a court may decide that wider disclosure to the general public is appropriate. In *Lion Laboratories,* for instance, the Court of Appeal considered that, given on the one hand the government's unbending public support for the intoximeter, and on the other the mounting public disquiet about its reliability, it was appropriate for the employees' fears to be aired through the media.

The requirement that any disclosure ordinarily be to a proper authority also helps to answer two further questions. The first is whether the person who wishes to rely on the defence must adduce evidence as to the accuracy of information whose truth is contested. It has been said that "a mere allegation of iniquity is not of itself sufficient to justify disclosure",[110] and that the confidant must make out a "prima facie case that the allegations have substance".[112] Where the disclosure is to an authority whose function is to investigate such allegations, however, it would seem that this principle does not and should not apply;[113] though by the same token there must be at least reasonable grounds for suspecting wrongdoing.[114] The second issue is whether the motive behind the disclosure is relevant. Again, although it may be that the defence would be refused to one who sought to publish information "out of malice or spite" or to "purvey scandalous information for reward,"[115] the worst of motives will be overlooked if disclosure is solely to the proper authorities.[116]

If an employee were dismissed for justified disclosure, they would have a strong case to assert before a labour tribunal that the termination was unfair. However, while the employee most likely would receive compensation, a tribunal might be reluctant to order reinstatement, especially if it was concluded that the employee/employer relationship had broken down. Fear of job loss, we suggest, is the primary sanction against employee external comment in Australian private sector employment. This is one reason why protective legislation for whistleblowers has been enacted, and to that we now turn.

107 Initial Serv. Ltd. v. Putterill, [1968] 1 Q.B. 396, 405–06 (C.A.); Attorney-General (U.K.) v. Heinemann Publishers Austl. Pty Ltd., 8 N.S.W.L.R. 341, 380–81 (1987).

108 *See, e.g.,* Francome v. Mirror Group Newspapers Ltd., [1984] 2 All E.R. 408 (C.A.).

109 *See, e.g.,* Duncan v. Medical Practitioners Comm., [1986] 1 NZLR 513.

110 Attorney-General v. Guardian Newspapers Ltd. (No. 2), [1988] 3 W.L.R. 776, 807 (H.L.).

112 *Id.* at 787. *See also* Butler v. Bd. of Trade, 1971 Ch. 680.

113 A v. Hayden (No. 2), 156 C.L.R. 532 (Austl. 1984); Re a Company's Application, [1989] 2 All E.R. 248 (Ch.).

114 Grofam Pty Ltd. v. KPMG Peat Marwick, 27 Intell. Prop. R. 215 (Fed. Ct. 1993).

115 Initial Serv. Ltd. v. Putterill, [1968] 1 Q.B. 396, 406 (C.A.).

116 Re a Company's Application, [1989] 2 All E.R. 248 (Ch.).

C. Whistleblowers Legislation in Australia

In the course of this decade three of Australia's States (South Australia, Queensland and New South Wales) and also the Australian Capital Territory have enacted whistleblowers protection legislation.[117] The legislation varies from jurisdiction to jurisdiction,[118] but the general purpose is to encourage employees to disclose to appropriate authorities corrupt practices and issues of maladministration within their agencies, to funnel disclosures to independent bodies, and to protect whistleblowing employees from reprisals including loss of their jobs. A "whistleblower" for this purpose generally refers to a public sector employee who makes disclosures concerning corrupt, improper or simply wasteful practices in her or his employing body. That body may be a State, Territory or local government, or some other statutory authority. Only in South Australia is protection extended into the private sector, with the statute applying to disclosure not only of maladministration by a public officer, but of any illegal activity, irregular or unauthorised use of public money, substantial mismanagement of public resources, or conduct causing a substantial risk to public health or safety or to the environment.

It is notable that the Australian government has not yet enacted legislation to cover the federal public sector, despite recommendations to that effect from parliamentary committees.[119] However changes have recently been made to the regulations governing employment in the federal public service in connection with the adoption of a new code of conduct for performance of duties. Departments are at least now required to put in place procedures to facilitate reports of breaches of the code and ensure they are investigated. It is also provided that public servants reporting such breaches are not to be victimised for doing so.[120]

It is difficult to know with any accuracy whether the legislation that now exists in Australia has encouraged employees to speak out. After all, some forms of reprisal, such as a failure to promote, can be carried out in a subtle manner which may defy detection. Employees are well aware of these subtle pressures which may have long-term effects on their careers. It would be fair to say that in Australia employees who become whistleblowers are brave individuals.[121]

---

117 Whistleblowers Protection Act (S. Austl. 1993); Whistleblowers Protection Act (Queensl. 1994); Protected Disclosures Act (N.S.W. 1994); Public Interest Disclosure Act (Austl. Cap. Terr. 1994). Although it is not strictly whistleblowers protective legislation, § 53 of the Official Corruption Commission Act 1988 (W. Austl.) also protects from reprisals those who disclose information.

118 *See* Lewis, *Employment Protection for Whistleblowers: On What Principles Should Australian Legislation Be Based?*, (1996) 9 AUSTL. J. LAB. L. 135; M. ALLARS, ADMINISTRATIVE LAW: CASES AND COMMENTARY 256–61 (1997); R. DOUGLAS & M. JONES, ADMINISTRATIVE LAW: COMMENTARY AND MATERIALS 137–45 (2d ed. 1996).

119 *See* SENATE SELECT COMMITTEE ON PUBLIC INTEREST WHISTLEBLOWING, IN THE PUBLIC INTEREST (1994); SENATE SELECT COMMITTEE ON UNRESOLVED WHISTLEBLOWER CASES, THE PUBLIC INTEREST REVISITED (1995).

120 Public Service Regulations, §§ 9–11 (Austl. 1998).

121 *See* B. MARTIN, SUPPRESSION STORIES (1997) and also the wealth of information collected at <http://www.uow.edu.au/arts/sts/bmartin/dissent/>.

References and suggested readings

ANDREW STEWART, STEWART'S GUIDE TO EMPLOYMENT LAW §§ 13.22–3 (4th ed. 2013).

A.J. Brown & Paul Latimer, *Symbols or Substance? Priorities for the Reform of Australian Public Interest Disclosure Legislation*, 17 GRIFFITH L. REV. 223 (2008).

Problem 12 discussion – Brazil

Ms. X's criticism touches two different situations: when she denounces the company's violation of environmental laws, she expresses concerns over the public good, while her comments on the managerial competence of her superiors are limited to her perception of their managerial ability. Due to the fact that there is no specific Brazilian law dealing with "whistleblowing" practices or regulating the exercise of free speech when it relates to employers' practices, both situations must be analyzed under the loyalty principle, which imposes on employees the obligation to refrain from practices that would impose some harm on employers.

As for the "whistleblowing" situation, employees may appeal to the Labor Inspection Office which is under an obligation to examine the situation and to take all necessary measures to ensure that employers meet all public regulation's requirements. If an employee decides to take the stand and carry out the denunciation himself/herself (which is the case with Ms. X), employers may argue that loyalty has been breached and as a consequence a labor contract cannot subsist. Still, a dismissal carried out under such conditions must be examined on its merits, especially if the criticisms are proved to be true.

As for the criticism of an employer's competence, what may be at issue here is the means used by the employee to express his/her voice. Before expressing it in a personal blog, employees may verbalize their criticism in proper forums, where improvement suggestions could also be forwarded. If an employee sidesteps such a possibility, employers may see it as a breach of loyalty and discharge the employee as a consequence. This was exactly what happened in

January, 2011, when *O Estado de Minas*, the biggest newspaper of Minas Gerais, dismissed a photojournalist for posting a comment on his personal blog criticizing the editor's choice of cover photo for the next day's paper which missed, according to his analysis, the best image of President Lula visit to Juiz de Fora, one of the major cities of Minas Gerais. Although the post never mentioned the editor's name, he expressed general criticism of newspaper editors in general, especially those who focus on the closing hour of the paper instead of on the quality of its contents. The following day, the photojournalist was dismissed by just cause, accused of dishonesty (article 482, *a*, *Consolidação das Leis do Trabalho*). The journalist's union immediately came forward to criticize the employer's conduct and to offer juridical support in any action taken by the employee. Case law on the matter, which is extremely scarce, has thus been enriched by this leading case in which the court has recognized the existence of a just cause for the employee's dismissal.

References and suggested readings

On the leading case of a blogger's criticism of his/her employer, see EMMANUEL PINHEIRO, *Das capas e etceteras …* , FOTODIÁRIO (personal blog). (Jan. 20, 2010), *accessed at* http://pinheironafoto.blogspot.com/2010/01/das-capas-e-etcteras.html (last visited Feb. 23, 2010). For the union's official note, see Sindicato repudia demissão de repórter-fotográfico do EM, SINDICATO DOS JORNALISTAS PROFISSIONAIS DE MINAS GERAIS, *accessed at* http://www.sjpmg.org.br/novo/gera_conteudo.asp?id_materia=2474 (last visited Feb. 23, 2010).

Problem 12 discussion – Germany

In contrast to some other countries, there is no specific law dealing with whistleblowing. An attempt by the former government (the so-called "grand coalition") to introduce such a provision into the civil code failed. More recent attempts by the opposition parties in the German Parliament (see, for instance, a Draft Act of 23.05.2012 which was presented by the Greens, Deutscher Bundestag Printing Matter 17–9782) have little prospect of success either. There is, however, some case law on the matter. In the year 2001 the Constitutional Court ruled that pressing criminal charges against the employer by the employee could not ordinarily lead to lawful dismissal if the charges were neither consciously wrong nor clearly negligently made (Federal Constitutional Court of 02.07.2001 – 1 BvR 2049/00). Later, the Federal Labor Court held that dismissal could be lawful if the pressing of criminal charges against an employer or its representatives was clearly disproportional. In order to establish disproportional behavior within this meaning the courts had to take into account whether the charges were true or false. Apart from that, they had to look at what motivated the employee to press charges and whether or not the employee had brought an internal complaint first (Federal Labor Court of 03.07.2003 – 2 AZR 235/02). Finally it should be noted that denunciations may justify a dismissal, in particular if they are clearly ungrounded. Each dismissal, however, must be judged on its merits. In particular, a diligent weighing of interests must take place in each case. In a case concerning Germany, the European Court for Human Rights (ECHR) recently ruled by judgment dated 21.07.2011 (28274/08, *Heinisch* case) that an employee could not be terminated without notice.

With regard to critical comments about the employer or its representatives it must be added that, if the comments do not amount to libel or slander, they are protected on the ground that Article 5 para. 1 sentence 1 of the Basic Law guarantees freedom of expression in stating that "every person shall have the right freely to express and disseminate his opinions in speech, writing, and pictures and to inform himself without hindrance from generally accessible sources" (Federal Constitutional Court of 16.10.1998 – 1 BvR 1685/92). Accordingly, an employee may criticize the employer or his representatives even in public (for instance, on the occasion of an open meeting) and in a polemic and/or pointed manner (Federal Labor Court of 17.02.2000 – 2 AZR 927/98 and 12.01.2006 – 2 AZR 21/05). This also applies when remarks are published on the intranet of the company (Federal Labor Court 24.06.2004 – 2 AZR 63/03). According to a recent judgment of the Labor Court Hagen 16.05.2012 – 3 Ca 2597/11, insulting a supervisor on Facebook may justify dismissal.

References and suggested readings

Andreas Ege, *Arbeitsrecht und Web 2.0*, *in* ARBEIT UND ARBEITSRECHT (AuA) 72 (2008); Andrew Király, *Whistleblower in Deutschland und Großbritannien – Lehren aus dem Fall Heinisch*, *in* RECHT DER ARBEIT (RdA) 236 (2012); Martin Brock, *Neue Regeln für Whistleblower im öffentlichen Dienst – Folgen der Heinisch – Entscheidung des EuGH vom 21.07.2011*, *in* öffentliches Arbeits- und Tarifrecht (öAT) 243 (2011).

Problem 12 discussion – Japan

As to the dismissal by reason of the employee's public criticism of the employer's dumping of waste, allegedly in violation of environmental law, two tier protections against dismissals should be examined: the protection stipulated in the Whistleblowers Protection Act of 2004, and general protection against abusive dismissals discussed in Problem 11.

First, whether or not Ms. X is protected by the 2004 Whistleblowers Protection Act should be examined. In Japan, illegal actions, fraud and non-compliance conducted by large food corporations and an atomic power plant were revealed in the early 2000s and became big scandals. In order to protect people's life, property and other interests, whistleblowing started to be encouraged and whistleblowers were to be protected against dismissals and other disadvantageous treatment by reason of whistleblowing. These circumstances brought forth the enactment of the Whistleblowers Protection Act in 2004.

The Act explicitly prohibits dismissals by reason of whistleblowing in the public interest (Art. 3 para. 1) and other disadvantageous treatment such as demotion and wage deduction (Art. 5). However, the Act encourages whistleblowing to the company for which the whistleblowers work and to a competent administrative organ. Ms. X's blog entry is directed to anonymous outsiders. Such whistleblowing to third parties or outside persons is protected only when there are justifiable reasons to do so, such as the risk of retaliation against whistleblowing to the administrative agency, or the risk that damage to the life or body of an individual has been caused or is about to be caused. If Ms. X fails to demonstrate such justifiable reasons, she will not be protected by the Act.

However, the failure to meet the application prerequisites of the Whistleblowers Protection Act does not exclude the application of the general rules on the prohibition of abusive dismissals. This is explicitly confirmed in Article 6 of the Whistleblowers Protection Act. Therefore, if Ms. X proves that the dismissal lacks reasonable grounds and is socially inappropriate, the discharge becomes null and void. Courts will review (1) whether the allegation is true or she had good reason to believe it was true, (2) whether the purpose of whistleblowing is proper, and (3) whether the manner of whistleblowing is appropriate. In the case of Ms. X, the appropriateness of the manner (blog entry open to the general public) would be questioned.

As to the second criticism of company's management, it raises the problem of a duty not to damage an employer's honor or reputation deriving from a duty of loyalty. It is generally agreed that an employee owes a duty of loyalty and faithfulness naturally deriving from an employment contract because employment relations are personal and continuous relations requiring confidence between the parties. Violation of this duty can justify disciplinary punishment by the employer.

For instance, if the employee participates in an organized boycott of the employer's products in his or her private life, he would violate this duty. Distributing handbills or letters harmful to the employer can violate the fidelity duty. In one case, an employee distributed handbills attacking the company in the employee's own time and away from the job. The Supreme Court held that he could be found to have violated the duty of faithfulness if the handbills distorted the facts and constituted slander or defamation (The *Kansai Denryoku* case, Supreme Court, September 8, 1983, 1094 HANREI JIHO 121). Similarly, sending libelous literature to the Lawyers Association was held to constitute just cause to discharge the employee (The *Keiai Gakuen* case, Supreme Court, September 8, 1994, 657 RODO HANREI 12). Disciplinary action against an employee who sent a letter criticizing the company's activity to a newspaper was held valid when the truth of the criticism is doubtful and problematic.[1] However, the dismissal of a doctor who reported improper medical consultation practice at his hospital to the public health center was held null and void (The *Shiseikai Tomisato Byoin* case, Tokyo District Court, November 27, 1995, 1562 HANREI JIHO 126). In the last case, the content of the report was true.

Compared with these cases, Ms. X's criticism of management is not so severe and does not cause any harmful effect to the company's sales or production. In Japan, therefore, Ms. X's remark does not constitute an objectively reasonable ground for discharge. Thus, the dismissal shall be invalid.

1 The *Shuto Kosoku Doro Kodan* case, Tokyo District Court, May 22, 1997, 718 RODO HANREI 17.

PRIMARY SOURCES

Whistleblower Protection Act

(Nullity of Dismissal)

Article 3

In the case a Whistleblower is dismissed by the business operator provided for in Item (i) of Paragraph 1 of the preceding Article on the basis of Whistleblowing provided for in each of the following Items in the respective case, the dismissal shall be void:

(i) In the case a Reportable Fact is considered to have occurred, occur or be about to occur: Whistleblowing to the said Business Operator, etc.;

(ii) In the case there are reasonable grounds to believe that the Reportable Fact has occurred, occurs or is about to occur: Whistleblowing to an Administrative Organ with the authority to impose Disposition or Recommendation, etc.; or

(iii) In the case there are reasonable grounds to believe that the Reportable Fact has occurred, occurs or is about to occur and when any of the following applies: Whistleblowing to any person to whom such Whistleblowing is considered necessary to prevent the occurrence of the Reportable Fact or the spread of damage caused by the Reportable Fact:
   (a) In the case the Whistleblower has reasonable grounds to believe that he/she will receive dismissal or other disadvantageous treatment if he/she does whistleblowing as provided for in the preceding two Items;
   (b) In the case the Whistleblower has reasonable grounds to believe that the evidence pertaining to the Reportable fact might be concealed, counterfeited, or altered if he/she does whistleblowing as provided for in Item (i);
   (c) In the case the Whistleblower was requested by the Business Operator, without any justifiable reason, not to blow a whistle provided for in the preceding two Items;
   (d) In the case the Whistleblower does not receive notice from the said Business Operator, etc., about the commencement of an investigation on the Reportable fact within twenty days from the day of the Whistleblowing provided for in Item (i) made in writing (including a record made by an electronic method, a magnetic method, or any other method not recognizable to human senses.; the same shall apply to Article 9), or the said Business operator, etc. does not investigate without any justifiable reason; or
   (e) In the case the Whistleblower has a justifiable reason to believe that some damage to the life or body of an individual is caused or about to be caused.

(Prohibition of Disadvantageous Treatment)

Article 5

(1) In addition to Article 3, the business operator provided for in Item (i) of Paragraph 1 of Article 2 shall not give any disadvantageous treatment such as demotion, a salary cut or other treatment to Whistleblower who is or was its employee on the basis of such Whistleblowing as provided for in the Items of Article 3.

(2) In addition to such disadvantageous treatment as provided for in the preceding Article, such business operator as provided for in Item (ii) of Paragraph 1 of Article 2 shall not give any disadvantageous treatment, such as asking the business operator dispatching the Whistleblower to replace him/her with another dispatched worker, to Whistleblower who is a dispatched worker working under the direction of the business operator on the basis of such Whistleblowing as provided for in the Items of Article 3.

(Provision on Construction)

Article 6

(1) The provisions of the preceding three Articles shall not preclude the application of the provisions of other laws and regulations (which shall mean Acts and orders based on Acts; the same shall apply to Paragraph 1 of Article 10) that prohibit a dismissal or any other disadvantageous treatment of worker or dispatched worker on the basis of the fact that the worker has blown a whistle pertaining to the Reportable Fact.

(2) The provisions of the Article 3 shall not preclude the application of the provision of Article 18–2 of the Labor Standards Act.

References and suggested readings

As to the Whistleblower Protection Act, see Kazuo Sugeno, *A New Law to Protect Whistle-Blowing: Changing Legal Consciousness in Japanese Industrial Society*, *in* EMPLOYEE INVOLVEMENT IN A GLOBALISING WORLD – LIBER AMICORUM MANFRED WEISS, 487 (Armin Höland, Christine Hohmann-Dennhardt, Marlene Schmidt & Achim Seifert eds., 2005).

Problem 12 discussion – United States

Although most employees in the United States work on an at-will basis, since the early 1980s many state courts have afforded tort relief for a discharge "violative of public policy," i.e. where the conduct giving rise to the employee's termination implicates the common good. Moreover, a number of states have enacted "whistleblower" laws to protect employees who speak out for the public good to reveal their employer's illegal or other wrongful activity. (One such federal law, the Sarbanes-Oxley Act, is dealt with in Problem 13, infra.)

Turning then to the employee's public criticism of the employer's dumping of waste, allegedly in violation of environmental law, absent statutory protection the vast majority of jurisdictions would decline to extend public policy to protect employee public speech critical of the employer even when there is a good faith belief in the company's wrongdoing. The federal constitutional protection of "free speech" on matters of public concern applies only to action taken by public authority, e.g. only by the state, not by private centers of power. Only two or three states – California, New Jersey, and, possibly, Pennsylvania – have applied their state constitutions' free speech clauses to private centers of power. South Carolina and Connecticut have legislated to extend state protection to the exercise of "political rights" (South Carolina) and to "rights guaranteed by the first amendment" (Connecticut), which might protect Ms. X's blog were she employed there.

Attention thus turns to state whistleblower statutes and these vary widely in coverage, i.e. as to what speech is protected and to whom it must be directed in order to secure protection. Invariably these protect reporting of a violation of law (or one "reasonably believed" to be such) to a public body, not a report to the press or direct public address.

Turning next to Ms. X's criticism of the company's management, in the English common law of master and servant, speech disparaging the master, his product or services, gave cause to dismiss as conduct inimical to the servant's implied obligation to do no act injurious to the master's business. This implied obligation has been carried over into the U.S. law of employment.

Under the National Labor Relations Act, speech critical of the company, especially of its labor policies or actions, uttered by or on behalf of a work group (and especially during the course of an effort to unionize) is protected as concerted activity for mutual aid or protection. But, even here, the courts have at times been chary of extending that protection to "disloyal" speech that centers on the quality of the product or the quality of management. Accordingly, if Ms. X's speech was spoken by her as an individual having no connection to or in anticipation of stimulating co-worker action it could not be protected by the NLRA as lacking in concert of action. And even were she to have spoken in a representative capacity it might not be protected as an act of unprotected disloyalty.

As noted in connection with Problem 9, three states – California, Colorado, and North Dakota – protect the employee's engagement in any lawful activity off the employer's premises and in the employee's own time so long as that activity does not have detrimental workplace consequences. Blogging would seem to be a perfectly lawful activity, but it remains to be seen, because there is almost no case law, what needs be shown in terms of detrimental workplace consequence to deprive this speech of that statutory protection. Curiously, a federal district court, predicting what Colorado law is, held that the statute did not protect an employee's letter to the editor in a local newspaper criticizing the employer's decision to replace full-time workers with independent contractors; but a decade later the Colorado Court of Appeals explicitly rejected that decision as inconsistent with the Colorado statute. Otherwise, there is no case law under these labor protective statutes.

References and suggested readings

See generally, BRIAN MALSBERGER et al., EMPLOYER DUTY OF LOYALTY: A STATE-BY-STATE SURVEY (4th ed. 2009).

The federal decision predicting Colorado law is *Marsh v. Delta Airlines*, 952 F.Supp.1458 (D. Colo. 1997). The Colorado court's reaction is *Watson v. Pub. Serv. Co. of Colo.*, 207 P.3d 860, 864–5 (Colo. App. 2008). The Connecticut Supreme Court has read into the state's extension of free speech to private sector employees the same limit the United States Supreme Court has regarding the free speech rights of public employees: an employee who speaks in the course of her employment is not protected by free speech at all. *Schuman v. Dianon Systems, Inc.*, 43 A.3d.111 (Conn. 2012). But as the employee in this problem is an accountant, it is unlikely that she has responsibilities for environmental matters.

Employer monitoring of social media has become an issue in the United States. *See* Pew Research Center's Internet's American Life Project, Privacy Management on Social Media Cites (Feb. 24, 2012) and Patricia Abril, Auner Levin & Alissa Del Riego, *Blurred Boundaries: Social Media Privacy in the Twenty-First Century Employee*, 49 AM. BUS. L. J. 63 (2012). *See generally*, Matthew Finkin, PRIVACY IN EMPLOYMENT LAW Ch. 5, §III (E) (3rd ed. 2009) (and the 4th ed., in press).

Exchanges among employees complaining about working conditions that involve or reasonably could lead to concerted activity vis-à-vis the employer are protected under the National Labor Relations Act. *Hispanics United of Buffalo*, 359 NLRB No. 37 (2012). But criticism of managerial competence has become beclouded. This is discussed by Matthew Finkin, *Disloyalty! Does* Jefferson Standard *Stalk* Still?, 28 BERK. J. EMP. & LAB. L. 541 (2007).

Ms. X's blog was open to the public. But much attention has been given to employer access to media accounts to which the applicant or employee restricts access. Currently eight states prohibit employers from requesting access. *See* the note on p. 201, supra.

> As social networking becomes more prevalent and as younger generations become more entrenched in it – what role do HR Departments/Educators/Mentor Managers play in helping shape the appropriate context of how to protect one's personal life? As a Facebook user, I have a standard simple rule – no work people on my Facebook friends list. I keep my private life separate and try to have healthy boundaries. The opposite is true for LinkedIn – very few of my personal friends are networked with me there. My spouse calls it my "never shall these two ships pass in the night" strategy. I can already count five times that as an act of kindness I've pulled aside a new employee and suggested that they may want to make their profiles private on Myspace/Facebook as they ought to consider if they really want the world to see their jello body shot pictures? Or create a perception among new colleagues about their behavior. In all cases they each came back and thanked me for it.
>
> Director, HR, Industrial Manufacturing Sector

Questions for Discussion – Problem 12

1. Note that all five countries hold that when a person enters into an employment relationship that person implicitly – that is, by operation of law – assumes an obligation to do that which furthers the employer's business interests and, per contra, to do no harm to it. At one time this was taken by management to trump any countervailing claim of either professional or public responsibility. As the chairman of the board of directors of the General Motors Corporation put it in 1971:

   > [T]he enemies of business now encourage an employee to be disloyal to the enterprise. They want to create suspicion and disharmony, and pry into the proprietary interests of the business. However this is labeled [sic] – industrial espionage, whistle blowing, or professional responsibility – it is another tactic for spreading disunity and creating conflict.

   Quoted in Kenneth D. Walters, *Your Employees' Right to Blow the Whistle*, in INDIVIDUAL RIGHTS IN THE CORPORATION 91, 93 (Alan Westin & Stephen Salsburg eds., 1980). But today, all these jurisdictions would accord a degree of autonomy for the disclosure of corporate wrongdoing – see Problem 13, infra – subject to bewildering differences in scope and application.

2. Your corporation has operations in all five countries and you have been tasked by your boss to develop a policy on blogging, web postings, twitter, and other statements in social media that will reduce the companies' exposure to adverse public relations while still complying with the law in all five countries. What should this policy state?

3. Ms. X's criticism of the layoff may stand on different ground than whistleblowing. Though she, her fellow workers, their families, and the local community all have a strong interest in the company's success, on its being managed well, her disparagement of the managers' decision, and so of their competence, triggers an old question couched by a labor arbitrator in a canine analogy: "Can you [an employee] bite the hand that feeds you, and insist on staying for future banquets?" *Forest City Pub. Co.*, 58 L.A. 773, 783 (Calvin L. McCoy Arb., 1972). The answer in the U.S. would seem to be a categorical "no," unless the speech constituted protected concerted activity for mutual aid or protection under the NLRA. The answer in Germany would be an equally categorical "yes," as a matter of free speech and personal autonomy. In Australia, Ms. X could have the possibility of persuading a tribunal that the discharge was excessive. This avenue would seem to hold promise of success in Brazil and Japan as well. Obviously, your company would not dismiss Ms. X in Germany. Would you do so in these other jurisdictions? Why?

PROBLEM 13: CONFIDENTIAL SECURITIES HOTLINE

The Sarbanes-Oxley Act deals with the functions of the auditing committees of the boards of directors of corporations whose securities are subject to regulation by the Securities and Exchange Commission (SEC). It provides, among other things, that the SEC direct the national securities exchanges and national securities associations to prohibit the listing of any security of an issuer that is not in compliance with the requirements of any portion of paragraphs (2) through (6). 15 U.S.C. §78j–m(1)(A). Paragraph (4) incorporated by this direction provides in pertinent part:

> (4) Complaints
>
> Each audit committee shall establish procedures for –
>
> …
>
> (B) the confidential, anonymous submission by employees of the issuer of [of the security] concerns regarding questionable accounting or auditing matters.

The Company is a multinational corporation whose stock is listed on a stock exchange subject to SEC regulation. It has asked you to set up an anonymous "hotline" which any employee in any of its facilities worldwide can call to report "questionable accounting or auditing matters." You have consulted legal counsel. Are there any obstacles to compliance outside the United States?

Problem 13 discussion – Australia

There is no reason why such a system could not be adopted in Australia. But it could not be used to preclude a whistleblower from going outside the company's system, for example to report wrongdoing to the police, or any other appropriate enforcement agency such as the Australian Securities and Investments Commission. Even if an employee signed an undertaking (for example, as part of their employment contract) to abide by the policy, this could not preclude such action. A contract cannot validly restrain a person's freedom to disclose "iniquity" or wrongdoing: *A v Hayden (No. 2)* (1984) 156 CLR 532.

Similarly, the presence of such a system could not preclude employees or others falsely accused of wrongdoing from initiating proceedings in defamation: see e.g. *SMEC Holdings Ltd v Boniface* [2007] NSWSC 1402, to which reference is made in the extract below from STEWART'S GUIDE TO EMPLOYMENT LAW.

References and suggested readings

ANDREW STEWART, STEWART'S GUIDE TO EMPLOYMENT LAW §13.23 (4th ed. 2013):

> Part 9.4AAA of the *Corporations Act* 2001 also protects employees (and others) who disclose information about what they suspect on reasonable grounds to be a contravention of the corporations legislation. No civil or criminal liability is to be imposed for making the disclosure, while any dismissal of such an employee will be unlawful. The discloser can also seek compensation for any harm threatened or caused by way of retaliation for the disclosure. In each case, however, the disclosure must be made in good faith, and only to the Australian Securities and Investments Commission (ASIC) or an appropriate person in the corporation itself. The legislation would not (even had it been in force at the time) have protected the 'disclosures' that were the subject of litigation in *SMEC v Boniface* (2007). There a manager had circulated anonymous e-mails falsely accusing a company and three of its directors of serious illegalities. He was found to have defamed them and was ordered to pay a total of $1.65 million in damages.

See also materials for Problem 12, supra.

Problem 13 discussion – Brazil

As mentioned in the discussion of Problem 12, there is no specific Brazilian law dealing with "whistleblowing" practices. Encouraging employees to come out and share their difficulties and problems is a practice "sold" as a valuable pedagogical tool in order to improve the working environment. Thus, some companies do provide a "hotline" where workers can blow the whistle on inappropriate employee actions. Yet, as Brazilian labor relations are extremely adversarial, employees rarely step up to share their co-workers' wrongdoings, but mostly come out to complain about managers and supervisors' mistreatment of subaltern employees. In addition to that, employers may have external "hotlines" for consumers to blow the whistle on inappropriate employees' actions. For instance, it is a very common practice adopted for employees whose work cannot be supervised (e.g. drivers).

Anonymity is a key issue. Employers usually say that anonymity has to be assured for the whistleblower vis-à-vis the employees as an incentive to "whistleblowing" practices. Yet as the "finger-pointed" employee has the right to confront the whistleblower, the problem here lies in the unacceptable suppression of defense rights as the accused would not be aware at first of any ongoing investigation against him/her. It gets worse if the information gathered by the company is used to dismiss an employee, as he/she has a right to confront the company's informer and sue – both company and whistleblower – for moral damages if it comes out that it was based on false grounds.

On the critical issue of extra-territorial application, it is not clear that the U.S. statutory requirement of anonymity in the initial report could prevent a judicially compelled disclosure of the hotline reporter's identity in Brazil.

References and suggested readings

For an example of a code of conduct with some guidelines on the use of a "hotline", see: ILLIX. *Código de Conduta & Ética (Ethics and Conduct Code), accessed at* http://www.illix.com.br/codigo.pdf (last visited Feb. 23, 2010).

Problem 13 discussion – Germany

"Codes of conduct" are (partly) subject to co-determination rights of the works council (Federal Labor Court of 22.07.2007 – 1 ABR 40/07; see also State Labor Court Hesse of 18.01.2007 – 5 TaBV 31/06). Establishing a "hotline" is subject to a co-determination right of the works council under either section 87 para. 1 no. 1 (dominating opinion) or section 87 para. 1 no. 6 of the Works Councils Act. Thus, if a works council exists, the employer is not allowed to act unilaterally. If, however, employees are not bound to notify breaches of compliance nor obliged to use the "hotline" – which appears to be the problem's purport – no co-determination right applies.

Data protection law may hold important restrictions, however. In any event, (non-binding) recommendations issued by the so-called "Article 29-Working Group," a group of European experts in this area, suggest that "whistleblower hotlines" might breach EU data protection law and, in particular, might not be in line with the principle of proportionality if, first, their use is not restricted to issues of financial accounting, auditing or fighting corruption; second, those employees who *are* obliged to use the hotline are not determined according to their responsibility; and, third, notification is not anonymous. In terms of US subsidiaries, particular problems arise if the hotline is technically established in the US and data is stored and processed there. Section 4b para. 2 sentence 2 of the Federal Data Protection Act requires that a country outside the EU guarantees reasonable data protection standards if personal data is to be transferred to such country. In the view of the European Commission, the United States does not guarantee the necessary standards. As a consequence, the transfer of personal data is restricted even within an international group of companies. Only if it can be shown in an individual case that the transmitted data is protected (e.g. by agreements between the companies concerned, participation in a so-called "safe harbour," substantiated and written consent by the concerned employees), would the transfer of data be permitted.

Apart from all that, a contractual "hotline clause" in a works agreement, though admissible in principle, may neither breach the fundamental personal right (*Allgemeines Persönlichkeitsrecht*) as enshrined in Articles 2(1) and 1(1) of the German Constitution, the Basic Law, nor may such clause breach the so-called "right to informational freedom" (*Recht auf informationelle Selbstbestimmung*), a right which was "invented" by the German Constitutional Court some time ago (Federal Constitutional Court of 15.12.1983 – 1 BVR 209/83) and is regarded as part and parcel of the right to privacy as guaranteed by Article 2(1) and 1(1) of the Basic Law.

As far as the establishment of an internal complaint procedure is concerned, there is a right to co-determination of the works council according to section 87(1) no. 1 of the Works Constitution Act (Federal Labor Court of 22.07.2007 – 1 ABR 40/07 and 28.05.2002 – 1 ABR 32/01).

References and suggested readings

Works Constitution Act § 87(1) (in Problem 1).

Anja Mengel & Volker Hagemeister, *Compliance und arbeitsrechtliche Implementierung im Unternehmen*, BETRIEBS-BERATER (BB) 1386 (2007); Gerlind Wisskirchen & Anke Körber/Alexander Bissels, *"Whistleblowing" und "Ethikhotlines" – Probleme des deutschen Arbeits- und Datenschutzrechts*, BETRIEBS-BERATER (BB) 1567 (2006); Thilo Mahnhold, *"Global Whistle" oder "deutsche Pfeife" – Whistleblowing-Systeme im Jurisdiktionskonflikt*, *in* NEUE ZEITSCHRIFT FÜR ARBEITSRECHT (NZA) 737 (2008); David Schneider, *Die arbeitsrechtliche Implementierung von Compliance- und Ethikrichtlinien*, Baden-Baden (2009).

Problem 13 discussion – Japan

As discussed in Problem 12, Japan enacted the Whistleblowers Protection Act in 2004. The Act explicitly prohibits dismissals by reason of whistleblowing in the public interest (Art. 3 para. 1) and other disadvantageous treatment such as demotion and wage deduction (Art. 5). Although establishing an anonymous hotline or other procedures keeping confidentiality is recommended, the Act does not explicitly require the setting up of such channels. However, of course, there is no obstacle to establishing an anonymous hotline.

A possible problem of an anonymous hotline might be that it would encourage irresponsible or malicious reporting for the purpose of damaging other persons. To be protected by the Whistleblowers Protection Act, reporting must be made without a purpose of obtaining wrongful gain, a purpose of causing damages to others, or any other wrongful purpose. Therefore, if the whistleblower made such wrong report for the malicious purpose of expelling or damaging his or her boss or colleague, he or she would be liable for tort if his/her name was disclosed by chance or for some other reason.

In Japan, since establishing an anonymous hotline is not legally required and employers want to secure responsible and trustful reporting and fear abusive usage of hotlines, anonymous hotlines have not been widely adopted. However, recently, several cases have attracted attention where whistleblowers' name that should have been kept confidential were carelessly revealed to the very person who had been named as being engaged in wrongdoing. Thus the importance of anonymous reporting will be more often recognized.

References and suggested readings

See Kazuo Sugeno, *A New Law to Protect Whistle-Blowing: Changing Legal Consciousness in Japanese Industrial Society*, *in* EMPLOYEE INVOLVEMENT IN A GLOBALISING WORLD – LIBER AMICORUM MANFRED WEISS 487–95 (Armin Höland, Christine Hohmann-Dennhardt, Marlene Schmidt, Achim Seifert eds., 2005).

Problem 13 discussion – United States

As Professor Richard Moberly has explained, there are basically two legal models in the United States to encourage employees to report corporate malfeasance: an "anti-retaliation" model – the most common form embodied in a variety of federal and state whistleblower laws; and what he has termed a "structural" model that, unlike the anti-retaliation model, which assumes the company is an adversary of the employee, seeks to enlist the employee as a participant in an effort to prevent wrongdoing. The major example of the latter is the Sarbanes-Oxley Act, the subject of this problem. As the other responses to this question indicate, what is problematic is the statutory requirement of anonymity. There has been no litigation on what the legal consequences are vis-à-vis erroneous (or malicious) reports of malfeasance.

The most obvious unanswered question is whether the subject of a wrongful report may learn the identity of the whistleblower and sue him or her for the state law tort of defamation or, should the employee reported-on be discharged, sue for intentional interference in economic advantage. It is possible that the federal statute, by conferring anonymity, preempts discovery of the speaker's identity under state law. And, even if the wrongly injured employee is able to learn who the speaker was, it may be that the law would be read to confer an absolute privilege – one that cannot be defeated even by proof of actual intent to injure or knowledge of the falsity of what was said.

Where an employer believes the structural model would be of benefit to it in areas where Sarbanes-Oxley does not apply – to set up an anonymous "hotline" with an express promise of confidentiality for reporting other violations of law, ethics, or company policy – these issues are very likely to be raised, this time, however, without the prospect of federally preemptive protections for the speaker. Such "hotline" systems have been voluntarily adopted by several U.S. companies.

References and suggested readings

MICHAEL DELIKAT & RENEE PHILIPPS, CORPORATE WHISTLEBLOWING IN THE SARBANES-OXLEY/DODD-FRANK ERA (2012); DANIEL WESTMAN & NANCY MODESETT, WHISTLEBLOWING: THE LAW OF RETALIATORY DISCHARGE (2004).

Professor Moberly's appraisal of these models in general and his particular critique of Sarbanes-Oxley is found in Richard Moberly, *Sarbanes-Oxley's Structural Model to Encourage Corporate Whistleblowers*, 2006 BYU L. REV. 1107 (comprehensively reviewing the literature).

On the structure of the law of defamation, including the role of privilege in the employment setting, *see* MATTHEW FINKIN, PRIVACY IN EMPLOYMENT LAW (4th ed.) (in press). New York has conferred an absolute privilege on the content of the U-5 Form, a public document that brokerages are required to file with the relevant stock exchange stating the reason for the termination of a broker. *Rosenberg v. Metlife, Inc.*, 866 N.E.2d 439 (N.Y. 2007). But Maine would accord only a qualified privilege – one that can be defeated by a showing of actual malice or knowing falsehood. *Galarneau v. Merrill Lynch, Pearce, Fenner & Smith*, 504 F.3d 189 (1st Cir. 2007).

We have a hotline – not for SOX specifically, but for violations of industry-specific federal/state statutes and the company's policies. One thing I find interesting is that the policy requires employees who have a "good faith belief" that a violation of law or company policy to report it and that retaliation is prohibited against any employee who has submitted a good faith report. Termination may result if an employee does not report a violation and if they knowingly provide false or misleading information. The hotline calls do not always lead to terminations or other disciplinary actions – many times people just have an ethical or policy question. The analysis of calls also highlights training and policy gaps. Our hotline is anonymous but there are very few calls where the caller's motivations are questionable. Our hotline policies would not be allowed (or difficult to implement) in Germany, Japan and Brazil for the reasons you mentioned

> related to anonymity. Because the company's officers and employees may be held personally liable (even if they are not directly involved) and the company can actually be prohibited from conducting business in the industry for legal violations, I think our hotline is really necessary as part of any defense against any possible legal action in the U.S.
>
> HR Consultant, Multiple Sectors

Questions for Discussion – Problem 13

1. Note the legally complex and sensitive treatment of this issue under both German co-determination and data protection law; and, should an accused employee be dismissed, under German wrongful dismissal law as well. The response to Problem 11 uses the term "denunciation" to characterize the whistleblower. To the drafters of Sarbanes-Oxley, the anonymous hotline reporter is a good corporate citizen who is best positioned to monitor the company's fiscal behavior in the public interest. In Europe generally, and especially in Germany, anonymous reporting of one's co-workers (or neighbors or family members) to those in authority has an odious history. *See* RICHARD GRUNBERGER, THE 12-YEAR REICH: A SOCIAL HISTORY OF NAZI GERMANY 1933–1945 Ch. 7 (1971) ("Denunciation"). Draft a one-page memo to your boss explaining the degree to which this hotline could operate in each of the four countries other than the U.S. and, where the hotline could not be set up, indicate why this is so.

2. In countries where you could not set up a hotline, what might you do instead (given your understanding of the law from the answers to Problem 13)?

A concluding note on alternate dispute resolution

As the introduction to the legal landscape in the United States in Part I noted, a feature of the contemporary legal scene has been the corporate adoption of employment arbitration policies that require employees to agree, as a condition of employment, that any legal claims they may have against their employers will not be heard in court but will be submitted to an arbitration system created by the employer. The rationale for these policies has been explained by an unsympathetic observer:

> Well-paid managerial and professional employees who believe themselves wronged by the corporation have little difficulty securing counsel and pursuing their legal rights,

> and lower-level employees with cases implicating potentially large damage awards are able to find lawyers willing to take these cases on a contingent basis. Lost in the legal system are those low-level employees with weaker claims or claims which, even if strong, are unlikely to produce high damage awards. These workers are less able to secure counsel and find it difficult, if not impossible, to vindicate their legal rights. And so the corporation offers the state a bargain, a bargain that a majority of the Court has been willing to accept: if the state will agree to stay the judicial hand, the corporation will unburden the state's courts by requiring its employees to arbitrate their legal claims. In this way, the jury – which is thought to be, if not biased against faceless corporations (with deep pockets), at least fickle – is eliminated. In return for greater predictability, a lessening of the potential for big damage awards, and the elimination of nuisance (or "strike") suits and of public litigation (with the attendant possibility of bad publicity), the corporation will make it practicable to hear cases that otherwise would have gone unheard. As a management lawyer put it, "[Arbitration is] faster, it's cheaper, and it's more manageable. If properly managed, it can provide a broader access to a neutral process."

Matthew Finkin, *Modern Manorial Law*, 38 INDUS. REL. 127, 131–2 (1999) (footnote omitted).

The United States Supreme Court has accepted the offer in a series of cases, all by closely divided votes. The legal theory is that the parties have consented merely to substitute one forum for another, the law to be applied being the same in either forum. To do so, the Court had to overrule a precedent of long standing, *Wilko v. Swan*, 346 U.S. 427 (1953), that had rejected that very argument in part on the ground that the choice of forum was itself an aspect of the law. Some effort at empirical research has been undertaken to find out whether arbitral results differ from what the courts produce. The state of empirical knowledge has been summarized by Alexander Colvin, *Empirical Research on Employment Arbitration: Clarity Amidst Sound and Fury?*, 11 EMP. POL'Y J. 405 (2007).

Could policy substituting arbitration for the courts be applied to the multinational company's foreign operations as well? The question can be tested in the sample surveyed here. Of *Australia*, Andrew Stewart has replied as follows:

> This is not an issue that has arisen in Australia, at least not publicly. As McCallum et al explain:
>
> > The early establishment of publicly-funded tribunals to deal with workplace disputes, by relatively informal processes, has meant that the profession of alternative dispute resolution (ADR) providers which regularly assists in other fields of law in Australia (notably family law disputes) has not made significant inroads into workplace dispute resolution in Australia. [U]nfair dismissal applications can be made relatively cheaply and without legal representation, and guarantee applicants

an assessment of the merits of their case by an expert tribunal. So there has been little incentive for employees to agree to the kinds of arbitration clauses commonly inserted into employment contracts in the United States.[2]

There are in any event some powerful legal obstacles to the establishment of any private arbitration regime. As explained in relation to Problem 11, Part 3–2 of the Fair Work Act 2009 creates a statutory right for most employees to apply to Fair Work Australia seeking reinstatement or compensation for unfair dismissal. An agreement that purported to preclude an employee from asserting this right would be treated as unenforceable, on the basis that it would be contrary to public policy: see generally *Brooks v Burns Philp Trustee Co Ltd* (1969) 121 CLR 432. The same would apply to rights arising under legislation, such as anti-discrimination statutes: see e.g. *Qantas Airways Ltd v Gubbins* 28 NSWLR 26 (1992).

Higher-paid non-award employees are excluded from the statutory unfair dismissal regime. To the extent they bring wrongful dismissal claims, this usually involves arguing that they have been dismissed in breach of contract. In principle, they could agree to submit such a common law claim to arbitration, rather than to a court. But under commercial arbitration legislation in each jurisdiction, the courts retain the power to review arbitral decisions for both procedural defects and errors of law: see e.g. Commercial Arbitration Act 2010 (NSW) ss 34, 34A.

Of *Brazil*, Roberto Fragale Filho has replied:

First of all, as labour rights are considered to be fundamental rights, the employee may not dispose of them in an arbitration system but has instead to go through the judicial system in order to validate whatever negotiation he/she wants to make with her employer. Secondly, an arbitration system "that the company creates" would be perceived as eliminating any if not all of the equality the parties must have in a labour conflict. Finally, it wouldn't be accepted because the right to file a claim is constitutionally guaranteed and cannot be revoked by any means. Not even statute has been able to change such perception. As a matter of fact, Previous Conciliation Committees (PCCs) were created by statute at the beginning of the 2000s and by law if an agreement is reached in a PCC, it has the same effect as a judicial decision. Still, the courts have constantly upheld that this provision is unconstitutional and that the right to file a suit is to be protected. Thus, returning to the question, I would say that such a provision is not enforceable.

The situation in *Germany* has been explained to similar effect:

Binding employment arbitration is allowed in two, but only two situations, governed by the Works Constitution Act (BetrVG) and the Labour Courts Act (ArbGG), respectively. In the former, the resolution of impasses between an employer and a works council, a form of collective dispute, must be submitted to an arbitration committee

2 Ronald McCallum, Joellen Riley & Andrew Stewart, *Resolving Disputes over Employment Rights in Australia*, 34 COMP. LAB. L. & POL'Y J. (forthcoming 2013).

> (*Einigungstelle*) where the dispute concerns a subject that must be co-determined, i.e. that requires the agreement of both parties, for example, the content of rules governing the modalities of working hours or the introduction and use of technical devices designed to monitor employee performance and behavior, such as the institution of surveillance cameras... These bodies do not decide questions of law; in fact, the labour court has jurisdiction to decide that a decision of an arbitration committee is in conflict with the law.
>
> In the latter, the Labour Courts Act allows for the use of binding arbitration in just two cases, but only where a collective agreement makes provision for it: (1) by submission of the parties to the agreement to decide questions arising under it and (2) by submission of the parties to a collective agreement on the grounds that an employment relationship is governed by it where the employment is of stage actors, film workers, variety artists and captains and crew covered by the seamen's act ...
>
> Disputes on the application of individual labour protective law, such as fair dismissal, maternal protection and so on, may not be submitted to arbitration even if the individual contract were to provide for it.

Matthew Finkin, *Privatization of Wrongful Dismissal Protection in Comparative Perspective*, 37 INDUS. L.J. 149, 157–8 (2009) (footnotes omitted).

Professor Araki has summarized the legal situation in *Japan* to the same effect:

> An agreement not to sue the employer but to entrust the arbitration system that the company creates is invalid in Japan. The Japanese Arbitration Act governing arbitration agreements stipulates that arbitration agreements concerning individual labor disputes shall be null and void. This regulation takes the unequal negotiation power between employer and employee into consideration and fears abuse of the arbitration agreement, depriving the employees of their right to go to court.

Discussion Comments and Questions

1. Note that Australia, Brazil, and Germany make available a labor court to which an individual may have resort without significant expense or legal counsel. The U.S. and Japan rely on individual litigation in which counsel is necessary. It might be well at this point to reconsider the statistics set out in the Note on Wrongful Discharge Litigation, supra.

2. It has been estimated that as many as 25–30 percent of non-unionized workers in the U.S. are covered by mandatory arbitration policies. Why "mandatory"? Why would these companies not give the employee a choice of forum – to litigate or to arbitrate?

3. Under some employment arbitration systems the employee relinquishes the capacity to bring or participate in a class or group claim. The National Labor Relations Board held that such waivers are unenforceable as being in violation of the Labor Act's non-individually waivable statutory right to engage in "concerted activity for mutual aid or protection." *D.R. Horton, Inc.*, 357 NLRB No. 184 (2012) *app. pending*. The issue is currently under judicial review. Why would a company institute such a restriction? What would be the practical consequences?

4. What are the benefits and drawbacks of private and public systems of employment legal claim resolution? If access to workplace justice is a public good, to vindicate the public policies found in the welter of federal and state employment protective law, would a publicly financed labor court be preferable to reliance on corporate decisions on the availability and structure of an alternative forum?

PART VI

COMPENSATION AND BENEFITS ADMINISTRATION

In Part VI, three compensation and benefit questions are posed. The first problem (Problem 14) involves the prospect of a common share ownership and supplementary pension scheme. The second problem (Problem 15) considers requests for equal treatment by members of a virtual team operating in different countries. The third problem (Problem 16) considers the extraterritorial implications of restrictions on executive compensation (in this case imposed by the U.S. government). Underlying most compensation and benefit issues are issues of internal and external equity in order to attract, retain and motivate a workforce, which are compounded by the need to have a consistent set of policies that spans national boundaries. A fourth problem (Problem 17) concerns the enforceability of an agreement not to disclose business information and to engage in competitive activity after the termination of employment.

Compensation and benefits vary considerably across nations. Wage levels vary with the degree of industrialization, though wages are rising rapidly in many newly industrialized nations. If we define the middle class as people earning between $10 and $100 a day, there are approximately 1.8 billion people in the middle class in the world today and it is estimated that there will be 3.2 billion by 2020 and 4.9 billion by 2030.[1] For multinational corporations, this means that a growing proportion of their global workforce will approach wages and benefits with middle-class expectations. Wage and benefit administration for a multinational corporation is complicated within the countries where they operate by fluctuations in the value of different currencies, differences in legislative rights with respect to pay and benefits, and contrasting assumptions about the regulation of labor markets. Moreover, the fundamental tension between local variation and global consistency is particularly acute in this context. At one extreme an HR professional described his multinational company's philosophy on wages and benefits as "what happens in Denmark, stays in Denmark" – reflecting a localized, country-by-country approach to compensation and benefits. While no company can be entirely at the other extreme because of nation-specific laws and regulations, most multinational

1 Source: Homi Kharas, "The Emerging Middle Class in Developing Countries," OECD Development Center, January 2010.

firms strive to have policies on compensation and benefits that are as consistent as possible for their entire workforce.

In the domain of compensation and benefits, it is helpful to think of the global workforce as segmented in a number of important ways in most multinational companies. This includes differentiation for executives, expats, people with specialized skills, middle managers, and the front-line workforce.

Policies on executive compensation are shaped by the norms for executive compensation in the corporation's home country, though the global market for executive talent is increasingly resulting in a "leveling up" to the standards where executive compensation is most generous. Executive compensation practices are most lucrative in the United States and that is seen as "infecting" standards in other parts of the world.

A second segment of the workforce in a multinational corporation includes expatriates (executives, managers, and subject matter experts). Here there are generally consistent policies across the global workforce for expat pay and benefits, though the role of expat assignments is shifting from a one-directional set of assignments emanating from the home country to multi-directional assignments, with expats potentially coming from any country where the company has operations to any other. This has required some calibration of expat policies, generally anchoring the policy in the pay and benefits of the individual's home country rather than the home of the corporation.

A third segment of the workforce includes individuals with skills, where the labor market for talent is becoming global. Here, the forces for standardization are more of the market, rather than corporate policy. Unlike the case of executive compensation, where the globalization of the market has had an upward effect on pay and benefits, there is not as clear a direction (up or down) in the overall trend, so much as a movement toward more standardization driven by the countries where there is a strong pool of the relevant talent.

Middle managers are a fourth segment of the global workforce and they are in roles that have traditionally been country specific, though their interactions and interdependence with counterparts in other countries are increasing, which does create additional internal pressure for increased consistency in pay and benefits. There is not necessarily a globalization of the labor marker as a driver in this case, but the issues of internal equity arise where work is becoming more interdependent.

Front-line workers, supervisors, and sub-contractors are additional segments of the global workforce. Here the pressure is generally a "leveling down" as work shifts toward lower labor cost regions of the world, though a number of nations are increasingly developing labor and employment policies aimed at building a larger middle class (and growing internal markets as a result).

Labor and employment laws only partly correspond to these segments of the workforce. That is, minimum wage and hour laws are primarily applicable to the front-line workforce, which policies addressing corporate governance (including corporate compensation committees) and executive compensation are primarily the concern of the executive segment of the workforce. Otherwise, the distinction is driven more by corporate policy and labor market dynamics, which we will see can be in tension with more general, transnational policies.

In addition to the problems and comments presented in Part VI, all of the country experts were asked about a possible multinational corporate policy of denominating all wages and benefits in a common currency. In principle this is possible in most countries, but does involve demonstrating that it is not making employees worse off than if they were paid in the local currency. At the same time, few companies are presently doing this or contemplating such an arrangement. The issue of a common currency is an issue, however, in the context of common share ownership or pension supplements, which may well be denominated in a common currency.

Set out below are some comparative data, first on wages, and second on the relationship between pay and productivity in our sample (see Tables VI.1 and VI.2).

Table VI.1 Average manufacturing wage (U.S. dollars, 2007) and gross domestic product (GDP) per capita and per employed person (U.S. dollars, 2010)

	Australia	Brazil	Germany	Japan	United States
Average manufacturing Wage, 2007 (U.S. dollars)	34.75	7.13	51.38	23.95	31.39
Gross domestic product per capita	39,137	11,210	36,635	32,424	45,854
Gross domestic product per employed person	78,061	21,640	74,482	65,364	99,624

Sources: U.S. Department of Labor, U.S. Bureau of Labor Statistics, Division of International Labor Comparisons; U.S. Bureau of Labor Statistics and the World Bank.

Table VI.2 Pay and productivity

United States	4.8
Japan	4.6
Germany	4.3
Australia	3.8
Brazil	3.8

Note: CEOs were asked "To what extent is pay in your country related to productivity?" (1 = not related to worker productivity; 7 = strongly related to worker productivity). Weighted average for 2011–12 is shown (mean for 144 nations is 3.0).

Source: World Economic Forum, Executive Opinion Survey, Global Competitiveness Report 2012–2013.

Table VI.3 Flexibility in wage determination

Japan	5.8
United States	5.4
Brazil	4.2
Australia	4.1
Germany	3.2

Note: CEOs were asked "How are wages generally set in your country?" (1 = by a centralized bargaining process; 7 = up to each individual company). Weighted average for 2011–12 is shown (mean for 144 nations is 4.9).

Source: World Economic Forum, Executive Opinion Survey, Global Competitiveness Report 2012–2013.

PROBLEM 14: SHARE OWNERSHIP AND COMMON SUPPLEMENTARY PENSION SCHEME

A company with operations in many different countries has introduced a common share ownership scheme and a single supplementary pension scheme, both designed to apply to all employees in all countries.

Problem 14 discussion – Australia

Share ownership

There is nothing unlawful in Australia about having employee share ownership schemes, provided they are used to supplement rather than substitute for payment of the minimum wage rates required by any applicable award or enterprise agreement (or, for non-award employees, the federal minimum wage). Wages must be paid "in money": Fair Work Act 2009 s 323(1)(b).

The company would also need to be aware of the tax treatment of employee share ownership schemes in Australia, which has changed in recent years: http://www.ato.gov.au/General/Employee-share-schemes/.

Supplementary pension

The company would need to ensure that its pension scheme complied with the requirements of the Superannuation Guarantee (Administration) Act 1992. Australian employers are effectively required to contribute a percentage (currently 9 percent) of their employees' earnings into a superannuation (pension) fund that complies with certain requirements. Strictly speaking, an employer can choose not to do this – but in that event a "shortfall" will be assessed and they will have to pay a "charge" or tax that exceeds what the contribution would have cost them. Employers are also required under this legislation to give their employees an option of choosing a fund other than the one the employer itself maintains, or would prefer to use.

References and suggested readings

ANDREW STEWART, STEWART'S GUIDE TO EMPLOYMENT LAW §§ 10.29–32 (4th ed. 2013).

Problem 14 discussion – Brazil

Foreign currency cannot be used for pension scheme payments in Brazil since foreign currency can't be used for salary payments. In fact, article 463 of the *Consolidação das Leis do Trabalho* explicitly states that salaries must be paid in cash and in Brazilian currency. Additionally, it indicates that salaries paid without observing such a rule are considered as not made. A Labor Ministry Ordinance has authorized (*Portaria* nº 3.281/1984) payments to be made by check (if they can be cashed on the same day) or money order in a savings account. Any wage stipulation on foreign currency in accordance with doctrine and case law should be converted to Brazilian currency based on the exchange rate of the celebration date of the contract and from that day on is subject to raises as stipulated in federal law or negotiated through collective bargaining. The only exception applies to non-resident foreign technicians who are hired for temporary services in the country.

The single pension scheme faces the same problem since payments in foreign currency are not allowed in Brazil. However, it is useful to remember that in the past, during the high inflation period, some companies stipulated a supplementary pension scheme based on foreign currency. Although the idea was to protect pensions from high inflation rates, it ended up creating a major problem as many asked for high percentage inflation rates to be used to recover the pension value which had already oscillated according to foreign currencies in order to protect it from inflation. Needless to say those numbers sky-rocketed, giving rise to astronomic values which were finally adjusted by the country's economic stabilization.

References and suggested readings

Portaria (Ordinance) No. 3.281 1984, *accessed at* http://www.fiscosoft.com.br/indexsearch.php?PID=80021 (last visited Feb. 24, 2010).

Problem 14: discussion – Germany

Whether section 107 para. 1 Gewerbeordnung is mandatory statutory law or whether employer and employee can agree on calculating and paying a supplementary pension scheme in a foreign currency has not yet been decided by the labor courts and is highly disputed between legal scholars. As another statute, section 2 para. 2 no. 2 Law of Proof of Substantial Conditions Applicable to the Employment Relationship (*Nachweisgesetz*), obliges the employer to inform the employee about the currency the wages are paid in, one can infer that section 107 para. 1 Gewerbeordnung is not mandatory. Therefore, the parties can in principle agree on a foreign currency. However, this is possible only if it is in accordance with the employee's interests. For example, both substantial losses because of rates of exchange and payment in a rather insecure currency (e.g. the Kenya shilling) would be unacceptable. Problems may arise regarding potential additional banking fees. In general, the employer has to bear only the bank transfer costs but not the account fees. However, a bank account that calculates in a foreign currency may cause additional costs. If it was the employer who wanted to calculate and pay wages in the foreign currency, a deviation from section 107 para. 1 Gewerbeordnung is probably legal only if he agrees to reimburse the employee for these additional costs.

If a works council was elected in the company such a policy could be implemented only with its consent, section 87 para. 1 no. 4 Work Constitution Act of 1972 (*Betriebsverfassungsgesetz*).

References and suggested reading

ERFURTER KOMMENTAR ZUM ARBEITSRECHT, §107 (12th Aufl. 2012); *Bauer & Opolony*, BETRIEBS-BERATER (BB) 1590 (2002); *Wisskirchen*, *Novellierung arbeitsrechtlicher Vorschriften in der Gewerbeordnung*, DER BETRIEB 1886 (2002); Henssler, Willemsen & Kalb, ARBEITSRECHT, §107 (35th Aufl. 2012).

Problem 14: discussion – Japan

Wage payments in Japan, under Article 24 of the Labor Standards Act (LSA), must comply with four principles: wages must be paid in cash, in full, directly to the worker, and in regular payments of at least once a month.

Share ownership raises the question of payment in cash and payment in full if the employer deducts some portion of the wages in exchange for giving shares. The exception of payment in cash becomes legal when a collective agreement concluded between the employer and a labor union allows such payment in kind. Deduction of wages is possible when the employer concludes a labor-management agreement with a majority representative at the establishment.

PRIMARY SOURCE

Labor Standards Act

(Payment of Wages)

Article 24

(1) Wages shall be paid in currency and in full directly to the workers; provided, however, that payment other than in currency may be permitted in cases otherwise provided for by laws and regulations or collective agreement or in cases where a reliable method of payment of wages defined by Ordinance of the Ministry of Health, Labour and Welfare is provided for; and partial deduction from wages may be permitted in cases otherwise provided for by laws and regulations or in cases where there exists a written agreement with a labor union organized by a majority of the workers at the workplace (where such a labor union is organized), or with a person representing a majority of the workers (where such a labor union is not organized).

(2) Wages shall be paid at least once a month on a definite date; provided, however, that this shall not apply to extraordinary wages, bonuses, and the like which will be defined by Ordinance of the Ministry of Health, Labour and Welfare (referred to as "special wages etc." in Article 89).

Problem 14 discussion – United States

The problem assumes the share sponsorship policy complies with U.S. law. Nevertheless, it may raise a complicated extraterritorial issue. In addition to reporting requirements for employers, the Employee Retirement Income Security Act of 1974 (ERISA) sets out provisions for vesting, benefit accrual and funding. While the coverage for employees in the U.S. must satisfy ERISA requirements, can this plan also satisfy the requirements of all other countries in which employees are provided with pension benefits? If the plan is maintained outside the United States and it is primarily for non-resident aliens (that is, the U.S. workforce is a small part of the global workforce), then it would not be subject to coverage under ERISA.

References and suggested reading

Employers have used payment systems to incentivize workers and that can result in different wages being paid to the employee from one pay period to the next. *See e.g.* B. Shearer, *Piece Rates, Fixed Wages and Incentives, Evidence from a Field Experiment*, 71 REV. ECON. STUDIES 513 (2004) and C. Brown, *Firms' Choice of Method of Pay*, 43 INDUS. & LAB. REL. REV. 165S (1990).

Questions for Discussion – Problem 14

1. While some countries require wage/salary payments in cash and most require use of the local currency, there are often exceptions for expatriate employees. What risks are involved for individuals *and* corporations when expatriate employees around the world have a common share ownership scheme and a common supplemental retirement scheme? Also, should these arrangements all be denominated in a common currency (such as the Euro) as compared with the local currency of the country in which they are working or the currency of their home country (which may or may not be the home country of the corporation)? Among other employee groups, including senior executives, middle managers, experts and specialists with a global labor market, and front-line supervisors and workers, which groups, if any, would you recommend have a common share ownership scheume and a common supplemental retirement scheme (and why)?

2. If the labor market for corporate executives and people with specialized skills truly becomes a global market, will any of the five countries have to re-examine and adjust the laws governing share ownership schemes and supplemental retirement schemes?

PROBLEM 15: PAY FOR MEMBERS OF A VIRTUAL TEAM

Employees with long-term assignments (six months or more) to work full-time on "virtual teams" with members in multiple countries are informed that they are each subject to the different standards in their home countries for the following:

- workplace health and safety;
- wage and hour laws;
- vacation leave;
- pregnancy and birth leave;
- family medical leave.

The employees protest – arguing that they are all doing equivalent work and should be entitled to equivalent working conditions. They insist that they should all be "harmonized upwards" to the most favorable standards of the countries represented within the team. Can the employer insist that the team function with different country standards? Is there any dimension on which the employer can be compelled to operate with a higher standard?

Problem 15 discussion – Australia

Australian law imposes more stringent standards on these matters than many of the other countries in this study – certainly the US. Accordingly the main issue in Australia would simply be complying with domestic requirements. But to the extent that the employees were demanding something more than the Australian minima, for example in relation to paid maternity leave (an area in which Australia trails many countries) the company would have no obligation to comply. If – but only if – the employees were seeking to enshrine such a commitment in a new enterprise agreement, to be registered under the Fair Work Act 2009, they could lawfully take industrial action in support of their demands. In any other situation, such industrial action would be unlawful.

Problem 15 discussion – Brazil

Brazilian employers are under no obligation to negotiate as they are free to accept the group demands and "harmonize upwards" their situations as long as the "harmonization" does not place them below any Brazilian labor law standards. What about the group argument that its members do equivalent work? As examined in Problem 3, the equal pay for equal work principle establishes that regardless of sex, nationality or age, in the same municipality, equal pay is assured for equal work, which corresponds to all work done with identical productivity and technical performance by different employees whose time difference in the same function is inferior to two years (article 461 of the *Consolidação das Leis do Trabalho*). Jurisprudence from the *Tribunal Superior do Trabalho* has extended the concept of "same municipality" to "same metropolitan region". In Rio de Janeiro, for instance, what was originally restricted to the city itself, has been extended by jurisprudence to 18 municipalities, covering the whole contour of *Baía de Guanabara* (Guanabara Bay). Yet, no matter the extent of the area covered, new technologies of information and communication present an important challenge for regulation of the equal pay for equal work principle as they efface the physical references that characterize "equal work". Legal reasoning on the matter (including Brazilian labor law) still thinks of workers at the same place, sharing the same assembly line. How to characterize then the "virtual teams" of the problem? Do they work at the "same place"?

References and suggested readings

BRASIL, TRIBUNAL SUPERIOR DO TRABALHO, *Súmula 6*, *accessed at* http://www3.tst.jus.br/jurisprudencia/Sumulas_com_indice/Sumulas_Ind_1_50.html#SUM-6 (last visited Oct. 2, 2012).

On the Rio de Janeiro Metropolitan Region, see: RIO DE JANEIRO STATE. *Lei Complementar No. 87 1997 (Braz.)*, *accessed at* http://alerjln1.alerj.rj.gov.br/contlei.nsf/0/eb26342129c7ae9203256571007be153?OpenDocument (last visited Feb. 25, 2010).

Problem 15 discussion – Germany

An employer may observe a higher standard of workplace safety and health as demanded by statutory law or pay higher wages voluntarily. Therefore, the employer may voluntarily grant a harmonization upwards. However, a single employee may demand such a harmonization only if the employer violates the equality principle by distinguishing between employees working in different countries.

The equality principle obliges the employer to treat all employees in a comparable situation equally unless he has a legitimate reason not to do so. For example the employer must not pay his favorite employee a bonus and exclude the other ones. However, the equality principle applies only if the workers are comparable or in a comparable situation.

In Problem 15 it is questionable if the employees working in different countries are "comparable." Although the scope of the equality principle is not limited to employees of one specific factory, workers from different premises are often not comparable. This is even truer of employees working in multiple countries since, for example, living expenses may be very different. As one has to assume that they are not in a comparable situation they can't demand harmonization upwards.

Under certain conditions employees working in European premises of the same company may hold elections to a European Works Council, based on European Directive 94/95/EC. However, such a council has only limited information and consultation rights. Therefore, it too can't demand harmonization upwards.

References and suggested readings

Richardi, ZEITSCHRIFT FÜR ARBEITSRECHT (ZfA) 30 (2008); Bepler, 18 SONDERBEILAGE ZU NEUE ZEITSCHRIFT FÜR ARBEITSRECHT (ZfA) (2004); Fastrich, RECHT DER ARBEIT (RdA) 65 (2000); Staudinger & Richardi, BÜRGERLICHES GESETZBUCH, Neubearbeitung ¶ 338 (2005);

BLANKE, EUROPÄISCHES BETRIEBSRÄTE-GESETZ (1999); MÜLLER, EUROPÄISCHES BETRIEBSRÄTE-GESETZ (1997); BLANKE, ARBEIT UND RECHT (AuR) 242 (2009); Melot de Beauregard & Buchmann, BETRIEBS-BERATER (BB) 1417 (2009); Thüsing & Forst, NEUE ZEITSCHRIFT FÜR ARBEITSRECHT (NZA) 408 (2009).

Problem 15: discussion – Japan

Japanese employers are free to discuss these matters and enhance working conditions as requested. However, there is no statutory obligation on the employer to accept their employees' requests.

Certainly, the Labor Standards Act (LSA) requires equal treatment of employees irrespective of nationality (LSA Art. 3). Therefore, if the multinational employees work on Japanese soil, the employer cannot differentiate their working conditions by nationality. However, the LSA is a public (administrative) law sanctioned by criminal penalties and administrative inspections, and thus its application is confined to Japan's territory. The LSA does not have any provision prescribing extraterritorial application. Therefore, in principle it does not apply to employees living and working in different countries than Japan.

Must the employer meet and bargain with the representative of these employees? The answer is in the negative. The Labor Union Act (LUA) sets out the employer's duty to bargain collectively with a labor union, but the LUA is also interpreted as not applicable across national borders. Of course, it is not prohibited to bargain and negotiate with them. Thus the employer is free to do so, but it is not his legal duty.

PRIMARY SOURCES

Labor Standards Act

Article 3 An employer shall not engage in discriminatory treatment with respect to wages, working hours or other working conditions by reason of the nationality, creed or social status of any worker.

Labor Union Act

Article 7 The employer shall not commit the acts listed in any of the following items:

...

(ii) to refuse to bargain collectively with the representatives of the workers employed by the employer without justifiable reasons;

...

References and suggested readings

As to the application of Japanese labor law in the international dimension, see Ryuichi Yamakawa, *The Road Becoming More Travelled: The International Dimension of Japanese Labor Law* 35(9) JAPAN LABOR BULLETIN 6–10 (1996).

Problem 15 discussion – United States

Nothing in the law of the United States would prevent an employer from: (1) observing more rigorous standards of health and safety than are established in federal or state law; (2) paying compensation above the minimum wage, overtime at greater than time-and-a-half, or forbearing to exercise its prerogative to assign mandatory overtime; (3) allow vacation time (as no federal or state law mandates any vacation time) or schedule vacations to accommodate the group's interest in leisure time activities; (4) provide for longer and/or paid pregnancy and birth leave beyond the 12 weeks of unpaid leave mandated by federal law or for other purposes. Indeed, employers do regularly exceed the legal floors established under the first three heads at least. Thus the U.S.

employees could insist on "upward harmonization" in all of these. But the employer is legally free to disregard their demands. As we have seen in the discussion of Problems 1 and 2, were the U.S. complement of employees to be unionized the employer would have to bargain over such demands. But U.S. law makes no provision for transnational bargaining as the NLRA has no extra-territorial application.

Were the U.S. employees in this work group not to be represented collectively, as is most likely to be the case, they could not be dismissed for collectively demanding upward harmonization for such would be concerted activity for mutual aid or protection protected by the NLRA; but the employer would be under no obligation to deal with them. (An employee who made such a demand as an individual only, with no connection to any current or expected group action, would not be engaged in concerted activity and so could be dismissed.) Were the company to desire to deal with the work group it would be free to do so long as that course of dealing were truly arm's-length. *See* Problems 1 and 2, supra. If the employees were unionized they could negotiate these higher standards, though there is nothing in U.S. law that would compel an employer specifically to take into account standards outside of the U.S. or to be part of a forum involving representatives of its workers outside of the U.S.

References and suggested readings

P. Marginson & G. Meardi, "Big Players, Different Rules? Multinationals and Collective Bargaining in Europe," Paper for the XX SASE Annual Meeting, Paris, 16–18 July 2009.

> In the push to launch cross-border rewards, employers can easily over-look pay-related discrimination laws in each affected country. In this context, discrimination is a broad concept – pay discrimination laws can encompass not only U.S. style protected group discrimination, but also a distinct type of job category discrimination unknown in the U.S.
>
> Head of Compensation and Benefits, Shipping/Natural Resources Sector

> [I]n each case, [including Problem 15], the laws of the respective countries have not begun to consider extraterritorial matters ... While the legal analysis of each country is rather straight forward, I believe the most interesting conversation is in regards to HR policy and the impact of such decisions in corporations that operate across multiple geographies ... [O]rganizations rely on focused virtual or dispersed teams to deliver on key

projects that could affect the entire organization. Primary examples of such projects could include large-scale information technology implementations, research collaborations, global marketing or even M&A integration projects. In consideration of policy, particularly when considering alignment of compensation and benefits, I believe it is important to focus on a definition of the types of teams, whether virtual or not, that might cause an employer to consider such alternatives. [W]ithout such consideration, broad "harmonizing up" of compensation and benefits could significantly add costs – both direct and indirect to any company with a broad international footprint.

Senior Vice President, HR, Biomedical Sector

The recent formation of International Human Resources function [in our company] is ... an example of the company's continuing effort to balance synergy and focus in labor practices. The purpose of International Human Resources function is to promote consistency in global corporate practices where needed while it promotes diversity by supporting local practices whenever possible. For instance, one of the big initiatives for the next 2 years is to implement its first global succession planning process in most countries. While people practices may be different in difficult cultures, the company has found that there are common elements in identifying and developing talent in most countries. Even as the corporation is implementing a harmonized way of developing our talent around the world, the corporation recognizes the need to give countries the flexibility to manage its own compensation and benefits at local levels. Managing compensation and benefits for our increasingly mobile workers around the world is not without its occasional challenges but due to the complexity of social and economic structures, managing these programs locally is a better alternative to harmonizing such programs at a global scale.

Director, HR, Electronics Sector

Questions for Discussion – Problem 15

1. As a multinational corporation, will the gains in productivity and retention that can be expected from "harmonizing upward" for all members of a virtual team be likely to make up for the additional cost? What data would you need to do a cost/benefit estimate on this issue? If more than 1 percent of workers around the world (approximately 46 million people out of 4.6 billion in the global workforce) were serving on cross-national virtual teams, would that be sufficient motivation for international employment standards associated with this work? If you disagreed at 1 percent, what is your view if it is 10 percent (approximately 460 million people) of the global workforce serving in some way on a cross-national virtual team?

PROBLEM 16: GOVERNMENT IMPOSED EXECUTIVE COMPENSATION RESTRICTIONS

The U.S. government has passed a law limiting executive compensation for the top officers of any company receiving government bail-out support. Do these limits apply to executives leading subsidiaries operating in other countries? Is this situation likely to change in the future (and, if so, how)?

Problem 16: discussion – Australia

It is unlikely a foreign law of this kind would be treated as applicable to an Australian-based employment relationship. There are no comparable limits on executive remuneration under Australian law, though recent legislation has strengthened the control of both company boards and shareholders over remuneration packages for "key management personnel" at listed companies: see Corporations Amendment (Improving Accountability on Director and Executive Remuneration) Act 2011 (Cth).

Problem 16: discussion – Brazil

Right now, there is no law in Brazil establishing a limitation of this kind. In 2009, during parliamentary debates over an Executive proposal to raise the loan capacity of the *Banco Nacional de Desenvolvimento Econômico e Social* (National Bank of Economic and Social Development), an attempt was made to introduce such a limitation, but it was not approved. Nevertheless, the idea germinated as the *Banco Central do Brasil* (Central Bank of Brazil) held a public hearing in April and May 2010 to discuss criteria for the remuneration policy for directors and employees of financial institutions and other institutions authorized to operate by the Central Bank. Later on, in November 2010, the Central Bank released a new regulatory system (Resolution 3,921) which established some limitations on the benefits for administrators of financial institutions under its supervision.

Brazilian law does not recognize the extraterritoriality of foreign legislation even for subsidiaries of foreign companies. Whether it relates to a top officer or a blue-collar worker, labor contracts are still to be regulated by Brazilian labor law. The major concern expressed by the *Consolidação* when it came to foreign labor related to its impact on the labor market. Thus, the foreign presence in Brazilian companies could not exceed the limit of one third of its workforce. When these questions were raised by the privatization wave of the 1990s, courts reaffirmed the prevalence of the national workforce and law. Nevertheless their decisions did not stop the changing process undergone by the foreign workforce operating in Brazil.

On the other hand, extraterritoriality for Brazilian labor law was put in place by Federal Statute nº 7.064/1982, also known as the *Mendes Júnior* Act. The name derives from the Brazilian engineering company which established itself abroad, in Angola, in the late 1970s, to participate in the building of basic infrastructure for the then new-born country. The extraterritoriality of Brazilian labor law was explicitly imposed on the company so as to encourage Brazilian workers to embark on such efforts. It still applies to Brazilian workers hired in the country or transferred to work abroad over periods of more than 90 days.

References and suggested readings

On the public hearing conducted by the Central Bank, see: BANCO CENTRAL DO BRASIL. *Edital de audiência pública No. 35 2010* (Braz.), *accessed at* https://www3.bcb.gov.br/audpub/Anexos/Download?caminho=/editais/edt_48/Edital-Audiência-Pública 35.pdf (last visited Feb. 25, 2010).

BRASIL. *Lei No. 7.064* (Federal Statute nº 7.064) 1982 (Braz.), *accessed at* http://www.planalto.gov.br/ccivil_03/Leis/L7064.htm (last visited Feb. 25, 2010).

Problem 16: discussion – Germany

It seems that in general foreign (US) law might be applicable in Germany if two conditions are met: first, that the foreign government has acted within the boundaries of its "sphere of control" and, second, that the said foreign law primarily or at least *pari passu* serves the interests of private persons and not only the interests of the state (Federal Civil Court of 16.04.1975 – I ZR 40/73); more "flexible" requirements may apply to the question of whether the law of other EU Member States has to be applied in Germany. Whether the US law limiting executive compensation passes this test is open to discussion.

References and suggested readings

Sonnenberger, *Introduction to EGBGB no 76 ff, in* MÜNCHENER KOMMENTAR ZUM BGB (4th ed. 2006).

Problem 16: discussion – Japan

As discussed in Problem 15, Japanese protective labor laws, such as the Labor Standards Act, the Minimum Wages Act, and the Equal Employment Opportunities Act, and collective labor relations laws, such as the Labor Union Acts and Labor Relations Adjustment Act, apply within the territory of the Japanese soil. These laws do not have any provisions allowing extraterritorial application.

Problem 16 concerns application of the domestic law to executives working in a foreign country. If the domestic law belongs to private law, the parties to the contract can choose the applicable law by agreement. However, if the domestic law falls under the category of public (administrative) laws, its application is confined to Japan's territory. The law in Problem 16 seems to be a public (administrative) law and thus, unless it has an extraterritorial application clause, it will not cover executives working in foreign countries.

In any event, the issue here is not the application of labor law because executives are not employees. When executives are regarded as employees at a higher echelon in the parent corporation, there might arise the so-called absolute application of labor protective laws via the special connection of mandatory laws (*Sonderanknüpfungstheorie*). However, the law in Problem 16 is not a labor protective one but concerns limiting executives' remuneration. Thus, such application by special connection theory would not occur here.

As for legislation limiting executives' salary, there has not been much discussion of this in Japan because the remuneration of Japanese executives is in general much lower than that of American executives. The fact that the annual salary of the president of Japan Air Lines was 9,600,000 yen (about 100,000 USD) and that he commuted by subway like ordinary employees was covered by the international media. Although the story also attracted attention in Japan, it was not because his salary was extraordinarily low, which was not very surprising to ordinary Japanese, but the international attention attracted was surprising and reminded the Japanese people of the comparatively narrow gap between labor and management in Japan.

As to the extraterritorial application of law this has not been an issue for active discussion so far.

References and suggested readings

As to the application of Japanese labor law in the international dimension, see Ryuichi Yamakawa, *The Road Becoming More Travelled: The International Dimension of Japanese Labor Law*, 35 JAPAN LAB. BULL. 6–10 (1996).

Problem 16 discussion – United States

The extraterritorial application of U.S. employment law is a complicated matter. Suffice to say that there is a strong presumption against the extra-territorial application of U.S. employment law. Nevertheless, Congress or the states can give their laws extraterritorial effect. Both the federal Age Discrimination in Employment Act and Title VII of the Civil Rights Act, prohibiting discrimination on grounds of race, religion, sex, or national origin, now apply to U.S. citizens employed abroad for U.S. or U.S.-controlled companies. (As one might imagine, there has been some litigation on what "control" means.) However, neither law may require an employer to violate the law of the country where the employee's workplace is located. A federal court of appeals held that the applications of mandatory retirement at age 65 to a U.S. citizen working for a U.S. company in Germany, as provided for in the German collective bargaining agreement covering those workers, was not actionable under the Age Discrimination Act: the German law of contract was "law" which would have been violated had U.S. law forbidding age-based mandatory retirement to have applied.

The presumption applies at the state level as well, but state law can also have extraterritorial application. In one case, for example, an employee of a Pennsylvania company, employed by it for 17 months, was assigned to work about six of those months abroad, in England and Canada, and brought suit under Pennsylvania's Minimum Wage Act for overtime pay incurred in that foreign service. (The federal Fair Labor Standards Act has an express non-extraterritorially clause, but it does not preempt state law.) A federal district court gave the Pennsylvania law extraterritorial application: the law applied to a Pennsylvania resident working for a Pennsylvania company who had been "given assignments outside of Pennsylvania."

The American Recovery and Reinvestment Act of 2009 authorizes the Secretary of the Treasury to limit the compensation of "senior executive officers" (the top five most highly paid executives of a public company) as well as "the next 20 most highly compensated employees" of entities in receipt of TARP (Troubled Asset Relief Program) funds. If one of these executives or employees works abroad for a TARP recipient there is no reason why they should not come under the Act. Note, too, that Sarbanes-Oxley has extraterritorial reach insofar as the company is one publicly traded in the United States under U.S. securities law.

References and suggested readings

See generally, *Extraterritorial Application of U.S. Laws*, 1B INTERNATIONAL LABOR AND EMPLOYMENT LAWS 34–1 (William Keller & Timothy Darby eds., 3d ed. 2009).

The Pennsylvania overtime case is *Truman v. DeWolff, Boberg & Assoc.*, 2009 U.S. Dist. LEXIS (W.D. Pa. 2009). The age case is *Mahoney v. RFE/RL, Inc.*,

47 F.3d 447 (D.C. Cir. 1994). The Recovery and Reinvestment Act is PL 115–5 with implementing regulations at 74 Fed. Reg. 63990 (Dec. 7, 2009).

> I find it interesting that the legal environment in the four countries outside of the U.S. do not address the issue of one country wanting to limit compensation to executives leading subsidiaries in their country. I strongly believe that in the future these countries may also want to establish similar laws for their executives. Even in countries like Germany and Japan, where executive compensation compared to U.S executives is much lower, discussions to limit compensation and hold executives responsible for creating a crisis have started to occur. We have learned from the economic crises in 2008–2009 that an event in one country can negatively affect the whole global economy. Also, limitations on executive compensation will probably occur through government actions toward the legal system of a particular country. For example, the response by Great Britain and France to the banks for creating chaos in their countries was to increase the tax on banker bonuses. This has the same effect as what was done in the U.S.; it just comes at it in a different way. Another example, while somewhat different, is the Greek financial crisis. The European Union countries demanded that Greece make changes to their pension system or they would not lend them money to deal with their economic crisis.
>
> Senior Vice President, HR, Information Technology Sector

> My employer was a recipient of TARP funds. After just over a year, we repaid every dollar of that investment. Our leadership didn't seek these funds. We agreed to accept the government's investment, as part of the plan to stabilize the overall financial system. The terms were not generous – 5 percent dividend per year for the first 5 years, 9 percent annually after that, plus … warrants allowing the purchase of our stock at [a price that was 10 percent above the closing price on that date]. These warrants function like stock options, and are active for up to 10 years. By paying off the TARP investment, our company is no longer bound by the executive officer compensation restrictions of the American Recovery and Reinvestment Act of 2009. However, populist rancor is fueling further legislative review as hearings continue on Capitol Hill. I believe it is very possible that additional compensation governance requirements will be codified that apply to all public companies in the U.S. As we consider the implications beyond the U.S., it becomes clear that this problem is solely a U.S. matter as presented. It cannot be expected that a "host country" of a subsidiary operation would move to enforce another nation's law. More likely, the host nation would choose whether or not to cooperate with the legislation's

originator, and perhaps consider a similar measure locally. However, take it a step further. Let's imagine a situation in which a government exerts pressure upon another country to accept its value/law/or judgment. Pressing to apply foreign laws in another's nation is clear infringement on that nation's sovereignty. This opens up an interesting line of discussion as I think about soccer balls being stitched by child labor, or sweat shops operated by US clothing manufacturers in Southeast Asia. At what point does an issue reach such a high level of common interest that international cooperation results? Perhaps that common interest could result in a situation in which foreign private law is not enforced, but rather adapted and replicated in the domestic country.

Vice President, HR, Financial Sector

I believe very strongly, as a CHRO, that while U.S. MNC do not have to impose limits on executives running foreign subsidiaries because they are outside of the U.S. or may not be U.S citizens, I think MNC should voluntarily put the same executive limitations on these executives. Any foreign executive who runs a subsidiary outside of the U.S, and is a foreign national should have their compensation limited using the following criteria:

(1) They had participated in the company's strategic plan.
(2) They have benefited from significant upside from the company stock.
(3) Their revenue contributes to 10 percent or more of the firm's revenue.
(4) They currently have a large equity stake of at least one times salary.

The reason for this point of view is that it can destroy the morale of a leadership group if some executives have their compensation limited and others do not. I also think it sends a better message to employees on the importance of a team that all leaders at certain levels will have their compensation limited.

Senior Vice President, HR, Information Technology Sector

Questions for Discussion – Problem 16

1. Is this just a U.S. law that is only relevant to U.S. corporations receiving government support during a recession, or does it have broader implications? If this law was held to apply to executives in subsidiaries around the world, would that be an intrusion into the sovereignty of other nations?
2. If there was a chance to submit testimony in advance of the potential application of this law to executives in foreign subsidiaries of U.S. corporations, how would you make the case on behalf of a multinational company that it should only apply to executives operating in the United States?

PROBLEM 17: NON-COMPETITION AND CONFIDENTIALITY AGREEMENT

The company had been a family-owned business, located in the state of Indiana, U.S.A. The company designs and manufactures specialized industrial heating and cooling equipment. It has been taken over by a hedge fund. The new management has a long-term business plan based on the success of recently developed computerized systems the company's engineers have devised. It plans to expand marketing nationally and worldwide, but in stages. So far, it has opened sales and service offices in Chicago, Los Angeles, Sao Paolo, Sydney, Hamburg, and Osaka, with more to follow in the U.S, Europe, Asia, and South America. The managers of these new offices have been asked as a condition of hire to have each salesperson sign the following contract:

Non-Competition by the Employee

The parties acknowledge that the Employee has gained and will continue to gain considerable confidential information about the businesses of the Employer, which could be injurious to the Employer if the Employee were to use such information for his own benefit. Therefore, the Employee agrees that during the term of his employment hereunder, and for a period of two (2) years after the effective date of the termination of the Employee's employment hereunder, the Employee shall not, directly or indirectly:

(i) in any capacity whatsoever, either as an individual or as a partner or joint venture, or as an employee, agent or representative for any person or business enterprise, or as an office, director, shareholder (having more than a nominal investment) or otherwise, engage in competition with the Employer, in the manufacture, marketing, leasing, distribution or sale of products in, or services related to, heaters or heating or air conditioning systems and related parts and components marketed in any state or possession of the United States or any foreign country where Employer currently does or in future will engage in sales of any of the above;

(ii) disclose, divulge, discuss, copy or otherwise use or exploit or attempt to use or exploit in any manner in competition with or contrary to the interests of the Employer any customer lists or records, methods, business and marketing plans and strategies, financial information or any other trade secrets or proprietary information of the Employer, it being acknowledged by the Employee that all such information regarding the business of the Employer is confidential information, the exclusive property of the Employer.

May the company require its sales people in these jurisdictions to sign this agreement? If there are problems with doing that, would these be resolved by having the contract specify that it will be governed by Indiana law where, presumably, the law is favorable to the lawfulness of the provision?

Problem 17 discussion – Australia

The Australian common law, like that of England, does not look favourably on any "restraint of trade", though such restraints are not completely prohibited. An agreed restriction on a worker's post-employment activities is presumed to be unenforceable as contrary to public policy, unless the employer can prove that it is no wider than reasonably necessary to protect some "legitimate interest" on the part of the employer: see e.g. *Lindner v Murdock's Garage* (1950) 83 CLR 628.

An employer cannot use a post-employment restraint merely to stifle competition from an ex-employee. But one of the legitimate interests it may seek to protect is the possibility of an ex-employee drawing upon confidential information (that is, information not generally available to the public) concerning the employer's business, products or customers: see e.g. *Brightman v Lamson Paragon Ltd* (1914) 18 CLR 331; *Rentokil Pty Ltd v Lee* (1995) 66 SASR 301. In principle, therefore, a restraint of the type described in the question *could* be enforceable. But this is subject to two important qualifications.

The first is that it would not be enough for the company merely to assert (or to rely on the recital in the non-compete clause itself) that each salesperson had access to confidential information. It must be shown that such information did indeed exist, that it was not generally available to the public, that the salesperson had access to the information, and that unless restrained they would be able to carry it away in their head and use it for the benefit of a competing business: see e.g. *Herbert Morris Ltd v Saxelby* [1916] AC 688; *Wright v Gasweld Pty Ltd* (1991) 22 NSWLR 317.

Second, even if there was a legitimate basis for having a restraint, the scope of this particular restraint would need to be shown to be reasonable, as of the time the restraint was originally agreed. There are two potential concerns with this particular restraint.

One is its geographical scope. The restraint would prevent an Australian salesperson from working for any of the company's competitors in any country in which the company operated. But this could only be valid if the particular information to which that salesperson had access had any relevance in those other countries: see e.g. *Minnesota Mining & Manufacturing (Australia) Pty Ltd v Richards* [1963] NSWR 1613; *Commercial Plastics Ltd v Vincent* [1965] 1 QB 623. The kind of customer or product information to which a salesperson has access is perhaps unlikely to qualify for global protection.

The other scope problem concerns the duration. Two years is a lengthy restraint. In *Miles v Genesys Wealth Advisers Ltd* [2009] NSWCA 25 a restraint of two and half years was upheld. But this involved a former executive who had valuable knowledge as to a financial services firm's operations, not a salesperson who is likely to have had access only to much lower-level information.

If a restraint is found to be wider in its operation than reasonably necessary, the common law will not allow it to be "read down" and enforced to whatever extent might otherwise have been reasonable. Severance of the "blue pencil" variety *is* allowed, if a court can simply strike out words or clauses that go too far. But a court will not add or change words to give a restraint a narrower or more reasonable operation: see *Lindner v Murdock's Garage* (1950) 83 CLR 628. For example, in this case the company might be able to show that it could validly have obtained a six or 12 month restraint on its sales staff, or a restraint that operated only in Australia, or selected parts of Australia. But at common law, a court would not grant an injunction to enforce the restraint as if it were limited in those ways.

In the State of New South Wales, however, it is different. There, the Restraints of Trade Act 1976 (NSW) expressly authorizes courts to enforce a restraint to the extent that it is reasonable to do so, even if at its widest the restraint would be contrary to public policy: see e.g. *Woolworths Ltd v Olson* [2004] NSWCA 372. The Act will apply wherever the "proper law" (see below) of the employment contract is that of New South Wales: see *KA & C Smith Pty Ltd v Ward* (1998) 45 NSWLR 702 at 719.

Since Sydney is in New South Wales, it is likely the company could rely on this Act to overcome any problem with the non-compete provision being cast too wide – provided it could meet the threshold requirement of showing that it had a legitimate basis for needing a restraint in the first place.

The other possibility for the company, if the non-compete provision in paragraph (i) were found to be unenforceable, would be to seek to enforce the more specific prohibition in paragraph (ii) on the use or disclosure of the company's information. But in practice, Australian courts only tend to grant injunctions restraining breaches of such provisions if the employer can identify with some precision a particular trade secret that can readily be distinguished from the employee's general "know-how": see e.g. *Pioneer Concrete Services Ltd v Galli* [1985] VR 675; *Triangle Corp Pty Ltd v Carnsew* (1994) 29 IPR 69; *Dais Studio Pty Ltd v Bullet Creative Pty Ltd* (2007) 74 IPR 512. Furthermore, if the prohibition were interpreted as seeking to restrain the use of information even after it had reached the public domain (that is, become publicly accessible), the prohibition would itself be unenforceable as a restraint of trade: see *Maggbury Pty Ltd v Hafele Australia Pty Ltd* (2001) 210 CLR 181.

The final issue is whether the restraints could be rendered enforceable if they were expressly made subject to Indiana law, assuming such law operated more favourably to the company's interests than the law of New South Wales. As explained in the article by Stewart and Greene referred to below, the general principle in Australia is that a contract is governed by its "proper law". This is the law of whichever jurisdiction has been chosen by the parties themselves, or which otherwise has the closest and most real connection to the contract: see *Vita Food Inc v Unus Shipping Co* [1939] AC 277; *Bonython v Commonwealth* [1950] AC 201 at 219. However, there is some authority to suggest that if a contract otherwise governed by a foreign law would operate in unreasonable restraint of trade, an Australian court might refuse to enforce the restraint as being contrary to Australian public policy: see *Rousillon v Rousillon* (1880) 14 Ch D 351; *Hawker de Havilland Ltd v Fernandes* [1996] ATPR ¶41–479 at p 41,912.

References and suggested readings

Andrew Stewart & Janey Greene, *Choice of Law and the Enforcement of Post-Employment Restraints in Australia*, 31 COMP. LAB. L. & POL'Y J. 305 (2010).

Andrew Stewart, STEWART'S GUIDE TO EMPLOYMENT LAW §§13.15–21 (3d ed. 2011).

Problem 17 discussion – Brazil

As freedom of work and the social values of labor are constitutionally guaranteed and therefore perceived as part of workers' fundamental rights, any limitations imposed on a labor contract, even as a post-employment condition that prevents the employee from engaging in a labor activity, is not well accepted under Brazilian law. It is not necessarily unlawful. The *Consolidação* establishes that habitual engagement by the employee in commercial transactions on his or her own account or for another without his or her employer's permission, if this involves competition with the undertaking in which he or she is employed or is prejudicial to the performance of his or her work (article 482, "c"), constitutes grounds for just cause, i.e. dismissal due to severe employee misconduct. Likewise, the disclosure of a company's secret constitutes grounds for just cause (article 482, "g"). Therefore, a clause to prevent employee competition or to secure confidentiality of a company's secrets during its labor contract would be acceptable as it only reinforces the statute on this matter.

On the other hand, the statute does address the situation of a post-employment non-competition clause. Still, employers are not entitled to use such a clause just to avoid competition, which as pointed out before is constitutionally protected as part of anyone's freedom to work. The reasonableness of such a limitation would have to be examined on a case-to-case basis as to its length, area and employment. In this problem, the clause seems unreasonable as it simply banishes the employee from the employer's economic activity anywhere in the world for two years without any compensation from the former employer. It also seems unreasonable to have this kind of limitation on employees such as salespeople that do not have managerial responsibilities.

As for the confidentiality clause, which is not outlawed by statute and therefore may be inserted in employees' labor contracts, reasonableness would also have to be examined on a case-by-case basis. Courts have upheld its reasonableness whenever the information was perceived as important to the employer's business, which is to say when its disclosure would have endangered the maintenance of the employer's activity. However, this is an issue which has not drawn a conclusive opinion from Brazilian labor courts. There are decisions both ways, either accepting or refusing the validity of such clauses, based respectively on the parties' good faith when they executed the contract or on the unconstitutionality of such limitations. When they were accepted, such clauses presented: (a) a length of time found to be reasonable and justifiable in terms of the restriction on the employee, (b) a geographical delimitation of the area in which the restrictions were enforceable, and (c) financial compensation paid to the employee as a counterpart for the limitations endured.

Finally, as *lex loci laboris* is the general rule for regulating labor contracts in Brazil, the attempt to use foreign legislation would only be appropriate if this resulted in regulation more favorable to the employee. As in the problem, if its use was to secure a more favorable regulation for the employer, its enforceability would most probably be refused by Brazilian labor courts.

References and suggested readings

Luís Alberto Gonçalves Gomes Coelho, *A tutela do conhecimento e dos segredos de empresa e as cláusulas de não-concorrência no direito do trabalho* (dissertação de mestrado), Curitiba: Centro Universitário Curitiba, Programa de Mestrado em Direito Empresarial e Cidadania (2008), *accessed at* http://www.google.com/url?sa=t&rct=j&q=coelho%20unicuritiba%20n%C3%A3o-concorr%C3%AAncia%20disserta%C3%A7%C3%A3o&source=web&cd=1&ved=0CCAQFjAA&url=http%3A%2F%2Ftede.unicuritiba.edu.br%2Fdissertacoes%2FLuisAlbertoGomesCoelho.pdf&ei=KgVvUJGWC4q20QWWtYHAAQ&usg=AFQjCNF1wUtwEOVL7gEJlF-M8m4WLeABig (last visited Oct. 5, 2012).

Problem 17 discussion – Germany

Assuming that the "salesmen" of the new offices are employees under German law, the following "guidelines" will apply:

Noncompetition clause for two years after the termination

After the end of the employment contract, competing with the former employer is not forbidden by German statutory law. It is therefore up to the parties to negotiate and agree on a noncompetition clause. Although such clauses are in principle permissible because of the basic principle of freedom of contract, §§74–5 f. German Commercial Code (*Handelsgesetzbuch*, HGB) impose restrictions in order to protect the employee's professional freedom. To be valid a noncompetition clause has to meet the following criteria:[2]

(1) It has to be in written form and the employer has to hand over a copy of it to the employee.
(2) The employee must not be a minor at the time of the signing of the noncompetition clause.
(3) The maximum noncompetition period that can be agreed on legally is two years following the termination of the employment contract.
(4) The noncompetition agreement must be designed and in fact function to protect the employer's legitimate interests. The employer has a legitimate interest in protecting his company secrets and in preventing his former employee from luring away his customers or providers.[3] The very interest in not having another competitor is not however so legitimate an interest as competition is one of the key elements of a free market economy.[4]
(5) The noncompetition clause must not infringe upon the legitimate employee's interests, in particular his professional freedom and right of personality.
(6) In the noncompetition clause the employer must agree to pay a waiting allowance (*Karenzentschädigung*) that amounts to at least 50 percent of the employee's last income during the period of noncompetition.

While criteria (1)–(4) are met in the present case, it is doubtful if the same is true for (5). Whether the noncompetition clause infringes in an inappropriate way on the employee's interests depends upon the following factors: How long is the period of noncompetition? What exactly is the employee forbidden to do – to compete at all or only to lure customers to his new employer/business? What geographical area is covered by the noncompetition clause? Is the noncompetition clause framed so widely that it encompasses all types of business that are (vaguely) related to the employer's business, or is it tailored to the specific products the employer is producing and selling? In the present case, the company not only wants the maximum period of two years but also a noncompetition clause that forbids not only luring customers away but all forms of competition. Moreover, the geographical area covered by the noncompetition clause is extremely wide. Although the intended noncompetition clause is tailored down to a specific market (heaters or heating, air conditioning systems and related parts and components), the before mentioned factors speak

2 For details see Staudinger/Richardi/Fischinger, BGB, §611, m.n. 632 ff.

3 BAG 1.8.1995 AP Nr. 5 zu §74a HGB.

4 BAG NZA 96, 310.

strongly against the validity of the intended noncompetition clause. In any event, whether criterion (5) is met need not be decided as the intended clause is plainly invalid because it does not state the employer's duty to pay a waiting allowance (*Karenzentschädigung*).

Confidentiality clause

Even without an explicit agreement an employee must not disclose company or business secrets of his former employer either during the term of his employment or afterwards.[5] It is possible to extend the ban to data that is not considered to be a company or business secret under German law. However, such an expansion is valid only if it does not constitute a "hidden" noncompetition clause that would not meet the criteria set out above. In the present case clause (ii) seems only to repeat the statutory law already in force. If so, it is, of course, valid.

Applicability of Indiana law

Although Art. 3 Rom I-Regulation stipulates the freedom of the parties of a contract to choose the law applicable, Art. 8 Rom I-Regulation restricts this freedom. In its para. 1 it states that the choice of law must not deprive the employee of the protection he would enjoy under the binding statutory law that would be applicable without the choice of law agreement. Both criteria are met here: (1) German law would apply, because the "salesmen" would work mainly in Germany; cf. Art. 8 para. 2 Rom I-Regulation; and (2) §§74 ff. HGB are binding statutory law which the parties must not deviate from in a way that is unfavorable for the employee, §75d HGB.[6] Conclusion: As the Indiana law would be unfavorable for the employee the choice of law would be invalid.

References and suggested reading

BAUER & DILLER, WETTBEWERBSVERBOTE (5th ed. 2009); Staudinger, Richard & Fischinger, BÜRGERLICHES GESETZBUCH, §611, ¶¶ 622 ff., 646 ff.; Thilo Mahnhold, *Choice of Law Provisions in Contractual Covenants Not to Compete: The German Approach*, 31 COMP. LAB. L. & POL'Y J. 33 (2010).

5 Cf. BAG 16. 3. 1982, 15. 12. 1987 AP Nr 1, 5 zu §611 BGB Betriebsgeheimnis; BAG 16. 8. 1988 – 3 AZR 664/87.

6 Cf. BAG 7. 9. 2004 AP Nr 11 zu §75 HGB.

Problem 17 discussion – Japan

Problem 17 relates to two issues: duty of non-competition and duty of confidentiality.

Duty not to compete

In Japan, there is no statutory provision that generally imposes a duty not to compete on employees during and after employment relations. One exception is a case of competition utilizing a "trade secret" which can be prohibited by the Unfair Competition Prevention Law (hereinafter "UCPL") as one form of unfair competition (UCPL Art. 2 para. 1 no. 7). Apart from this exceptional case, many legal issues remain highly controversial: for instance, whether a duty not to compete is naturally derived from an employment contract or whether an explicit agreement to that effect is required. And if such an agreement exists, should that agreement be given literal effect or should it be scrutinized in the light of its impact on employees' free choice of occupation or the public interests of fair competition?

Duty not to compete during employment relations

It is generally accepted that an employee bears a duty not to compete with his employer during employment relations in the light of the loyalty inherent in an employment contract. Therefore, explicit agreements or provisions in work rules are not necessary to impose such a duty during employment.

Japanese employers can resort to various counter-measures against employees' violation of a non-competition duty during employment relations. In some cases, employers have claimed damages for violation of the non-competition duty. However, disciplinary actions, including disciplinary dismissal, normal dismissal, and/or a reduction or forfeiture of severance pay, are more common measures.

Duty not to compete after termination of employment contract

The most controversial issue is whether the employee owes a duty not to compete after the employment relationship has ceased. A non-competition duty significantly infringes employees' freedom to choose their occupation.

Article 22 of the Japanese Constitution prescribes "every person shall have freedom… to choose his occupation to the extent that it does not interfere with the public welfare." Though constitutional provision does not have a direct effect on contracts between private persons, the freedom to choose one's occupation constitutes public policy (Civil Code Art. 90) and a private person's contract contrary to public policy is held null and void. A non-competition duty may also distort fair competition. Therefore, post-employment non-competition covenants are scrutinized with great care in the light of employees' interest, especially freedom to choose their occupation and the need for employee protection against loss of livelihood.

Validity of the non-competition agreement

The leading case on the validity of a covenant not to compete is the *Foseco Japan* case (Nara District Court, Oct. 23, 1970, 624 HANREI JIHO 78). The court held as follows: "Since covenants not to compete deprive livelihood of economically weak employees, endanger their existence, restrain employees' freedom to choose their occupation, and entail the possibility to cause unfair monopoly through limitation of competition, it should be scrutinized whether there existed reasonable circumstances for the parties to conclude such a covenant… In defining the reasonable scope of the covenant, it is required to carefully scrutinize the temporal limitation, geographical limitation, the type of business that is restricted, and whether or not compensation was paid, taking the three viewpoints of the employer's interests (protection of the business secrets), employee's interests (restraints on finding a new job) and public interests (danger of monopoly and interests of general consumers) into consideration." Though there are some exceptional cases,[7] courts generally review the reasonableness of the non-competition agreement.

According to the majority of court decisions, the validity of a post-employment non-competition agreement is scrutinized in the light of (1) whether the purpose of the non-competition agreement is to protect the former employer's peculiar information and secrets, (2) the employee's status in the former company, (3) whether the restriction on the employee's activities is proper in terms of types of job, temporal and geographical scope, and (4) whether the former employer provided compensation for the restriction.

Most labor scholars deem compensation as essential to recognize the validity of a non-competition agreement. However, courts regard compensation as just

7 The *Tokyo Gakushu Kyoryokukai* case, Tokyo District Court, April 17, 1990, 1369 HANREI JIHO 69 (ordered damages to be paid based on the provision in the work rules that imposed a three-year non-competition duty after termination without scrutinizing the reasonableness of the provision).

one of the factors in determining the reasonableness of the agreement, and do not automatically nullify non-competition agreements that do not provide compensation.

Therefore, managers may request the salesperson to sign the non-competition agreement in Problem 17. However, its validity and enforceability is questionable because compensation for non-competition is not explicitly provided in the agreement and the geographical scope of the restriction is vague and wide.

Duty of confidentiality

Under current Japanese law, the duty of confidentiality to keep trade secrets and the duty to keep confidential other information should be distinguished since the former is regulated by the UCPL, whereas the latter is not covered by the UCPL but is based solely on employment contracts.

Trade secrets protected by the Unfair Competition Prevention Law

As for trade secrets protected by the UCPL, employees have a duty of confidentiality both during and after their employment relations. Although until the 1990 revision of the UCPL there was no statutory regulation, the 1990 revision of the UCPL makes the duty to keep trade secrets confidential a statutory obligation, and thus enforceable *without contractual provisions* to that effect.

Therefore whether certain information is part of a trade secret and is protected by the UCPL or not is vitally important. To be protected by the UCPL, several requirements must be met. First, to be protected as a "trade secret" in the sense of the UCPL, the information must meet three requirements: being controlled as secret, being useful for business activities, and being publicly unknown (UCPL Art. 2 para. 6). Second, the UCPL requires that the trade secret must be provided by an owner thereof, namely the employer in employment relations (UCPL Art. 2 para. 1 no. 7). Therefore, customer information which an employee has gathered himself is interpreted as his own and not information provided by the employer. Third, the UCPL requires an employee's purpose of making an unfair profit or of inflicting damages on the employer by using or disclosing the trade secrets (UCPL Art. 2 para. 1 no. 7). More concretely, in order to determine the unfairness of the deed, the following four factors are considered: (1) the extent of confidence between the parties, (2) the owner's (employer's) interest, (3) the employee's interest, and (4) the characteristics of the trade secret.

Other confidential information

Apart from special regulations on trade secrets, there is no statutory provision that imposes a general duty of confidentiality on employees during and after employment relations. Parties to employment contracts can establish a duty of confidentiality concerning information which is not regarded as a trade secret and not protected under the UCPL by agreeing or by so prescribing in work rules. Such an agreement is valid unless it is regarded as against public policy.

Whether employees should owe a duty of confidentiality without such explicit provisions differs during and after employment relations.

During employment relations, it is universally agreed that an employee bears a duty to keep confidentiality as a duty of loyalty naturally deriving from an employment contract. In the case of violations of confidentiality, Japanese employers can resort to disciplinary actions including disciplinary dismissal,[8] normal dismissal,[9] as well as claiming damages[10] for the breach of contracts or as a tort liability. It is thought that injunction is also possible when the content of a duty of confidentiality is clearly specified.

By contrast, after termination of employment relations, it is unclear whether a former employee is subject to the duty to keep confidential information other than trade secrets. When there is an explicit agreement on confidentiality after termination and their content is not against public policy, it is thought that such an agreement is enforceable. In the absence of such an explicit provision, the majority opinion among academics is that employees do not bear a duty of confidentiality concerning information other than trade secrets since the ancillary duty of employment should be terminated at the end of the contract. However, even if contractual liability is denied, disclosure of confidential information in extremely bad faith can cause tort liability.

In Problem 17, if information concerned is regarded as a "trade secret" in the meaning of the UCPL, the salesperson owes a duty of confidentiality without signing the agreement. If information is not regarded as a "trade secret" under the UCPL, salespersons will, as a matter of principle, bear the duty only when they sign the agreement.

---

8 The *Furukawa Kogyo* case, Tokyo High Court, February 18, 1980, 31 ROMIN-SHU 49. Employees who happened to acquire secret information on the production plan, cost price and profits with detailed numbers made it public at a cell meeting of the Communist Party. The employer's disciplinary dismissal of those employees was held legal because employees bear a duty to keep business secrets as an ancillary duty of employment contracts.

9 The *Misasa Denki* case, Tokyo District Court, July 16, 1968, 226 HANREI TIMES 127.

10 The *Mino Yogyo* case, Nagoya District Court, September 29, 1986, 499 RODO HANREI 75.

Even when the parties to the non-competition agreement choose Indiana law that governs the agreement, according to Article 12, Act on General Rules for Application of Laws, mandatory provision concerning labor contracts shall apply to the matters stipulated in the mandatory provision with regard to the formation and effect of the labor contract. Thus, it depends on the interpretation as to whether the restrictive rules on non-competition shall be regarded as mandatory provision in the meaning of Article 12, Act on General Rules for Application of Laws. Since the reasons for the restriction on the non-competition agreement is to secure freedom to choose an employee's occupation guaranteed by the Constitution, the rule would more than likely be regarded as mandatory.

PRIMARY SOURCES

Constitution

Article 22 Every person shall have freedom to choose and change his residence and to choose his occupation to the extent that it does not interfere with the public welfare.

Unfair Competition Prevention Act

(Definitions)

Article 2 (1) The term "unfair competition" as used in this Act shall mean any of the following:

. . .

(vii) use or disclosure of a trade secret disclosed by the business operator holding such trade secret (hereinafter referred to as the "holder") for the purpose of acquiring an illicit gain or causing injury to such holder;

. . .

The term "trade secret" as used in this Act shall mean a production method, sales method, or any other technical or operational information useful for business activities that is controlled as a secret and is not publicly known.

Act on General Rules for Application of Laws

(Choice of Governing Law by the Parties)

Article 7 The formation and effect of a juridical act shall be governed by the law of the place chosen by the parties at the time of the act.

(Special Provisions for Labor Contracts)

Article 12 (1) Even where the applicable law to the formation and effect of a labor contract as a result of a choice or change under Article 7 or Article 9 is a law other than the law of the place with which the labor contract is most closely connected, if a worker has manifested his/her intention to an employer that a specific mandatory provision from within the law of the place with which the labor contract is most closely connected should be applied, such mandatory provision shall also apply to the matters stipulated in the mandatory provision with regard to the formation and effect of the labor contract.

(2) For the purpose of the application of the preceding paragraph, the law of the place where the work should be provided under the labor contract (in cases where such place cannot be identified, the law of the place of business at which the worker was employed; the same shall apply in paragraph (3)) shall be presumed to be the law of the place with which the labor contract is most closely connected.

(3) In the absence of a choice of law under Article 7 with regard to the formation and effect of a labor contract, notwithstanding Article 8, paragraph (2), the law of the place where the work should be provided under the labor contract shall be presumed to be the law of the place with which the labor contract is most closely connected with regard to the formation and effect of the labor contract.

References and suggested readings

Takashi Araki, *Legal Issues of Employment Loyalty in Japan*, 20 COMP. LAB. L. & POL'Y J. 267 (1999); Ruichi Yamakawa, *Transnational Dimension of Japanese Labor and Employment Laws: New Choice of Law Roles and Determination of Geographical Reach*, 31 COMP. LAB. L. & POL'Y J. 347 (2010).

Problem 17 discussion – United States

Two issues are presented: a contractual non-disclosure (or confidentiality) agreement; and a covenant not to compete. Both are governed by state law. On the former, the law tends to be fairly uniform. On the latter, far less so.

As a preliminary matter the legal background should be brought to the fore. It is invariably said – though it is sometimes observed more in the breach in some states – that the law looks askance at restrictions on an employee's ability to exploit his or her knowledge, skills, and experience: that restraints that deprive the employee of the capacity to develop his or her "human capital," and deprive the public of the benefits of her or her services, are strongly disfavored. Nevertheless, the common law does impose an obligation to respect trade secrets and other confidential business information the employee has acquired even in the absence of a contractual obligation to do so; trade secret obligations have been codified in a widely adopted Uniform Trade Secrets Act. However, the common law implies no obligation not to work for a competitor. That is a matter of contract. With that as background we turn to the two provisions at hand.

The non-disclosure agreement. The agreement must meet the requirements of any contract – of offer, acceptance, and consideration. If the agreement is tendered the salesperson and executed at the time of hire, the latter should not be a problem. The agreement's substance is concerned with customer lists, marketing and financial information and business methods, plans and strategies that are either trade secrets or designated as confidential business information. Such may not be disclosed for a two-year period in competition with or "contrary to" the interests of the employer. To the extent the restricted information is a trade secret or meets the legally defined standard of confidentiality – as not otherwise attainable from other sources and which the company has made legally satisfactory efforts to protect from disclosure – the agreement would seem to be lawful. The duration of the restraint is not problematic. Neither is its scope to the extent it restricts disclosure of protected information for competitive reasons.

However, cautious counsel might be concerned about the prohibition of disclosure that is not competitive but that is "in *any* manner… contrary" to the company's interests. The breadth of the prohibition may be problematic to the extent it could be read to limit whistleblowing – disclosure of malfeasance to a public authority – or to the giving of counsel to parties seeking to litigate, perhaps in the public interest, that would include such information. *See e.g. Union Pacific Railway v. Mower*, 219 F.3d 1069 (9th Cir. 2000). It is not clear that the non-disclosure provision would be allowed to trench quite that far. *See* Terry Dworkin & Elletta Callahan, *Buying Silence*, 36 AM. BUS. L.J. 151 (1998).

The non-competition agreement. The general common law approach to a covenant not to compete is to weigh the employer's asserted need for the restriction, the reasonableness of it in terms of duration and geographic scope, the nature of what jobs are restricted, against the public's as well as the individual's interest. But, given the amorphous nature of this multi-faceted balancing test, each state (and, even each court within it, as we will shortly see) can weight these factors rather differently. How that is so will be illuminated by running this agreement through the laws of the states where the company currently has offices – California, Illinois, and Indiana. But before doing so mention needs be made of the consequences of a finding of unreasonableness. In some states, a court drawing that legal conclusion will excise those features that render the agreement unreasonable, will "blue pencil" these provisions, if possible, and enforce the agreement as judicially revised. In other states, the courts eschew that authority on the assumption that such power would only encourage employers to attempt to overreach, failing which they can rely on judicial salvation after the dust settles. Let us see how *this* covenant would fare.

California. The California Business and Professional Code, §16600, provides:

> Except as provided in this chapter, every contract by which anyone is restrained from engaging in a lawful profession, trade, or business of any kind is to that extent void.

The only exception the statute sets out is for the sale of a business, dissolution of a partnership, or the like. Some courts had crafted a "narrow restraint" exception to what would seem to be the otherwise unequivocal sweep of the statute: that it only forbade a *total* restriction on an employee's ability to engage in her trade, occupation, or profession; that, in other words, the statute allowed for *reasonable* restrictions. In 2008, the California Supreme Court rejected that allowance: "Section 16600 is unambiguous, and if the Legislature intended the statute to apply only to restraints that were unreasonable or overbroad, it could have included language to that effect." *Edwards v. Arthur Anderson LLP*, 81 Cal. Rptr. 3d 282, 291–2 (2008). This non-compete agreement could not be enforced under Cal. law.

Illinois. In 2011, the Illinois Supreme Court, reiterating the injury done by a "total and general restraint" worked by a covenant having that effect, reiterated as well the tripartite test applied in New York:

> A restrictive covenant, assuming it is ancillary to a valid employment relationship, is reasonable only if the covenant: (1) is no greater than is required for the protection of a legitimate business interest of the employer-promisee; (2) does not impose undue hardship on the employee-promisor, and (3) is not injurious to the public.

Reliable Fire Equp. Co. v. Arredondo, 965 N.E.2d 393, 396 (Ill. 2011).

However, many Illinois courts had cabined the legitimate business interests necessary to support a non-competition agreement to the protection of trade secrets (or other confidential business information) or the maintenance of "near-permanent" customer relations. This, the Illinois Supreme Court rejected:

> [W]hether a legitimate business interest exists is based on the totality of the facts and circumstances of the individual case. Factors to be considered in this analysis include,

> *but are not limited to*, the near-permanence of customer relationships, the employee's acquisition of confidential information through his employment, and time and place restrictions. No factor carries any more weight than any other, but rather its importance will depend on the specific facts and circumstances of the individual case.

Id. at 403 (emphasis added).

This rather muddies the water and complicates the ability of counsel to give advice. Suffice it to say, to the extent the interest supporting the provision in this problem is the protection of trade secrets, confidential information, and customer contact, the first prong of the test would be met. So, too, would the two-year limit appear to be reasonable as in line with what the Illinois courts have approved. The difficulty lies in the scope of the prohibition: it reaches employees in markets the company does not yet serve and it prohibits the salesman from working for a competitor "in any capacity" in such places. The salesman, for example, could not become an office manager for a heating/cooling design company anywhere in the world where the company decides to do business in future. There is a rich texture of law in Illinois on these issues and it seems clear that for these reasons the contract would be unlawful under Illinois law.

In Illinois, blue penciling is not foreclosed, but the Illinois courts view it skeptically depending upon how unfair the restraint is, how broad or ambiguous. It seems unlikely the Illinois courts would undertake to narrow this provision.

Indiana. We need not speculate about Indiana law for this problem is adapted from a decision of an Indiana intermediate appellate court from which the text of this contract was taken. *Coates v. Heat Wagons, Inc.*, 942 N.E.2d 905 (Ind. App. 2011). Indiana, too, follows the tripartite test set out by the Illinois Supreme Court save that a "legitimate protectable interest" is defined rather more broadly: as "an advantage possessed by an employer, the use of which by the employee after the end of the employment relationship would make it 'unfair to allow the employee to compete with the former employer'." *Id.* at 913 (citation omitted). In the *Heat Wagons* case, the salesman's knowledge of customer requirements learned by his contacts was such an interest. (Even though the former employee consulted a freely available trade list for customers, he was faulted for not removing his prior employer's customers from the list.) In addition, his knowledge of the heater parts market developed in his work for the prior employer was a protected interest which the court distinguished from "general skills or knowledge" developed on the job.

On geographic scope, although the covenant was nation-wide, the prior employer appended a list of states where it did or expected to do business. Indiana courts do blue pencil such covenants; but, the Supreme Court of Indiana had disallowed the exercise of that power when a covenant covered the entire United States as being, in effect, no restriction at all. In this case, however, the appended list included the 19 states where the prior employer did business and on that basis was held to be sufficiently restrictive: the trial court could strike the other states not among the 19 and enforce the covenant as so restricted. In addition, the scope of the work prohibition ("in any capacity") was blue penciled by the trial court and affirmed on that basis. One judge on the three member panel dissented:

> The purpose of the covenant here at issue is not to protect the employer's trade or business secrets. Rather, its purpose is solely to prevent competition by restricting the employee from engaging in competition with employer "in any capacity whatsoever" and would prevent the employee from competing in any way with the employer. Included in the prohibited actions is owning stock in any company engaged in the heating and air conditioning business. This could include owing stock as an investor. Also prohibited would be working in manufacturing in any heating and air conditioning business even though the employee never worked for employer in manufacturing.
>
> In regard to geographic scope, the restriction applied to all states in which the employer does or has done business, without regard to whether the employee has ever had any involvement in such states. While the trial court invoked the blue pencil doctrine to exclude thirteen of the thirty-two states listed on the exhibit because the employee had had no contact with businesses in such states, there was no showing of the extent of employees' involvement in the remaining states.
>
> I also question the re-writing of a contract as a matter of policy. A restrictive covenant in an employment contract is to be strictly construed against the employer.

Id. at 921–2 (Kirsch, J. dissenting).

Obviously, this non-competition agreement (as narrowed) would be enforceable in Indiana.

The choice of law clause. The parties are free to designate the law that governs the contract, but whether the court of the forum state will accede to that provision is an open question. Some states would refuse to enforce a choice of law provision where the law chosen would violate the public policy of the forum state. But most states would address the issue by posing two questions; if the answer to either is negative the contact's choice of law will not be accepted. First, the state court

> will not defer to the choice of law clause if the chosen state has no substantial relationship to the parties or the transaction and there is no other reasonable basis for the parties' choice. Second, it will not apply the law of the chosen state if that law would be contrary to a fundamental public policy of a state with a materially greater interest than the chosen state in the determination of the particular issue, and which ... would be the state of the applicable law in the absence of an effective choice of law by the parties.

Gillian Lester & Elizabeth Ryan, *Choice of Law and Employee Restrictive Covenants: An American Perspective*, 31 COMP. LAB. L. & POL'Y J. 389, 397 (2010) (footnotes omitted).

To enforce the covenant a court would have to have both subject matter and personal jurisdiction over the defendant, the former employee. Thus the employer would have to sue the employee in the state where he or she has located. This could be any state in the U.S. or any of the Company's foreign operations. But, for ease of analysis, let us assume the former employee were to be working for a competitor in California or Illinois. These states would have a materially greater interest than Indiana. It is most *un*likely that they would accede to the contract's choice of law as it would be contrary to the public policy of the forum state. *See e.g. Brown & Brown, Inc. v. Mudron*, 887 N.E.2d 437 (Ill. App. 2008).

In sum, it is likely that the confidentiality agreement would be enforced in all three states. The covenant not to compete would be enforced in Indiana, if narrowed. It would not be enforced in California. And it is unlikely that it would be enforced in Illinois.

References and suggested readings

BRIAN MALSBERGER et al., TRADE SECRETS: A STATE-BY-STATE SURVEY (4th ed. 2011).

BRIAN MALSBERGER, et al., COVENANTS NOT TO COMPETE: A STATE-BY-STATE SURVEY (8th ed. 2012).

Questions for Discussion – Problem 17

1. It has been argued that covenants not to compete should be limited to those employees most likely to be in possession of business information that requires protection, perhaps by limiting enforceability by rank, salary, and expertise. Norman Bishara & Michelle Westermann-Behaylo, *The Law and Ethics of Restrictions on an Employee's Post-employment Mobility*,

49 AM. BUS. L.J. 7 (2012) (with a good survey of the legal and economic literature). Would the salesmen in this problem meet that test? How does Bishara & Westermann-Behaylo's proposal match up with what our sample of non-U.S. countries do?

2. Some researchers have found the absence of covenants not to compete in California has contributed to the velocity of information exchange which has conduced accordingly toward the more rapid development of new ideas and new products. Ronald Gilson, *The Legal Structure of High Technology Industrial Districts: Silicon Valley, Route 28, and Covenants Not to Compete*, 74 N.Y.U. L. REV. 575 (1999). See generally, ALAN HYDE, WORKING IN SILICON VALLEY: ECONOMIC AND LEGAL ANALYSIS OF A HIGH VELOCITY LABOR MARKET (2003). Other researchers have found a connection between employee mobility and economic growth especially in the context of innovation clusters and start-up enterprises. It has been argued that these militate toward the non-enforcement of non-competition agreements not involving the disclosure of protected information. *See* Catherine Fisk & Adam Barry, *Contingent Loyalty and Restricted Exit: Commentary on the Restatement of Employment Law*, 16 EMP. RTS. & EMP. POL'Y. J. No. 2 (in press) (comprehensively surveying the literature).

3. Germany views a covenant not to compete, even if meeting all other standards of enforceability, to be, in effect, an option inasmuch as specified compensation has additionally to be paid should the employer choose to invoke it. Brazil would also look to whether there was adequate, separate compensation paid for the covenant. Could this be a generalized approach? Note, however, that German law takes no account of the public interest.

4. Assess the arguments for the employer's property interests, the employee's interest in self-advancement, and the public's interest in better and less expensive goods and services against what these countries – or, in the U.S. case, what the various states – do.

PART VII

GLOBAL SUPPLY CHAINS AND LABOR STANDARDS

A global multinational corporation will have various divisions and lines of business, each of which will depend on an array of suppliers around the world. Increasingly, suppliers are responsible for high value-added parts of the business, not just component parts or low value-added services. As the extended enterprise includes suppliers playing crucial roles, broader questions are posed around the need for consistency in labor and employment policies as they apply across the entire enterprise. Indeed, employees in these distributed operations are increasingly making claims that corporate policies apply in their various circumstances. Concurrently, the consuming public and even some governments are holding corporations responsible for working conditions in the supply chain. Indeed, companies that advertise their projects as "fair trade" or that otherwise highlight aspects of working conditions among their suppliers are seeking a market advantage based on the supply chain employment practices.

Part VII poses four problems that center on the complexities of setting employment policy across the extended enterprise of a corporation. The first problem (Problem 18) centers on an integrated lean/six sigma system across a corporation and its suppliers. The second problem (Problem 19) centers on an integrated safety operating system and the third problem (Problem 20) centers on a global "zero tolerance" policy on discrimination, again applying across suppliers in a global corporation. At stake here is the challenge of national labor and employment policies and administrative procedures being applied not just to a multinational corporation, but also to its suppliers. The fourth problem (Problem 21) deals with the engagement of transnational unions and works councils in seeking to secure compliance with international labor standards, with a special emphasis on "freedom of association" – the right to engage in collective bargaining. An underlying theme is that there are efficiencies, operational advantages, and ethical reasons for corporations to have integrated global systems, but they are not well matched to the structure and operation of the labor and employment legal context in countries.

The changing nature of work and technology is a theme throughout all of the problems in the preceding parts of the book, but the shifts in entire work systems become particularly evident in Part VII. Variously termed a post-industrial economy, a service economy, an information age, a knowledge economy, among other things, it is clear that what Piore and Sabel termed "The Second Industrial Divide" in 1984 represents as distinct a shift as the first divide more than a century ago between a craft and an industrial economy.

Emblematic of the change are a set of what are termed "lean" and "six sigma" corporate initiatives. These terms refer to systematic initiatives and underlying principles where the distributed knowledge and expertise of the workforce is harnessed to drive continuous improvement in operations. First emerging in manufacturing and now extending across enterprise operations, the idea of "lean" reflected the elimination of waste (such as excess inventory, extra steps in a process, etc.) in order to improve what is termed the "flow of value" to the customer. Early thinking came from Dr. W. Edwards Deming, OUT OF THE CRISIS (1986) and Joseph Juran, QUALITY CONTROL HANDBOOK (1951), while it was James Womack, Daniel Jones & Daniel Roos, THE MACHINE THAT CHANGED THE WORLD: THE STORY OF LEAN PRODUCTION (1991), that coined the term "lean" in reference to the new ways of fostering efficiency in the auto industry. The term "six sigma" refers to a standard of quality that is six standard deviations from the mean or about 3.4 defects per million instances. In contrast, a three sigma operation is only dependable 93.3 percent of the time, with 66,807 defects per million "opportunities" – good for some cases and unacceptable for others. Tools such as using statistical sampling for process control, mapping entire "value streams" and targeting opportunities for improvement (based on data), design for manufacture, and others are at the heart of this approach. The terms "lean" and "six sigma" have come to be used in different industries and different firms, but drawing on the same set of tools, methods, and principles. Though not always fully appreciated, the heart of these systems involves a fundamental shift in thinking by managers – systematically to value and engage the distributed knowledge and expertise of the workforce in the service of continuous improvement (J. Cutcher-Gershenfeld et al., KNOWLEDGE-DRIVEN WORK: UNEXPECTED LESSONS FROM UNITED STATES AND JAPANESE WORK SYSTEMS (1998)).

As we will see in the Part VII problems, these new work systems afford levels of precision and control in business operations that have direct implications for employment policy. Indeed, new research on global labor standards in supply chains finds that organizations with robust lean/six sigma initiatives in their supply chains have a far greater impact on ensuring decent wages, working hours, and working conditions than is achieved through voluntary international standards or local government inspection regimes (Richard Locke, Fei Qin & Alberto Brause, *Does Monitoring Improve Labor Standards?: Lessons from Nike*,

61 INDUS. & LAB. REL. REV. (2007)). These and other related changes in the nature of work raise fundamental questions regarding the roles of corporations and governments with respect to monitoring and improving labor and employment relations.

PROBLEM 18: REQUESTED WAIVER OF INSPECTIONS

A company has instituted lean/six sigma systems across its first, second and third tier suppliers. The result has been increased productivity by the suppliers, as well as less use of overtime, increased investment in training, better safety performance and reduced turnover. Based on more than a year of demonstrable success with this new model, the company argues that it need not be subject to inspections by government representatives enforcing labor standards. Will it find a receptive audience with the government agencies? If it makes the same argument to any of the leading non-governmental organizations (NGOs) focused on labor standards, will they be receptive? If it asks local, regional or national governments for funding to train suppliers in lean/six sigma tools and methods, is it likely to be successful?

Problem 18 discussion – Australia

As in the US, an Australian (or Australian-based) employer would not be able to argue that its use of lean/six sigma practices superseded its need to comply with its obligations under the Fair Work Act 2009 or other labour statutes.

Over the past decade, various Australian employer associations have promoted the concept of "self-regulation", but without notable success. If anything, there has been a dramatic increase recently in the funding, activity and effectiveness of the main federal inspectorate, now part of an agency known as the Fair Work Ombudsman. A company reputed to be a "good employer" might expect not to be targeted in any of FWO's random audits, but it would still be vulnerable to the investigation of any employee-initiated complaint. The same would apply in relation to the enforcement of occupational health and safety standards under State or Territory law (see Problem 19). Trade unions – the most obvious type of NGO with an interest in the enforcement of labour standards – would seem even less likely to be interested in accepting the notion of self-regulation.

As for training, a number of organisations in Australia already provide lean/six sigma courses that attract government subsidies. The organisations concerned are accredited training providers, operating within the general framework for vocational education and training. It would seem unlikely that an Australian government would go outside that framework to fund company training programs directly.

References and suggested readings

Sean Cooney, *Exclusionary Self-Regulation: A Critical Evaluation of the AMMA's Proposal in the Mining Industry*, *in* Labour Law and Labour Market Regulation, 187 (C Arup et al. eds., 2006).

Tess Hardy, *A Changing of the Guard: Enforcement of Workplace Relations Laws Since Work Choices and Beyond*, *in* Fair Work: The New Workplace Laws and the Work Choices Legacy, 75 (Anthony Forsyth & Andrew Stewart eds., 2009).

Problem 18 discussion – Brazil

Whatever may be the quality of a working methodology and the impressive results obtained, companies are still subject to the Labor Inspection Office supervision, which may be implemented by any of its officials. They enjoy the right to enter premises, make inspections, demand information, examine documents, and question employees. If labor standards are not respected they are entitled to issue infraction notification and fines, to interdict places and to embargo construction sites. The use of lean/six sigma systems will have no impact on their work as they are extremely zealous of their prerogatives and not inclined to allow its replacement by organizational methods as good as they may be. Brazilian NGOs are not really focused on labor standards in general, but are more concerned with specific issues such as contemporary slavery. The use of lean/six sigma systems seems be extremely far from their major concerns. Public funding in the labor field aims by preference at workers' reinsertion in the labor market and may rarely be available for such training, which corresponds to a very specific company demand.

References and suggested readings

On the Labor Inspection Office officials' prerogatives, see: *Decreto No. 4.552 (Ordinance No. 4.552) 2002 (Braz.) accessed at* http://www.planalto.gov.br/ccivil_03/decreto/2002/D4552.htm (last visited Feb. 27, 2010).

Problem 18 discussion – Germany

Monitoring compliance with labor standards is mainly the task of commercial regulatory authorities (*Gewerbeaufsichtsämter*). Under section 22 of the Employment Protection Act (*Arbeitsschutzgesetz*) these authorities enjoy the right to enter premises, make inspections, demand information, look into relevant documents, obtain expert advice, make examinations and so on. There is no evidence that the establishment of lean/six sigma systems impacts in a way which could prompt commercial regulatory authorities to consider refraining from inspections altogether. German NGOs rarely have a focus on labor standards (at home). As a consequence it is difficult to say whether they would be impressed. As far as state funding is concerned, participating in further education with regard to, for instance, six sigma seminars may be paid for by a so-called "formation voucher" (*Bildungsgutschein*) according to section 81 of Social Code III. Apart from that there are many other possible sources of government funding at both state and federal level (the latter including funding by the so-called "labor agencies", *Agenturen für Arbeit*). Funding, however, is essentially individual in the sense that individuals willing to engage in further education can apply for subsidies.

Problem 18 discussion – Japan

The individual employment relationship between an employer and an employee is regulated by protective laws such as the Labor Standards Act (LSA), the Minimum Wages Act, the Security of Wage Payment Act, the Industrial Safety and Health Act, and so forth. Among these, the most fundamental and important is the LSA which establishes minimum working standards. The LSL regulates fundamental rights of workers, payment of wages, working hours, paid leave, special protection of young workers and pregnant women, workers' compensation for work-related accidents, work rules, and so forth.

The Ministry of Health, Labor and Welfare (MHWL) was responsible for the administration of labor protective laws. The Labor Standards Bureau within the MHWL administers labor standards established by the Labor Standards Act, the Minimum Wages Act, the Industrial Safety and Health Act. Actual implementation of this labor protective legislation occurs through the Labor Standards Inspection Offices in each prefecture. Approximately 3,500 Labor Standards Inspectors work at 343 Labor Standards Inspection Offices throughout Japan. The Labor Standards Inspectors are authorized to inspect workplaces, to demand the production of books and records, and to question employers and workers (LSA Art. 101). Furthermore, with respect to a violation of the LSA, Labor Standard Inspectors shall exercise the duties of judicial police officers under the Criminal Procedure Law (LSA Art. 102).

An employee may report violation of labor protective laws to the Labor Standards Inspection Office. Dismissal and other disadvantageous treatment by reason of such employee's having made a report is prohibited by criminal sanctions (LSL Art. 104, 119 no. 1).

Working conditions prescribed in the LSA are the minimum labor standards. Therefore, an employer in Japan cannot argue that its use of lean/six sigma practices superseded its need to comply with these minimum working conditions established by the LSA. To provide flexibility, the LSA allows derogation from the mandatory norms based upon a "labor-management agreement" or "majority-representative agreement." A labor-management agreement is a written agreement between an employer and the "representative of the majority of workers at an establishment," namely a union organizing a majority of the workers in the establishment or a person representing a majority of the workers in the absence of a majority union. Deviation from the mandatory minimum standards is allowed when the Act explicitly prescribes such derogation. For instance, the LSA requires a labor-management agreement for deduction of wages, hours-averaging schemes or overtime work. Such deviation is explicitly allowed by the Act. The use of lean/six sigma makes no legitimate and successful argument to deviate from the minimum working conditions and to evade state supervision through labor standards inspectors.

Domestic regulatory measures are insufficient to improve working conditions of supply chains located in other, developing countries, because such domestic laws are not applicable across the national border as discussed in Problems 14 and 15. Therefore, it is here that the measures adopted in the context of Corporate Social Responsibility (CSR) most effectively work. CSR is not legally sanctioned but relies on stakeholders' voluntary actions. In this arena, NGOs will play an important role. The employer has no duty to meet and bargain with NGOs, but reputational criticism made by NGOs would significantly affect the company's activities.

Problem 18 discussion – United States

In the United States the Fair Labor Standards Act's (FLSA) basic requirements are:

- payment of the minimum wage;
- overtime pay for time worked over 40 hours in a workweek;
- restrictions on the employment of children; and
- record-keeping.

The FLSA has been amended on many occasions since it was first passed in 1938. The U.S. Department of Labor states that workers covered by the FLSA are entitled to the minimum wage and overtime pay at a rate of not less than one and one-half times their regular rate of pay after 40 hours of work in a workweek. Various minimum wage exceptions apply under specific circumstances to workers with disabilities, full-time students, youth under age 20 in their first 90 days of employment, tipped employees and student-learners. Special rules apply to state and local government employment involving fire protection and law enforcement activities, volunteer services, and compensatory time off (instead of cash overtime pay). Employers are required to keep records on wages, hours, and other items which are generally maintained as an ordinary business practice. The FLSA child labor provisions are designed to protect the educational opportunities of youth and prohibit their employment in jobs and under conditions detrimental to their health or safety. The child labor provisions include some restrictions on hours of work for youth under 16 years of age and lists of hazardous occupations too dangerous for young workers to perform.

An employer in the U.S. would not be able to argue that its use of lean/six sigma practices superseded its need to comply with these basic labor standards in its operations. Further, U.S. multinational corporations are not held accountable for compliance with U.S. labor standards by firms in their supply chain, whether in the U.S. or abroad. Under the North American Free Trade Act of 1994 (NAFTA), there was an intent to raise labor standards among suppliers in Mexico (rather than lower standards in the U.S. and Canada). The actual impact of NAFTA is still a matter of some scholarly debate – it has clearly expanded trade, but it is less clear that there is a causal relationship with labor standards and working conditions in firms that are operating under the auspices of this law. The law imposes few specific restrictions on a U.S. employer with respect to labor standards for suppliers in Mexico or Canada.

At the same time, there is new research suggesting that the use of lean/six sigma practices is positively associated with higher levels of pay, lower levels of turnover, increased investment in training, and reduced reliance on overtime. Moreover, this research indicates that lean/six sigma practices have a much greater impact than either government inspection practices or monitoring by non-governmental organizations. Further, there is evidence to suggest that current administrative practices relative to labor standards do not achieve their full potential in ways that might advance the interests of both workers and employers. Thus, there is a policy question as to whether agencies responsible for administering labor standards should provide more autonomy or even increased support to employers with robust lean/six sigma operations.

Government support for training on lean/six sigma principles is often available through local and state level economic development agencies in the U.S., usually drawing on federal training funds that are supplemented with additional local and state resources.

References and suggested readings

Richard Locke & Monica Romis, *The Promise & Perils of Private Voluntary Regulation: Labor Standards and Work Organizations in Two Mexican Factories* (MIT Sloan, Working Paper No. 4734–09 January 2009).

Richard Locke, Matthew Amengual & Akshay Mangla, *Virtue out of Necessity?: Compliance, Commitment and the Improvement of Labor Conditions in Global Supply Chains* (MIT Sloan, Working Paper No. 4719–08, MIT October 2008, updated March 2009).

Richard Locke, Fei Qin & Alberto Brause, *Does Monitoring Improve Labor Standards?: Lessons from Nike*, 61 INDUS. & LAB. REL. REV. 3 (2007).

David Weil, *Protecting the Vulnerable Workforce in the US: A Sector-Based Approach*, 51 J. INDUS. REL. 411 (2009).

David Weil, *A Strategic Approach to Labour Inspection*, 147 INT'L. LAB. REV. 349 (2008).

David Weil & Amanda Pyles, *Why Complain? Complaints, Compliance, and the Problem of Enforcement in the U.S. Workplace*, 27 COMP. LAB. L. & POL'Y J. 101 (2007).

David Weil & Carlos Mallo, *Regulating Labour Standards via Supply Chains: Combining Public/Private Interventions to Improve Workplace Compliance*, 45 BRIT. J. INDUS. REL. 805 (2007).

David Weil, Archon Fung, Mary Graham, & Elena Fagotto, *Regulation by Transparency: The Effectiveness of Government Mandated Disclosure Policies*, J. POL'Y ANALYSIS & MGMT. 155 (2006).

My company … is currently undertaking a widespread initiative to join OSHA's Voluntary Protection Program through its obtainment of VPP status. Our corporation is ultimately focused on generating profits for shareholders, and we continue to streamline and cut back many redundant areas throughout the company including centralizing our safety functions across the enterprise. The biggest cost to our corporation, outside of payroll, is workers' compensation. Part of the philosophy of VPP is getting employee involvement to establish a safety culture. We feel we can implement both cost-saving measures *and* investment in safety concurrently through VPP.

Director, HR, Food and Beverage Sector

The company that I work for has committed to lean initiatives, and we are committed to conducting lean Kaizen events in which employees are encouraged to bring solutions to the table to improve productivity and efficiencies. Many of the "green" sustainment actions that we have undertaken have surfaced from employees and they deliver cost savings in lowering electrical power consumption in our sites. Therefore while it's not mandatory by law that we make these changes, it is the right thing to do for our employee's engagement in the business and for controlling costs.

Vice President, HR, Electrical Manufacturing Sector

Especially when it comes to labor standards in the area of safety, I do not think corporations can be trusted to regulate themselves or their suppliers. The reason is that there is too much pressure on line managers to meet their quarterly and annual revenue and profit numbers. When revenue goes down due to industry or macroeconomic conditions, line managers are forced to cut expenses. The first area they go to is our staff functions which may manage safety or enforce standards for suppliers. These are the first jobs to be cut and is why corporations cannot be trusted to self-regulate. An example of this is Amoco Corporation ... [which] was purchased by British Petroleum. Due to the need to meet investor and the market's expectations on profits, BP drastically cut back on expenses over the years in their safety function, ... [which] contributed to major refinery explosions in Joliet, IL and Texas City, Texas. In sum, profit pressures are the reason companies cannot be trusted to regulate themselves.

Senior Vice President, HR, Information Technology Sector

MNCs have more compelling reasons to implement proactive employment practices than just avoiding regulatory inspections ... . MNCs would want to step up standards in particular amongst their suppliers, including "doing the right thing" through being a good corporate citizen, avoiding negative scrutiny from the public, and ensuring that supplier-customer partnerships are maximized as customers increase their investments in trusted suppliers in return for higher quality and cost-efficient products and processes ... MNCs that proactively self-regulate and encourage their suppliers to adopt higher levels of labor standards are fast-tracking to what would normally occur in the marketplace over time without their initiatives. As technology and the speed of change increase exponentially, companies that have shifted their thinking to this more proactive mindset will be better equipped to succeed in the competitive global economy.

Director, HR, Food and Beverage Sector

Voluntary programs may not be as effective as the companies would like you to believe and may be quickly dropped/cut to meet financial goals, but I think relying on government inspections/audits may not be the panacea either. A look at the recent news regarding the Massey Energy Upper Big Branch coal mine disaster demonstrates that government regulations, audits, violation notices and fines alone are not enough to create a workplace/corporate culture which values the safety of their employees. Many companies value safety and see the financial benefit to related investments, however, this has to be more than a "safety program" (which can be cut) and more than lip service, it has to be interwoven into work streams and processes and the core business. It has to be something that is internalized by the employees and management, not just the "safety team". Easier said than done, right? Absolutely, but I don't think safety can be achieved by external regulation only (from the government or company on suppliers). It has to be part of the corporate culture, the way the company does business, the values the employees demonstrate. Although self-regulated and voluntary programs may be more PR than a core aspect of a company's business, I think the long-term financial and employee welfare value of effective, continuous improvement safety plans can only be achieved if it comes from within the company.

HR Consultant, Multiple Sectors

For the past 15 years I have been a CHRO for two different service companies who have been suppliers to fortune 1000 firms... In my 15 years at both companies we have never been audited on our employment practices, never been asked how many discrimination complaints were filed against us, never been asked about discrimination settlements, etc. All we get asked is whether we communicate annually a code of ethics policy to employees which includes a discrimination statement. We reply "yes" [on] all of the "requests for a proposal," but when we get the business we are never audited by the customer. It has never happened where a customer has audited our practices and we generally were the largest supplier to our customers.

So why in both situations were my firms never audited by our customers? First, ... [c]orporations are in the business of making money and delivering goods and services to customers. Their focus is to win in the marketplace, and beat their competitors. It is not to enforce [Corporate Social Responsibility] initiatives with their suppliers. Second, resources would rarely ever be available to enforce CSR initiatives. I cannot see any CHRO asking their CFO during a budget process or a budget reforecast to have resources to monitor the employment or safety practices of our suppliers. The CHRO would be laughed out of the C suite. It just does not happen in the real world based on my experience. In addition, I doubt corporations have any good metrics to show CSR benefits.

Moreover, why do corporations who have CSR policies for their suppliers do not have the same policies for their customers who provide revenue to them? At both of my employers we had situations where we had strong anti-discrimination policies for our suppliers. However, at both firms we had situations where one of our employees complained they were being sexually harassed by a senior manager who worked for a customer. In both cases the senior manager was either the decision maker for our services or an influencer. When I requested that we contact the customer's General Counsel or the senior manager's boss to file a complaint, the line executives at my firms refused to do so. They were ... fearful that filing a complaint would result in a loss of revenue. The fact that the two employees were being harassed, while serious, was not serious enough to lose potential revenue. In both cases my CEO agreed that we would immediately move both employees away from that specific customer into other jobs.

In summary, the above example is how Corporate America really works. Corporations can never be expected to do a quality job in self-regulating businesses in their supply chains. This is not the focus of their business, and will eventually conflict with their sole purpose of generating profits for their owners.

Senior Vice President, HR, Information Technology Sector

Questions for Discussion – Problem 18

1. Experts in all five countries indicated that the presence of lean/six sigma systems is not a substitute for regulatory oversight on issues of workplace health and safety. On the other hand, the readings by David Weil, Richard Locke, and others clearly point to the potential value of some form of public/private partnership in which the presence of lean/six sigma systems are taken into account by government agencies. Based on the five expert responses and other information that you might have, which of the five

countries would you pick as the target to try to build support for such a partnership structure and why not any of the others? What non-governmental organizations might you enlist as partners in such an initiative (including NGOs focused on labor standards, health and safety community action organizations, unions, and others)?

2. One lesson from the application of lean/six sigma systems to workplace safety is that not all variables move in the same direction at the same time. For example, an increase in reported "near misses" and minor incidents typically corresponds with a reduction in the more serious "lost time incidents" and fatalities. This is because the reporting of near misses and minor incidents allows for increased attention to prevention. Since none of the countries sees the lean/six sigma systems as a substitute for regulatory oversight, how receptive do you think the regulatory authorities will be to the argument that it is OK to have an increase in some categories (the more minor ones) since it will lead to a reduction in the more serious categories later on (if there is a lean/six sigma system in place)?

3. Based on the expert responses and any other information that you might have, which country or countries would you target as the most likely to provide public resources for lean/six sigma training and what would be the basis for your request for public resources?

PROBLEM 19: GLOBAL SAFETY

A company has established a "Global Safety Operating System" that provides common tools and methods supporting continuous improvement in safety in all operations around the world, including all of its suppliers. Must the company conduct a detailed analysis of ensuring consistency with health and safety rules, regulations and procedures in each country before instituting this new safety operating system?

Problem 19 discussion – Australia

The company would need to ensure its system met the requirements of any applicable Australian occupational health and safety (OHS) law. There are separate statutes in each State and Territory: see e.g. Work Health and Safety Act 2011 (NSW); Occupational Health and Safety Act 2004 (Vic). Under an intergovernmental agreement, each State and Territory had agreed to harmonise these laws by the beginning of 2012. This was meant to involve the enactment of a "model" Work Health and Safety Act. At the time of writing, the States of Victoria and Western Australia had each failed to pass the necessary legislation. Some degree of harmonisation had already been achieved, however, through the adoption and cross-jurisdictional recognition of standards on specific workplace hazards.

Australian OHS laws typically provide for the declaration of "codes of practice" that provide practical guidance for dealing with health and safety issues of a particular type, or in a particular type of workplace. In some jurisdictions, individual employers have been allowed to propose such codes, provided they embody standards that are no less stringent than those that would otherwise be imposed under the legislation in question. The relevant provisions in Division 2 of Part 14 of the Model Work Health and Safety Act simply state that the Minister can approve a code of practice, without indicating the source of each code. Section 275 makes it clear that compliance with a code may be taken into account by a court in assessing whether there has been a breach of the law's requirements, though it is not determinative.

References and suggested readings

ANDREW STEWART, STEWART'S GUIDE TO EMPLOYMENT LAW Ch. 15 (4th ed. 2013).

Problem 19 discussion – Brazil

As mentioned in the discussion of Problems 2 and 16, health and safety rules are strictly regulated by the Ministry of Labor and Employment and supervised by the Labor Inspection Office. While worldwide coordination may be welcomed as it may result in an improvement in health and safety labor conditions, on the one hand, it does not derive from any Brazilian legal requirement and, on the other hand, it does not eliminate the applicability of all Brazilian *Normas Regulamentadoras* (regulatory standards), which set national standards on the matter.

References and suggested readings

BRASIL, MINISTÉRIO DO TRABALHO E EMPREGO, *Normas Regulamentadoras*, *accessed at* http://www.mte.gov.br/legislacao/normas_regulamentaDORAS/Default.asp (last visited Feb. 27, 2010).

On labor inspection, see Adalberto Cardoso & Telma Lage, *A Inspeção do Trabalho no Brasil*, 48 DADOS 451 (2005), *accessed at* http://redalyc.uaemex.mx/redalyc/pdf/218/21848301.pdf (last visited Feb. 14, 2010).

Problem 19 discussion – Germany

Legal rules on health and safety, in particular the provisions of the Act on Health and Safety (*Arbeitsschutzgesetz*), are applicable to the territory of the

Federal Republic only. Coordination with foreign laws is not required. As far as possible issues of workers' co-determination are concerned it should be noted that the Works Councils Act is not applicable outside the territory of the Federal Republic either.

Problem 19 discussion – Japan

Japanese employers must abide by the detailed provisions of the Industrial Health and Safety Act protecting workers' safety and health. There is no provision which relieves employers who adopt a well-developed safety system of government inspection and oversight.

The Industrial Health and Safety Act does not have any provisions which require harmonization or coordination with other national laws on workplace safety. Thus, the Global Safety Operating System in Problem 19 can be implemented without any coordination with other countries.

Problem 19 discussion – United States

Two questions are implicit in this problem: How would U.S. law treat the establishment of a Global Safety Operating System; and must there be a country-by-country analysis before such a system could be launched?

While there is no formal definition of a safety operating system, this approach to safety draws on lessons from quality operating systems (such as lean and six sigma systems) which achieve continuous improvement in outcomes through standardized tools and methods, the use of regular feedback with performance data, and the engagement of the distributed knowledge of the full workforce. Key guiding principles include a focus on prevention before incidents occur (rather than inspection afterwards), reducing variance in an operation before instituting improvements, and a learning process centered on Deming's "plan, do, check, adjust" (or PDCA) approach. Thus, a global safety operating system would likely include providing front-line workers with data on safety incidents and near misses, engaging the workers and their representatives in the analysis of these data, identifying improvement options for implementation and analysis, and surfacing underlying root cause factors (such as workplace design, training systems, safety culture, etc.).

In the U.S., employers are responsible for protecting the safety and health of their employees, consistent with the provisions of the Occupational Safety and Health Act of 1970, the Mine Safety and Health Act of 1977, the Fair Labor Standards Act (which addresses safety with respect to child labor), and cognate state laws. Under the Occupational Safety and Health Act of 1970, the employer must provide a workplace free from recognized hazards that are causing, or are likely to cause, death or serious physical harm to employees regardless of the size of the business. The Occupational Safety and Health Administration (OSHA) develops standards and regulations to implement the Act.

At various times in recent decades, there have been U.S. Department of Labor initiatives centered on allowing employers with demonstrated, well-developed safety systems to be relieved of a certain measure of government inspection and oversight. At present, however, there is no special dispensation provided to U.S. employers for having an integrated, safety operating system.

There is nothing in U.S. law that would require any harmonization or coordination with other national laws on workplace safety. Thus, aspects of the planned "Global Safety Operating System" could be implemented on a pilot basis in the U.S. without waiting for a country-by-country analysis. Of course, the planned system might have to be modified based on the requirements of different jurisdictions, so a pilot launched in the U.S. might not be able to be diffused without modification in other locations and then it would not be a single international safety operating system. There is nothing in U.S. law that would allow for more flexible standards in the U.S. so that the system could be consistent across different national jurisdictions.

Note that ever since the United States joined the International Labor Organization (ILO) in 1934, it has generally only ratified ILO conventions that are consistent with U.S. law and practice. Thus, there are no ILO conventions that would serve as the basis for increasing the consistency of U.S. regulation on workplace safety with practices in other countries.

References and suggested readings

Neil Gunningham, *Towards Effective and Efficient Enforcement of Occupational Health and Safety Regulation: Two Paths to Enlightenment*, 19 COMP. LAB. L. & POL'Y J. 547 (1998).

> The implementation of [our company's] Global Safety Operating System is one example of harmonizing global policies and practices. As discussed during the course, there is no legal reason to harmonize safety across countries and such self-governing will not exempt the company from meeting legal requirements at local level. In addition, determining the common denominators among countries, especially emerging countries such as China and India, where there are lower standards set by the government, is proving to be a challenge. The implementation of the system has just begun and the company is committed to this initiative [since] building a common language in the area of safety is strategically important to the organization's sustainability.
>
> Director, HR, Electronics Sector

> [In my company we have] clear and established rules for safety procedures to ensure employees are working properly and avoiding injuries. While we have strict OSHA reporting standards in the US, many other countries do not have such requirements ... regardless of what the local laws require, if it's the right thing to do, or the best practice in other locations that go above and beyond [what is required], then we take the higher level of expectation in all other locations too.
>
> Vice President, HR, Electrical Manufacturing Sector

> One of our US locations was viewed as a highly inefficient and costly operation with high accident and injury rates. Several years ago, the leaders and the employees had a wake-up call when it was audited by OSHA. Today, the same facility turned itself around and has a reputation to have a highly safety minded culture with employees who are deeply involved in continuously improving safety practices and leaders who promote and support the team. The lowest accidents and work related injuries among the US operations are the main factors in this location's high productivity rate in recent years. In addition, when some of its product lines were outsourced to China and Mexico in order to make room for new product lines at its location, in an effort to help build the solid foundation in these new operations, the US team trained their counterparts in China

> and Mexico in implementation of similar high-quality safety programs that are sustainable. As its first step towards establishing a global safety operation system, our corporate in Europe recently created a global safety team with the representatives from countries around the globe. This US location had an opportunity to share their best practices and their success stories to demonstrate not only the higher labor standards beyond legal requirements but also the financial impact on the bottom line.
>
> Director, HR, Electronics Sector

Questions for Discussion – Problem 19

1. Given that the reporting requirements in each country are distinct, which record keeping strategy would you recommend pursuing as a multinational corporation and why? Option 1: Implementing a separate, country-by-country record-keeping system focused only on the reporting requirements in each country; Option 2: Integrating all the reporting requirements of each country into one common, integrated record-keeping system that would involve some record-keeping in each country that is not required; Option 3: A hybrid model (and spell out what that would be).

2. Assuming you were a multinational corporation able to generate data that would demonstrate better safety performance under a single, standardized global system, which country would you pick (and why) as the best place to try to achieve dispensation from a national standard, so long as you were operating consistently with the standards of a global system? If you were a government official responsible for workplace health and safety, what arguments would be most likely to persuade you that a global safety operation system would merit dispensation from some country-specific standards.

PROBLEM 20: ZERO TOLERANCE POLICY

A company is deeply committed to valuing diversity and opposing discrimination in all of its operations. It establishes a "zero tolerance" policy for any discrimination based on race, gender, religion or sexual identity in any of its suppliers – notifying suppliers that supply contracts will not be renewed if they are found guilty of any of these forms of discrimination. Will it encounter any legal barriers to implementing this policy with suppliers around the world? If it also encourages the formation of "affinity groups" among its suppliers for different sub-groups based on racial, gender, religion, or sexual identity (such as the African American Women's Engineering Group or the Lesbian, Gay, Bi-sexual, and Trans-sexual group or the Muslim Prayer Group), will that create any legal complications?

Problem 20 discussion – Australia

There is no obvious reason why these strategies could not be adopted in Australia. Even if the company failed to enforce its zero tolerance policy with suppliers, it is hard to see how anyone could legally complain. As for affinity groups, there is nothing in the Fair Work Act 2009 that would prevent the company "dealing with" them, even over wages or working conditions. The company would of course need to make sure that it did not discriminate against suppliers or workers not members of these groups. But it should be noted that anti-discrimination laws often contain an exemption for "special measures" (including affirmative action programs) that are intended to meet the needs of a particular group or to reduce their disadvantage.

Problem 20 discussion – Brazil

There will be no legal barriers to a company establishing a "zero tolerance" policy for any discrimination based on race, gender, religion or sexual identity in any of its suppliers. However, if the supplier is an outsourced service, once the policy is set, disobedience of its rules by the company may bring undesirable consequences as to its liability, especially because of jurisprudential-made subsidiary liability (see Problem 9). The formation of "affinity groups" may be a problem as it may be perceived as a barrier to employment equal opportunities. Due to the fact that identity issues are not so intense in Brazilian labor, case law is scarce and such conduct would most probably be perceived as a peculiarity of a foreign corporative culture.

Problem 20 discussion – Germany

Establishing a "zero tolerance" policy may be in the spirit of section 12 para. 4 of the General Act on Equal Treatment (*Allgemeines Gleichbehandlungsgesetz*), according to which the employer has to take suitable, necessary and reasonable measures if workers are discriminated against by "third parties." In addition, section 17 para. 1 of the Act states that partners to collective agreements, employers, workers and workers' representatives are called upon to participate, within their tasks and means, in efforts to implement the goals of the Act. This implies that the employer should design his contractual arrangements in line with what is required by the principle of non-discrimination.

Encouraging the formation of "affinity groups" as such might not trigger legal problems.

Problem 20 discussion – Japan

Since the Japanese Labor Union Act does not contain a provision analogous to §8(a)(2) of the NLRA in the US prohibiting an employer from creating or supporting an employee organization that "deals with" it, establishing "affinity groups" itself would not raise any legal problems in terms of collective labor relations.

Whether the company can impose anti-discrimination policies on its foreign suppliers is a new issue for most Japanese companies. In Problem 18, a private company voluntarily adopts a "zero tolerance" policy and declares that supply contracts shall not be renewed when a supplier violates the anti-discrimination policy. Even if the "zero tolerance" policy and the policy of cancelling supply contracts in the event of non-compliance were incorporated in the supply contract, a contractual obligation would be established between the company and its suppliers, not between the company and the supplier's employees or other stakeholders. Thus it would be difficult for the supplier's employees and other stakeholders to sue against the company, based upon the company's "zero tolerance" policy.

Problem 20 discussion – United States

In terms of U.S. law, two concerns would have to be allayed in accommodating "affinity groups." First, they would have to pass muster under §8(a)(2) of the NLRA were the employer to "deal with" such a group over wages, hours, and working conditions. (See the discussion of Problems 1 and 2.) Proposals made by such groups to improve hiring, retention, promotion, and training for persons of color or on the basis of sex, religion, gender identification, or the like, or proposals better to accommodate religious observance or practice by rescheduling work or by institution exemptions from dress codes, deal with statutory subjects of collective bargaining. Under §8(a)(2) the employer could not create or establish such a group and then deal with it on those issues: that would be "domination" of labor organizations. If spontaneously generated, the employer would have to deal with it at arm's-length: the allocation of company space for group meetings or the use of company facilities for its communications would have to walk a fine line between statutorily impermissible "interference" and arm's-length cooperation. The second concern is the role of the various civil rights acts; that is, insofar as the availability of such a group is a benefit of employment, the employer could not allow one protected class the possibility of group formation and disallow another. Otherwise, there is no prohibition of an employer's enforcement of broader non-discrimination policies than federal or state law requires.

Questions for Discussion – Problem 20

1. Given the expert comments from the five countries, will a "zero tolerance" policy on workplace discrimination be successful? Rank order the five countries to indicate where you anticipate the most success down to the greatest risk of the policy not being successful. Indicate the reasons for your choices.

2. What would you recommend as a common corporate policy on affinity groups that will maximize their impact, while not running afoul of the law in all five countries?

3. Given the comments of the experts, what can you infer about the discrimination issues that are going to be most salient in each of the five countries? (It might be useful to review the material in Part III, supra.) In what ways does the very concept of discrimination vary country by country?

PREFACE TO PROBLEM 21

The growth of international trade, the reduction or elimination of barriers to the flow of capital, goods, and even persons across national borders has had an enormous economic impact. It has also been taken to challenge the capacity of the nation state to control the domestic labor market, to protect workers from downward pressure on wages and working conditions. The multinational enterprise (MNE) or transnational corporation (TNC) is seen by many as sitting astride the world, above the nation states and unaccountable to them in its capacity to shift capital in a race to the bottom on labor standards.

The concern is not new. Since its creation in 1919, the International Labour Organization (ILO) has addressed labor standards via the promulgation of conventions (and recommendations) for nations to legislate, few of which have been ratified by the United States. But since the 1980s, labor rights have been placed higher on the public agenda by the European Community (EC) (now the European Union), the Organisation for Economic Co-operation and Development (OECD) (whose 1976 Declaration on International Investment and Multinational Enterprises dealt in part with labor rights and freedom of collective bargaining), the Organization for Security and Co-operation in Europe (OSCE) (formerly the Conference for Security and Co-Operation in Europe (CSCE)), the World Bank, numerous public and non-governmental organizations (NGOs), international union federations, and individual nation states. In fact, it has been argued that the growth of labor law in accelerating industrial economies was always a transnational affair. Michael Hoberman, ODD COUPLE: INTERNATIONAL TRADE AND LABOR STANDARDS IN HISTORY (2012).

Whether labor rights should be accounted for on a transnational plain – or how that can be best accomplished – has been a rich subject of debate and commentary. *See generally*, Bob Hepple, LABOUR LAW AND GLOBAL TRADE (2005). *See also* Christian Barry & Sinjay Reddy, INTERNATIONAL TRADE & LABOR STANDARDS: A PROPOSAL FOR LINKAGE (2008); and, most recently (and provocatively), Harry Arthurs, *Making Bricks Without Straw: The Creation of a Transnational Labour Regime*, Osgoode Hall Research Paper No. 28 (2012). What follows will touch, lightly, on an aspect of the global presence that may cross the desk of multinational human resource management and their lawyers.

PROBLEM 21: SIGNING AN INTERNATIONAL FRAMEWORK AGREEMENT

You are the Vice-President for Human Resources of an American multinational company. It has hundreds of suppliers worldwide in almost 90 countries and maintains manufacturing, sales or service offices in each of the countries under study here that contract with these suppliers either domestically or across borders. The CEO has received a letter from an international federation of 120 unions representing workers in 80 countries, including unions active in the five countries under study here. The federation has requested that the company sign a Global Agreement taken verbatim from the International Federation of Chemical, Energy, Mine, and General Workers Union (ICEM) Global Agreement with Norske Skog, set out below. The CEO has asked for your recommendation on whether the company should sign it. You have asked for an opinion of legal counsel in the U.S., Australia, Brazil, Germany, and Japan on the legal consequences to the company of signing the agreement: for its application to the company in those countries, to its legal responsibilities for suppliers in those countries, and, most especially, for its legal responsibility in those countries for the behavior of its suppliers abroad with which it or its subsidiaries contract. Their opinions are attached. Now that you have been put on the legal map, what advice would you give? Would you advise that the company be a signatory, or not? Why?

(An edited text of the ICEM – Norske Skog Global agreement on "The Development of Good Working Relations in Norske Skogindustrier's World-wide Operations" (June 24, 2002) is set out below. For ease of analysis some key passages have been *italicized.*)

1. PREAMBLE

This agreement has been concluded between Norske Skogindustrier ASA, hereafter referred to as Norske Skog, and Fellesforbundet (The Norwegian United Federation of Trade Unions), and the ICEM (International Federation of Chemical, Energy, Mine and General Workers' Unions).

The agreement is based on the signatories' joint commitment to respect basic human rights and trade union rights in the community, and to achieve continuous improvements within the areas of working conditions, industrial relations with the employees of Norske Skog, health and safety standards at the workplace and environmental performance.

On the basis of the company's core values – openness, honesty and co-operation – the parties agree that they should actively co-operate locally, nationally, and internationally. Co-operation is to be built on mutual respect, confidence and freely available and honest information. This ensures the possibility for the employees to influence decisions through consultation with the management.

This agreement relates to all Norske Skog operations where the company has direct control as owner. *Where Norske Skog does not have a controlling interest it will use its fullest influence in order to secure compliance with the standards set out in this agreement.*

Norske Skog will notify its *subcontractors and suppliers of this agreement and encourage compliance* with the standards set out in paragraph 2 below:

2. CONDITIONS OF EMPLOYMENT

Both parties underline the fact that they respect fundamental human rights *and trade union rights*, both in the community and at the workplace. The parties also wish *to promote* these rights in the company's supply chain and with customers.

Within the company's own field of business the top manager for each business unit is responsible for ensuring that the following minimum rules and ILO conventions are not broken:

(a) Freedom of association and collective bargaining

All workers shall have the right to be members of trade unions. These unions shall have the right to be recognized for the purpose of collective bargaining in conformance with ILO Conventions 87 and 98. Workers' representatives shall not be subjected to any discrimination and shall have access to all necessary workplaces in order to carry out their duties as representatives (ILO Convention 135 and Recommendation 143). *The employer shall take a positive attitude to trade union activities, including organizing.*

(b) Discrimination

Equality of opportunity and treatment shall be guaranteed regardless of race, colour, gender, religion, political conviction, nationality, cultural origin or other irrelevant factors (ILO Conventions 100 and 111).

(c) Health & Safety

The parties believe that every employee has the right to a healthy and safe working environment. Norske Skog is committed to providing this. To achieve industry best practice the company will involve and work with the employees, their representatives and trade unions, to continually improve the company's health and safety performance.

(d) Forced labour

Forced labour, including slave and penal labour (ILO Conventions 29 and 105), shall not be used, neither shall employees be required to pay any deposit or leave their identity papers with the employer.

(e) Child labour

Child labour shall not be used. Only workers over the age of 15 – or over legal school age or the age of 18 in connection with hazardous work – may be employed (ILO Conventions 138 and 182). If this commitment is, or has been, violated by Norkse Skog, the company will ensure that adequate educational opportunities and adequate interim financial support will be given.

(f) Wages

Wages and benefits paid for a standard working week shall at least be sufficient to cover the basic needs of the worker and his or her family.

Deductions shall not be made from wages as a disciplinary measure. All employees shall receive clear information in writing about the wage scales and deductions from pay before they are employed. Information regarding pay and deductions should be provided to employees each time wages are paid, and these should not be changed other than by written consent of the individual worker or by collective agreement.

(g) Employment conditions

Employment shall, as a main rule, be based on permanent employment. Temporary and part-time employees should as a main rule receive the same relative terms and conditions as fulltime permanent employees. All employees shall have the opportunity to take part in relevant educational and training programmes.

3. IMPLEMENTATION

(a) Norske Skog will ensure that appropriate translations of the agreement are accessed at all workplaces. The agreement will also be made public on Norske Skog's website and Intranet.

(b) Both parties accept that effective local monitoring of this agreement must involve the local management, the workers and their representatives, health and safety representatives and local trade unions.

(c) To enable local representatives to play a full role in the monitoring process, they will be given adequate time for training and involvement in the monitoring process. The company will ensure that local representatives are provided with information, access to workers, and rights of inspection necessary to effectively monitor compliance with this agreement.

4. INFRINGEMENTS OF THE AGREEMENT

In the event of a complaint or an infringement of the agreement the following procedure will normally apply:

(a) Firstly, the complaint should be raised with the local site management.

(b) If the complaint is not resolved with local management, it should be referred to the appropriate national union who will raise the issue with the company's regional president.

(c) If still unresolved, the complaint will be referred to the ICEM Brussels office who will raise the matter with the company's Corporate Management.

Where infringements are found, these shall be reported to the responsible member of management, *who will ensure that relevant corrective measures are implemented.*

(Omitted are provisions for annual review of the effectiveness and impact of the agreement, for its implementation, and for its distribution to unions, employees, contractors, local management, and more broadly.)

Problem 21 discussion – Australia

There is nothing in Australian law that would either prohibit the making of such an agreement or, on the other hand, give it any automatic legal effect.

The Global Agreement would not qualify as an enterprise agreement that could be registered under Part 2–4 of the Fair Work Act 2009 (Cth) (see Problem 1), since it is not an agreement between the company and its (Australian-based) employees.

To have any direct legal effect, therefore, it would need to be argued that the agreement was enforceable as a contract. Collective agreements on labor conditions have not usually been treated in Australia as having contractual effect, though admittedly the point has only occasionally been tested in court. In the leading decision, *Ryan v Textile, Clothing and Footwear Union of Australia* [1996] 2 VR 235, a number of unregistered collective agreements concerning redundancy entitlements were held not to satisfy the common law tests for an enforceable contract. The court could see nothing to suggest that the parties involved intended the agreement to be legally binding, as opposed to having "industrial" effect. Nor could the court detect that any "consideration" had been provided by the unions who made the agreement, in return for the employer's commitment to provide certain severance benefits.

In relation to the ICEM Agreement, the element of consideration (or "quid pro quo") can be satisfied through the joint commitments in clauses 4–7 concerning dispute resolution, review, information and administration. But there is nothing in the Agreement itself that conclusively establishes an intent to create legal relations (that is, an intent for it to be binding as a contract). The vague or aspirational language of many of the commitments might well tell against a finding of such intent.

Even if the Agreement were found to be legally binding as a contract, under Australian law it could only be binding on, and enforceable by, the parties who had actually made the Agreement: that is, the company and ICEM. The doctrine of privity of contract remains much stronger under Australian law than in the US. In most States, the common law still has the effect that a contract cannot be enforced by a "third party" even if they are intended to benefit from its performance: see e.g. *Coulls v Bagot's Executor and Trustee Co Ltd* (1967) 119 CLR 460. Hence the Agreement could not be enforced either by the company's employees or by any Australian unions representing them. Furthermore, ICEM would have only limited remedies available to it if it sought to sue the company for breach. It could not, for instance, claim damages, because it itself would not have suffered any pecuniary loss.

There would, however, be three possible ways around this enforcement problem. One would be to argue that any contract was governed not by Australian law, but by the law of the country in which it was signed. If that were the US, then the privity doctrine would present less of a barrier to enforcement actions by employees (to the extent that they could establish themselves as "intended beneficiaries" of the company's commitments).

The second possible argument is that even if the Agreement itself were not legally binding as a contract, the commitments in it should be regarded as impliedly incorporated into the employment contracts of the company's workers. Although this notion is nothing like as well established as in the UK, arguments of this type have occasionally succeeded in Australia: see e.g. *Gregory v Philip Morris Ltd* (1988) 80 ALR 455.

The third possible argument would be to invoke s 18 of the Australian Consumer Law (see Competition and Consumer Act 2010 (Cth) Sch 2). This prohibits conduct in trade or commerce that is misleading or deceptive, or that is liable to mislead or deceive. Although there is some controversy as to how far conduct relating to employment conditions can be said to occur "in trade or commerce", the provision has been successfully relied upon to secure remedies against employers, generally for misleading an employee about the security or benefits of a particular job: see e.g. *O'Neill v Medical Benefit Funds of Australia* (2002) 122 FCR 455. In this particular case it might be said that in signing the Agreement, or in subsequently publicizing or acknowledging it, but then not complying with its terms, the company had misrepresented its commitment to the Agreement. Alternatively, the breach might lie in the company leading its employees or others to believe that the Agreement was legally binding, when in fact it had no such effect: see e.g. *Forrest v Australian Securities and Investments Commission* (2012) 86 ALJR 1183 (a case involving representations as to the status of a commercial agreement, rather than a labor agreement).

References and suggested readings

ANDREW STEWART, STEWART'S GUIDE TO EMPLOYMENT LAW §§5.8; 8.51–4 (4th ed. 2013).

Problem 20 discussion – Brazil

Obviously, the company is under no obligation to negotiate the proposed International Framework Agreement, but it is free to do so. As to enforcement in Brazil, the employer will be bound by the Brazilian minimum labor standards which may not be derogated from or reduced in any way. For instance, a provision stipulating that "only workers over the age of 15 – or over legal school age or the age of 18 in connection with hazardous work – may be employed (ILO Conventions 138 and 182)" would have to be adapted to Brazilian law which provides that children between 14 and 16 years old may only work as apprentices. No one under the age of 16 may be hired as a regular employee.

Assuming that the International Framework Agreement has been signed, what would be its impact on the company's Brazilian employees? Would it be enforceable? An International Framework Agreement might not qualify as a *collective* agreement under Brazilian laws since both parties (the international union federation and the international company), or at least one of them if the international company is a Brazilian one, are not entitled to negotiate working conditions under Brazilian law, but their incorporation into individual labor contracts may be easily argued as a valid circumstance. They would thus have a similar impact as an internal code of conduct that adheres to the employees' contracts. To avoid such incorporation, the recent Global Framework Agreement signed on December 2011 by the Petróleo Brasileiro S/A (Petrobras) and the International Federation of Chemical, Energy, Mine and General Workers' Unions established that its object "is to seek understanding on good labor relations at Petrobras abroad".

As for the provisions concerning company suppliers, it is clear that a Global Agreement cannot create duties for third parties. Its careful writing usually eliminates liability as the company's engagement is to "use its fullest influence in order to secure compliance with the standards set out in this agreement." It is just a moral engagement, even though it might have some impact on individual labor contracts.

References and suggested readings

Petrobras & ICEM, TERMS OF UNDERSTANDING OF GOOD LABOR RELATIONS (2011) *accessed at* http://www.icem.org//files/PDF/Global_agreements_pdfs/1201.Petrobras%20GFA%20Text%20English.pdf.

Problem 21 discussion – Germany

The primary question that has to be addressed is whether or not the Global Agreement gives rise to concrete rights and duties. Some scholars argue that the provisions of International Framework Agreements (IFA) are generally of a non-binding nature. The majority view might be, however, that rights and duties can arise from such agreements if this results from an interpretation of the individual agreement under the ordinary rules of construction.

If an IFA has legal effects, the signatory parties can enforce it. Third parties, on the other hand, are by no means empowered to do so. As a consequence, individual employees cannot rely on the agreement (if the individual contract does not explicitly refer to it). Though it is true that collective agreements take normative effect under German law, IFAs do not qualify as collective agreements in this sense. Even if international trade union federations were to be regarded as in principle being capable of concluding such agreements (which is doubtful), it would have to be noted that umbrella organizations do not meet the requirements for concluding viable collective agreements under German law because they are neither mandated accordingly by their members nor foresee conclusion of such agreements in their by-laws.

Apart from that it must be noted that IFAs cannot create duties of third parties (other companies of a group or independent suppliers). It may, however, be that a company by entering into an IFA promises to influence another company to achieve a certain aim as defined in the agreement. It depends then on an interpretation of the agreement itself when the company is supposed to act and how far it has to go. Remarkably enough, the language to be found in IFAs is mostly cautious in this regard. Hence, IFAs can hardly be interpreted as creating some sort of strict liability for a company in case of any violation of its provisions by suppliers anywhere in the world.

References and suggested readings

Gregor Thüsing, *International Framework Agreements: Rechtliche Grenzen und praktischer Nutzen*, *in* RECHT DER ARBEIT (RdA) 78 (2010); Rüdiger Krause, *International Framework Agreements as Instruments for the Legal Enforcement of Freedom of Association and Collective Bargaining? The German Case*, 33 COMP. LAB. L. & POL'Y J. 749 (2012).

Problem 21 discussion – Japan

As the legal status of an International Framework Agreement (IFA) is not much discussed in Japan, the answer is not clear. If the IFA is regarded as a collective bargaining agreement (CBA) under the Labor Union Act (LUA), it can have a binding effect on members of the contracting organization. However, whether the IFA concluded outside Japan can be regarded as a CBA under the Japanese LUA is questionable.

If the LUA applies to the IFA, a question is whether the parties must be employers or an organization of employers and labor union or federation of labor unions. As to the labor side, the union in Japan joins the global federation.

In order to conclude a CBA under the LUA, the global federation must be an organization meeting the five requirements discussed in Problem 1. This might be possible.

As to the management side, the contracting party is the multinational company. The Japanese supplier is a different legal entity and is not a member of the contracting company. In other words, the relationship between the company and the Japanese supplier is not that of an employers' association and its member company. Therefore, the contract between the company and the global federation cannot have a binding effect on the Japanese supplier as a CBA.

If the contract cannot be a CBA, it would be difficult to find legal grounds binding the Japanese supplier.

Certainly, the company itself promises the global federation to implement various matters pertaining to the workers of its suppliers. Thus, not to implement these matters might be regarded as breach of contract and might cause tort liability. However, this is a legal effect between the contracting parties and different from the legal effect on the supplier and its workers.

Problem 21 discussion – United States

The legal status of IFAs under U.S. law has recently been analyzed by Professor Alvin Goldman, *Enforcement of International Framework Agreements under U.S. Law*, 33 COMP. LAB. L. & POL'Y J. 605 (2012). The most obvious legal avenue of enforcement is in contract. Goldman concludes that these agreements would meet the legal requirements of contract – offer, acceptance, and consideration flowing between the parties – either as "contracts between an employer and a labor organization" under federal law, §301 of the Labor Management Relations Act, or under state law. Nevertheless, other obstacles remain: of the capacity to contract, of standing to sue, and the availability of effective remedies. The question may arise of whether the parent corporation signatory to the IFA binds those of its foreign subsidiaries that are separate legal entities.

Insofar as suit is brought by a U.S. union that is a member of the global federation against the contracting company for its action vis-à-vis *its* employees in the United States, none of these would seem to be problematic. The union would argue on agency principles that the international federation was acting for it, that it had standing to enforce an agreement made for its benefit, and that the company's obligation, "to take a positive attitude" toward union organization, though seemingly too vague to provide an ascertainable contractual standard, would be akin to terms commonly found in neutrality agreements in the labor setting which have been enforceable. *See* the discussion of the United States law in Problem 1, *supra*, dealing with employer neutrality.

Far less clear is the status of a suit in contract brought by the global federation and such other parties as might be meaningful – the U.S. union, a foreign union, an employee of a foreign contractor or supplier – against the company in the U.S. to redress its actions – or inaction – vis-à-vis a *foreign* supplier or contractor, e.g. a suit brought in the U.S. against the company because its supplier in Central America is repressing union activity by brutal means.

A second obstacle Goldman identifies is whether the company undertook any enforceable contractual obligation because the obligation in the text, being only to "encourage" compliance by suppliers and contractors, is subject only to a monitoring system that makes no provision for judicial action. These two features make contractual intent and standing to enforce questionable. Prof. Goldman points to *Doe v. Wal-Mart Stores, Inc.*, 527 F.3d 677 (9th Cir. 2009), in which the United States Court of Appeals for the Ninth Circuit upheld the dismissal of a complaint against Wal-Mart brought by a number of workers in foreign factories supplying Wal-Mart for Wal-Mart's failure to abide by its "Standards for Suppliers," a unilateral corporate policy statement. These standards governed its suppliers' working conditions: child and forced labor, pay, and discrimination. But the court held that as Wal-Mart's Standards made no promise to these employees, Wal-Mart assumed no duty to them to enforce its policy.

Professor Goldman's caution is, obviously, well placed; but, even so, the *Wal-Mart* case would seem to be distinguishable insofar as what is under consideration here is not a unilaterally-issued policy – a Corporate Code – but what calls itself a contract (or "agreement") made with an international trade union federation. Moreover, "best efforts" clauses have been held to be contractually enforceable in other contexts. An obligation to "encourage" compliance by suppliers and contractors can be read as more than aspirational; that is, as a commitment – at least to attempt to do something meaningful, though provision for a separate monitoring system could be read as an intent to preclude external, i.e. judicial, intervention. On that, it should be noted that the instrument makes no express preclusion of judicial enforcement, however.

Goldman goes on to discuss other potentially applicable legal avenues for non-compliance: consumer protection law, citing *Kasky v. Nike, Inc.*, 27 Cal. 4th 939 (Cal. 2002), holding that public representations about labor conditions in Nike's supplier plants was commercial speech subject to liability for factual misrepresentation; and possible action under securities law, for deceiving investors on the basis of the company's public assurances of its social responsibilities.

An aspect of U.S. labor law that is often neglected in that context is the so-called "hot cargo" clause, section 8(e) of the Labor Act, which renders unenforceable an agreement between an employer and a labor organization whereby the employer agrees to "cease doing business with any other person." To the extent the IFA is read as an agreement by the employer not to subcontract to or purchase from contractors or suppliers *in the United States* who refuse to observe the labor standards the IFA sets out, the enforceability – but only the enforceability – of that obligation could be challenged before the NLRB. One element of analysis here echoes what was just discussed above: whether the global union federation is a "labor organization" under the Labor Act; that is, whether, to track the definitional requirements, employees participate in it and whether it acts in whole or part for the purpose of dealing with employers over wages, hours, and working conditions. But another element derives from the fact that §8(e) has not been read literally by the United States Supreme Court in other settings and its application in the effort to increase adherence to international labor standards has no legal precedent, one way or the other. At least this much is clear: inasmuch as US labor law has no extraterritorial application, §8(e) would be no bar to the enforcement of the IFA in the United States in application to contractors and suppliers abroad.

PRIMARY SOURCES

The National Labor Relations Act, 29 U.S.C. §152(5):

> The term "labor organization" means any organization of any kind, or any agency or employee representation committee or plan, in which employees participate and which exists for the purpose, in whole or in part, of dealing with employers concerning grievances, labor disputes, wages, rates of pay, hours of employment, or conditions of work.

The Labor Management Relations Act, §301(a):

> Suits for violation of contracts between an employer and a labor organization representing employees in an industry affecting commerce as defined in this Act ... may be

brought in any district court of the United States having jurisdiction of the parties, without respect to the amount in controversy or without regard to the citizenship of the parties.

References and suggested readings

The section 8(e) issue is discussed by Matthew Finkin, *Employer Neutrality as Hot Cargo: Thoughts on the Making of Labor Policy*, 20 NOTRE DAME J. L. ETHICS & PUB. POL'Y 541 (2006).

On June 19, 2012, a new organization, IndustriAll Global Union, was created bringing together the affiliates from former global federations including ICEM. *See* http://www.industriall-union.org/about-us. Its mission includes the bringing together of workers across supply chains.

Questions for Discussion – Problem 21

1. An ILO Convention bears upon the domestic law of the nation that ratifies it; that is, the ratifying country obligates itself to bring its law into conformity. There is scant means to compel it to do so, however; and its labor law remains domestic law.

   Most of the effort to connect labor rights to trade has centered on "soft law" – the complaint processes of the OECD, or under multilateral or bilateral trade agreements, and the like – which are ultimately of a political character. In addition, the movement for corporate social responsibility has pressed for the adoption of corporate codes – sometimes drafted by non-governmental organizations (NGOs), sometimes drafted by companies unilaterally, some with internal, some with external monitoring mechanisms, and some with no provision for monitoring at all.

   Yet another feature of the scene, pressed especially in Europe by European Works Councils (EWCs) and global union federations (GUFs) are International Framework Agreements (IFAs) of which the ICEM-Norske Skog agreement is but one. Sir Bob Hepple has supplied an overview:

   > Distinct from codes of conduct are framework collective agreements negotiated by trade unions. The fundamental problem is that international trade union structure cannot match the globalized activities of TNCs [transnational corporations] to negotiate framework agreements covering all the countries and sectors in which a TNC operates. The main international federation is the ICFTU, and there are 10 sectoral federations. Between 1994 and 2004, five of these sectoral federations negotiated a total of 31 agreements with TNCs. All but two of these TNCs are European-based and one of the critical factors in persuading these TNC to

negotiate has been the European Works Councils Directive compelling the establishments of EWCs. The agreements are, in the ICFTU's words, only "the first building blocks in an international system of industrial relations".

An analysis of the content of the 31 framework agreements... shows that their main point is to commit the TNCs in question to the core international labour standards of eliminating child and forced labour, the principle of equality and non-discrimination, and rights to freedom of association and collective bargaining. ... The number and scope of these agreements is likely to increase rapidly in those sectors where TNCs are vulnerable to consumer and shareholder pressures. For beleaguered international union federations, they present an opportunity to raise their profile. These unions have been able to take advantage of the EWCs to initiate such agreements. With few exceptions, it seems unlikely that US-based TNCs will be ready to bargain with unions on these issues.

BOB HEPPLE, LABOUR LAW AND GLOBAL TRADE 76–7 (2005) (footnotes omitted).

2. Two prominent students of the question have this to say in the opening of a discussion well worth reading in full:

[W]e see IFAs, individually and collectively, as contested terrains, some leading in a positive direction, some leading in a negative direction, and some leading nowhere at all.

IFAs are not only about regulating multinationals. They are also about the relations between unions within and across countries and sectors. They are not only about unionizing workers in the United States and elsewhere in the world. They are also about the future of industrial relations within and across countries. IFAs, therefore, have political and organizational implications regarding both transnational regulation and transnational collaboration and it is because of all these sets of concerns that we should care about the paths that they are creating and those they are closing.

Dimitris Stevis and Michael Fichter, *International Framework Agreements in the United States: Escaping, Protecting, or Globalizing Social Dialogues?*, 33 COMP. LAB. L. & POL'Y J. 667, 667 (2012).

3. If some form of transnational labor regulation is socially and economically desirable – toward what end and by what means? Prof. Alan Hyde poses a useful starting point for discussion:

Global labour regulation should focus on labour conditions that are not the source of national comparative advantage (such as child labour and very unsafe work practices), which persist because collective action problems impede their eradication, and should not focus on labour conditions that are legitimate sources of comparative advantage, since such regulation will be ineffective and destroy the trust necessary for regulation to function in the absence of meaningful sanctions ...

> What is needed is a blurring of the boundaries, so that commercializing work [by outsourcing to contractors and other labor market intermediaries] is not understood as total relief from legal liability, and a targeted approach to make the ultimate consumer of labour responsible for some, but not all, of the worst labour conditions.

ALAN HYDE, *Responsibility for Labour Conditions Down the Production Chain*, *in* CHALLENGING THE LEGAL BOUNDARIES OF WORK REGULATION Ch. 5 (Judy Fudge, Shae McCrystal & Kamala Sankran eds., 2012).

4. Are the standards the IFA proposes your company require its suppliers and contractors to address of any concern to the company? If not, why not? If so, why so? Is it as a matter of good public relations, because of your firm's brand name, its reputation among consumers is of importance? What if the company's situation does not make it vulnerable to publicity or corporate campaigns generated by groups concerned about labor rights?

5. Before drawing up your recommendation, would you be concerned about: (1) how representative the global federation is? Whether the U.S. unions who are members of it have been involved in drafting the IFA – or have an interest in unionizing your company's employees? (2) Whether you should consult your contractors and suppliers before deciding? (3) Whether your contractors and suppliers should be asked to consult their national unions – or whether your company should? (4) How the monitoring system will be implemented at the local level?

6. What purpose would be served by executing the IFA that would not be served by a corporate code? See generally, IVANKA MAMIC, IMPLEMENTING CODES OF CONDUCT: HOW BUSINESSES MANAGE SOCIAL PERFORMANCE IN GLOBAL SUPPLY CHAINS (2004).

7. Is Hepple correct that, as a U.S.-based transnational, you would be reluctant to deal with the global union federation? Why? To what extent does the foregoing advice on the legal aspects of the IFA play a role in your recommendation? What is your recommendation?

PART VIII

IN LARGER COMPARATIVE CONTEXT

Twenty-one specific problems in six separate areas that multinational corporate human resource managers are likely to confront have been posed. These have been worked through the laws of five very different countries. The analyses and discussion of them has wanted in neither detail nor nuance. The time has come to step back from the welter of detail to placc what has been learned about these legal systems in a larger comparative context. To begin with we will offer six conceptual categories to guide the discussion: (A) legal origin or family; (B) legal culture; (C) the political economy of capitalism; (D) national values; (E) the transmission and transplantation of law; and (F) the diffusion of corporate culture and managerial practice across borders. We will conclude with (G) on the overall implications for practice and policy.

A. LEGAL ORIGIN, LEGAL FAMILY

From the nineteenth century, at least, legal scholars have taken to devising a taxonomy of European legal systems. As Jaakko Husa observes:

> Comparative law is and has always been fascinated by the idea of thinking and conceiving of law as a representative of a larger category of being. The epistemic need to draw a global map of law has been the undeniable motivational force; there is even today an urge to rise above the micro-level complexities and a desire to try to conceive law as a global phenomenon. For some comparative lawyers to think globally equals to stress the commonalities, i.e. that which is similar (integrative comparison), whereas, to others this means to appreciate and to underline the differences (contrastive comparison) between legal systems.

Jaakko Husa, *Legal Families* in ELGAR ENCYCLOPEDIA OF COMPARATIVE LAW 491, 492 (Jan Smits ed., 2d. ed. 2012) (reference omitted.) *See also* H. Patrick Glenn, *Comparative Legal Families and Comparative Legal Traditions* in OXFORD HANDBOOK OF COMPARATIVE LAW Ch. 12 (Mathias Reimann & Reinhard Zimmermann eds., 2006).

A traditional taxonomy, but one that has received renewed attention in recent years, deals with the emergence of two different legal traditions in Western Europe: the common law, with roots in England, and the civil law, with roots on the Continent. (Some see a further distinction within the civil law tradition between that rooted in France and that rooted in Germany.) Each was extended by borrowing to Eastern Europe and more widely abroad by colonial rule. The common law is characterized as privileging the role of judicial discretion over code-making by legislatures and by the role of juries. In contrast, the civil law is characterized by less judicial independence, the unimportance of juries, and the greater role of legislated codes – notably the French *Code Napoléon* and the German *Bürgerliches Gesetzbuch* (BGB).

On this ground, some argue further that common law countries tend to rely more on markets and contracts, and civil law countries tend to rely more on direct state intervention and regulation. Thus, it is argued, civil law countries tend to regulate markets – including the labor market – more extensively than do common law countries, the latter accordingly preserving (or reserving) greater room for freedom of contract. By the same token, common law countries should have less generous social security benefits by virtue of greater reliance on markets for their provision.

Similar claims have also been made for connecting a nation's legal origin – its family – to its economic efficiency and productivity. Simon Deakin and Katharina Pisto have collated some of the leading arguments advancing and critiquing the legal origin theory, with an emphasis on the economic aspects of the argumentation. Students of the subject will find it an invaluable resource. LEGAL ORIGIN THEORY (Simon Deakin and Katherina Pisto eds., 2012). Of particular concern here is the application of that theory to the labor market and to the employment relationship. Juan Botero and his colleagues have taken that on. They have coded and indexed the labor and employment laws of 85 countries, including the five represented here: the higher the number of their index, the greater the degree of employee-protective legal intervention. Their results for the five countries represented here are set out in Table VIII.1.

Table VIII.1 Legal origin and labor regulation

Country	Employment Law Index	Collective Relations Law Index	Social Security Law Index	Log GNP per capita (1997)	Legal origin
Australia*	0.3515	0.3720	0.7820	10.0010	English
Brazil	0.5676	0.3780	0.5471	8.4638	French
Germany	0.7015	0.6071	0.6702	10.2608	German
Japan	0.1639	0.6280	0.6417	10.5545	German
U.S.	0.2176	0.2589	0.6461	10.3129	English

Note: *These data pre-date the Fair Work Act. The numbers assigned to Australia in the first two columns would be higher today.

Source: Juan Botero et al., *The Regulation of Labor*, 119 Q.J. ECON. 1339 (2004) Table III.

The methodology of coding and indexing, the historical grounding of the common law–civil law distinction, and the claimed empirical consequences of it have been criticized by Beth Ahlering and Simon Deakin, *Labor Regulation, Corporate Governance, and Legal Origin: A Case of Institutional Complementarity?*, 41 LAW & SOCIETY REV. 865 (2007). A close reading of both the Botero group's paper and the Ahlering & Deakin response is *strongly* recommended. Ahlering and Deakin's summary might serve to instigate that closer examination:

> There is no reliable basis on which it can be said that common law institutions are more conducive to economic growth than their civil law counterparts, and the more careful analyses of the legal origin school do not in fact claim that there is such a link. To the extent that it serves as a proxy for the social and economic effect of laws, the labor index could be used to throw light on the welfare and efficiency effects of regulation and to provide some indications of the likely strength of national-level complementarities between labor law and corporate governance. However, the pointers provided by the legal origin approach would need to be supplemented by more detailed institutional accounts of individual country systems for the findings to be regarded as reliable.

Id at 892. The complementarities between labor law and corporate governance will be discussed under the rubric of "Varieties of Capitalisms" below.

An equally rigorous critique of the theory not connected specifically to labor law but focused on its general connection to the promotion of efficient outcomes has been mounted by Nuno Garoupa and Andrew Morriss, *The Fable of the Codes: The Efficiency of the Common Law, Legal Origins, and the Codification Movements*, 2012 U. IL. L. REV. 1443 (2012). They painstakingly unpack the claimed connection between legal family and economic efficiency. They propose instead that analysis proceed by asking specific questions of a legal system's ability to generate economic growth: (1) the costs of identifying and applying efficient rules, (2) the system's ability to restrain rent-seeking in rule formulation and application, (3) the cost of adapting rules to changing circumstances, (4) the transaction costs to parties needing to learn the law, (5) the ease of contracting around rules, and (6) the costs of transitions between systems.

Comments and Questions for Discussion

1. Garoupa and Morriss share Ahlering and Deakin's criticism of the distinction between judge-made law (common law) and legislation or code-based regulation (civil law) on the ground that the latter relies as much as the former on adjudication for implementation and refinement. Nor, they argue, does the form in which the law is embodied say much

about the degree of flexibility that is actually allowed. As Ahlering and Deakin put it, "The social or economic effect of a given legal rule can only be understood by seeing legal rules as part of a system of interlinked norms, some of which are extralegal in nature." *Id.* at 883.

2. A crude "first cut" on the claims made about and for legal origin could proceed thusly: Australia and the U.S. have common law derived labor law systems. Germany and Japan have German civil law derived labor law systems. Brazil has a French civil law derived system of labor law. Go back over each of the problems dealing with employee voice, discrimination, privacy, dignity, and dismissal:
   (a) Do Australia and the United States regulate in each of these areas less extensively than do Brazil, Germany, and Japan? i.e. do they leave more room for contract?
   (b) In regulating, do Australia and the United States rely more on judges and less on statutes or codes than Brazil, Germany, or Japan?
   (c) Do Australia and the United States rely more on lay judgment (juries) in the application of law than do Brazil, Germany, and Japan? If so, what is the relationship of lay judgment to economic efficiency?
   (d) Do the common law countries rely more on individual litigation than direct government intervention?

3. Again, go back over each of these problems. How much flexibility does management actually have in effecting its desired ends?

4. Return to the questions Garoupa and Morriss pose. Which legal system conduces toward more efficient labor market outcomes? (Do we need to think more about what efficiency means?)

B. LEGAL CULTURE

David Nelkin has observed that the concept of a legal culture "can help make comparisons of legal systems more sociologically meaningful by alerting us to the way aspects of law are themselves embedded in larger frameworks of social structure and culture that constitute and reveal the place of law in society." David Nelkin, *Legal Culture* in ELGAR ENCYCLOPEDIA OF COMPARATIVE LAW 480, 483 (Jan Smits ed., 2d ed. 2012). This includes the very conception of what is meant by "law" – as we saw in connection with Problem 21 – and the role of precedent or the role of general clauses vis-à-vis more detailed regulation, even of the detail in the drafting of legal instruments – as we saw in the plant closure agreements in Problem 10 – as well as the role of lawyers in society, and a good deal more.

> Legal culture can be discerned in different approaches to regulation, administration and dispute resolution. There may be important contrasts in the degree to which given controversies are subject to law, the role of other expertises, the part played by "alternatives" to law, including not only arbitration and mediation but also the many "infrastructural" ways of discouraging or resolving disputes. Attention must also be given to the role of other religious or ethical norms and the ambit of the informal.

Id. (reference omitted). *See generally*, COMPARATIVE LAW AND SOCIETY (David Clark ed., 2012) (Pt. I) (on other disciplinary approaches) and David Nelkin, *Legal Cultures*, *id.* Ch. 15.

One aspect of a nation's culture is the extent to which it is "juridified," i.e. insofar as law might pervade – or drench – social and economic life; here, as it bears upon the employment relationship. "Juridification" has been identified as "the pretention to engineer and control social change through law. Jürgen Habermas sees a 'colonization' of the lifeworld by law. Taking a more neutral stance one could speak of an increasing penetration of legal rules and procedures into all walks of life." Willibald Steinmetz, *Introduction* in PRIVATE LAW AND SOCIAL INEQUALITY IN THE INDUSTRIAL AGE: COMPARING LEGAL CULTURES IN BRITAIN, FRANCE, GERMANY, AND THE UNITED STATES 1, 23 (Willibald Steinmetz ed., 2000). However, it can be argued more positively that tolerably clear and well administered legal rules can facilitate exchange and efficiency or, on the other hand, that the actual penetration of law can be rather shallow notwithstanding a well-developed texture of rules. One of the questions Garoupa and Morriss pose is how accessible the legal system really is and what the transaction costs attendant on the application of law are.

Questions for Discussion

1. Consider the extent to which the countries under study here are "juridified": of the extent to which employers might find their freedom of action constrained by law, of the likelihood of those constraints actually being resorted to and applied, and of the costs of that application. In that connection it might be well to reconsider the material set out in the *Note on Wrongful Discharge Litigation* in Problem 10 and in the *Concluding Note on Alternate Dispute Resolution* in Problem 13.

2. Consider also the extent to which non-legal constraints – communal norms which may be expressed in disapproval, protest, and other individual and group action – may also and, perhaps, more effectively limit managerial action. Return to the *Note on Dignity: The Case of Captive Audition* at the end of Part IV. It is unheard of – simply "not done" – for employers in Australia, Brazil, or Germany to oppose unionization, or particular unions, by conducting a captive audience speech; that is why there is no case law in these countries on the question of legality. But, as there are no judicial precedents, why don't these employers test the law by holding captive audience assemblies?

C. POLITICAL ECONOMY: VARIETIES OF CAPITALISM

Another comparative approach to macroeconomic institutions looks to the identification of institutional complementarities: one institution may raise the return from another and when it does so it can be said to complement it; and, where they are complementary, they can combine to add to a nation's economic performance. This manner of thinking embodies what has come to be called a "varieties of capitalism" approach. *See generally*, VARIETIES OF CAPITALISM: THE INSTITUTIONAL FOUNDATIONS OF COMPARATIVE ADVANTAGE (D. Soskice & P. Hall eds., 2001).

Students of this approach have posited two ideal types: Liberal Market Systems and Coordinated Market Systems. The United States and Germany are taken to be archetypical of these models. The focus is on the intersection of the institutions of corporate governance with the institutions of labor law and employment relations. The intersection can be examined at the firm level – how the two interact in the governance of the enterprise – or it can be examined at the level of the market, for example, whether labor markets are regulated across the board or left for collective (or individual) agreement.

This approach has been explained by Peter Hall and Daniel Gingerich. Taking the United States as the archetypal Liberal Market Economy, they note of it that

> firms face large equity markets marked by high levels of transparency and dispersed shareholding, where firms' access to external finance depends heavily on publicly assessable criteria such as market valuation. Regulatory regimes allow hostile takeovers that depend on share price, rendering managers sensitive to current profitability. Because trade unions are relatively weak and employment protection low, labor markets are fluid and wage-setting primarily a matter of contract between workers and individual employers. Because labor markets are fluid, workers have incentives to invest in

general skills that can be taken to other jobs, and, because industry associations are weak, firms lack the capacity to mount the collaborative training programs that confer industry-specific skills ... Top managers enjoy substantial authority over all aspects of firm strategy, including layoffs.

Peter Hall & David Gingerich, *Varieties of Capitalism and the Institutional Complementarities in the Macroeconomy*, MPIFG Discussion Paper No. 04/5 (2004) at pp. 8–9.

Taking Germany as the archetypical Coordinated Market Economy, they explain that firms there are

> closely connected by dense networks of cross-shareholding and membership in influential employers associations. These networks provide for substantial exchanges of private information, allowing firms to develop reputations that permit them some access to capital on terms that depend more heavily on reputation than share value. Accordingly, managers are less sensitive to current profitability. In the presence of strong trade unions, powerful works councils, and high levels of employment protection, labor markets are less fluid and job tenures longer. In most industries, wage-setting is coordinated by trade unions and employers associations that also supervise collaborative training schemes, providing workers with industry-specific skills and assurances of available positions if they invest in them ... Hemmed in by powerful workforce representatives and business networks, top managers have less scope for unilateral action, and firms typically adhere to more consensual styles of decision-making.

Id. at 9.

The two archetypes have been displayed graphically (see Table VIII.2).

Table VIII.2 Complementarities in corporate governance and labor law

	Pattern of shareholder ownership	Protection of minority shareholders	Employee representation at firm level	Regulation of the labor market
Liberal Market Systems	dispersed	high	voluntarist	partial
Coordinated Market Systems	concentrated	low	integrative	universalist

Note: *Integrative* denotes the incorporation of employee voice directly into firm decision-making. *Voluntarist* denotes a reliance on collective bargaining, whether agreed to or required by law. *Partial* stands for a limited scope accorded to labor market regulation by law. *Universalist* denotes a more wide-ranging role for law.

Source: Ahlering & Deakin, supra, Table 1 of 876.

Hall and Gingerich test for the complementarity of corporate governance and labor relations *within* each of these models and conclude that the effects are positive in terms of economic growth. They conclude that

> rates of growth are highest where competitive markets coordinate both spheres *or* where institutional support for strategic coordination is high in both. Where labor relations are strategically coordinated, substantial efficiencies seem to be available from strategic coordination in the sphere of corporate governance. Where corporate governance is dominated by fluid equity markets, however, rates of growth are substantially higher when labor markets are also fluid and competitive.

Hall & Gingerich, supra at 26–7 (emphasis added).

Complementarity has implications for the portability of law, to be discussed in the next section. But it is well here to return to Garoupa and Morriss. They suggest that there may be costs in transferring rules that are efficient in the context of one system into another system that functions along different lines. Whether that might be so and if so, to what extent and with what cost offsetting benefits is considered in the discussion in Section E, infra.

To illuminate what the theory suggests, let us compare the two paradigmatic states – Germany and the U.S. If managers in Germany, not driven by shareholder value, need not be as concerned as their U.S. counterparts about the firm's performance in this quarter vis-à-vis the same quarter in the previous year, if they are less driven by stock prices, if it is difficult to dismiss employees, and if employees expect long-term commitments, the firm is more likely to invest in skills training and upgrading – even general skills that are not firm specific, that are portable – because those employees will remain with the firm and the firm will recoup the sunk costs over time by greater employee productivity. If, however, employees are easy to dismiss and do not expect long-term commitments, and if firms are influenced more by stock price and short-term economic gains, firms will be reluctant to invest in employee training for fear their sunk costs will not be recouped and that employees will be poached by competitors or – ever with a weather eye on the labor market – will seek out better-paying jobs. Thus, a law requiring firms to devote resources to its workforce's general skills development would either echo or reinforce an institution already common in a Coordinated Market System, but might not be *firm* cost effective – despite a potentially large macroeconomic boost – in a Liberal Market System.

> The pursuit of financial performance is a central principle of corporate governance and interest to shareholders. This presumption favours letting a CEO follow the financial tail of profits. When times are favourable, the interests of shareholders and employees are much aligned. However, when times change their interests diverge. The differences [are reflected] in how law and corporate governance structures protect those different interests. The interests of employees are protected by labour law, workplace health and safety laws, but they have no guarantees of permanent employment. The case is almost the opposite for shareholders, who can be permanent if they wish, but they have almost no other legal protections. Shareholders get the promise of corporate executives to do their best to make a profit. The lack of other legal protections makes that promise important.
>
> Head of Compensation and Benefits, Shipping/Natural Resources Sector

> By virtue of their ability to locate operations in other countries, MNCs have a new bargaining chip for negotiating with their home governments – the threat of moving current business out of the country. Similarly, they have a bargaining chip to wield with other governments (as well as their home government): the promise of locating new business within the country. This bargaining chip brings power to MNCs to extract tax incentives or rebates, subsidized training programs for workers, free land and even involvement in setting of labor laws.
>
> Manager, International Benefits and Compensation, Consumer Goods

Comments and Questions for Discussion

1. These materials do not attend to comparative corporate governance. But as the varieties of capitalism approach suggests, the employment relationship and employment law are embedded in a social fabric that includes corporate governance – just as, in terms of an economy's macroeconomic performance, regulation of the labor market cannot be disaggregated from the regulation of the product market. *See* the papers collected in 19 COMP. LAB. L. & POL'Y J. 280–329 (1998). For a more wide-ranging comparative overview, further recommended reading would include HANDBOOK ON INTERNATIONAL CORPORATE GOVERNANCE (C.A. Mallin ed., 2d ed. 2011), with chapters on Australia, Brazil, Germany, and Japan. For further reading on *Australia*, Richard Mitchell et al., LAW, CORPORATE

GOVERNANCE AND PARTNERSHIPS AT WORK: A STUDY OF AUSTRALIAN REGULATORY STYLE AND BUSINESS PRACTICE (2011); on *Brazil*, Robert McGee, *An Overview of Corporate Governance Practices in Brazil* in CORPORATE GOVERNANCE IN DEVELOPING ECONOMIES Ch. 31 (Robert McGee ed., 2009). On *Germany*, Dieter Sadowski, Joachim Junkes & Sabine Lindenthol, *The German Model of Corporate and Labor Governance*, 22 COMP. LAB. L. & POL'Y J. 33 (2000); on *Japan*, Takashi Araki, *A Comparative Analysis: Corporate Governance and Labor and Employment Relations in Japan*, 22 COMP. LAB. L. & POL'Y J 67 (2000); and on the *United States*, Marleen O' Connor, *Labor's Role in the American Corporate Governance Structure*, 22 COMP. LAB. L. & POL'Y J. 97 (2000). *See generally*, Sanford Jacoby, *Corporate Governance in Comparative Perspective: Prospects for Convergence*, 22 COMP. LAB. L. & POL'Y J. 5 (2000).

2. As assisted by the readings referenced above on the issues of corporate governance, and considering the analyses of the problems on the regulation of the labor market, where would you place Australia, Brazil, and Japan on a scale of liberal or coordinated market systems?

3. Based on the cases and the country responses, do you believe that the liberal markets will, over time, "liberalize" the coordinated markets, or will the coordinated markets increasingly "coordinate" the liberal markets, or will they be on separate, parallel tracks with relatively little cross-influence in the years to come?

D. NATIONAL VALUES

Nations have been distinguished one from another by their embrace of particular sets of values. These have been measured by survey data of samples of their populations or subsets of them. But, as a reading of David Hume's rumination of two centuries ago reminds us, the underlying assumption of "national character" can be treacherous ground insofar as it may so easily lend itself to stereotyping, or worse. David Hume, *Of National Character*, in 1 DAVID HUME, ESSAYS MORAL, POLITICAL, AND LITERARY, Essay XXI at 244 (T.H. Green & T.H. Grose eds., 1898). Nevertheless, survey data are there. How we interpret them – and how and why they change over time – is the stuff of social science. *See e.g.* THE CULTURAL VALUES OF EUROPE (Hans Joas & Klaus Wiegandt eds., Alex Skinner trans. 2008).

With due circumspection, a question worth briefly considering here is whether a country's labor laws tell us something about its national values, at least at a particular moment in time. This, in turn, demands that we engage with what is meant by national "values." The late sociologist, Seymour Martin Lipset, in a study that focused on a comparison of the United States with Japan, had this to say:

> Values are well-entrenched, culturally determined sentiments produced by institutions or major historical events … They result in deep beliefs, such as deference or antagonism to authority, individualism or group-centeredness, and egalitarianism or elitism, which form the organizing principles of societies. Value-based explanations may relate to institutional differences to other countries, for example, constitutional constraints on state power, divided or united authority structures, religious systems. They also bear on behavioral outcomes, such as litigiousness or propensity to use government to deal with social problems – welfare, health, unemployment.

Seymour Martin Lipset, AMERICAN EXCEPTIONALISM: A DOUBLE-EDGED SWORD 25 (1996).

While an appreciation for societal values is key to understanding the many observed differences in the laws governing the workplace problems presented in this book, the law in each country is an incomplete and possibly lagging reflection of national values. A full analysis of the underlying values in the five nations selected is beyond the scope of this book, but survey responses on selected values covered in the World Values Survey and other sources may be instructive for the student puzzling through the legal differences.

First we present some selected data from the World Values Survey, which is administered by a global network of social scientists through the World Values Survey Association.[1] The data involve stratified random samples, with data presented here on each of the five countries in this book.[2] Note that in some places we do not present all of the possible categories of survey responses on a given item, but just a particularly salient category (such as the percentage responding "agree" to a statement). We have deployed some of this in considering Problems 3, 5, and 6, and it might be well to return to those references and to those discussions in considering this section.

While the responses presented below reflect distinct national tendencies in the values of each country, the data should be treated with some caution as there can also be substantial variation within a country by region, gender, age, race,

1 http://www.worldvaluessurvey.org/index_organization.

2 Sample sizes are: Australia N = 1,238; Brazil N = 1,042; Germany N = 1,408; Japan N = 1,496; United States N = 2,014. The surveys in Australia and Japan were in 2005 and the surveys in Brazil, Germany, and the United States were in 2006.

economic status and other factors. Also, these are simple percentages, not more extensive, theory-driven multivariate analysis such as research with the World Values Survey on issues of religion,[3] democracy,[4] and other topics.

Figure VIII.1 presents responses on a scale of one to ten, with the low numbers reflecting the view that "incomes should be made more equal" and high numbers reflecting the view that "we need larger income differences as incentives." As the figure indicates, income equality is most highly valued by respondents in Germany, while respondents in Japan and the United States place the lowest value on it.

Figure VIII.1 Views on income inequality

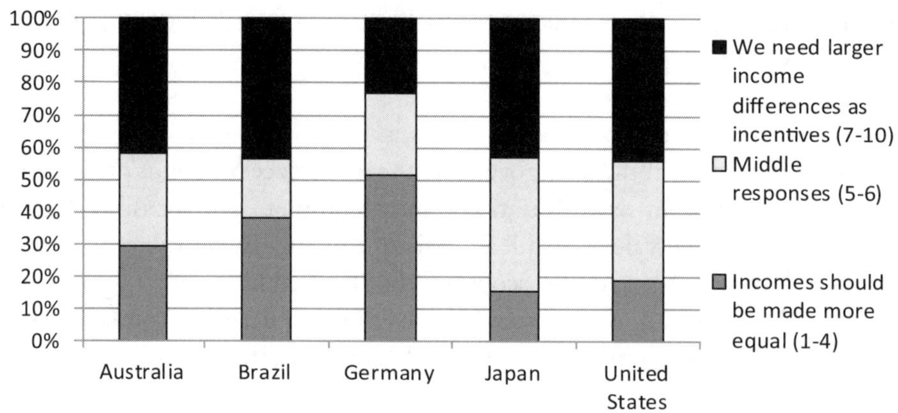

Source: Chart developed from World Values Survey Online Data Analysis (weighted responses), http://www.wvsevsdb.com.

Views on individual and government responsibility are highlighted in Figure VIII.2, with low numbers indicating that government should take more responsibility and high numbers indicating that individuals should do so. Respondents in Brazil, Germany, and Japan give the highest support for government responsibility, while respondents in the United States and Australia accord greater responsibility to individuals.

3 Nate Breznau, Valerie A. Lykes, Jonathan Kelley, M. D. R. Evans, *A Clash of Civilizations? Preferences for Religious Political Leaders in 86*, Nations, 50 J. FOR THE SCIENTIFIC STUDY OF RELIGION 671 (2011).

4 Ronald Inglehart and Christian Welzel, *Changing Mass Priorities: The Link between Modernization and Democracy*, 8 REFLECTIONS 551 (2010).

Figure VIII.2 Views on individual and government responsibility

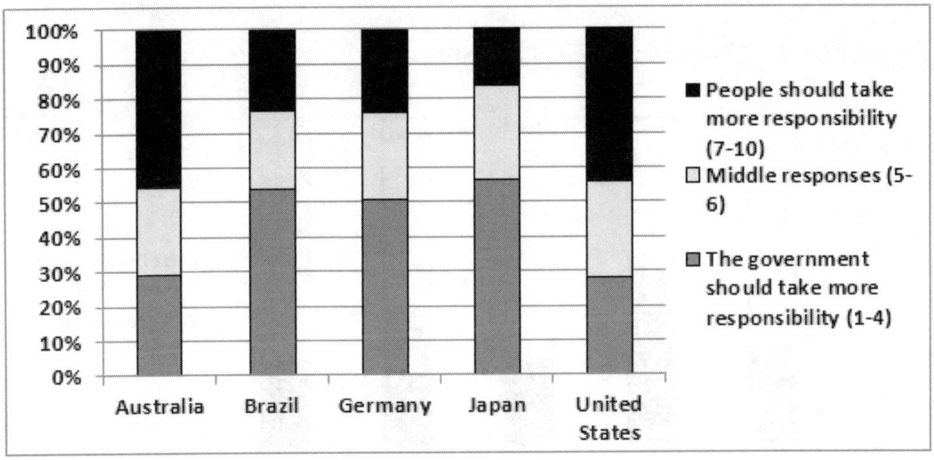

Source: Chart developed from World Values Survey Online Data Analysis (weighted responses), http://www.wvsevsdb.com.

Confidence in government is indicated in Figure VIII.3, with responses of "A great deal" and "Quite a lot" combined together. Respondents from Japan indicate the greatest confidence in government, though at least half of the respondents in all the countries express confidence.

Figure VIII.3 Confidence in government

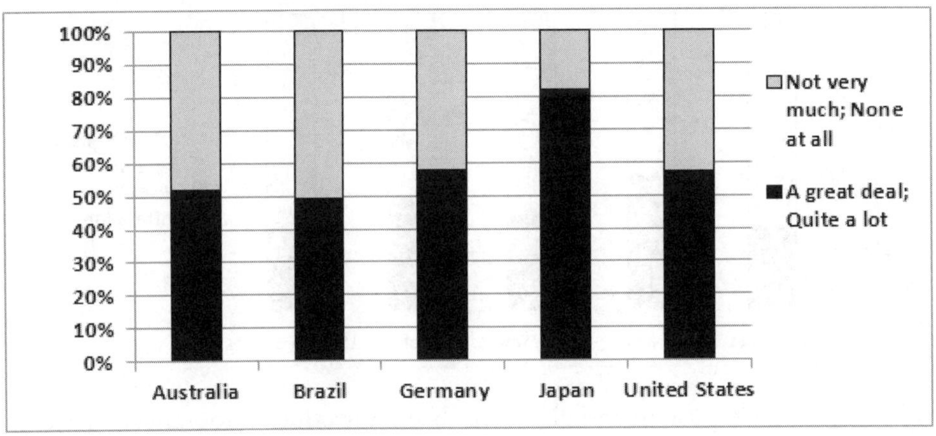

Source: Chart developed from World Values Survey Online Data Analysis (weighted responses), http://www.wvsevsdb.com.

Confidence in major companies is indicated in Figure VIII.4, with responses of "A great deal" and "Quite a lot" combined together. Only Brazil has more than half of the respondents expressing confidence in major companies, with less than 30 percent of respondents from Australia, Germany and the United States expressing confidence.

Figure VIII.4 Confidence in major companies

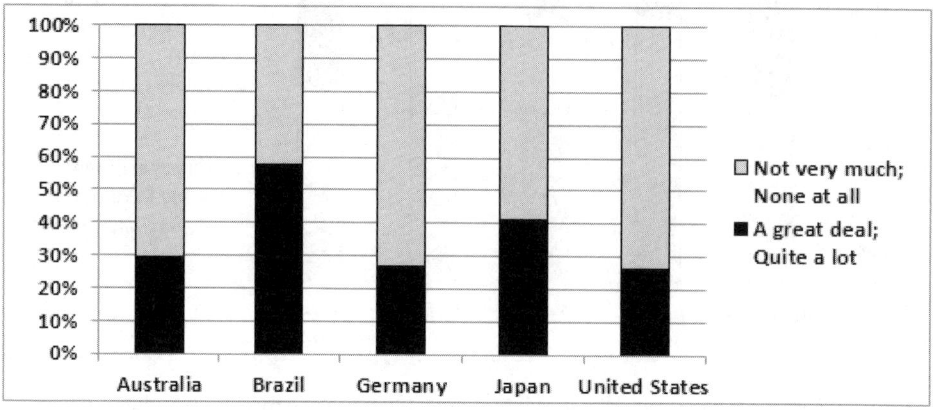

Source: Chart developed from World Values Survey Online Data Analysis (weighted responses), http://www.wvsevsdb.com.

Confidence in labor unions is indicated in Figure VIII.5, with responses of "A great deal" and "Quite a lot" combined together. Interestingly, the confidence in labor unions closely parallels the confidence in major corporations in each case.

Figure VIII.5 Confidence in labor unions

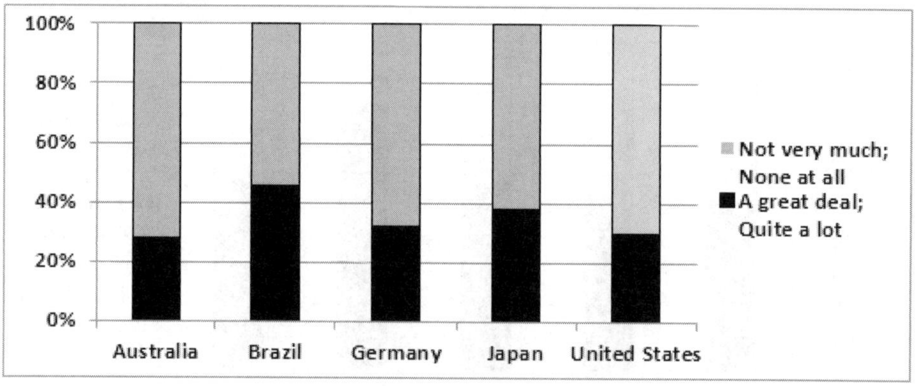

The concept of post-materialism has been introduced to reflect views in societies that go beyond economic and physical security to focus on autonomy and self-expression. A combination of responses to survey questions from the World Values Survey are added together to reflect these views – the value accorded autonomy and self-expression – and these are presented in Figure VIII.6. Australia and Germany stand out with the strongest post-materialist views, though only about 20 percent of the population hold strong views in this direction. The United States, Japan, and Brazil have stronger views on the materialist dimension, though a number of Australian respondents have more post-materialist views (indicating a bimodal distribution).

Figure VIII.6 Materialist and post-materialist views

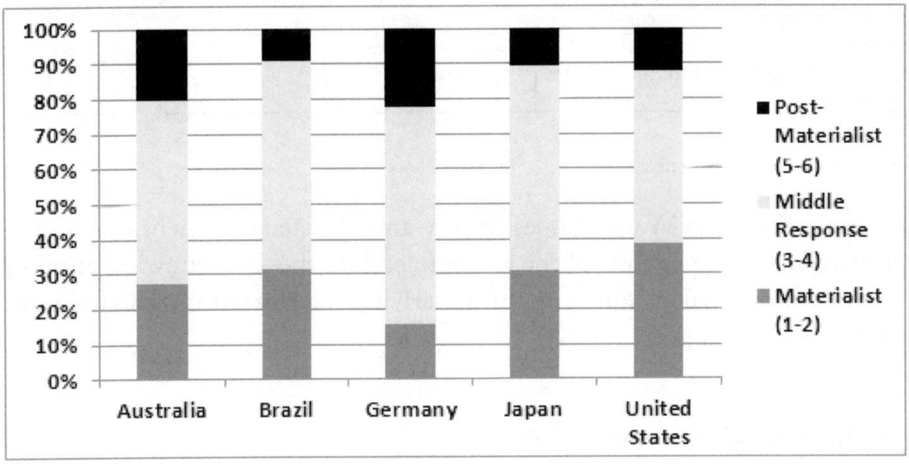

Source: Chart developed from Work Values Survey Online Data Analysis (weighted responses; Inglehart 12 item post-materialism scale), http://www.wvsevsdb.com.

In addition to the World Values Survey, another indicator of national cultures can be found in dimensions of culture advanced by Geert Hofstede.[5] Figure VIII.7 features three cultural dimensions that are commonly used in cross-cultural comparisons, power distance, individualism, and long-term orientation. In each case, the ratings are on a scale from a low score of zero to a high score of 100. Brazil and Japan stand out as having higher levels of acceptance of inequality in the distribution of power, as well as having a longer-term orientation. The United States and Australia stand out as being more individualistic. This classification is broadly consistent with the results from the World Values Survey.

5 Geert Hofstede, CULTURE'S CONSEQUENCES: INTERNATIONAL DIFFERENCES IN WORK-RELATED VALUES (2d ed. 1984).

Figure VIII.7 Comparison of national cultures along three of Hofstede's dimensions

	Australia	*Brazil*	*Germany*	*Japan*	*United States*
Power Distance (acceptance by less powerful members of unequal power distribution – high score)	36	69	35	54	40
Individualism (degree of interdependence of members of society – high score)	90	38	67	46	91
Long-Term Orientation (future-oriented – high score, versus short-term, historically oriented – low score)	31	65	31	80	29

Source: http://geert-hofstede.com.

The results from the World Values Survey and Hofstede's dimensions do not represent definitive portraits of the values in each of the five countries, but they do provide additional insights into the underlying cultures within which the law operates in each country.

Questions and Comments

1. Return to the problems we have discussed. To what extent do these countries' labor and employment laws match up with the survey data on:
   (a) the role of individual contracting and self-representation in contract as opposed to reliance on the government to assure acceptable employment outcomes;
   (b) acceptance of the employer's power to act unilaterally in contrast with the role of collective voice;
   (c) the desire for autonomy or privacy-respecting measures in contrast to the desire for pay and benefits.

2. Seymour Martin Lipset's study a generation ago compared the U.S. to Japan on several scales:
   (a) equalitarian/hierarchy;
   (b) rights/duties;
   (c) independence (inner directed)/dependence (other directed);
   (d) heterogeneity/homogeneity;
   (e) active/reactive;
   (f) open/closed.

   Some of these are echoed in some of the laws treated in the foregoing problems: the extent to which a nation's laws are influenced by the law in foreign jurisdictions would be an indication of openness, for example; or a more expansive approach to classes protected from employment discrimination would be an indication of the value attached to heterogeneity.

Again, though this overlaps with question 1, asked in this section above, it might be instructive to reflect back on the problems and the laws they take up from the perspective of the values they reflect.

E. LEGAL TRANSMISSION AND TRANSPLANTATION

David Gerber reminds us of a feature of a taxonomic approach to comparative law, whether of legal origin or even of varieties of capitalism, that it

> has relatively little to say about how to categorize new issues or about categorizing "law in action" rather than "law on the books." Most of the attention has involved formal characteristics of legal systems. That is part of the picture, but … [it] … provides little guidance in dealing with change.

David Gerber, *Comparative Law and Global Regulatory Consequence: The Usage of Competition Law* in PRACTICE AND THEORY IN COMPARATIVE LAW 120, 127 (Maurice Adams & Jaco Bomhoft eds., 2012).

But law, including labor and employment law, does change; and, as the Australian case evidences, sometimes the change can be radical and accomplished with astonishing rapidity. Why change occurs presents a larger question than this little coursebook can take on. But one feature of it is the role of non-domestic legal influence – of the capacity for the law in one state to be influenced by or even to borrow law from another. Such influence and borrowing in labor law has long been a feature of the European scene. *See generally*, THE MAKING OF LABOUR LAW IN EUROPE (Bob Hepple ed., 1986) and THE TRANSFORMATION OF LABOUR LAW IN EUROPE (Bob Hepple & Bruno Veneziani eds., 2009). Japan's civil code was taken from the German BGB and its law of collective bargaining was taken from the United States, even as it became Japanified in the process, as we have seen. And much of labor protective law enacted in the United States from the Progressive Period to the New Deal looked to Europe. *See generally*, Daniel Rodgers, ATLANTIC CROSSINGS (1998).

A classical approach to the issue of legal transplantation in labor law has been to distinguish the degree of "fit" between that which would be borrowed and the domestic legal context. This was set out in a classic article by Otto Kahn-Freund, *On Uses and Misuses of Comparative Law*, 37 MOD. L. REV. 1 (1972); but it has come in for criticism more recently.

> This approach ... seeks consistency and rationality but by doing so, it distorts reality. One problem is that it pays insufficient attention to the reasons why transplants succeed or fail. They may fail on rather specific grounds, rather than simply on lack of "fit," for example, because they are opposed by vested interests that would be adversely affected by legal change. Another problem is that this approach does not explain how transplants actually occur.

Michele Graziadei, *Comparative Law as the Study of Transplants and Receptions* in OXFORD HANDBOOK OF COMPARATIVE LAW 441, 472 (Mathias Reimann & Reinhard Zimmermann eds., 2006) (reference omitted) (comprehensively reviewing the literature). And, Graziadei stresses, transplantation does occur.

A more open-ended approach has been essayed by Jörg Fedtke:

> [T]ransplants can take place on different levels of a legal system and for a variety of reasons. Though far more often a result of decisions made by national legislators, legal borrowing can also come in the guise of judicial activity or, more gradually, through the backdoor of commercial practice ... [R]easons for using legal transplants include the harmonization of law within the framework of international agreements; the influence of attractive political ideas and concepts ... [among others]. Economic pressures create further incentives for the introduction of changes based on foreign [law] ... Finally, the global spread of increasingly similar working and living conditions has raised equally similar legal problems in societies all over the world, and – in their wake – a trend towards similar and often even identical legislative and judicial responses.

Jörg Fedtke, *Legal Transplants* in ELGAR ENCYCLOPEDIA OF COMPARATIVE LAW 550, 550–51 (Jan Smits ed., 2d ed. 2012). He goes on to explain that

> Borrowing legal ideas is a dynamic process which can take several years. The initial phase involves the identification of an appropriate model and (in most cases) more or less comprehensive adjustments of the chosen material in order to merge it successfully with the existing rules of the borrowing system. Even mere translation will thereby often increase the differences between the original and the "imitated" provision. Once they have found their way into a new environment, foreign legal ideas are then likely to be subject to substantial further change.

Id. at 551.

Discussion Comments and Questions

1. More than twenty years ago, Paul Weiler, steeped in Canadian labor law, argued that U.S. labor law could create space for a system of non-union employee participation, influenced, in part, by the German system of works councils. Paul Weiler, GOVERNING THE WORKPLACE 287–95

(1990). Stephen Befort and John Budd argued subsequently that the German works council system could and should be transplanted to the United States. Stephen Befort & John Budd, INVISIBLE HANDS, INVISIBLE OBJECTIVES: BRINGING WORKPLACE LAW AND PUBLIC POLICY INTO FOCUS 181–8 (2009). Review the discussion of German law in Part II. Note the relationship of works councils to labor unions which, as a practical albeit non-legal matter, are (or are supposed to be) mutually supportive. Note also the role of fair dismissal law in Germany (Part V) and of the additional job protections afforded works councillors. As a purely legal matter, German works council law could be enacted in the U.S. But would such a transplant take root? (On the comparative problematic of the question in a different context *see* Anthony Forsyth, *The "Transplantability" Debate Revised: Can European Social Partnership be Exported to Australia?*, 27 COMP. LAB. L. & POL'Y J. 305 (2006).) If some U.S. employers have successfully resisted unionization, why would they embrace works councils? Absent employer support, would that transplant take root?

2. In employment discrimination law, Europe has borrowed the American concept of "disparate impact," adopted by the U.S. Supreme Court in *Griggs v. Duke Power Co.*, 401 U.S. 424 (1971). In Europe, it is called "indirect discrimination." Dagmar Shiek, Lisa Waddington & Mark Bell, NON-DISCRIMINATION LAW §3.3.2 (2007). So, too, has the legal controversy in the United States surrounding "affirmative action," which commenced with a 1961 presidential Executive Order governing federal contractors, and has subsequently been echoed in Europe, where it is called "positive action." *Id.*, Ch. 7. This transplantation suggests that there might be portable responses to similar problems thrown up by advanced global capitalism of the sort Fedtke adverts to. Reconsider the data appended to Problem 5. Why is Australia more expansive than the U.S. in the scope of its non-discrimination protections, while Japan and Brazil are less so? Are there any legal – or other – barriers to an expansion of the categories in the latter jurisdictions? On the other hand, why is federal law in the U.S. less protective in scope than Australia? If the U.S. is an exporter of antidiscrimination law, why would it be impervious to importation, or, less strongly, to foreign influence?

3. The EU Data Protection Directive forbids the transmission of personally identifiable information to a state whose laws do not provide adequate protection as measured by European standards. Review those standards. Note that a number of non-European countries have brought themselves into compliance, but the United States has not. (The "safe harbor" set out

previously has been little availed of.) The more widespread acceptance in non-European states of these European-based legal principles suggests that they are, in fact, transplantable. Why has the U.S. not complied?

4. Reconsider the responses to Problem 9, to the *Note on Dignity: The Case of Captive Audition*, and, especially, to the *Note on the Concept of Personality*. Is there any legal obstacle to a U.S. court adopting a notion of personal dignity as a matter of public policy that would disallow an employer the power to control an employee's intimate association not involving a superior-subordinate relationship? If not, why has no court done so? (You might care to return to Section D, supra.)

5. Return to the discussion of the casualization of work in Problem 4. Does the shift of uncertainty in income and working time to employees (affecting millions of employees in the aggregate) present a social problem. If yes, why? If no, why not? Does it call for legal redress? If so, what might that address be? Consider the approaches taken in Australia, Germany, and Japan. Would a mandatory minimum notice period (e.g. 48 hours) ameliorate the harshness? A guarantee of minimum hours? A requirement of a pay premium? Some combination of these?

6. In view of the near ubiquitous provision for protection against arbitrary dismissal elsewhere in the developed world, what explains the absence of fair dismissal law in the United States?

F. THE DIFFUSION OF CORPORATE CULTURE AND MANAGERIAL PRACTICE

In the cross-cultural diffusion of innovation there are invariably early adopters and others that come along subsequently. Not only is the innovation important, but there is only diffusion where there are channels of communication embedded in social systems. Everett Rogers, DIFFUSION OF INNOVATIONS (1962). Further, in the diffusion of innovation and corporate culture it is predictable that there will not just be the intended results, but unintended consequences as well. *See* Robert K. Merton, *The Unanticipated Consequences of Purposive Social Action*, 1 AM. SOCIOLOGICAL REV. 894 (1936). The problems discussed in the preceding parts reveal key cross-cultural (and legal) barriers facing what can be termed "early adopters" of innovative human resource management practices, the importance of the social systems context, and a variety of unintended consequences as multinational corporations set up operations in diverse legal contexts. No corporation invests in other cultural contexts expecting to fail, but the landscape is littered with failed attempts to import culturally bound work systems.

In addition to diffusion within the "four walls" of a multinational corporation, MNCs can adopt practices from one another. It happens directly through a practice known as "benchmarking" where teams of representatives visit counterparts at firms seen as having leading practices in order to study and learn. Transmission also happens through consulting firms, movement of individuals from firm to firm in the labor market, visibility in the business press, and other means. The overall effect has been characterized as a process of institutional "isomorphism" where firms in a given industry or sector tend to look like one another. *See* P.J. DiMaggio & W. Powell, *"The Iron Cage Revisited": Institutional Isomorphism and Collective Rationality in Organizational Fields*, 48 AM. SOCIOLOGICAL REV. 147 (1984).

An astute and prominent Canadian observer of the scene has cautioned that multinational corporations generate their own "law" which is diffused throughout their operations and, in that sense, has extraterritorial effect. The "law of the workplace," he opines,

> comprises not only state labor law but also (and more importantly) formal contractual understandings; workplace customs explicitly acted on and implicitly accepted as binding by workers and managers; and low-visibility behavioral norms embedded in operating manuals, daily routines, and workplace cultures. The law of the workplace has long been understood by industrial relations practitioners and socio-legal scholars to exist apart from – and sometimes in contravention of – state law.

Harry Arthurs, *Extraterritoriality by Other Means: How Labor Law Speaks Across Borders, Conquers Minds, and Controls Workplaces Abroad*, 21 STAN. L. & POL'Y REV. 527, 528 (2010). Based on interviews with a number of labor lawyers representing multinational corporations he concluded that: the clients, not the lawyers, were the prime generators of transnational norms; and, for structural and economic reasons it was most unlikely that these would generate a common international body of labor law, a *lex laboris*.

> On the whole, it seems, transnational corporations – which tend to think globally in most respects – seem to act locally when they deal with workers. But this is not an invariable rule: when local labour standards are less favourable to their off-shore employees than conditions in the home country, a TNC will naturally take advantage of the local *status quo*; but when they are more favourable, it will argue that local operations must be made "competitive" and local labour standards brought into line with a supposed global norm.

> In a backhanded fashion, the lawyers interviewed confirmed the existence of this contradiction. They said, for example, that dealing with transnational clients presented special challenges, which differed from those of dealing with domestic clients. A very common account of relations with their US-based transnational clients centered on the necessity of "educating" these clients who generally arrived in a new host country with established human resources policies but no knowledge of local law or industrial relations practices.

Harry Arthurs, *The Role of Global Law Firms in Constructing or Obstructing a Transnational Regime of Labour Law* in RULES AND NETWORKS: THE LEGAL CULTURE OF GLOBAL BUSINESS TRANSACTIONS 273, 284 (Richard Appelbaum, William Felstiner & Volkmar Gesser eds., 2001).

Nevertheless, and as the preceding problems so richly illustrate, the diffusion of corporate culture – and policy – can break against the wall of domestic law as well as domestic custom and practice. A rather obvious failure of education – or the client's unwillingness to be educated – is evidenced in some of Wal-Mart's experience in Germany. It did establish a works council at a newly opened store. (Because white collar and non-executive managerial employees can vote for works councilors and can serve in that capacity, the establishment of a new facility staffed initially by such employees creates space for a company to found a favorable works council, where there is little or no independent union presence.) Even so, Wal-Mart did not seek the council's consent in applying its company-wide "no fraternization" and "no beard" grooming policies. These were enjoined straightaway by a German Labor Court on the failure to have sought works council consent. But, the decision was merely an interim or stop gap for even had its consent been sought the works council could not have agreed to company rules that violate the right of personality. To American lawyers that prohibition was "most startling" (Marissa Anne Pagnattaro & Ellen Purie, *Between a Rock and a Hard Place: The Conflict Between U.S. Corporate Codes of Conduct and European Privacy at Work Laws*, 28 BERKELEY J. EMP. & LAB. L. 375, 418–19 (2007)), when to any German lawyer it would be Wal-Mart's policies, not the court's decision, that would be startling.

A more successful effort to transplant employment policies in tension with local culture and law is exemplified by McDonald's experience in Europe. By a heavy reliance on franchising and a staffing model using part-time students, housewives and retirees, it was able for the most part to avoid the creation of works councils in Germany. Tony Royle, WORKING FOR MCDONALD'S IN EUROPE (2000). It was able to do that, however, in part due to the indifference of German unions at the time, in contrast to its experience in Denmark where it was compelled by boisterous union and public pressure to conform to Danish law and expectations. *Id.*

Over the past 30 years, there have been waves of automobile assembly and component plants transplanted from Japan, Germany, Korea, and other nations to the United States. The experiences with these plants reveal many complications associated with cross-cultural diffusion. For example, in Flat Rock, Michigan, what was originally a Mazda plant (now operated by Ford) was a physical replica of the Mazda plant in Hiroshima. Duplicating the physical layout was not a problem; however, when the intensive work pace and cultural assumptions around "fair treatment" were also imported from Japan by the Mazda managers, the plan experienced what came to be termed the "long, hot summer." A hard driving work pace, combined with a Japanese view of fairness, centered on treating each person differently based on their particular circumstance (young versus old, married versus single, male versus female, etc.), culminated in a series of wild cat strikes that ultimately prompted the needed dialogue on a social system that would work in the U.S. context. J. Cutcher-Gershenfeld et al., KNOWLEDGE-DRIVEN WORK: UNEXPECTED LESSONS FROM UNITED STATES AND JAPANESE WORK PRACTICES (1998). Interestingly, other aspects of the Japanese system, such as team-based processes driving continuous improvement in quality, safety, and other dimensions of performance, were initially seen as specific to the clan-based culture of Japan and unlikely effectively to transfer to the U.S. In fact, these "kaizen-teian" systems (the term roughly translates as "continuous improvement based on knowledge") are now ubiquitous across U.S. manufacturing operations and can be found in many other parts of the world.

Embedded in these three company examples are lessons on cross-cultural diffusion as having "tangible" features of the system (technology, policy, procedures, etc.) and "intangible" features (values, assumptions, relationships, etc.). Cutcher-Gershenfeld et al., supra. Whereas the tangible aspects of the Wal-Mart, McDonald's, and Mazda work systems were well-developed and highly successful in their home country contexts, success or failure hinged on the intangible aspects in each case.

The intangible aspects of work systems are challenging in that they are interwoven with both national and organizational cultures. In considering organizational culture with tools and methods derived from the study of national cultures, Schein distinguishes superficial cultural artifacts (how people dress, how offices are laid out, etc.) from a deeper level of policies, practices, and procedures, which are further undergirded by deep (often unspoken) values and assumptions. Edgar Schein, ORGANIZATIONAL CULTURE AND LEADERSHIP: A DYNAMIC VIEW (1992).

Moreover, diffusion is not a one-time or unidirectional process. There is what is termed "primary diffusion" from the home country, which happens with the establishment of a new operation in a new cultural setting. Subsequently there can be waves of what is termed "secondary diffusion" as ideas and practices spread out to suppliers, customers, and even neighbors in the community. Further, there can be "reverse diffusion," where innovations in the new setting return *to* the home country (Cutcher-Gershenfeld et al., supra). But, as Arthurs' interviews with labor lawyers evidenced, reverse diffusion can abut a strong headwind when a worker-favorable foreign practice (or law) confronts a less worker-favorable environment. Consider this illustrative story of the power and limits of reverse diffusion based on an interview with a Japanese manager after a multi-year assignment in the United States:

> He indicated that he had learned a valuable management lesson from his American counterpart, which involved the use of positive reinforcement [or feedback]. He explained that managers in Japan use more negative than positive reinforcement. As it happens, the negative reinforcement in Japan is non-blaming, which is in contrast with negative reinforcement that is commonly given in the United States ... Back in Japan, he indicated that he continued to use more positive reinforcement with Japanese workers and he found it very effective.

The manager was then asked if this practice might be adopted more broadly in his company. He instantly responded that he would never let others know he was doing this; he would be seen as presuming to have a better way of managing than his superior and he would never want that to happen. Thus, the reverse diffusion of innovation had occurred, but an overlay about respect for senior authority placed a boundary on just how far the diffusion might go.

The range of the possible in innovation and diffusion is not just a two-way street. In studying cross-cultural business negotiations, Jeswald Salacuse documents the emergence of what he terms "third cultures" in joint ventures and other settings. Jeswald Salacuse, THE GLOBAL NEGOTIATOR: MAKING, MANAGING AND MENDING DEALS AROUND THE WORLD IN THE TWENTY-FIRST CENTURY (2003). These are instances where the deep values and assumptions are no longer those of the parent company (its culture and its home country culture) or those of the subsidiary cultural context, but a hybrid blend featuring elements of each and possibly new patterns of interaction, all with sufficient coherence for it to be called a new culture of its own.

To sum up, a half-century ago, the forces of industrialization and globalization were seen as driving a convergence or homogenization of employment systems. Clark Kerr, John Dunlop, Fred Harbison & Charles Myers, INDUSTRIALISM AND INDUSTRIAL MAN: THE PROBLEMS OF LABOR AND MANAGEMENT IN

ECONOMIC GROWTH (1960). But this thesis was subsequently rejected based on the persistence of variation in employment relations systems. B.J. Punnett & O. Shenkar, HANDBOOK OF INTERNATIONAL MANAGEMENT RESEARCH (1996).

An emerging line of scholarship suggests that there are simultaneously forces of convergence and forces driving persistence in variation. Harry Katz & Owen Darbishire, CONVERGING DIVERGENCES: WORLDWIDE CHANGES IN EMPLOYMENT SYSTEMS (1999); Sanford Jacoby, *Corporate Governance in Comparative Perspective: Prospects for Convergence*, 22 COMP. LAB. L. & POL'Y J. 5 (2000); Shyh-Jer Chen, John J. Lawler, & Johngseok Bae, *Convergence in Human Resource Systems: A Comparison of Locally Owned and MNC Subsidiaries in Taiwan*, 44 HUMAN RESOURCE MANAGEMENT 237 (2005). In this sense, the problems studied here reveal both the forces driving a desire for increased consistency across nations and the combined legal and cultural barriers to the diffusion of change – further validating the view that there is a concurrent mixture of convergence and divergence to be found at the intersection of multinational human resource management and the law.

As HR executives, the [key] question ... is: "What approach to the issue in question protects and promotes the organization's interests the best?" This should be balanced with environment factors, including public scrutiny, corporate reputation, and employee perception of such policy or operational decisions. Expanding and promoting employee rights is a valid societal pursuit, but is often the focus of plaintiff's attorneys, interest groups, and public policy advocates. If an HR practitioner advocates for employee interests to the detriment of the employer's interests, that individual is emphasizing the legacy of Organizational Development ... There are certainly valid roles of an ombudsman office, or a third-party employee relations organization that possesses stronger connection to the interests of the company as a whole, versus alignment with local management. However, again, if an HR practitioner in the role of Business Partner takes on an Organizational Development mindset, as described by humanism, democracy, and values which are superordinate to priorities of the business, that individual's value and credibility as a business partner can be diminished. Our position as internal policy-makers places us in a unique position to impact society through workers' rights issues. I suggest that we should attempt to remain "politically neutral" in our roles. Our priority should be advancing our employer's interests within the existing law. To be clear, when considering the environment that the employer operates within, it can often be advantageous to offer additional promises, rights, or protections to employees. I merely suggest that those corporate policy decisions should be made based upon the interests of the business, rather than an overarching political or humanistic viewpoint.

Vice President, HR, Financial Sector

One implication for HR is to not assume that one set of policies or practices can be upheld across multiple countries. HR needs to try and integrate, or at least take into consideration, a country's culture versus creating strategies and making employment decisions solely through the lens of the MNC's home-country's culture. This may mean establishing a "baseline" policy to treat all employees with dignity and respect, and to provide uniform treatment that upholds these values. Policies would need to be analyzed on a case-by-case level within each operating country so that MNCs can avoid costly legal violations, and so that national employees' and cultural beliefs are not trodden upon.

HR Director, Food and Beverage Sector

Discussion, Comments and Questions

1. Assume it is ten years from now and present trends – as best you can glean from the essays you have read – continue at their current pace of change. Consider the six basic areas under which the problems that have been raised cluster. What employment policies and practices in multinational corporations do you predict will have moved toward greater standardization and consistency across national boundaries? What practices will most resist such standardization?

2. Are there technological forces or social forces that might prove to be massively disruptive to the whole system of laws governing employment relations in all five nations considered here – what might they be and how might such impacts be manifest?

G. IMPLICATIONS FOR POLICY AND PRACTICE

For leaders in multinational corporations and policy makers, the implications of these 21 cases can be profound. While some corporations operate with considerable differentiation in policies and procedures across business units and within different national markets, most have overarching policies, principles, and practices that are intended to be consistent throughout the corporation.

The cases in this volume suggest that maintaining such consistency will often run aground on contrasting legal considerations that reflect deep underlying differences.

While most policy makers struggle mightily to maintain and incrementally adjust labor and employment laws as they affect domestic stakeholders, the task is further complicated by the situations of those who work domestically for foreign multinational firms, and by the extraterritorial implications for domestic firms and their expatriates operating abroad. These must be folded into the mix of emerging cross-national standards and policies – at least in some markets, such as the European Union, or with respect to bilateral or multilateral trade agreements. Just as corporate leaders often seek consistency in policies and practices across their global operations, so policy makers often seek consistency within national boundaries.

What is to be done? As noted earlier, one manager in a French multinational company reported that his corporation had developed an approach that they somewhat lightly termed, "what happens in Denmark stays in Denmark." To some degree, country-by-country customization of human resource management practices is necessary and, arguably, even optimal. However, there are additional competitive advantages and social benefits to consider with respect to bridging across the legal variation to some degree.

With the increased interdependency of teams and functions across national boundaries, a pure country-by-country model may well stumble on issues of fairness and efficiency. What is required, however, is a focus that goes beyond the surface-level legal requirements and prohibitions, and appreciates the underlying values and assumptions. Then it is possible to know where the law will bend to enable cross-national consistency and where it won't. For example, there may be less flexibility with respect to policies that violate the integrity of the person in Germany than in Japan where the balance is more likely to respect the interests of employers.

As one student summed up the implications of these case materials, observing: "The implications are clear: multinational companies must have cultural awareness and must respect and adhere to the local policies and cultural values in the countries in which it operates while still maintaining its own corporate responsibility and basic standards where possible." (Vice President, HR, Electrical Manufacturing Sector). Note the concluding caveat, "where possible." This reflects the ways in which local law and culture predominate.

> I take issue with [the view that] "law drives HR Policy." I find this to be a pervasively frustrating perspective. My belief is that company values (and conversely how we want to be viewed) should drive policy. While in the course of evaluating and constructing these policies we should consult and consider the legal perspective, the ultimate decision process should reflect a larger weight in company values. Companies with strong value systems should be encouraged to go beyond the laws (and they often do – see specs on Best Places to Work and their policies) and companies that are less value conscious can seek to work within the letter of the law (likely attempting to do so to their advantage). Too often, I think we've been in rooms with executives and especially mid-level managers where they ask "what does the law say we have to do?" I'd challenge each of us to respond with "What do our values say we have to do?"
>
> Director, HR, Industrial Manufacturing Sector

> Despite of rapid technology advancement, rising living standards and converging global market place, it is not likely that we will see harmonization of culture and social norms resulting in harmonization of employment laws and people practices across the globe any time soon.
>
> Director, HR, Electronics Sector

As the velocity of change in a post-industrial society accelerates, many of the inherited institutional arrangements incompletely match what is taking place in markets, technology, and social relations. We have documented a great deal of variance with respect to governance of relations between labor and management, the movement of work across national boundaries, the role of religion in the workplace, the intersection of privacy and technology, the basic principles of performance management, the protections for "whistleblowers," the role of executive compensation when firms impact entire economies, the impact of global safety and quality operating systems, the emergence of international framework agreements, and many other matters.

The various conceptual frameworks offered in this concluding part of the book provide some signposts for the path ahead – both in what they tell us and what we have learned that goes beyond the legal frameworks. The origins of a legal system (highlighted in Section A) are revealed as less informative than local practice and customs. For example, a captive audience presentation by an employer may not be proscribed under the law, but it might well be anathema in Australia. Even though this book provides a comprehensive window into the law on the 21 problems, the combination of the borrowing of "legal" concepts (identified in Section E) and the cross-cultural diffusion within and across firms (discussed in Section F) suggests that managers will need to continually attend to the dynamic nature of law and local practice.

Ultimately, we see that there are limits to pure market-based solutions, just as there are limits to pure regulatory solutions. In this respect, the answers to the problems by labor law experts and the comments by industry executives set the stage for a full engagement with these many challenges if we are to have well-functioning systems of employment relations in the twenty-first century – systems that effectively take into account the interests of workers, unions, managers, corporations, suppliers, customers, communities, and nations.

Overall, a certain humility is suggested in the face of the evidence presented in this volume. It is humility with respect to both the plasticity and endurance of culture. Operating at the intersection of national cultures and organizational cultures, as the many problems and responses in this volume do, surfaces deep values and assumptions. *See* Schein, ORGANIZATIONAL CULTURE AND LEADERSHIP, *supra*. For leaders operating within large multinational firms, these are taken as fixed and even as immutable. The same is true for policy makers, workers, union leaders, and other stakeholders with respect to their national values and assumptions. But when these clash – as they often do – it can be something of a clash of the titans. However, as many of the highlighted executive comments reveal, this intersection of values and assumptions can also generate reflection, learning, creativity, and action. Twenty-one problems, it turns out, need not be entirely problematic.

INDEX